Sustainable Development in the 21st Century

Volume 1

Philipp Lange

Sustainability Governance

Exploring the Potential of Governance Modes to Promote Sustainable Development

Nomos

© Coverpicture: NASA Earth Observatory image by Joshua Stevens, using MODIS data from the Land Atmosphere Near real-time Capability for EOS (LANCE). Caption by Kathryn Hansen.

The Deutsche Nationalbibliothek lists this publication in the Deutsche Nationalbibliografie; detailed bibliographic data are available on the Internet at http://dnb.d-nb.de

a.t.: Basel, Univ., Diss., 2016

ISBN 978-3-8487-3991-2 (Print)
978-3-8452-8330-2 (ePDF)

British Library Cataloguing-in-Publication Data
A catalogue record for this book is available from the British Library.

ISBN 978-3-8487-3991-2 (Print)
978-3-8452-8330-2 (ePDF)

Library of Congress Cataloging-in-Publication Data
Lange, Philipp
Sustainability Governance
Exploring the Potential of Governance Modes to Promote Sustainable Development
Philipp Lange
321 p.
Includes bibliographic references.
ISBN 978-3-8487-3991-2 (Print)
978-3-8452-8330-2 (ePDF)

1. Edition 2017

Foreword

This study was accepted as a dissertation in the field of sustainability research by the Faculty of Humanities and Social Sciences at the University of Basel in the Fall semester of 2016. I want to thank the editors of the series »Sustainability in the 21st Century« for accepting the study as the first title of the series and in particular Prof. Dr. Andreas Rechkemmer for very helpful comments. I also thank Nomos for the good collaboration.

The study could not have been written without the support of several people. In the following, I want to express my gratitude.

First of all, my greatest thanks go to my supervisor Prof. Dr. Paul Burger. Paul, I deeply appreciate how you accompanied me throughout the whole process - from the very first ideas to the research proposal, until the final discussions. It has been a long road and I am really happy how we managed it. Thank you for all your helpful support!

Particular thanks also go to my co-supervisor Prof. Dr. Peter Driessen. Peter, thank you for supervising me. Your experience in the field helped a lot - in the discussions during the project and especially for the specification of the subject matter at the beginning!

I would like to give special thanks to Dr. Basil Bornemann. Basil, I always appreciated the hours together in our office! Thanks for both interpersonal and professional support - you are far more than just a colleague!

I also want to thank David Schreiner for proofreading. David, thanks for the professional collaboration!

I am furthermore grateful to the whole Sustainability Research Group. Thanks for the nice time over the years, guys!

Not least, I want to express my gratitude to my family and my friends. Your lasting support gave me the stability for conducting this work!

Finally, I acknowledge the physical pain, which accompanied me when writing the study. It taught me that thought is the only thing that can disturb the contentment of the now ...

Thanks!
Basel, June 2017 *Philipp Lange*

Abstract

Within scholarly and political debates, there is a broad consensus that governance is pivotal for the realization of societal transformation processes towards sustainable development (SD). Yet, in view of a variety of existing modes of governance in modern societies, it is an open question how to govern in such a way that SD is best fostered. Within sustainability governance literature, there is an influential normative claim that the promotion of SD calls for so-called ′new′ modes of governance, i.e. non-hierarchical forms that feature participative or self-governing characteristics. However, thus far there is lack of empirical evidence to support this claim. One of the most important research desiderata is thus to explore whether certain modes are in fact generally superior to others when it comes to governing societies towards sustainable tracks.

This study contributes to filling the knowledge gap regarding the potential of governance modes to promote SD by exploring the sequence of governance and its results. Addressing existing conceptual confusion on ′governance′, ′modes of governance′ and ′governance results′, it develops a theoretical framework consisting of four elements: (i.) a governance conceptualization that covers the inherent complexity of real-world arrangements and enables understanding of their workings and possible ways to induce change; (ii.) a formal frame for meaningfully differentiating among governance modes; (iii.) a scheme for grasping the societal changes induced by governance, i.e. governance impacts, as changes in the action strategies of affected actors; and finally (iv.) a normative frame for appraising impacts in light of SD. Guided by this framework, the study follows a comparative case study approach of a qualitative nature to empirically explore five real-world arrangements in Swiss energy policy. The arrangements represent the full range of governance modes - from hierarchically centralized and decentralized governance, to public-private and interactive modes up to self-governance.

The empirical research provides a differentiated picture of the workings of governance modes and their inducement of societal changes towards SD. Findings reveal no differences among the modes indicating that certain modes are per se better suited to promote SD than others. In contrast, the superiority of ′new′ to hierarchical modes as proclaimed in mainstream literature is put into perspective. Results indicate that interactive governance can easily fail to induce actions towards SD at all, and a ′shadow of hierarchy′ in self-governing can be required as leverage. Moreover, public-private modes can easily fail when there is no threat of a more stringent mode and participatory elements can also hinder faster and more sustainable results. Furthermore, hierarchical modes can be potent in contributing to SD, and certain aspects thought responsible for the supposed superiority of ′new′ modes can occur through hierarchical governance, too. Findings also indicate that other factors, such as the particularities of involved actors or the nature of the embedding context, can have a large influence on the potential of governance to promote SD. Based on the findings, hypotheses for future research are formulated.

Overall, the study adds to the discourse on how to govern towards SD in theoretical and empirical respects. It provides conceptual clarification on governance, its modes and results in light of SD and offers empirical insights on the relation between governance modes and SD. In view of the findings, future sustainability governance research should shift its focus from concentrating on ′new′ modes to the interplay of modes and the meta-governance of an appropriate mix of modes in different contexts. Likewise, practitioners should increasingly conceive sustainability governance as a meta-governed situational interplay of modes, so that the best of today`s variety to govern can be made.

Keywords: Sustainability Governance; Governance Modes; New Modes of Governance; Sustainable Development; Swiss Energy Policy

Contents

List of figures and tables

Abbreviations

ASIA	Association of Swiss car importers
cf.	compare (latin: confer)
CHF	Swiss franc
CO_2	Carbon dioxide
DETEC	Federal Department of the Environment, Transport, Energy and Communications
e.g.	for example (latin: exempli gratia)
et al.	and others (latin: et alia)
EnAW	Swiss Energy Agency of the Economy
FOEN	Swiss Federal Office of the Environment
g	gram
ibid.	in the same place (latin: ibidem)
i.e.	that is (latin: id est)
IWB	Industrial Works Basel
kg	kilogram
km	kilometer
kWh	kilowatt hour
l	liter
NGO	Non-Government Organization
SD	Sustainable Development
SDGs	Sustainable Development Goals
SFOE	Swiss Federal Office of Energy
TJ	terajoule
transl.	translated
UN	United Nations
WCED	World Commission on Environment and Development

Part I: Introduction

1 Overview

1.1 Point of departure

Modern societies have become increasingly complex, both in terms of existing problems and in terms of dealing with them. Facing unstructured, persistent problems of unsustainability, the notion of sustainable development (SD) calls for putting societies on a more sustainable path. This entails ensuring the well-being of present and future generations in view of the limitedness of resources and fragility of ecological and social systems - a goal that requires deep societal transformation processes. Within scholarly and political discourses, there is a broad consensus that the far reaching changes in human-nature relations implied by SD need to be actively shaped. Accordingly, governance is regarded as pivotal for the realization of the needed transformation processes (cf. e.g. Adger & Jordan, 2009; Meadowcroft et al., 2012; Barnes & Hoerber, 2013; Ayre & Callway, 2005; Petschow et al., 2005; OECD, 2007). It is vividly argued that 'SD' and 'governance' have to go hand in hand. Some authors also consider the lack of sustainability that characterizes existing development patterns to be mainly a crisis of governance (e.g. Van Zeijl-Rozema et al., 2008; Farrell et al., 2005; Mahanti & Manuel-Navarrete, 2015). It is thus further argued that governance practices have to be reoriented towards SD. Along this line, it is even claimed that »*sustainable development is really all about governance*« (Meadowcroft, 2011, p. 536; cf. also e.g. Frödin, 2015).

'Governance' has emerged as a concept in political science, sustainability science and other fields as a response to the growing awareness that over the past decades governing has increasingly become a shared responsibility of state, market and civil society (e.g. Pierre & Peters, 2000; Kooiman, 2003; Stoker, 1998; Rhodes, 1997). Resulting from these changes in governing, a variety of modes of governance have emerged in modern societies. These modes range from hierarchical governance to formalized public-private partnerships, up to multi-actor networks and more or less autonomous self-governance by societal actors.

In view of the variety of co-existing modes, the question arises how to govern in such a way that SD is best fostered. Governance modes are at the core of the debate on sustainability governance and there is a lively discussion regarding the suitability of certain modes for promoting SD. Within mainstream sustainability governance literature, there is a strong and highly influential normative claim that dealing with sustainability problems requires so-called 'new' modes of governance (see e.g. in Newig et al., 2008; Bäckstrand et al., 2010; Hogl et al., 2012). Such modes are marked by non-hierarchical governing that exceeds 'traditional' government control and features participative or self-governing characteristics. Typical examples are collaborative, deliberative and multi-level governance modes that emphasize partnership among multiple actors. In fact, the realm of SD governance has increasingly become an experimental field for new modes of governance within recent years (cf. also e.g. Meadowcroft, 2011; Bressers, 2004). These modes are commonly regarded as being able to handle the complex, dynamic, multi-scale, cross-sectoral and long-term temporal aspects of SD in a more adequate manner than hierarchical ones. According to this perspective, new modes should thus be explicitly advocated in practice. Frequently mentioned key terms associated with suitable sustainability governance are closely related to the characteristics of new governance modes: participation, adaptiveness, reflexiveness, integration of policies and scales, deliberation and social learning (cf. e.g. Steurer, 2010; Kemp et al., 2005; Huh, 2011; Shiroyama et al., 2012; Voss et al., 2007; Meadowcroft et al., 2005; Rist et al., 2007; Dedeurwaerdere, 2005; Monkelbaan, 2015; Sajeva et al., 2015; OECD, 2002). Some scholars, for instance, argue that in view of uncertainty, ambivalence about goals and distributed power, sustainability governance should be organized as a reflexive and experimental process (e.g. Voss et al., 2006; Loorbach, 2010; Grin et al., 2010).

Overall, it is claimed that new modes of governance are generally better suited to promoting SD than traditional hierarchical steering. However, thus far there is lack of reliable empirical evidence supporting this claim (cf. e.g. Jordan, 2008; Filho et al., 2016; Bäckstrand et al., 2010; Hogl et al., 2012). There are hitherto no empirical studies that comparatively explore the merits of the range of different governance modes with regard to their contribution to SD on the ground. Seeing certain modes as generally superior to others - and thus as a panacea that is not questioned - entails the danger that empirical scrutiny is pushed into the background. Griffin (2010, p. 366) points exactly to this knowledge gap when highlighting that »*many governance and sustainability scholars have argued that governance work is short on studies that assess the sustainability potential [...] of new governance initiatives*«.

Empirical research in the sustainability governance field frequently adopts a rather static perspective, exploring solely the presence or absence of certain modes in specific sectors (cf. also Adger & Jordan, 2009). Moreover, there is often a failure to clearly separate procedures from results. Arguing for a specific way of organizing governance processes in light of the challenges coming along with SD seems to have given rise to the assumption - and some scholars tend to assume a priori - that these arrangements also perform best with regard to results. While procedures and results are naturally linked, a ′good′ governance process in light of SD does not necessarily ensure that an actual contribution to SD is made on the ground. Apart from this, the research field is characterized by a lack of conceptual clarity regarding ‘governance‘, ‘modes of governance‘ and ‘governance results‘. This has clearly hampered empirical inquiries of normative claims.

Against the backdrop of these shortcomings, one of the most important research desiderata within contemporary sustainability governance research is to explore if certain modes of governance are in fact generally superior to others when it comes to governing societies towards sustainable trajectories.

1.2 Research objective and questions

The knowledge gap on the relation between governance modes and SD forms the point of departure for this study. My research objective is to comparatively explore the potential of the range of different governance modes to promote sustainability. Therefore, I include the entire continuum of existing modes, from hierarchical governance at different levels, to public-private collaborations, deliberative networks and self-governing. In so doing, I aim to contribute to clarifying whether certain modes are generally superior to others in fostering SD (though I only aim at qualitative conclusions and thus do not aspire generalizations in terms of which mode performs better, cf. below). My overall motivation is to make a contribution to the debate on how to govern societies towards sustainable pathways.

The crucial aspect in order to scrutinize the merits of a governance mode in terms of SD are the induced results on the ground. Although I regard governance procedures, i.e. how governance is conducted, as important, I primarily view governance - especially in the field of sustainability - as a means to an end (cf. also e.g. Young, 2009, p. 30: »*Governance is not an end in itself. We seek to create governance systems [...] in order to steer human societies toward advantageous outcomes.*«). Since governance aims to bring about societal changes to resolve collective problems, it is crucial what 'ultimately comes out'. Thus, the complex sequence of governance and its results has to be addressed. Desirable for exploring the merits of modes would be capturing their *end* results, i.e. changes in environmental and socio-economic conditions, in this study called *governance outcomes*. However, when the notion of SD is taken seriously in its broad societal and holistic meaning, the assessment of such macro-level outcomes raises vast research challenges. This especially concerns data availability, long time horizons and multiple interacting variables (cf. also e.g. Koontz & Thomas, 2006).[1]

Taking this into account, this study aims to explore the potential of modes to promote SD by focusing on the *interface* between governance and its outcomes: the societal changes occurring in the meantime of governance workings and end results. Thus far, this linkage - the entire range

1 Assessing SD means more than assessing environmental effectiveness. The attainment of environmental targets can be measured more easily (for instance, the question if participatory governance leads to more environmentally benign results is increasingly being investigated in the literature, cf. chapter 2.4). However, SD represents a complex challenge and calls for considering numerous environmental and socio-economic goals in different sectors across multiple temporal scales. Furthermore, the influences of governance modes on SD are difficult to isolate as multiple consequences from other governance arrangements may intervene. Altogether, sustainability governance represents a field with a multitude of interdependencies. Accordingly, an overall sustainability assessment would require a long-term analysis that gives consideration to countless sectors, scales and side-effects.

of societal changes induced by governance - represents some sort of a ′black box′ within (SD) governance research. While usually behavioral change of target groups is considered, other aspects are neglected. I conceive of this intermediate missing link as *governance impacts*[2].

Based on this, the following *background assumption*, on which this study relies, can be formulated. In order to promote SD, a governance mode must fulfill two requirements. On the one hand, it has to induce certain impacts, i.e. changes in societal conditions. Only if societal changes are induced (such as institutionalization processes, changes in infrastructures or behavioral change of actors) does governance have an actual influence in practice. On the other hand, the induced impacts must be in line with the goals associated with SD (i.e. reflecting its functional and normative prerequisites). When a governance mode induces impacts that are consistent with sustainability goals, the mode will ultimately lead to sustainable outcomes. Overall, the potential of governance modes to promote SD is thus determined by its ability to induce impacts that are in line with SD.

Against the backdrop of the research objective, this study addresses the following *overall research question*:

Q 1: Are there differences among modes of governance indicating that certain modes are generally better suited to promote SD than others?

In order to answer this overall research question, four theoretical tasks have to be addressed first. This is required in light of missing conceptual clarity on ‘governance‘, ‘modes of governance‘ and ‘governance results‘. The first theoretical task is to develop a sound conceptualization of governance. As a prerequisite to exploring the sequence of governance modes and their results, a deepened understanding of the multifaceted phenomenon of real-world governance is needed. The conceptualization shall enable understanding the workings of governance and reveal possible

2 To avoid confusion, it should be noted here that in the literature there is also a contradictory use of the terms, where outcomes are conceived as intermediate results and impacts as end results (cf. chapter 3.3).

ways for inducing societal change. In view of existing conceptual vagueness on 'modes of governance', the second theoretical task is then to find a way to meaningfully distinguish among governance modes. Likewise, a heuristic device for grasping the range of impacts of governance must be developed. Finally, for appraising impacts in light of SD, a normative frame with sustainability criteria has to be at hand. Taken together, these tasks are addressed in the following four *theoretical sub-questions*:

Q 1.1: How can governance be conceptualized in a way that covers the inherent complexity of real-world governance?
Q 1.2: How can modes of governance be meaningfully differentiated?
Q 1.3: How can the impacts of governance be grasped?
Q 1.4: How can governance impacts be appraised in terms of sustainability?

The four theoretical sub-questions each have a counterpart addressed in the empirical part of the study. The subjects of this empirical part are five real-world governance arrangements within Swiss energy policy that display the full range of different modes of governance. To answer the overall research question, first of all, an understanding of governance workings in these different real-world arrangements is needed. This means to retrace by which means, actor constellations, institutional rules and so forth certain policy outputs are achieved. In so doing, it can be revealed how the arrangements induce change - as the foundation for understanding the chain of governance and results. Second, the arrangements each have to be allocated to a specific governance mode. These two steps together reveal a detailed picture of the workings of different modes while disclosing their specific characteristics. Afterwards, the impacts of the governance arrangements need to be determined. In this regard, it is also necessary to establish the link between the identified impacts and the specific characteristics of governance modes. Accordingly, it has to be explored how the impacts were actually induced through governance. In this way, it is disclosed, which role the characteristics of the pertinent governance modes actually played. Finally, the impacts must be appraised in light of sustainability goals. Overall, this leads to the following four *empirical sub-questions* that are addressed in the empirical part of the study:

Q 1.5: How does governance unfold within five real-world arrangements in Swiss energy policy that display the range of different governance modes?
Q 1.6: Which governance modes do these arrangements represent?
Q 1.7: What are the impacts of the arrangements and how were these induced?
Q 1.8: To what extent do the identified impacts meet the criteria of a sustainable development?

Taken together, the questions explore whether the mode of governance makes a difference when it comes to inducing sustainable impacts (i.e. investigating the specific characteristics of governance modes and their role for promoting SD). Based on this, insights regarding normative claims can be deduced, i.e. if there are indications that the characteristics of certain modes make them generally superior to others in light of SD. The proceeding also helps to disclose other influencing factors that determine the potential of governance to promote SD.

In the following, two important remarks are given in view of the demarcation of the research interest. First of all, since the focus of this study is on the result side of governance, I do not aspire to an assessment of 'the governance mode itself', e.g. based on certain 'good' governance criteria. Instead, I am interested in whether a governance mode promotes SD in terms of changes in society. Apart from that, the study does not aim at producing generalizable conclusions in terms of which mode performs best. My goal is not to identify causal relationships between modes and (un)sustainable results. Rather, I aim at qualitatively shedding light on the characteristics of modes and their potential to promote SD. The goal is to provide a differentiated picture of the workings of different modes and their triggering of societal changes towards SD. Against the background of the normative claim in the literature putting emphasis on new modes, the study aims to explore if there are differences among modes that would support such a claim. This proceeding serves as a basis for formulating hypotheses at the end of the study to be tested in future research.

1.3 Research strategy

Having elaborated on the research objective and questions, I will in the following introduce the research strategy, i.e. how to reach the objectives and answer the questions (cf. also e.g. Verschuren et al., 2010, on general project design). In *theoretical respects*, I develop a framework that consists of four elements - as addressed by the theoretical sub-questions elaborated above: a conceptualization of governance, a formal frame for differentiating governance modes, a scheme for grasping governance impacts, and a normative frame for appraising impacts in terms of SD.

The development of this theoretical framework is supported by relying on different literature strands: governance research and the broader political science literature, sustainability governance literature (both empirical-analytical and normative) and normative foundations of sustainability. The framework then serves as the foundational basis for the empirical research.

With regard to the *empirical part*, I follow a comparative case study approach of a qualitative nature. As already mentioned, it consists of five in-depth case studies in the realm of Swiss energy policy that display the range of different governance modes. The cases are each explored through the four elements of the theoretical framework.

Accordingly, the study unfolds along the following main steps of research: The five cases are first of all investigated by means of the governance conceptualization to reach a deepened understanding of governance workings in each case (*research step 1*). Based on this, the formal frame for modes is used to allocate each case to a specific governance mode (*research step 2*). Subsequently, via the scheme for governance impacts, the particular societal changes within each case are identified (*research step 3*). Finally, with the help of the normative frame for sustainability appraisal, the impacts are appraised in terms of SD (*research step 4*). Figure 1 illustrates the research steps by highlighting the interplay of theoretical investments and milestones in the empirical part.

The general process of the case study research is geared towards the steps of planning and preparing the cases as well as collecting, analyzing and interpreting the data (cf. e.g. Yin, 2009). It is important in this respect to note that the function of the cases is directed at illuminating the research question and to enable the formulation of hypotheses (and thus not to explicitly validate the theoretical framework). Also, they are to be seen as exemplary cases that were selected in light of the overall research goal.

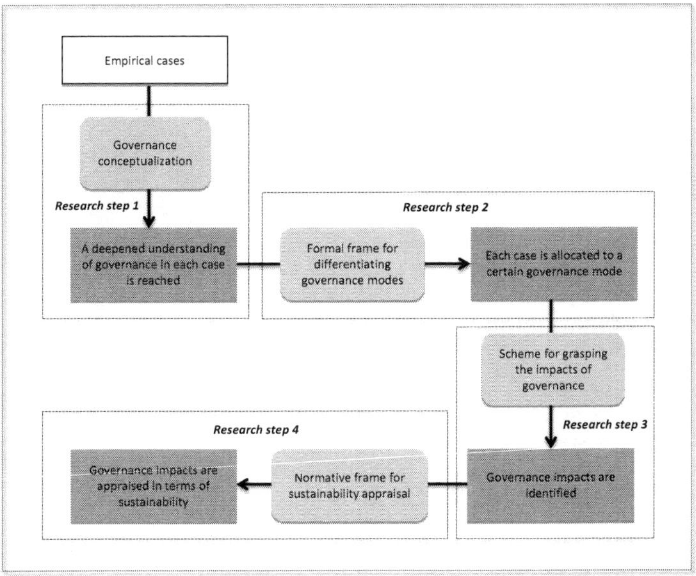

Figure 1: Research steps - interplay of theoretical investments and milestones in the empirical part. Theoretical investments: light grey, milestones for empirical research: dark grey (own illustration)

With regard to *data collection*, I make use of a triangulation of both methods and sources. Three primary techniques are combined to provide different sources of evidence for each of the five cases. First, existing research on the cases is reviewed. Second, official political-administrative documents and documents from societal bodies participating in governance, such as firms and other initiatives, are studied (e.g. laws, programs, evaluations, plans and strategy papers). Finally, qualitative expert-interviews (semi-structured) with key representatives from governments, administration, the market and civil society are conducted.

For the first two research steps sketched out above, I make use of the same data set extracted through all three techniques of data collection (see also table 1 below). The third step is also based on all three techniques, yet the focus lies on gaining data by means of expert-interviews (due to limited available information on governance impacts through desk research). The fourth step in turn consists of an interpretation of the data gathered in step three.

Table 1: Overview of data collection and analysis techniques (own illustration)

<table>
<tr><th>Research step</th><th>Methods for data generation</th><th>Method for data analysis</th></tr>
<tr><td>Research step 1:
The five empirical cases are explored by means of the governance conceptualization to reach a deepened understanding of governance in each case</td><td rowspan="2">• Review of existing research related to governance within the cases
• Studying of official documents related to governance within the cases
• Expert interviews with key participating actors in the governance arrangement in question</td><td>The governance conceptualization is translated into a deductive category system. The analysis of the data is conducted by means of the content structuring technique.</td></tr>
<tr><td>Research step 2:
Each case is allocated to a specific mode of governance via the formal frame for governance modes</td><td>The formal frame for governance modes is translated into a category system and data analysis follows the content structuring technique.</td></tr>
<tr><td>Research step 3:
The impacts in each case are identified by making use of the scheme for governance impacts</td><td>• Review of existing research related to impacts of the cases
• Studying of official documents related to impacts of the cases
• Expert interviews with key actors that are either affected by the governance arrangement in question or general experts for its results</td><td>The scheme for governance impacts is translated into a category system and data analysis follows the content structuring technique.</td></tr>
<tr><td>Research step 4:
The identified impacts are appraised in terms of SD</td><td>No additional generation of data</td><td>Interpretative appraisal of results from research step 3 in light of the normative frame for sustainability appraisal.</td></tr>
</table>

In terms of *data analysis*, I apply a qualitative content analysis, i.e. category guided text analysis. More specifically, I follow the procedure of deductive category application (also known as directed content analysis, cf. e.g. Mayring, 2015; Hsieh & Shannon, 2005). Therefore, the first three elements of the theoretical framework (the governance conceptualization, the frame for modes and the scheme for impacts) are translated into deductive category systems. On that basis, I use the content structuring technique to analyze the data. Finally, I interpret the findings in light of the normative frame for sustainability appraisal. Table 1 gives an overview of data collection and analysis techniques in connection with the four introduced research steps.

1.4 Structure

The formal structure of the study unfolds as follows. The following *Part II* is dedicated to providing the theoretical groundwork. In this part, *chapter two* first of all works out the state of research regarding the field of sustainability governance, and clarifies the understanding of respective key terms in this study. The chapter starts with an introduction to the key concepts of sustainability (chapter 2.1), governance and governance modes (chapter 2.2). After that, the overlap of these notions is addressed by consolidating the sustainability governance discourse (chapter 2.3). In light of the research perspective of this study, a particular focus is then set on the linkage between modes of governance and sustainability as well as further connected research fields (chapter 2.4). In relation to the foundations laid in chapter two, the *third chapter* develops the theoretical framework, consisting of four elements: a conceptualization of governance (chapter 3.1), a formal frame for differentiating governance modes (chapter 3.2), a heuristic for capturing governance impacts (chapter 3.3) and finally a normative frame for sustainability appraisal (chapter 3.4).

Based on this theoretical groundwork, *Part III* of the study then deals with the empirical case studies. At first, *chapter four* will go into detail with regard to the research methodology used - in terms of the general case study approach (chapter 4.1), data collection (chapter 4.2) and data analysis (chapter 4.3). The *fifth chapter* then provides an introduction to the five case studies. First of all, an overview is given to the embedding of the cases in terms of Swiss energy policy, which relates the cases to each other (chapter 5.1). This is followed by an elaboration of the individual cases in the subsequent chapters (chapter 5.2-5.6). After that, in *chapter six*, the results of the case studies are presented. This includes the deepened understanding of governance workings within the cases (chapter 6.1), the allocation of the cases to specific governance modes (chapter 6.2), the identification of governance impacts (chapter 6.3), and finally their sustainability appraisal (chapter 6.4). An overview of the empirical findings concludes this part (chapter 6.5).

Subsequently, *Part IV* of the study provides a discussion of the results gained and elaborates implications of the findings in *chapter seven*. The chapter starts with a discussion of whether the mode of governance indeed makes a difference when it comes to promoting sustainability (chapter 7.1). Based on this, hypotheses that are to be tested in future research are formulated (chapter 7.2). In view of the findings, overall implications with regard to the field of sustainability governance are deduced (chapter 7.3).

Finally, *Part V* concludes the study in *chapter eight* with a summary (chapter 8.1), a reflection on the research in substantive and methodological terms (chapter 8.2), and ultimately an outlook on the directions for future work in the field (chapter 8.3).

In addition to this overview of the formal structure, figure 2 illustrates in more detail the logical procedure of the study, i.e. the successive development of the argument.

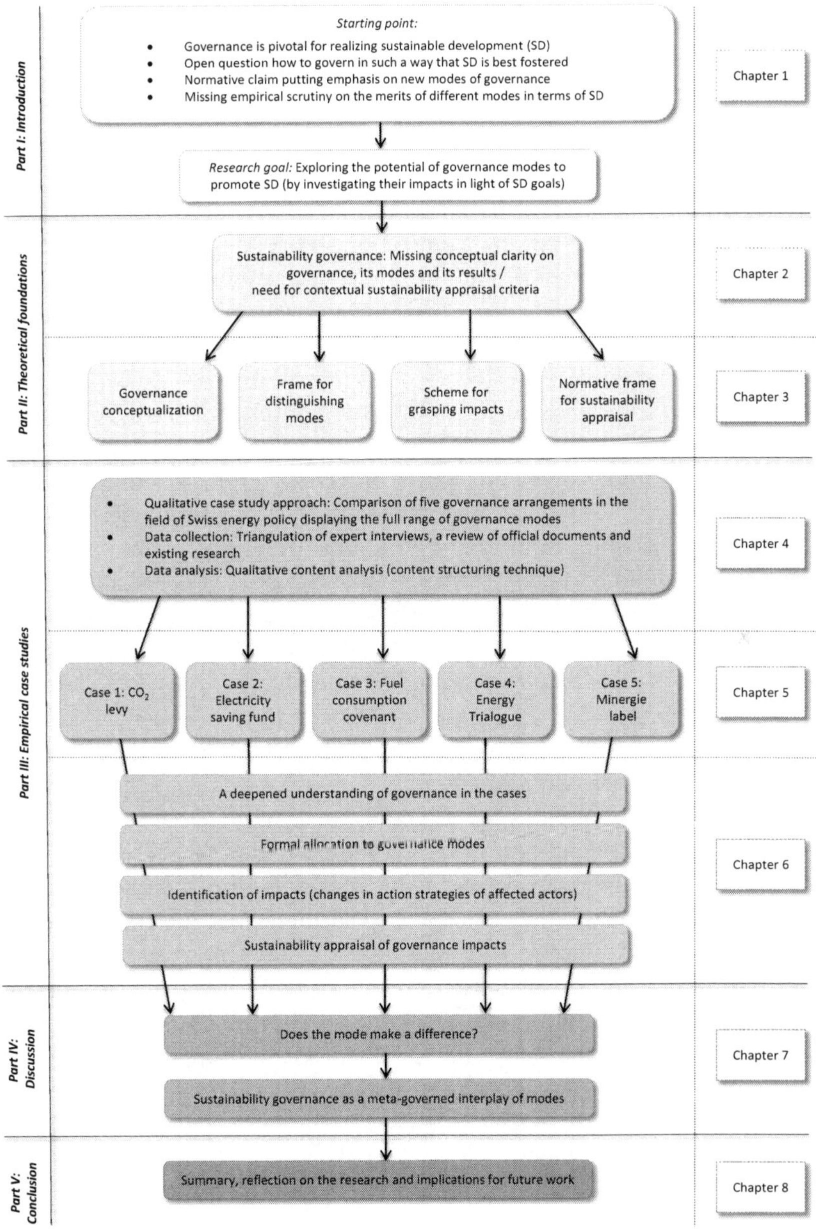

Figure 2: Proceeding of the argument (own illustration)

Part II: Theoretical foundations

2 Sustainability governance

As a foundational basis for the study, this chapter provides an overview of the state of research regarding the field of sustainability governance. In so doing, this section will also demonstrate the research desideratum addressed by this study as well as the need for the development of the theoretical framework.

Within academia, the concepts of both sustainability and governance serve as bridges among disciplines, thus provoking interdisciplinary debates. The number of publications comprising both notions has grown remarkably over the past decades, indicating the increasing relevance of the rapidly developing field. Yet, both terms are characterized by significant conceptual ambiguities. Kemp et al. (2005, p. 13) accordingly argue with regard to SD and governance that »*neither of these terms is yet mature or clearly defined. Perhaps more importantly, the overlaps between their wider meanings remain understudied.*« In line with this, Jordan (2008) characterizes the notions as two of the most contested terms in the entire social sciences. In light of this, this chapter will clarify the understanding of the two terms in this study, alongside the more specific notions of modes of governance and new modes of governance.

I will in the following first provide an introduction to SD (chapter 2.1), governance and governance modes (chapter 2.2), and then address their overlap by consolidating the discourse of sustainability governance (chapter 2.3). Finally, I will focus on the linkage between governance modes and SD - and further connected research fields (revealing what kind of work already exists in the wider sense connected to the research objective and thus positioning the study in the multi-faceted field) (chapter 2.4).

2.1 Sustainable development

Against the backdrop that the current global development trajectory can be characterized as unsustainable, the notion of SD has become increasingly prominent in scholarly and political debates as well as in the public domain. Since the publication of the landmark Brundtland Report »Our Common Future« in 1987 (WCED, 1987), SD has become a broadly accepted mission statement and nowadays commands almost universal support (for a recent overview cf. e.g. Michelsen et al., 2016).

Despite this, the particular meaning of sustainability[3] remains regularly contested (cf. e.g. Jacobs, 1999; for a recent synthesis of different understandings see e.g. Bolis et al., 2014). A large discrepancy exists between the intuitive version of the regulative ideal that frames public and political debates and its theoretical conceptualization and operationalization (cf. e.g. Kates et al., 2005; Dobson, 1996; Christen & Schmidt, 2012; Burger & Christen, 2011; Franklin & Blyton, 2011). While it is on the one hand argued that the concept of SD is elusive and marked by arbitrariness, it is also proclaimed that the act of debating the meaning of SD entails a value itself. In this sense, implementing SD is also concerned with a societal process of deliberation and negotiation on shaping humanity′s future. Yet, a clear distinction has to be made between SD as a societal discourse and the theoretical approach to SD within sustainability science. The latter contributes to rationalizing the societal discourse and to informed decision-making by providing reliable knowledge (for recent overviews on sustainability science cf. e.g. Wiek et al., 2012; Miller, 2013; Kajikawa et al., 2014).

The literature on SD is generally vast, characterized by a broad scope and multi-dimensional heterogeneity (cf. e.g. Redclift, 2005). It can be roughly mapped in terms of two different poles of understandings (cf. e.g. Van Zeijl-Rozema et al., 2008; Bornemann et al., *forthcoming*). One the one hand there is a 'well-being perspective' (where societal concerns and uncertainties shape the normative SD concept related to quality of life). This understanding stands in the Brundtland tradition and conceives SD as a comprehensive trajectory of societal development towards safeguarding the well-being of present and future generations. On the other hand, there is a narrow 'ecological sustainability perspective' (wherein ecological

3 In this study, the two terms ′sustainable development′ and ′sustainability′ are used synonymously.

limits determine SD and the concept is objectified based on scientific evidence). Contributions in this vein perceive SD as an improved management of ecological resources, furthering resilience in light of limited carrying capacities. Apart from this distinction, there are differences in terms of substantive or procedural interpretations. While the former identify a fixed and universal normative core of SD, the latter regard it rather as a contested idea that needs to be specified in different contexts.

Since within this study I am not dealing with the concept of SD itself but with the relation of SD and governance modes - directed towards a better understanding of governing for promoting SD - I refrain from presenting a full outline of the sustainability discourse here. For the more specific conceptualization of sustainability, I refer to recently published contributions particularly dealing with this (e.g. Christen & Schmidt, 2012; Burger & Christen, 2011). Yet, what is important here is (i.) the pertinent understanding of SD, and (ii.) why governance is pivotal for reaching a more sustainable development.

(i.) The basic understanding of sustainability within this study builds upon the framing of the notion in the Brundtland tradition (*»development that meets the needs of the present without comprising the ability of future generations to meet their own needs«*, WCED, 1987, p. 43). The report related the satisfaction of needs with the idea of limitations. It connected the political goal of global justice and the discourse on human development with the fact of restricted environmental resources and the fragility of ecosystems. Accordingly, the pursuit of SD is connected with decoupling the pressures of existing socio-economic drivers on natural systems and thus embraces a balance of social, economic and environmental goals.

More specifically, I perceive of SD as a hybrid term linking normative, i.e. intra- & intergenerational justice, with systemic foundations, i.e. mechanisms of human-nature-interaction (coupled human-nature systems). It is thus about shaping development given the risks emerging from present activities and upholding societal abilities to (re)act. With this as the point of departure, SD is conceived in this study as a societal role model aimed at *ensuring the well-being of present and future generations within the frame conditions of finite environmental and social resources as well as fragile social-environmental systems*. Based on this understanding, in chapter 3.4, a frame for SD appraisal in the context of energy policy is developed.

(ii.) In terms of why governance is pivotal for reaching SD, it already became apparent above that SD is about directing development in light of the dissatisfaction with existing, unsustainable patterns. The notion of SD can thus basically be seen as an answer to a practical problem. It claims that the international development path needs to be reoriented in the direction of SD (this includes the implicit assumption that it is basically possible to direct societies on a desirable path, a supposition that is shared by the governance discourse, cf. below). As a means for organizing this reorientation, governance for organizing collective action is a necessary condition. The fundamental societal transformation processes need to be actively shaped (cf. also Meadowcroft, 2007, p. 302: »*Sustainable development is not a spontaneous social product: it requires goal-directed intervention.*«). This emphasizes the importance of steering when addressing SD, i.e. a purposive endeavor to lead a system from a certain state to another by influencing its development. Sustainability science in general is thus not interested solely e.g. in systems knowledge in terms of understanding and explanation but also in how societal transformation can be achieved, i.e. knowledge for action. Moreover, sustainability is an issue not only on the individual level, but on a societal level as a whole (cf. also Burger & Christen, 2011, p. 2: »*The scope of actions towards sustainability comprises not only individual, but also institutional, i.e. high level strategic actions decided by structural agents. Accordingly, sustainable development includes structural and political elements.*«). Moreover, as flawed governance practices encourage unsustainable development patterns, improved governance is needed. Overall, governance plays a vital role in shifting the societal development trajectory on to more sustainable lines.

The policy content of SD was amongst others developed at the UN summits of Rio in 1992 (United Nations Conference on Environment and Development) and Johannesburg in 2002 (World Summit on Sustainable Development), boosting sustainability to the role of being a key principle for policy action across levels (from the local to the global level) and sectors. The concept gained recognition in international policies and gave rise to sustainability strategies on different political-administrative levels. It has also extended beyond the realm of governments to businesses, other institutions and civil society. These developments depict the generally acknowledged action-guiding power of the concept. This was recently strengthened by the Rio+20 conference in 2012 as well as the '2030

Agenda for Sustainable Development‘ and its ‘Sustainable Development Goals‘ (SDGs) adopted at the UN summit 2015 in New York (United Nations Sustainable Development Summit).

When construing SD as a policy objective, it becomes apparent that the need to govern a process of deep social transformation requires action across a variety of spatial, structural and temporal scales. The steering logic in light of SD exhibits a multi-dimensional character, which takes place in the context of uncertain and ambivalent objectives (that might also change and develop over time), a long-term perspective, as well as multiple levels and sectors (cf. e.g. Baker, 2009; Kemp et al., 2005). Accordingly, when governance addresses sustainability problems, it is confronted with what has also been characterized as ‘wicked problems‘. Such problems are usually described as containing several interdependencies, being socially complex and unstable and including value differences, with a disputed knowledge base for defining their nature and possible solutions (cf. e.g. Rittel & Weber, 1973; Head, 2008; cf. also the description of problem structure types, such as unstructured problems, by Hoppe, 2010).

Overall, the attributes coming along with SD - i.e. uncertainty, complexity, ambiguity and future orientation, as well as functional and spatial interdependencies - pose several steering challenges. The pursuit of SD has thus triggered the scientific and political debate on ′governance′. The endeavor of implementing sustainability in different fields has promoted a range of novel governing forms. As a matter of fact, the pursuit of SD represents a paradigm case with respect to what motivated the governance approach in general: the increasingly complex, dynamic and interdependent nature of contemporary policy-making. In the following chapter, I will go into detail with regard to the governance concept.

2.2 Governance and its modes

This chapter first of all deals with the notion of governance (i.), and then elaborates on the terms of modes (ii.), and new modes of governance (iii.).

(i.) The *governance concept* has become increasingly prominent over the past decades in both scholarly and political debates, especially from the early 1990s onwards. ′Governance′ has become one of the most commonly used terms in social sciences, encouraging scholars to call it a ‘magic concept‘ (Pollitt & Hupe, 2011). Most generally speaking, the notion refers to practices through which societies are governed - whereas governing is usually understood as activities that make a purposeful effort to guide facets of societies[4] (e.g. Kooiman, 1993; cf. also Torfing et al., 2012). Traditionally, governing has been associated with formal hierarchical intervention and control by governments as the single decision-making authority. Governance in turn refers to something broader than this conventional authority-based governing style. It emerged as a concept to include novel dynamics - with the potential of including different forms of how society is steered (e.g. Pierre & Peters, 2000; Stoker, 1998; Rhodes, 1997; Kooiman, 2003). The notion thus first and foremost has been a response to the growing awareness, that state actors and institutions are not the exclusively relevant ones when it comes to dealing with societal issues. From this perspective, governance can be seen as an attempt to grasp broader patterns of state-societal interactions (e.g. Levi-Faur, 2012; Hajer & Wagenaar, 2003; Chhotray & Stoker, 2009).

According to the literature, over the past decades, governing has increasingly become a shared responsibility of state, market and civil society. This is putting increasing emphasis on societal actors (including private actors from the market and actors from civil society) and institutions (e.g. Bevir, 2011; Steurer, 2013). The extension of policy-making to society at large is associated with the rise of non-hierarchical forms, such as network, collaborative and participatory arrangements that feature co-operative and 'horizontal' elements (e.g. Bellamy, 2011; Héritier & Rhodes, 2011). These arrangements allow a plurality of interests to be merged into collective action. They are also frequently characterized by multi-centered interactions, occurring at different spatial scales and across multiple policy levels (e.g. Bache & Flinders, 2004; Hooghe & Marks, 2001). Accompanied by autonomous self-governing arrangements by societal actors, this entails a blurring of boundaries between steering subjects and objects, questioning the distinction between state and societal sectors (cf. e.g. Mayntz, 2003).

---

4 The notions of 'steering' (cf. above) and 'governing' are in this study used synonymously - since I follow a broad governance perspective, i.e. governance is viewed as 'the steering of society'.

While it is generally not questioned that different forms of governance have emerged, it is contested in the literature to what extent these developments have had an impact on the steering capacity of the state (cf. e.g. Bevir & Rhodes, 2016). Likewise, there is a debate about the question of whether forms of hierarchical governance have increasingly given way to non-hierarchical ones. Generally speaking, there is a state-centric and a society-centric viewpoint (cf. Pierre, 2000; for a recent overview see e.g. Capano et al., 2015b). Some authors regard the developments as signs of a weakening, retreat or hollowing out of the state - through the dispersion of authority both vertically to actors located at other territorial levels, and horizontally, to non-state actors (e.g. Rhodes, 1997). However, this 'power relocation assumption' has been challenged, both empirically and theoretically (cf. e.g. Mol, 2016; Arts, 2014). Instead of a weakening, several authors thus speak of a shifting role of governments, in which the state's constitutional power is altered towards facilitation and cooperative partnering (e.g. Kooiman, 2003). It is further argued that the state remains a central actor, especially with respect to aspects like legitimacy and accountability (cf. e.g. Goetz, 2008; Börzel & Risse, 2010).

Despite the prominence of the term governance, there is huge conceptual ambiguity when it comes to its exact meaning. It is thus a highly elusive and imprecise concept. Some authors argue that the vagueness of the term may have contributed to its abundant popularity. Scientific and political discourses cover a broad range of different understandings and there is no generally accepted definition (cf. e.g. Van Kersbergen & Van Waarden, 2004; Robichau, 2011; Ruhanen et al., 2010). For instance, as far as political sciences are concerned, the usage of the notion greatly differs in the sub-disciplines of international relations, comparative politics, public administration and public policy (cf. e.g. Kjær, 2004).

What is more, there is not even consensus on the range of phenomena that can be grouped under the term. As it is frequently used for a wide variety of aspects, it is difficult to get a clear picture of what it is all about. Capano et al. (2015b, p. 312) argue that »*the unanswered questions can only be resolved through a more clearly focused conceptualization of, and more rigorous empirical research into, current governance arrangements than presently exists.*« Against this backdrop, I will in chapter 3.1 disclose a substantiated way of approaching 'governance' and develop a sound conceptualization.

In most basic terms, there is an encompassing and a narrow understanding of governance (cf. e.g. also Colebatch, 2014). In the encompassing sense, it includes all kinds of practices and mechanisms through which societies are governed. This covers hierarchical state steering, governing where the state co-operates with societal actors and governing where the state plays little or no role (governing by, governing with and governing without the state). In contrast, in the narrow sense, governance only includes non-hierarchical forms. The narrow perception of governance is thus explicitly established in contrast to traditional state steering. It can then be equated with 'new' governance and upholds a government - governance dichotomy (cf. also Bell & Hindmoor, 2009). Apart from this, there are on the one hand single-dimensional governance concepts with a restricted focus on certain aspects of governing (such as interaction processes or used steering instruments), alongside multi-dimensional approaches that follow a broader perspective (cf. also Lange et al., 2013).

In this study, the notion of governance is used in a broad sense in both respects. I restrict it neither to non-hierarchical steering nor to a specific dimension of governing. From theoretical and empirical points of view, I hold that the concept can unfold its full value when used to denote all forms and dimensions of steering (for a similar argumentation in this regard cf. also e.g. Benz & Dose, 2010; Pierre & Peters, 2000). The governance approach then entails the ability to cover the whole range of institutions and actors involved in today's variety to govern.

At a general level, I conceive of governance as all forms of coordinating collective action in order to realize common objectives (or create societal opportunities) against the backdrop of a problem of public interest. More specifically, in this study, governance is defined as *coordinated and more or less institutionalized interactions of state and/or societal actors ultimately aiming at the realization of collective goals*. Following this perspective, governance encompasses interaction processes related to the coordination of actors, guided by formal and informal institutions in the pursuit of common goals (cf. further the conceptualization in chapter 3.1).

(ii.) Having introduced the concept of governance, I can in the following address in more detail the notion of *governance modes*. 'Modes of governance' are at the core of the discourse on governance. Yet, the missing conceptual clarity of governance goes hand in hand with confusion regarding its modes. This holds true for both sustainability governance literature and governance literature in general. In light of this, chapter

3.2 explicitly deals with finding a way for meaningfully distinguishing among governance modes.

In general, there are various different understandings and no universally accepted definition of the term. Diedrichs et al. (2011, p. 1) recently complained: »*Still, there is little consensus on what modes of governance exactly are.*« (cf. also Bulkeley et al., 2007; Knill, 2004; Smismans, 2008; Tömmel, 2009; Homeyer, 2006; Pahl-Wostl, 2015). When authors use certain labels for signifying particular modes, it is frequently not clear what they are really referring to and the labeling remains at a rather vague level. In many studies, there remains a pretty undifferentiated picture. A unified typology or a coherent taxonomy is accordingly very much in its beginning stages (cf. also Hillman et al., 2011, p. 409: »*Past attempts to conceptualize modes of governance have sometimes led to more confusion than clarity [...] Better analytical clarity is needed to arrive at operationalizations useful for empirical research.*«). As conceptual frames usually form the fundament for guiding empirical research, the non-existent conceptual agreement goes hand in hand with missing empirical scrutiny. Both the richness of prevalent real-world governance arrangements and the nuance embedded in these are far from sufficiently understood.

Different proposals for classifications of governance modes exist (cf. e.g. Kooiman, 2003; Fenger & Bekkers, 2007; Blatter, 2007; Howlett & Ramesh, 2015; Pierre & Peters, 2005). In most basic terms, authors conceive 'modes of governance' as forms of social order, i.e. basic coordination principles. On an abstract, aggregated societal level, the term then refers to three general ideal types of institutions of hierarchies, markets (more generally competition systems) and networks (more generally negotiation systems) - with partly different terminology and modifications (e.g. Lowndes & Skelcher, 1998; Thompson et al., 1991).[5] However, for the purpose of this study to understand real-world governance arrangements and their relations to SD, one needs to go beyond these abstract types of

5 While hierarchies are associated with authority exercised by governments, operating through administrative orders and sets of rules, markets feature self-organization of private actors. Networks in turn are based on resource dependencies between state and societal actors (cf. in more detail e.g. Meuleman, 2008).

co-ordination on a highly aggregated level. Apart from this, other contributions use the term governance modes to denote certain individual aspects of governing (such as policy instruments) or make use of such aspects for differentiating governance modes (e.g. Jordan et al., 2005). Although such studies give useful insights, they do not by themselves help to grasp the complexity of real-world arrangements. In contrast, several authors from the (sustainability) governance discourse have recently made efforts to consider this complexity by including multiple aspects in their analyses (e.g. Tollefson et al., 2008; Howlett et al., 2009; Pahl-Wostl, 2009; Van de Meene et al., 2011; Van Leeuwen & Van Tatenhove, 2010; Weber et al., 2011). Among these contributions, there are three coherent proposals that aim to meaningfully differentiate among modes of governance (Driessen et al., 2012; Arnouts et al., 2011; Hysing, 2009). These proposals are addressed in detail in chapter 3.2.

The basic understanding of the term governance modes in this study is based on the governance definition presented above. I accordingly perceive of governance modes as *forms of realizing collective goals by means of coordinated action* (this understanding will be specified in chapter 3.2). This covers the whole scope of steering societies - from hierarchical governing by centralized governments (top-down intervention) to joint action (e.g. collaborative and network governance) up to societal self-organization (without direct governmental interference). Basically, modes of governance can thus be described as the specific appearance that a certain governance arrangement takes. The term *governance arrangement* is accordingly used to denote a specific empirical real world setting that can be allocated to a certain mode.

(iii.) The missing conceptual clarity regarding the concepts of 'governance' and 'governance modes' comes along with confusion about the more specific term of '*new modes of governance*'. The notion has become a buzzword within (sustainability) governance literature over the last decade and is especially used in conjunction with various normative claims. However, within the literature, its meaning differs and it frequently remains unclear what is exactly 'new' about new governance (cf. also Gunningham, 2009, p. 146: »*The term is defined more by what it is not, than by what it is. And where it is defined, this is often done in such broad terms that it does little to narrow the scope of inquire or to identify what is distinctive about this form of governance.*«).

The variety of examples of governance forms that are (or can be) labelled as 'new modes' is expansive. Most prominent examples are participatory governance (e.g. Heinelt, 2002), network governance (e.g. Dedeurwaerdere, 2005), collaborative governance (e.g. Ansell & Gash, 2008), reflexive governance (e.g. Voss et al., 2006), adaptive governance (e.g. Folke et al., 2005), multi-level or polycentric governance (e.g. Hooghe & Marks, 2001), interactive governance (e.g. Driessen et al., 2001), public-private partnerships (e.g. Lowndes & Skelcher, 1998), deliberative governance (e.g. Pattberg, 2007), and self-governance (e.g. Sørensen & Triantafillou, 2013).

While there is accordingly no common definition of 'new modes' in the literature, it is possible to identify recurring characteristics. The common core of new modes descriptions - and the understanding of the notion in this study - is that the term labels non-hierarchical governing forms that incorporate societal actors (from market or civil society), either exclusively or together with governmental actors.

Apart from this, several scholars identify key characteristics frequently associated with new governance modes (see e.g. Van der Heijden, 2013; Nelissen, 2002; Gunningham, 2009; Holley et al., 2012; Tollefson et al., 2012). According to these authors, new modes are rather characterized by participatory deliberation, polycentric and multi-level collaboration, devolved decision-making, consensus-building as well as heterarchy through power sharing. Further associated characteristics are flexibility, experimentalism, ongoing readjustment, and non-coerciveness - coming along with embedded values like learning, adaptability and integrative solutions.

The inclusion of 'new' implies that such governing forms have become implemented only recently. There seems to be a trend that these forms increasingly have become more common over the past two decades (cf. e.g. Bäckstrand et al., 2010). However, it must be clearly pointed out that some governance arrangements may have historically been relatively new in some policy sectors but long-established practices in other contexts (cf. also Treib et al., 2007). Thus, generally speaking, I hold the juxtaposition of 'old' traditional modes and 'new' modes as principally misleading - just as a government-governance dichotomy. Accordingly, I adopt the popular terminology of 'new' modes only for the purpose of labeling.

Having clarified the concepts of SD, governance and governance modes, I can in the next chapter address the overlapping field of sustainability governance by consolidating its discourse.

2.3 Consolidating the sustainability governance discourse

The field of sustainability governance has received concerted attention in an immense amount of studies within the last decades (for an overview see e.g. Adger & Jordan, 2009). A general rationale for linking SD and governance can be expressed as follows. When SD is discussed, the question arises of how it can be put into practice (and governance plays a decisive role in this regard). Likewise, when governance is addressed, the overall purpose behind governing is of central concern (and sustainability has become a frame of reference in this respect).

Sustainability governance can be basically understood as socio-political governing oriented towards the attainment of SD (Meadowcroft, 2007) or as purposeful action to change (facets of) society in a more sustainable direction (Voss et al., 2007). As introduced above, the field addresses the endeavor of governing in view of complex and long-term sustainability problems, including ambivalent goals and uncertain knowledge. Since promoting societal transformation processes towards SD includes multi-dimensional challenges, sustainability governance represents a 'wicked' endeavor itself. It principally covers the joint promotion by political-administrative, market and civil society actors and takes place on various levels (local, regional, national and international). Moreover, it affects different policy fields (such as the energy, water or the agricultural sector), is situated within and among socio-economic and ecological spheres, and its future orientation crosses temporal scales.

Against this background, literature within the multi-facetted sustainability governance discourse explores or prescribes the requirements, designs and means, as well as potentials and limits of governing towards SD in different contexts (cf. also Bornemann et al., *forthcoming*; for recent specific conceptual frameworks on sustainability governance cf. e.g. Huh, 2011; Wydra & Pülzl, 2013; Shiroyama et al., 2012; Iribarnegaray & Seghezzo, 2012). The diversity within the discourse thereby reflects the ambiguities associated with 'governance' and 'sustainability' as well as the variety of problems addressed. In thematic terms, there are moreover several adjacent discourses that exhibit a certain intersection with the sustainability governance discourse. Examples are the research fields of environmental governance, earth system governance, governing commons, global governance or governance of wicked problems. The lines in this regard are blurred, since contributions in these fields frequently refer to the concept of sustainability.

As a first basic orientation to structure the discourse, literature on sustainability governance can be distinguished according to whether it is oriented towards normative or to empirical-analytical contributions (see also Jordan, 2008; Steurer, 2010; this characteristic is shared with governance literature in general). The *normative literature strand* exhibits an explicit prescriptive agenda, i.e. arguing for something that should be adopted in order to achieve preferred goals (e.g. Voss et al., 2006; OECD, 2002). It is thus headed towards prescribing ideal forms of governance that match ideas associated with SD. This literature strand is frequently subsumed under the term 'governance *for* sustainable development'. One of the most prominent approaches in this regard is the reflexive governance approach - together with the connected examples of transition management and adaptive management, which address dealing with socio-technical and socio-ecological systems respectively (cf. e.g. Kemp et al., 2005; Brousseau et al., 2012; Voss et al., 2006; Grin et al., 2010; Loorbach, 2010 - and Armitage et al., 2009; Foxon et al., 2009). A more general strand is the debate on 'good' governance. Several principles have emerged on how governance should be conducted (such as openness, legitimacy, effectiveness, transparency, accountability, predictability, participation and the rule of law, cf. e.g. UNDP, 1997; Lockwood, 2010; Griffin, 2008). These principles share some similarities with the normative principles from the particular sustainability governance discourse.

In contrast, the *empirical-analytically grounded strand* focuses on analyzing and explaining existing real-world sustainability governance arrangements (cf. e.g. Baker & Eckerberg, 2008; Evans et al., 2006). Publications in this regard, for instance, examine how SD has been interpreted and implemented in distinct governance systems (e.g. the implementation of national SD strategies or the manifestations of SD within international governing). This literature strand is often termed 'governance *of* sustainable development'.

However, overall the lines between the normative and the empirical-analytical strand are frequently not clearly cut (for instance, when studies entail an implicit normative perspective, hidden in certain underlying assumptions - e.g. rooted in notions such as new modes of governance).

This study clearly follows an empirical-analytically grounded sustainability governance research perspective. Accordingly, sustainability governance and its modes are addressed as an empirical phenomenon to shed light on the relationship between governance modes and SD. This can in turn serve as a basis for critically discussing normative claims on modes of governance (as Capano et al., 2015b, p. 319, put it: »*The governance concept, freed of its ideological connotations and preferences for non-governmental modes of governing, is a powerful conceptual tool which can help to order and analyze the multifaceted ways through which policies are coordinated.*«).

Besides the distinction between normative and empirical-analytical contributions, literature on SD governance can be distinguished according to *other dividing lines* (cf. in the following in more detail, e.g. for respective references to example studies, Bornemann et al., *forthcoming*). A first basic distinction can be made in light of the context from which the contributions originate and the context in which they are applied. Both contexts can be either scientifically or practically based. As the boundaries are frequently blurred, the discourse seen as a whole exhibits a hybrid character.

Second, there are variations in terms of the addressed subject area of approaches. This concerns spatial scales (concerned with the global, supra-national, national, regional or multiple levels) and thematic fields (including encompassing approaches dealing e.g. with sustainability strategies or work on specific policy sectors or sector transcending problems).

Finally, there are variations in the rationale of approaches in terms of framing 'SD' and 'governance'. On the one hand, there is work that tends to see sustainability governance as a rather result-oriented technocratic endeavor to govern along fixed sustainability goals. On the other hand, there are approaches that rather highlight deliberation and discourse in view of dynamic and contextual sustainability understandings. In between these extremes, there are intermediate approaches that exhibit a mixed character in terms of this framing.

Despite these variations on the surface of the discourse, having a look at its deeper structure reveals that all the contributions in the field of sustainability governance build on certain *epistemic building blocks*, i.e. a recurring knowledge base. This includes both the more general governance and the sustainability discourse, as well as empirical knowledge from different fields, theoretical accounts (about society, politics and nature as well as their interplay) or practical knowledge in terms of implementing SD. All these knowledge bases entail specific potentials for illuminating and substantiating the field of sustainability governance.

2.4 Governance modes and sustainability

Having outlined the SD governance discourse, I will - in light of the research perspective of this study - elaborate in the following on the linkage between governance modes and SD. I will first go into detail with regard to normative claims in the literature and the lack of empirical evidence in this regard. After that I will broaden the perspective and elaborate on further connected research fields, i.e. illustrating what kind of empirical work already exists.

As already sketched out in the introduction, the normative SD governance literature strand has come up with a range of assumptions on governance modes and sustainability, bearing in mind the steering challenges associated with the pursuit of SD. This entails certain claims on the merits of governance modes, accompanied by guiding principles for appropriate sustainability governance. Generally speaking, the assumptions entail the idea that 'forms should follow functions'. Referring to the classical form-follows-function debate, Lafferty (2004) states that governance is never established in a societal vacuum and that forms of governance tend to reflect the dominant functions of the system to be governed (e.g. basic values and goals or interests of actors). Applying this logic of functional interdependence to the realm of SD, he argues that in order to be effective, governance for SD requires an adjustment of the form of governance according to stipulated SD functions (i.e. the governance form has to reflect and serve the functional prerequisites of SD).

When screening the literature, it seems that there is a pretty clear answer to the question which governance modes are best suited for governing societies towards SD. There is a strong and highly influential *normative claim for new modes*. Following this perspective, such modes should thus be advocated in governing practices. In light of proclaimed failures of hierarchical steering, new modes are commonly regarded as being able to handle the challenges of SD in a more adequate manner (see e.g. in Newig et al., 2008; Bäckstrand et al., 2010; Hogl et al., 2012). Behind this claim are assumptions such as that integrating multiple perspectives increases the flexibility to adapt to unexpected circumstances.

As Bressers (2004, p. 285) argues: »*The discourse on sustainable development governance has been dominated by a search for new and innovative steering mechanisms.*«

Normative assumptions also abound in the adjacent discourses mentioned above. Several claims are made with regard to the appropriate design of environmental governance (e.g. Jänicke, 2006), the governance of socio-ecological and socio-technical systems (e.g. Armitage et al., 2009; Borras & Edler, 2015), earth system governance[6] (e.g. Biermann, 2007), global governance (e.g. Commission on Global Governance, 1995), as well as the governance of wicked problems in general (e.g. Head, 2008).

Sustainability governance literature also shares the 'enthusiasm' for new modes with the more general governance discourse. Several studies in this regard put high expectations in such modes, e.g. in terms of effective and legitimate problem solving (»*Much is expected from such new governance arrangements. Scholars repeatedly refer to these as providing an opportunity for greater legitimacy and effectiveness than traditional modes of governance.*«, Van der Heijden, 2013, p. 454). Following a general perspective, scholars also explicitly praise the advantages of networks. Partly, there is a positive bias, since certain authors hold them more effective than hierarchies and markets per se (see in more detail e.g. Fotel, 2013; Larsson, 2015; for a recent overview in this regard see also e.g. Ramesh et al., 2015).

While some authors make explicit claims in terms of new modes and SD, other scholars put forth certain principles of how to govern in view of sustainability. As already introduced above, specific features are proclaimed to be closely connected with sustainability governance - such as participation, reflexiveness, adaptiveness, integration of policies and scales, deliberation and social learning (see e.g. Kemp et al., 2005; Huh, 2011; Shiroyama et al., 2012; Meadowcroft et al., 2005; Rist et al., 2007;

---

6 Especially with regard to environmental governance, the blurring of lines mentioned above gets expressed in contributions. For instance, while in Bäckstrand et al. (2010) the publication title refers to environmental governance, the authors explicitly elaborate on the concept of SD, including case studies stemming from the field of sustainability governance (cf. also Hogl et al., 2012; Newig & Kvarda, 2012; cf. in general also Brand, 2002).

Monkelbaan, 2015; Sajeva et al., 2015; Dedeurwaerdere, 2005; OECD, 2002). All these aspects can be associated with the characteristics of new modes of governance (cf. chapter 2.2).

For instance, Steurer (2010) recapitulates what he calls basic normative governance principles of sustainable development. Arguing that SD is above all an integrative challenge, he highlights the principles of integrating stakeholders, horizontal and vertical integration in terms of sectors and levels as well as reflexivity in terms of integrating different types of knowledge. Voss et al. (2007) proclaim an inadequacy of traditional steering approaches in light of ambivalent goals, uncertain knowledge and distributed power (cf. also Newig et al., 2008). They argue that only reflexive and participatory approaches address all these challenges. In accordance with this, the approach of 'reflexive governance for sustainable development' relies amongst others on six requirements to further continuous reflection and readjustment: integrated knowledge production, experimentation and adaptivity of strategies, anticipation of long-term effects, interactive participatory goal formulation and strategy implementation, as well as a congruency of governance and problem space (Voss et al., 2006; cf. also Brousseau et al., 2012; Kemp et al., 2005). More specifically, Loorbach, (2010) elaborates on what he terms a 'new governance approach for sustainable development', proclaiming the potential of transition management. Key characteristics of this highly influential approach in the broader sustainability governance discourse (developed in the realm of transition research; cf. e.g. Grin et al., 2010) are system innovation as well as experimentation and envisioning in multi-stakeholder transition arenas.

In order to demonstrate the omnipresence of assumptions regarding new modes of governance, an overview of recent key citations from the literature is given in the following (table 2). Note that some authors refer to the discourse as a whole and do not necessarily share the assumptions.

Table 2: Recent references to assumptions regarding new modes of governance (own illustration)

Reference	Citation
Newig & Kvarda, 2012, p. 29	*»Traditional modes of collective decision-making for complex [...] sustainability problems are increasingly questioned. More and more, representative-democratic, top-down administrative procedures are challenged by participatory, collaborative and network-like modes of governance involving civil society actors [...] These problems may be addressed by more flexible, adaptive forms of governance that help broaden the societal basis.«*
Meadowcroft, 2011, p. 537	*»Issues related to sustainability can be cited as typical of the kind of complex and deep-seated societal problems which traditional - state-centered and hierarchical - modes of governance are ill equipped to handle.«*
Jordan, 2008, p. 27	*»These [new modes of governance] are widely held to be better at dealing with something like sustainable development.«*
Griffin, 2010, p. 366	*»Sustainability is said to require a climate of 'dialogue', 'partnership' and 'shared responsibility', rather than centralized 'command and control' policies.«*
Dijk, 2015, p. 136, 138	*»New governance approaches, such as interactive arrangements, networks and partnerships, have emerged [...] Although the quest for a sustainable society cannot be managed in terms of command and control, it can be managed in terms of influencing and adjusting: a more subtle, evolutionary way of influencing the direction and pace of developments [...] We see the need for a further shift from government (and its state-centric approach) to governance (and its more pluralistic approaches). The nature of sustainability issues [...] requires a more dynamic governance approach.«*
Bäckstrand et al., 2010, p. 12, 15	*»In the sustainability governance literature, new modes are seen as examples of deliberative and collaborative governance. These governance modes are claimed to be functional, to handle the complex [...] aspects of modern [...] problems. Uncertainty and risk requires participation of a multiplicity of actors.«*
Webb, 2005, p. 246	*»Top-down, state-centered approaches to regulation [...] are particularly vulnerable to failure [...] The suggestion being made is that multivariate, multiparty governance approaches have a better likelihood of success in such choppy waters because they harness the energies and experience of multiple parties and perspectives and are therefore likely to be more robust, flexible, responsive, efficient, and effective. In a word, they are more likely be sustainable in today's operating environment.«*
Lockwood et al., 2010, p. 987, 990	*»These governing arrangements are especially evident in policy arenas informed by the discourse of sustainability, which has an explicit ethical foundation in notions of participation, responsibility, stewardship, and duty of care, and which makes novel demands on institutions and policy [...] New governance modes therefore provide opportunities to address problems characterized by complexity, uncertainty, interdependency, and deficiencies in resources, expertise, and knowledge.«*
Meuleman & Niestroy, 2015, p. 12300	*»Together with the complex causal chains and uncertainties that the SD challenge entails, these requirements have led to a general preference for 'networking' [...] The preference for networking as a governance style seems to make sense for the challenges of sustainability, which are impossible to 'control' from a single center.«*
Loorbach, 2010, p. 161, 164	*»Sustainable development is used here as a common notion referring to those persistent problems in [...] societies that can only be dealt with on the very long term [...] through specific types of network and decision-making processes [...] Dealing with persistent societal problems in the long term will require approaches that give special attention to learning, interaction, integration, and experimentation on the level of society.«*

Kardos, 2012, p. 1168	*»The traditional models of governance, dominated by regulatory control of formal state institutions, are not well equipped to carry out the shifts that sustainable development implies and proved their limitations.«*
Capano et al., 2012, p. 57	*»These are examples of those wicked or even 'super wicked' problems, which originally spurred governance experiments and for which new governance arrangements are supposed to be uniquely well adapted.«*
Zhang, 2015, p. 380	*»In the past two decades, scholars have both advocated for and expected a transition from hierarchical governance modes dominated by governments to non-hierarchical governance modes (market and network governance) [...] Growing uncertainty and complexity in these policy domains has given rise to a host of 'wicked problems' that require much greater flexibility and responsiveness in regulatory instruments and governing processes than can be offered by the hierarchical governing model that states traditionally relied on.«*
Ferlie et al., 2013, p. 4	*»Networks may well be the most suitable governance mode in those many and expanding policy arenas characterized by 'wicked problems'.«*
Bell & Morrison, 2015, p. 519	*»Scholars argue that only an adaptive governance style is sufficiently flexible to deal with sudden changes, complexity and uncertainty. Within this paradigm, it is assumed that governing in general should move from precaution and hierarchy to adaptiveness and networks.«*
Buizer et al., 2011, p. 23	*»Governance is a response to the mounting complexity and multilayered nature of [...] problems, which are assumed not to have been adequately addressed by hierarchical government. As a consequence, scientists observe and often advocate various new modes of governance.«*
Pahl-Wostl, 2009, p. 357	*»This reflects the need for new modes of governance and knowledge generation to deal with increasing uncertainty and complexity.«*
Booher & Innes, 2010, p.10	*»We believe that this emergent governance form is more resonant with effective approaches [...] than are traditional government practices [...] Self-organizing processes can make governance systems more resilient in the face of change and complexity.«*
Gunningham, 2009, p. 146	*»New governance is claimed to be more responsive, legitimate, and effective than top-down approaches because deliberation, cooperation, and learning at local level may lead to responses which better take account of local circumstances, build on local knowledge and capacities, and result in greater stakeholder ownership and 'buy in'. It is also, arguably, better able to transcend jurisdictional boundaries than traditional approaches.«*
Adelt et al., 2014, p. 437	*»There is some consensus in governance literature that modern ways of self-organized coordination perform better than traditional ways of hierarchical control.«*
Hogl et al., 2012, p. 9	*»New modes of governance typically come with high expectations. With their enhanced levels of inclusiveness, participation and reflexivity, they are perceived to ensure policy-making that is both more effective and legitimate.«*

Overall, the normative claim putting emphasis on new modes has become so influential that a decisive part of the sustainability governance discourse is clearly marked by it. This includes not only the normative strand, but also the empirical-analytical strand with implicit, hidden assumptions. This part of the discourse treats the idea that 'sustainability governance means governing through new modes' as almost common sense and self-evident without questioning it - and in so doing it is reproduced.

As this is a common belief that is taken for granted, in this part of the discourse it could be characterized as what Bourdieu (1977) called a 'doxa' (see also Bourdieu's specific illustration of the notion, Bourdieu & Eagleton, 1992). Based on this 'doxa', more particular claims for designing sustainability governance are made. Critical studies are in the minority - and drawbacks of new modes are frequently neglected. Against this backdrop, Arnouts and Arts (2009) recently argued that the 'dark side' of new governance remains undertheorized.

The prominence of the normative claim has been strengthened by certain other influences. For instance, there is a connection with the established general assumption in SD literature that the pursuit of sustainability requires participation (as for instance proclaimed in Agenda 21 approaches, cf. UNCED, 1992). This pursuit of participation has been transferred to the governance realm, e.g. by arguing that both legitimacy and effectiveness become increased (see in more detail e.g. Newig & Kvarda, 2012). Moreover, there is a mutual reinforcement with actual practices - since the field of sustainability governance has become a crucial experimental arena for new modes (cf. also e.g. Meadowcroft, 2011; Bäckstrand et al., 2010; Bressers, 2004). This potentially reproduces an unquestioned assumption that new modes generally perform better than traditional ones.

Aspects like participation, and thus facilitating to co-create the evolution of societies, may entail an intrinsic value. Furthermore, e.g. flexibility in courses of actions to uphold adaptation options is without doubt crucial in light of SD and its future orientation (cf. also chapter 3.4). However, in this regard, it is important to make a distinction in terms of the level of governance and the level of society. The question is whether e.g. reflexive governance is inevitable for upholding societal adaptation options, or if hierarchical governance is potent in doing so, too. This leads us to the distinction between governance processes and results.

As already introduced above, within the literature there is a frequent lack of distinction between the processes of governance and its results (see e.g. Emerson & Nabatchi, 2015, who explicitly highlight a conflation of process and result performance, cf. also Young, 2009). The sustainability governance literature has been more oriented on processes thus far (cf. also the related debate on 'good governance', cf. also e.g. Holley et al., 2012). In line with this, Bell & Morrison (2015) point to the danger that governance studies focus so much on processes that they tend to overlook results. Yet, although governance processes and results go hand in hand (cf. also Dang et al., 2015, on the concept of governance capacity), a ′good′ process in view of SD - whatever this may look like - does not automatically lead to sustainable contributions on the ground. While a ′good′ process might be desirable in itself, it is important to clearly differentiate between ′sustainable processes′ and ′sustainable results′.

The existing conflation of process and result performance is also due to a lack of conceptual clarity in terms of the chain of governance results. Thus far there is no consistency in the use of key terms in the literature. This will be addressed in chapter 3.3, in which I will clarify the chain of governance results and conceptualize governance impacts.

Despite the normative claims putting emphasis on new modes in terms of promoting SD, several scholars do explicitly point to the fact that such assumptions have not been approved by sound evidence. They argue that there is thus far a *lack of empirical studies* on the relation between governance modes and SD (cf. e.g. Griffin, 2010; Jordan, 2008; Filho et al., 2016; Adger & Jordan, 2009; Bäckstrand et al., 2010; Hogl et al., 2012). The high normative appeal may in this regard have slowed down the needed empirical scrutiny. A lack of evidence is also prevalent with regard to the general merits of modes, as elaborated in the broader governance literature. Table 3 provides an overview of recent citations referring to shortcomings of empirical scrutiny on the merits of governance modes.

Table 3: Recent references to missing evidence on the merits of governance modes (own illustration)

Reference	Citation
Filho et al., 2016, p. 755	*»There is a paucity of research which explore the links between governance and sustainability.«*
Howlett & Ramesh, 2015, p. 23	*»Lost in the pursuit of these ideologically preferred alternatives, however, is the understanding of whether or not a preferred governance mode can actually address a particular sector's problems.«*
Adger & Jordan, 2009, p. 20	*»There is a need for more work which sees the governance of sustainability in terms of both processes and outcomes [...] We need to know what forms of governing lead to what sorts of outcomes.«*
Mahanti & Manuel-Navarrete, 2015, p. 416	*»However, the concrete relationship between governing processes and sustainability outcomes remains obscure.«*
Vodden, 2015, p. 2	*»[There is a] lack of empirical evidence that collaborative governance is better able to avoid unsustainable pathways than traditional governance approaches. [This calls for] more rigorous, empirical assessment of collaborative governance approaches and their performance.«*

Klijn, 2012, p. 294	»*The question whether [new governance] delivers what it promises (i.e. more effective, efficient and legitimate dealing with complex problems) is one of the most important questions.*«
Hogl et al., 2012, p. 18	»*[It is the] empirical evaluation of new modes of governance, which has been called for in the literature.*«
Holley et al., 2012, p. 10	»*There is little evidence that [new governance] actually delivers on its normative promises.*«
Newig & Kvarda, 2012, p. 30	»*Whereas the ideological basis for new forms of governance has already reached a mature state, their actual performance is far from evident.*«
Bäckstrand et al., 2010, p. 4	»*[There is a] lack of critical-empirical studies of the promise of new modes.*«
Emerson & Nabatchi, 2015, p. 719	»*The normative appeal of collaborating across boundaries to solve complex public problems or deliver public goods and services may have slowed the needed scrutiny of these rapidly proliferating forms of governance.*«
Ansell & Gash, 2008, p. 549	»*Is collaborative governance more effective? Very few of the studies we reviewed actually evaluated governance outcomes [...] Systematic comparisons were rarely explicitly made.*«
Duit et al., 2010, p. 366	»*We currently have very little systematic knowledge about how different types of real-world governance systems differ in their ability to cope with different types of complex change.*«
Hey et al., 2007, p. 1860	»*It is far from evident whether or not the 'new modes of governance' have a greater problem-solving capacity than the old ones, which is often taken for granted.*«

Overall, the overviews illustrate both the claim that certain modes are generally better suited to promote SD and the lack of empirical evidence. This study deals with this research desideratum by comparatively shedding light on governance modes in terms of promoting sustainable results.

In the following, I will *broaden the perspective* and address 'the bigger picture' of further connected research strands - in order to reveal what kind of work already exists in the wider sense connected to the research objective of this study.

There are several scholars who deal with the performance of governance modes (the notion of performance can mean different things according to different criteria; cf. e.g. Kenis & Provan, 2009; Heinelt, 2010; Anheier & List, 2013 - in this study the notion is used in a general manner, in the sense of denoting the merits of governance, cf. also e.g. Bäckstrand et al., 2010). However, there are differences with regard to the focus. A distinction has to be made in terms of three - partly overlapping - respects. This contrasts the already existing work from this study, and in so doing also positions the study in the broader multi-faceted field. To start with, a distinction has to be made between work that strives to scrutinize the performance of single governance modes and work that comparatively explores different modes. Furthermore, studies that assess the merits of modes in general terms have to be differentiated from work with a certain focus, e.g. in terms of environmental effectiveness or promoting SD, which in turn is a decisive difference. Finally, the merits of governance modes in terms of sustainability can be looked at by exploring governance and its procedures (respectively the mode of governance itself), or by addressing the contributions to SD in terms of results. In the following overview, these partly overlapping distinctions will become apparent.

A first field to be considered for seeing 'the bigger picture' is the broader governance literature, in which both theoretical and empirical studies address the general performance of modes - such as their ability of effective and legitimate problem solving (while, as indicated, the conceptualization of 'performance' varies; see e.g. Emerson & Nabatchi, 2015, Fawcett & Daugbjerg, 2012; cf. also Sørensen & Torfing, 2009, who argue that there is a lack of understanding what 'effective' means in terms of new governance modes).

Alongside the long established performance measurement of government programs and policy evaluation (cf. e.g. Hatry, 2006; Knoepfel et al., 2011), a prominent emerging strand of studies deals with the merits of collaborative, network or public-private governance (e.g. Koontz & Thomas, 2012; Kenis & Provan, 2009; Klijn et al., 2012). The lines among these studies are frequently blurred due to the similar characteristics of the modes and unclear terms (»*We lack clear, standardized definitions of terms such as 'network', 'governance' and 'collaboration'.*«, Emerson & Nabatchi, 2015, p. 718). This is conflated with the mentioned elusiveness in terms of process and results performance (cf. above and chapter 3.3).

The empirical studies in this broader field of governance research reveal a diverse picture with regard to the performance of collaborative, network and public-private governance (cf. e.g. Andrews & Entwistle, 2010; Speer, 2012; Kvartiuk, 2016). »*The evidence presented by the literature is at best mixed*« (Börzel & Panke, 2007, p. 158) and »*which of these modes of governance [...] is likely to function effectively, however, remain under-examined*« (Howlett & Ramesh, 2014, p. 318). There is thus no clear answer to the question if these modes of governance deliver what they promise - for instance, more effective and legitimate problem solving, compared to hierarchical governance (for a critical analysis cf. also Grande, 2012).

In view of the research objective of this study, it must be said that research in this broader field of governance studies can provide useful general insights.[7] However, with the broad focus, it does not contribute to illuminating the relation between governance modes and SD. Moreover, these studies mostly address only single governance modes and do not compare different modes in opposition (especially new to traditional ones). There is a general shortcoming in the literature in light of comparative empirical research on different modes (cf. also Howlett & Ramesh, 2015).

In contrast, for instance, Adelt et al. (2014) comparatively assess the merits of different governance approaches based on a simulation experiment. Decentralized coordination is compared to hierarchical control and soft control to strong control in view of their ability to cope with complex systems. The authors conclude that the examination produced a rather ambiguous picture and that the question of which governance forms are best suited cannot be answered generally.

Ramesh et al. (2015) furthermore compare the experience of the three broader forms of hierarchies, markets and networks in a case study regarding different countries and covering three decades. They conclude that non-hierarchical governance is not a substitute for state steering in situations where government failures exist.

However, in light of this study, these studies do not cover the full range of meaningfully differentiated governance modes and again do not strive at a sustainability appraisal.

Apart from this, there is work that explicitly deals with the endeavor of evaluating sustainability governance (or adjacent work focusing on environmental governance, earth system governance and so forth). Several scholars approach this topic by proposing evaluation criteria of governance for SD. For instance, Adger et al. (2003) propose the criteria of equi-

7 Useful insights can in turn also be provided not only by more general, but also by more specific literature. This is true e.g. in terms of the established more specific literature on the evaluation of policy instruments, for instance, the effectiveness of voluntary (environmental) agreements. However, a policy instrument reflects only a part of a governance mode (cf. in more detail chapter 3.1 and 3.2).

ty, efficiency, effectiveness and legitimacy. Biermann et al. (2010) argue to look at architecture, agency, adaptiveness, accountability, allocation and access.

An illustrative empirical investigation following such criteria is provided by Den Uyl (2014, cf. also Den Uyl & Driessen, 2015), who comparatively explores three different new modes of governance. She first of all points to a lack of studies comparing more than one governance mode in view of sustainability. Taking up this shortcoming, she evaluates the modes 'adaptive management',' transition management' and 'payments for environmental services' in terms of a set of criteria (equity, democracy, legitimacy as well as handling issues of scale and uncertainty).

Yet, in light of this study it must be noted that this part of the literature mostly focuses on governance processes or the mode of governance itself. As highlighted above, this study is not addressing this field - but the contribution of modes to SD in terms of results.

On the other hand, there are studies that do address results by exploring the environmental effectiveness of (new modes of) governance, i.e. the attainment of environmental targets. A prominent strand in this regard addresses participatory and collaborative governance (e.g. Scott, 2015; Biddle & Koontz, 2014; Newig & Fritsch, 2009; Gerlak et al., 2013; Young et al., 2013; Koontz & Thomas, 2006; Dupius & Knoepfel, 2015). There is also work dealing more generally with the environmental performance of new modes (e.g. Van der Heijden, 2013 and 2015; Arnouts & Arts, 2009; De Ona & Morales, 2013).

The results of empirical studies in this line reveal no straightforward answer to judge whether e.g. participative and collaborative modes perform well with regard to environmental effectiveness. The overall picture remains rather fragmented with conflicting evidence. Nearly all scholars explicitly argue that more studies are needed that explore the link between new modes and environmental results (while e.g. Scott, 2015, p. 537, states that »*we still know very little about the relationship between collaboration and environmental outcomes*«, Newig, 2012, p. 59, concludes that »*there is much belief on the merits of participation in environmental governance, but little evidence*«).

Yet, in light of the research objective of this study, it has to be clearly pointed out in this regard that the promotion of sustainability means more than environmental effectiveness (as elaborated in chapters 1.1 and 2.1, cf.

also chapter 3.4) (apart from that, the studies also frequently lack a comparison of different modes).

Taking everything into account, there is a lack of empirical studies that comparatively explore the merits of different governance modes with regard to SD in terms of results. There are neither studies that cover the full range of governance modes, nor studies that holistically strive to scrutinize the merits of modes in view of sustainable results. As already mentioned above, empirical studies in the field of sustainability governance frequently reduce their research on exploring the presence or absence of certain modes in specific sectors (cf. also Adger & Jordan, 2009). It is thus an open question whether certain modes are in fact generally preferable to others, and there is a need for exploring the relation of modes and SD.

The *state of research* in sustainability governance relevant for this study and thus the point of departure for the upcoming theoretical framework can be summarized as follows. It is generally acknowledged that governance is pivotal for catalyzing and coordinating societal transformation processes towards SD. However, in view of a variety of existing modes in modern societies, it is an open question how to govern in such a way that SD is best fostered. There is an influential normative claim that new modes are superior to hierarchical ones in this regard, but a lack of sound empirical evidence.

Apart from that, there is little conceptual clarity on governance, its modes and results - which hampers empirical inquiry. In order to address the knowledge desideratum of exploring the potential of modes to promote SD, it is thus first necessary to develop a sound conceptualization of governance and find a way to meaningfully distinguish modes. Furthermore, it is essential to clarify the field of governance results and find a way to grasp them. Finally, there is a need to develop particular (context-specific) sustainability criteria for appraising results (in a certain field). All this will be addressed in the upcoming chapters.

3 Theoretical framework

In light of the theoretical desiderata revealed in the last chapter, this part of the study is concerned with developing the theoretical framework that serves as a basis for the empirical part. The framework is composed of four building blocks. I will start with the conceptualization of governance (chapter 3.1), followed by the formal frame for meaningfully differentiating among modes of governance (chapter 3.2), the heuristic device for grasping governance impacts (chapter 3.3) and finally the normative frame for the appraisal of impacts in terms of SD (chapter 3.4).

3.1 Conceptualization of governance

As introduced in chapter 2.2, there is no generally accepted definition of 'governance' - and what is more, no agreement on the aspects that are covered by the term. Some authors use it to denote a specific facet of steering, while others employ it to grasp several facets. Against the backdrop of missing conceptual clarity, the first theoretical desideratum - that the research question of this study is calling for - is a sound conceptualization of governance.

My point of departure is the definition of governance as provided in chapter 2.2 (*coordinated and more or less institutionalized interactions of state and/or societal actors ultimately aiming at the realization of collective goals*). The conceptualization shall enable a deepened understanding of the social phenomenon of real-world governance (in other words, governance as an empirical phenomenon shall be grasped by certain deductively derived determinants). More specifically, the conceptualization shall allow the reconstruction of the inner functioning of governance, i.e. to explore how governance works in different arrangements and settings. Accordingly, it must cover the inherent complexity of real-world arrangements. Within the broader logic of this study, this step is needed as a prerequisite to fully comprehend the sequence of governance and results. It will provide indications for the possible ways through which governance can induce societal changes. The more the complexity of arrangements is understood, the better one is able to explore relations to SD.

With this in mind, conceptualizing governance involves considering a complex set of interacting facets. In what follows, I will thus first provide a foundation for the conceptualization (chapter 3.1.1). In this regard, I systematize the diversity of governing facets by reinterpreting the prominent discourse 'from government to governance'. This will reveal a range of basic aspects identified within governance literature that should be covered by the conceptualization. Subsequently, I will argue that an orientation on the established structuring of the political via the dimensions of polity, politics and policy allows to meet the demand of covering this range of aspects. Based on this, I develop the conceptualization (chapters 3.1.2 and 3.1.3) (cf. in the following also Lange et al., 2013).

3.1.1 A foundation

The contemporary complexity of the real-world phenomenon of governance is closely connected to multi-faceted changes in governing over the past decades. As a foundational basis for the governance conceptualization, there is thus a need to look at this diversity of changes.

As introduced above, the increasing use of the governance concept is connected to the development over the past decades that governments are not the exclusively relevant entities when it comes to collective action and managing public goods. Accordingly, it aims to capture something broader than government. This is illustrated by the prominent storyline 'from government to governance', as frequently referenced in (SD) governance literature (cf. e.g. Fenger & Bekkers, 2007; Jordan et al., 2005; Pierre & Peters, 2005; Hackett, 2013; Arts, 2014; Jordan, 2008; Bell & Hindmoor, 2009; Hysing, 2009; Capano et al., 2015b; Torfing et al., 2012). However, this storyline remains at a very abstract level. While there is a consensus that 'governance' typically includes a broader spectrum of steering beyond 'conventional' government control, there is no agreement on what it is actually about. Changes in the way society is governed are frequently proclaimed in a very broad manner. Overall, the inflationary spread of the elusive storyline contributed to the confusion surrounding 'governance' and hampered the building of a coherent understanding.

In what follows, I will thus explore the storyline 'from government to governance' by having a deeper look at the (SD) governance literature and in this sense provide a reinterpretation. This is in line with other authors, who argue that the reality of modern governance is much messier and more complex than the storyline suggests (e.g. Tollefson et al., 2012;

Howlett et al., 2009). I will scrutinize it by closer looking at the two axes of (i.) the direction of the changes in governing and (ii.) the objects of change.

(i.) First of all, in terms of the *direction of changes*, 'from government to governance' implies that forms of hierarchical governance have increasingly given way to non-hierarchical ones. This indicates that authorities and competencies have moved away from the state to other bodies: a shift from state-centric to multi-centric governing. In this vein, the mainstream academic debate has presented changes in governing in a fairly unidirectional way. However, there is little empirical evidence supporting this widespread assumption (cf. e.g. Arts, 2014; Van Kersbergen & Van Waarden, 2004; Adger & Jordan, 2009; Kjær, 2004). Moreover, empirical research indeed indicates that the supposed storyline is too superficial and represents an oversimplification, disguising the richness of co-existing governance forms (Hysing, 2010; Koch, 2013; Tollefson et al., 2008; Jordan et al., 2005; Driessen et al., 2012; Weber et al., 2011). This research suggests that changes in governing are frequently not unidirectional but bidirectional movements - along a continuum between the two opposing extremes of state intervention (traditional hierarchical government control through authoritative allocation of values to society) and societal autonomy (self-organizing networks of co-coordinating societal actors).

Also, real-world arrangements could be placed in most cases somewhere along this continuum, rather than at the extreme poles. Along this line, Jordan et al. (2005, p. 484) argue that »*government and governance [...] are actually much more intertwined than is implied by some governance theorists*« (cf. also Hill & Lynn, 2005). Using the terminology of the storyline, 'government' and 'governance' thus are rather not fixed and clearly separated entities, but could be interpreted as two poles on a spectrum of different forms for realizing collective action.

Yet, in principle I regard a 'governance - government' dichotomy as misleading. As introduced in chapter 2.2, in this study, 'governance' is used as a concept that includes 'government' as a specific form (this point of view as an umbrella concept also helps to overcome the competing society-centered and state-centric perspectives in governance literature; cf. chapter 2.2, for an overview cf. e.g. Bell & Hindmoor, 2009; Capano et al., 2015a).

The discourse 'from government to governance' as a uniform shift towards non-hierarchical forms, is then rather to be interpreted in terms of multiple shifts between two poles on a continuum of state intervention and societal autonomy. Overall, contemporary real-world governing displays a plurality of simultaneously co-existing modes of governance resulting from various shifts in governing. Yet the question remains: what has actually changed?

(ii.) In terms of the *objects of change*, the discourse 'from government to governance' tends to ignore internal differences, especially with regard to which changes it actually entails. It implies that governing evenly shifts away from hierarchical to non-hierarchical forms with regard to all kinds of aspects. By failing to clearly differentiate among these aspects, it neglects the complex and multifaceted nature of real-world governing (in the words of Howlett et al., 2009, p. 384: »*What makes new governance something new and different is not always clear in accounts provided of the government to governance shift.*«). The general discourse thus has to be specified with regard to the objects of change.

Distilling the (SD) governance literature in more depth, scholars point to several changes in governing that have taken place within various different spheres (cf. e.g. Tollefson et al., 2008; Van Leeuwen & van Tatenhove, 2010; Capano et al., 2015a; Howlett et al., 2009; Pahl-Wostl, 2009; Van de Meene et al., 2011; Weber et al., 2011). The changes can be subsumed under the headings of shifts in the locus of governance (such as novel actors and increasing levels of policy-making) as well as shifts in the focus (like changing rule systems and new policy instruments). This entails an influence on different facets of governing, such as power relations between actors, decision-making structures, the way policy is made, how problems are defined and which solutions are considered legitimate.

All the different spheres of changes have an interdependent character (cf. in this regard empirical findings pointing to complex mutual influences of certain governance facets, e.g. Craik et al., 2012; Capano et al., 2012; Doelle et al., 2012; Howlett, 2009). For instance, increasing participation of non-state actors tends to foster a more pronounced multi-level character of processes and non-coercive power relations. These trends in turn provoke new practices of policy-making, challenging the conventional types of law and leading to new, e.g. more informal, rule systems and novel types of soft law, such as voluntary agreements (see also the traditional debates in political sciences on the relationships among political processes, policies and institutions, e.g. Lowi, 1972; Heinelt, 2007, cf. furthermore discussions on the relation between structure and agency as well as actor-institution configurations, e.g. Marsh & Smith, 2000; North, 1990).

Accordingly, instead of regarding governance changes as one-dimensional shifts (as proclaimed by the storyline 'from government to governance'), it must be pointed out that changes in governing are a good deal more complicated. They should be regarded as a consequence of complex and variable interrelations between several facets (e.g. who governs by which means and conditions, in pursuit of which goals, based on what kind of knowledge and with which results). Due to these various facets that mutually influence each other, today's reality of the phenomenon of governance is highly diverse and variegated, showing a 'messy' and complex picture. It is characterized by an intrinsic multi-dimensionality with interdependent aspects. In order to understand real-world governance arrangements, this has to be taken into account. I will address this challenge of capturing the aspects from various different spheres of governing in the following part.

3.1.2 Basic structure: three dimensions and their interplay

The reinterpretation of the discourse 'from government to governance' along the two axes of the direction and objects of changes has revealed a multitude of governing facets, related in a nested fashion. Against this backdrop, I hold that a satisfactory governance conceptualization has to fulfill two requirements. On the one hand, it has to provide a sufficiently nuanced picture to capture the inherent complexity sketched out above. On the other hand, it must be able to adequately address the interrelations and feedback loops among the different facets.

To meet these two demands, I propose to conceptualize governance by means of the three interdependent dimensions of *governance structures*, *processes* and *contents* with a particular focus on their *interplay*. The logic behind this trilogy corresponds with the long-established structuring of the political via the dimensions of polity (structures), politics (processes) and policy (contents) (see e.g. Pennings et al., 2006; von Prittwitz, 1994; Lauth & Wagner, 2010). Recently, a range of studies has emerged that argue for using this tripartition in order to analyze real-world governance arrangements (e.g. van Leeuwen & van Tatenhove, 2010; Treib et al., 2007; Kritzinger & Pülzl, 2008; Wydra & Pülzl, 2013; Benz & Dose,

2010; Zürn, 2008; von Blumenthal, 2014). Other scholars also propose a division of governance into a structural, procedural and substantive dimension, yet without explicitly referring to polity, politics and policy (e.g. Tollefson et al., 2008 and 2012; Driessen et al., 2012; Hysing, 2009).

My conceptualization thus fits with a recent development in the literature to use all three dimensions of the political for grasping the complex phenomenon of governance. However, the specific elaboration of the three dimensions in light of steering, i.e. what aspects the dimensions specifically should include to shed light on real-world arrangements, is far from clear in the literature. I will accordingly address this question in detail in the following. The basic structure of the governance conceptualization unfolds as follows:

(i.) With the dimension of *governance structures* I refer to the framing conditions of governance, i.e. to the institutional architecture composed of formal and informal rule systems and the resulting roles, relations and mechanisms of social interaction among actors on different institutional levels.

(ii.) The dimension of *governance processes* incorporates the actual decision-making and implementation processes of interaction taking place during governing. This dimension thus entails how the interests of different state and/or societal actors with varying resources, power and influence are transformed into coordinated action.

(iii.) With the dimension of *governance contents* I refer to the substantive policy setting of governance. This dimension refers to the appearance of problem definitions, decisions, objectives and steering instruments as well as of general characteristics such as the degree of the pursuit for learning and integration or the policy-science interface.

(iv.) The *interplay* of the interdependent dimensions of governance structures, processes and contents finally highlights three two-sided linkages: the structures-processes interplay, the processes-contents interplay and the structures-contents interplay. This aspect thus allows a differentiated analysis of the interrelations among the dimensions.

The entirety of the three dimensions is referred to in this study with the umbrella term *governance workings* - as together they depict how governance works in different arrangements. The term thus covers the dynamic relations among institutional structures, interaction processes and substantive components.

Capturing the complexity of governance arrangements by means of three interrelated dimensions and their interplay is a tangible approach that at the same time allows sufficient nuance within each dimension. The conceptualization can serve as a heuristic lens to reconstruct the contextual realities of the co-ordination of actors and institutions in policy systems in detail. Yet, it must be considered that the tripartite division is an analytical distinction. This means that certain complex empirical phenomena can frequently not be reduced and allocated to only one particular dimension but rather transcend the dimensions. Having this in mind, I explicitly do justice to the real-world interconnectedness of the dimensions by clearly considering their interplay.

Apart from being able to grasp the range of governance facets sketched out in the previous chapter, the particular choice of the three dimensions can be further rationalized as follows. First of all, I argue that all three dimensions are constitutive for governance. As argued above, I regard the ultimate aim of governance as realizing common objectives against the background of collective problems. Following this understanding, it becomes apparent that each of the three dimensions is a crucial component. In order to realize collective goals, governance necessarily includes some form of decision-making and implementation processes, presupposes a certain institutional set-up that provides an embedding frame and is supposed to yield certain material products (that ultimately address the problem at hand).

Moreover, the three dimensions also allow the integration of different spheres that are associated with the notion of governance in the literature. Authors frequently point to certain structural facets (e.g. Rosenau, 1992; Biermann et al., 2010), procedural features (e.g. Rhodes, 1997) or substantive aspects of governance (e.g. Héritier, 2002) (see also in general Pierre & Peters, 2000; for an overview cf. also Levi-Faur, 2012).

While studying particular facets can indeed give useful detailed insights, I hold that the full picture of governance can only be understood when the different focal points of interest are brought together. In line with this, several authors point to the importance of a multi-dimensional perspective for understanding governance (e.g. Hufty, 2011; Mees et al., 2013; van Assche et al., 2014b; Lin et al., 2014; Hillman et al., 2011;

Newell et al., 2009; Christou & Simpson, 2009; Bressers & Kuks, 2003; Van Trung Ho et al., 2014). Rayner (2015) also argues that within the literature, there is an increasing recognition of governance as a multi-dimensional concept.

Accordingly, I am rather critical of approaches that neglect certain facets in their governance analyses (such as substantive aspects; for a critical discussion on neglecting content-related settings cf. also e.g. Heidbreder, 2009). In contrast, by integrating the different strands that are frequently explored separately in governance literature, my conceptualization is both differentiated and comprehensive. Thus, it potentially depicts a way towards a more unified theory of governance.

Since the conceptualization simultaneously analyzes governance from three different angles, it furthermore can bring together different disciplinary research strands within governance research and beyond (e.g. the legal scholarship that focuses on the role of law and strands with a focus on institutions or actors). As the logic behind the approach builds on the traditional structuring of the political, it is furthermore connectable with more general approaches (e.g. the 'Institutional Analysis and Development framework'; e.g. Ostrom, 1998, the 'Advocacy coalitions framework'; e.g. Sabatier, 1998; or the 'Actor-centered institutionalism framework'; e.g. Scharpf, 1997 - for an overview on different approaches that study the political see e.g. Sabatier, 2007). Moreover, since the approach is not reduced to one specific theoretical perspective, it can also be connected to general theories such as power- and interest-based, institutional or discourse theories.

3.1.3 The conceptualization in detail

Having outlined and justified the basic structure of the conceptualization, I can now elaborate the three dimensions and their interplay in more detail. The question of how to conceptualize the dimensions to shed light on the logic of different governance arrangements is far from trivial. For instance, the studies that pursue a multi-dimensional perspective mentioned above point to various aspects that could be assigned to the dimensions. My aim is to incorporate sufficient nuance within each dimension to arrive at a thorough picture of real-world governance.

Apart from that, in view of demarcating the different facets among the dimensions, it has to be considered that the division lines in real-world governance are blurred. As noted above, when separating the dimensions, their overlapping character (a highly interconnected nature with dynamic relations among each other) has to be born in mind.[8] Accordingly, the dimensions should be conceived as one interwoven complex that is only disentangled for analytical reasons. I will consider this in the presentation of the dimensions by already referring to certain interrelations (note that while the three-dimensional picture would also allow three distinct analyses, I hold that the inherent complexity of governance can best be understood when all dimensions and relations are studied together).

In order to reach a comprehensive picture of each of the three dimensions, I will make use of an extensive literature review. In this review, I consider both the (SD) governance literature that transcends the dimensions and the broader literature that addresses aspects within the dimensions individually. The following three important clarifications specify my focal point in this respect. First, as a basic background assumption I stress that, since governance implicates organizing collective action, the dimensions and their interplay are looked at from a steering perspective (while steering is understood in a wide sense as the goal-oriented influence of societal developments, cf. chapter 2; for a detailed discussion on the notion of steering, see e.g. Stoker, 2000). Accordingly, the background question for conceptualizing the dimensions is: which aspects are able to illuminate steering in terms of the dimension in question?

Second, the object that the conceptualization addresses is governing occurring in particular arrangements, i.e. specific real-world settings in view of a certain collective action problem. I accordingly have a particular focus on such governance arrangements, as opposed to e.g. whole policy

---

8 As indicated above, I demarcate the line between structural and procedural aspects, which is frequently blurred in the literature, as follows: While the procedural dimension refers to actual decision-making and implementation processes, the structural dimension comprises the framing conditions for these processes. This means that, for instance, structures predetermine the *division* of power and resources, which are then actually *mobilized* in processes.

sectors. This focus arises from the basic research objective of this study to explore different modes, from hierarchical to non-hierarchical ones.

Third, against the background of this research objective - and since governance in my perception covers the whole spectrum from state intervention to societal autonomy - the question of how governance works necessarily has to consider this entire continuum. When demonstrating the logic of governance in terms of certain structural, procedural and substantive elements, I will thus sketch out these characteristics in terms of hierarchical and non-hierarchical arrangements as the most general distinction on this continuum. This is only to be seen as an orientation for illustrating the form of appearance these characteristics can take (the particular allocation of governance arrangements to specific modes is in turn the goal of the formal frame that I deal with in chapter 3.2 - only here, parameter values of certain characteristics become relevant). With the conceptualization in this chapter, I will provide a heuristic device that illuminates governance workings in different arrangements, and the ways they could induce change. For this, an understanding of the interdependency of governance facets is crucial.

In the following, I present each dimension in detail. My aim is to disclose governing as an unfolding interplay of the three dimensions. I start with explicating governance structures (i.), since this dimension can be seen as the 'architecture' of governance (cf. e.g. Biermann et al., 2010), followed by governance processes (ii.), and governance contents (iii.). Finally, I explicitly elaborate on the interplay among the dimensions (iv.).

(i.) Governance structures

Governing always includes a structural component that provides its embedding frame. This framing of an arrangement is determined by its institutional architecture. For my purpose, *institutions* are understood as both formal procedures and informal routines, which structure social interaction by constraining and enabling the behavior and courses of actions of actors (cf. e.g. North, 1990; Knight, 1992; March & Olsen, 1989). Governance is not only embedded in institutions but also produces them. The distinction between formal and informal institutions thereby points to their nature of development, codification, communication and enforcement. *Formal institutions* refer to regulative rules that are codified in legally binding documents and thus officially established (what is formally allowed and what is not allowed?). They are usually associated with channels of governments and constitutional structures. In contrast, *informal institutions* comprise social norms as well as culturally stabilized customs, expectations and systems of meaning that are commonly accepted throughout society. These are typically not codified and instead developed, communicated and enforced outside of legally sanctioned channels (cf. e.g. Pennings et al., 2006, p. 25; Pahl-Wostl, 2009, p 356f.; Van Trung Ho et al., 2014, p. 12). Within the literature, there are different attempts to distinguish among specific sub-categories of informal institutions (see e.g. Ostrom et al., 1994). A distinction at a basic level is provided by Scott (2001, p. 34 ff.), who subdivides normative and cultural-cognitive institutions. The former refer to shared values that have a moral basis judged by societal standards, i.e. rules of good practice (what is right and what is wrong?). The latter denote rules constituting the nature of reality and the frames through which meaning is made (what is thinkable and what is unthinkable?).

While governance arrangements usually exhibit both formal and informal rule systems that mutually influence and shape each other (cf. e.g. Helmke & Levitsky, 2004), the overall *degree of institutional formality* varies among different arrangements (cf. e.g. Howlett et al., 2009, p. 385f.; Hardiman & Scott, 2010, p. 171 ff.). This is reflected, for instance, in the respective origin and nature of the institutional mandate and the formalities with regard to the procedures of consultation (cf. e.g. Tollefson et al., 2012, p. 12; see also Craik et al., 2012). There are governance arrangements with clearly prescribed legal foundations and a well-established rule-based approach as well as arrangements with more informal and experimental approaches that also cross multiple jurisdictions and levels.

Regardless of their formal or informal nature, institutions exert a *structuring character on actors*, influencing what these actors do and refrain from doing in their dealings with one another (cf. e.g. Hajer, 2006, p. 47; Rhodes & Murray, 2007, p. 83; Liefferink, 2006, p. 53; van Assche et al., 2014b, p. 1125). Although this influence is not absolute or linear, participating actors in governance make use of institutions to coordinate collective decision-making (I will elaborate the actor field of governance in more detail below). They draw upon the predominant 'rules of the game' of exchange and interaction to act properly and legitimately. In this regard, different levels of institutions can be distinguished. For instance, rules of procedure for a specific focal process of interactions (micro level) can be separated from structural patterns on the level of a policy domain (meso level) and broader constitutional rules or the political culture (macro level). While the first level directly influences a governance arrangement, the latter two levels can have an indirect effect (cf. Voss & Bornemann, 2011; for general hierarchies of institutions see e.g. Knoepfel et al., 2011, p. 126).

The structuring character of institutions on actors and their interactions unfolds in different ways. I will explore these ways in the following. First of all, the institutional embedding determines which actors are actually allowed to take part in a governance arrangement. These rules can be described as boundary or *access rules* (cf. e.g. Timmermans 2001, p. 320; Ostrom & Crawford, 2005, p. 194 ff.). They can result, for instance, in either relatively closed governance arrangements that are only accessible by a particular set of selected actors; or more inclusive ones, which are occasionally open to almost every actor willing to participate.

Moreover, institutions shape the division of *responsibilities and roles* among participating actors in governance through certain domain rules (cf. e.g. Van Buuren & Klijn, 2006, p. 400; Arnouts, 2010, p. 32). Such rules result in a particular allocation of competencies among the actors for different tasks. These tasks might be formally allocated through official mandates or informally taken, for instance through voluntary action. Different governance arrangements vary in the role divisions among actors, e.g. in terms of who is in charge for implementing decisions or the extent to which results are formally monitored and reviewed. While in hierarchical governance, the role of managing actors is rather that of an organization controller, in non-hierarchical governance this role becomes more a mediator and process manager (cf. Booher & Innes, 2010, p. 50). Also, in hierarchical arrangements, responsibilities are frequently rather static with lower flexibility, while in non-hierarchical these are more flexible and context dependent (cf. e.g. Van de Meene et al., 2001, p. 1120, Van der Windt, 2008, p. 150 ff.). Likewise, institutions determine the *models of representation* among actors participating in governance. Driessen et al. (2012, p. 146) distinguish among three different types that help to understand how representation can look (cf. also Hysing, 2009, p. 651). While pluralist arrangements exhibit a representation that follows the logic of the political linked to official channels of government, i.e. democratic elections with lobbying of societal actors, corporatist arrangements show formalized public-private representations. In contrast, partnership models of representation exhibit voluntary participation of actors from the market or civil society, resulting in either public-private or private-private structures.

Against this backdrop, it becomes apparent that institutions also define the specific *relationships among actors* in governance. In this vein, there are governance arrangements with vertical relations between a lead actor and other actors, as well as arrangements with horizontal relations among all actors involved. The former are based on relationships of domination and subordination (significantly constraining the autonomy of subordinate actors). In the latter, no actor is subject to the commands of others. This comes along with the degree of structural *coupling of actors*. While in hierarchical governance, actors are frequently tightly coupled, non-hierarchical arrangements show looser couplings (cf. e.g. Börzel & Risse, 2010, p. 114; Van Zeijl-Rozema, 2008, p. 413; Kronsell & Bäckstrand, 2010, p. 41; cf. in this respect also the network analysis approach, e.g. Blum & Schubert, 2011, p. 65; Schneider & Janning, 2006, p. 117).

The way in which the relationships among actors unfold is closely related to the *access to resources and the division of power*. The institutional set-up thereby defines both the locus of resources and power among the actors participating in governance (I will further specify the aspects of resources and power below). This locus varies among different governance arrangements. While hierarchical arrangements are characterized by more centralized resource control, non-hierarchical arrangements rather exhibit distributed resources, resulting in mutual resource dependencies among actors (cf. e.g. Fenger & Bekkers, 2007, p. 25; Hysing, 2009, p. 651; Marsh & Smith, 2000, p. 7). The former then exhibit hierarchical power relations with a centralized locus of power and a single authority. In the latter, power is more distributed and thus exhibits polycentric characteristics, leading to non-hierarchical power relations and shared authorities (cf. e.g. Craik et al., 2012, p. 28 ff.; Howlett et al., 2009, p. 384 ff.; Booher & Innes, 2010, p. 50).

The structure of the relations among actors in turn influences the mechanisms of their interactions. Institutions predetermine the particular *patterns of interaction* occurring within governance. A basic distinction in this respect can be made between top-down and bottom-up approaches (see e.g. Sabatier, 1986; Hanf & Scharpf, 1978). While the former exhibit hierarchical command and control structures, the latter show a more flexible character (cf. e.g. Kooiman, 2003, p. 11 ff.). A differentiated picture for understanding how interactions can play out is provided by Scharpf

(1997, p. 97 ff.), who distinguishes among four different forms. While hierarchical direction includes a single actor with the power to make collectively binding decisions, in majority vote, the plurality of actors adopt decisions that apply for all actors. In turn, in negotiated agreement, actors unanimously agree on a course of action, while in unilateral action, actors choose among alternatives without coordinating their actions (e.g. Kritzinger & Pülzl, 2008, p. 295 f.; Treib et al., 2011, p. 104 ff.; Wydra & Pülzl, 2013, p. 89; Gale, 2009, p. 11). These four forms each differ in terms of structure (hierarchical or non-hierarchical), the degree of formal institutionalization, and the locus of authority (centralized or dispersed).

According to the predominant locus of authority, the interactions of actors can then be situated at different *institutional levels* (cf. e.g. Hillman et al., 2011, p. 409; Hysing, 2010, p. 44 ff.; Bressers & Kuks, 2003, p. 65 ff.; Baker, 2009, p. 6). This represents a final important aspect to understand how governance works in structural terms. There are governance arrangements that primarily rely on global or supranational institutional levels, as well as arrangements that are mainly located at the national, regional or local level. The latter two are frequently characterized by devolved and decentralized decision-making structures. Moreover, there are also arrangements that transcend these settings and exhibit multilevel characteristics (see e.g. Bache & Flinders, 2004; Hooghe & Marks, 2001).

(ii.) Governance processes

The structural characteristics provide the frame for the actual decision-making and implementation processes taking place in a governance arrangement. These processes are based on the interplay of different actors. The term actor here denotes all social units that possess agency or power of action and can be possibly involved in governance - including individual, collective or corporative actors[9] (cf. e.g. Scharpf, 1997, p. 51 ff.; von Prittwitz, 1994, p. 14; Blum & Schubert, 2011, p. 52). This ranges from

9 While collective actors are highly dependent on and guided by the preferences of their members, corporate actors are typically ′top-down′ organizations under the control of an owner or hierarchical leadership (see in more detail e.g. Scharpf, 1997, p. 51 ff.).

governmental actors to actors from the market and civil society (cf. e.g. Steurer, 2013; Glasbergen & Driessen, 2002), such as laypersons and non-governmental organizations as well as scientists and other experts. All these actors can stem from the different levels mentioned above - from global to local or multiple levels. Actors in governance usually establish certain *coalitions*, i.e. more or less stable forms of cooperation that are bound by common discourses, resources and rules (cf. e.g. Arts et al., 2000, p. 57ff.; cf. also the notion of advocacy coalitions, e.g. Sabatier, 1998). Thus, apart from actors operating individually, there are also tight, extensive groups of actors working together and smaller coalitions acting beside each other (cf. e.g. Arnouts, 2010, p. 29).

Predetermined by the institutional access rules referred above, each governance arrangement exhibits a particular configuration of actors and coalitions (cf. e.g. Pierre & Peters, 2005, p. 10 ff.; Kritzinger & Pülzl, 2008, p. 295, Treib et al., 2007, p. 7). This denotes the *actor field* of an arrangement. It refers to those actors, who commonly address the common problem at hand by means of coordinated action. They come together in various spatially and temporally different settings to achieve shared objectives (cf. also the notion of actor networks, e.g. Rhodes & Marsh, 1992; Kenis & Schneider, 1991; or action arenas, e.g. Ostrom et al., 1994). The actors are thus interrelated in a more or less systematic way and have an influence on the problem situation and its development (as opposed to actors that are affected by the problem, cf. chapter 3.3.2) (cf. e.g. Hermans & Cunningham, 2013, p. 187). Different governance arrangements vary in the number and nature of actors interacting in decision-making and implementation. The closed or open character of an arrangement mentioned above results in processes with only an exclusive actor configuration or procedures that feature a range of different actors with various backgrounds (see in general e.g. Bevir, 2011; Kronsell & Bäckstrand, 2010; Kooiman, 2003). During the different phases of interaction, the actor field may also vary in the case of actors joining or leaving an arrangement.

The actors belonging to this field strive to get their interests incorporated into decision-making. Different governance arrangements vary in the ways in which interests are taken into account in the initiation, formulation and adoption of policies (see generally e.g. Kohler-Koch, 1999; Falkner & Leiber, 2004; Scharpf, 1997; Schmitter, 1981). These ways of *interest intermediation* go hand in hand with the models of representation referred to in the structural dimension above. In the case of overlapping interests among actors, coordination is generally easier to achieve than in the case of diverging interests (cf. also the influence of particular actor con-stellations, e.g. Scharpf, 1997, p. 69 ff.; cf. also the distinction on the constellations of interests between coordination, agreement and defection, Knill, 2004). During the struggling for dominance, controversy over problems and solutions may lead to conflicts (cf. e.g. Driessen et al., 2001, p. 324; Scharpf, 1997, p. 69 ff.). Different governance arrangements then vary in the ways of *conflict resolution* and strategies for overcoming problems of coordination (cf. e.g. Kritzinger & Pülzl, 2008, p. 293 ff.). In hierarchical coordination there is more dominant authoritative order, with which actors have to comply. In turn, in non-hierarchical coordination, conflicts of interest are rather solved by negotiating compromises, bargaining or arguing to develop common interests (cf. e.g. Börzel & Risse 2010, p. 115).

A factor that greatly influences how interests of participating actors are incorporated in governance processes is the *mobilization and exchange of resources*. Resources cover the practical means that actors have to realize their objectives (cf. e.g. Coleman, 1990, p. 28). Within a governance arrangement, the exchange of resources represents the basis for the interactions among actors. Different general categories of resources can be differentiated that are relevant for the actions of state and societal actors in different stages of governance (such as economic, political, informational or personal types). Knoepfel et al. (2011, p. 67) provide a detailed distinction of resources including: law, personnel, money, organization, consensus, cognitive skills, time, infrastructure, political support and force (see in general also e.g. Dente, 1995; Buizer, 2008). The use of resources (exclusivity versus non-exclusivity) and its quantity (rivalry versus non-rivalry of consumption) are each influenced by the institutional setting. Different arrangements vary in terms of which resources are most crucial among actors. For instance, in some cases, legislation might be central, while in others, infrastructure or financial means may be more essential (cf. e.g. Liefferink, 2006, p. 54 ff.; Arnouts, 2010, p. 31).

The mobilization and exchange of resources is closely linked to the *power that actors exercise* during different phases of interaction processes. Power can be interpreted in different ways (for an overview see e.g. Arts & Tatenhove, 2005, p. 347). Since governance as coordinated action always incorporates more than one actor (cf. e.g. Stoker, 1998, p. 18 f.), the relative power of actors vis-à-vis each other is most relevant to understand how governance works. This refers to the capacity of an actor to achieve a desired objective in cooperation or competition with others (cf. e.g. Schmidt, 2005, p. 524f.), and is closely linked to the relative portfolio of resources that an actor possesses. Determined by the specific power relations among actors sketched out in the structural dimension, power can be exercised in different ways: either through coercion, administrative and legal expertise in hierarchical relations or through trust, cooperation and respect in non-hierarchical relations (cf. e.g. Van de Meene et al., 2011, p. 1120; Craik et al., 2012, p. 28 ff., cf. also more generally Hyden, 2001, p. 18). In these different cases, the *basis for legitimacy* varies. While in the former, legitimacy is normally founded on democratic representation; in the latter, actions are rather legitimized by an agreement on the predominant roles, relations and procedures (cf. e.g. Driessen et al. 2012, p. 146).

When participating actors of a governance arrangement actually mobilize the resources and power they have at their disposal, they make use of their capacity to take action. This defines the *amount of influence* that actors actually exert (cf. e.g. Willer et al., 1997, p. 580 ff.; Von Prittwitz, 1994, p. 33 ff.), also called ′agency′ (e.g. Dellas et al., 2011). A basic distinction in terms of influence can be made between central actors that continuously get involved (dominating the evolution of governance processes), and more peripheral actors. In this respect, different governance arrangements vary with regard to the actors taking the lead during decision-making and implementation (cf. e.g. Cristou & Simpson, 2009, p. 605; Driessen et al., 2012, p. 146). There are arrangements with state actors as the leading actors and also self-regulating arrangements, in which multiple actors from the market or civil society dominate during initiation and coordination (see in general also e.g. Kickert et al., 1997; Stoker, 2006).

The overall *process character* of governance is heavily influenced by this degree of state and societal actor initiative vis-à-vis each other (for a detailed characterization of different types of processes cf. e.g. Von Prittwitz, 1994, p. 36 ff.; Hufty, 2011, p. 414). Van der Windt (2008, p. 151) argues that hierarchical arrangements show a rather coercive process character with less flexibility. In contrast, non-hierarchical arrangements with societal actors in the lead tend to exhibit deliberations that include visions and values. Several scholars argue that such arrangements are more transparent and flexible with a focus on communication, arguments, and a trust-worthy atmosphere. Here, there is an emphasis on reciprocity, cooperation, exchange of information and unanimous decisions (cf. e.g.

Van de Meene, 2011, p. 1120; Christou & Simpson, 2009, p. 602; see also generally Homeyer, 2006; Börzel, 2006).

(iii.) Governance contents

The processes of governance are supposed to yield certain products that are directed at solving the collective problem addressed. Accordingly, each governance arrangement usually exhibits a particular policy setting with different content-related issues. In principle, I argue that the *substantive components of governance* can be roughly distinguished by an orientation on basic results of the traditional policy cycle (cf. e.g. Parsons, 1995; Fischer et al., 2007; for an overview on different products of the cycle see e.g. Knoepfel et al., 2011, p. 117 ff., cf. also Pierre & Peters, 2005, p. 14 ff.). For the sake of simplicity, I follow the argumentation of Schneider and Janning (2006, p. 50 ff.) to reduce the core of the cycle to the three main phases of agenda setting, policy formulation and policy implementation. Certainly, not all governance arrangements, especially those near to the latter end of the 'state intervention to societal autonomy continuum', follow the ideal-typical stages of the policy cycle (even with regard to traditional hierarchical policy-making, the heuristic represents a simplification with several limitations, see in more detail e.g. Sabatier, 2007). However, I hold that at least similar substantive components can be found in all different kinds of governance arrangements.

First of all, corresponding with the initial stage of 'agenda setting', governance processes usually lead to certain *problem definitions* in view of the challenges addressed (including their demarcation, causes and effects), as well as the choice to take action or intervene in specific ways. Subsequently, according to the phase of 'policy formulation', there are certain programs, plans or strategies that establish particular *objectives* and targets with specific priorities and associated responsibilities. Different governance arrangements can vary with regard to the appearance of these substantive issues (see in general e.g. Bressers & Kuks, 2003; Kooiman, 2003; van der Windt, 2008). There are, for instance, variations in the nature of problem definitions (e.g. in the clarity of demarcation and degree of appraisal of cause and effects) as well as in the type of goals, i.e. which solutions are regarded as legitimate and how these are dealt with during different phases of governance processes. In this regard, De Búrca and Scott (2006, p. 3) argue that compared to hierarchical governance, non-hierarchical arrangements put an emphasis on provisory and revisable problem definition and anticipated solutions, accompanied by ongoing review. Similarly, Van der Windt (2008, p. 151) states that hierarchically oriented arrangements rather follow a product orientation with fixed standards and issues - while within non-hierarchical arrangements, a process orientation is dominant with a wider range of issues. Here, a larger amount of problem definitions and solutions is discussed within deliberation rounds. In a similar vein, Vermeulen (2002, p. 69), points to rather static and singular goal-driven policies as opposed to dynamic and inclusive ones. Driessen et al. (2012, p. 146), furthermore, highlight different degrees of uniformity in terms of goals and targets formulated in governance. While in hierarchical arrangements goals and targets tend to exhibit a rather uniform character, in non-hierarchical governance they are more sensitive to the respective context, for instance, leading to actor or level specific targets or tailor-made goals (see also Booher & Innes, 2010).

Corresponding with the phase of 'policy implementation', the formulated programs, plans and strategies are usually implemented and translated into certain approaches of problem solving (i.e. intervention or creation of opportunities). In this sense, governance arrangements produce formal and informal outputs that include certain implementation activities and the application of measures. Different arrangements thereby vary with regard to their respective approaches (see e.g. Treib et al., 2011; Hysing, 2009; Mees et al., 2013; Tollefson et al., 2012). In general, hierarchical governance is associated with more rigid forms of implementation, defining detailed procedures and standards, while non-hierarchical governance implies more flexible, modifiable implementation with adjustments to circumstances (cf. e.g. Bartolini, 2011, p. 11). The differences in implementation become most obvious in terms of the nature and form of *policy instruments* that governance arrangements implement for achieving their formulated goals (cf. e.g. Howlett et al., 2009, p. 386; Wydra & Pülzl, 2013, p. 89; cf. also Jordan et al., 2005). Different typologies can be found within the literature. Usually a distinction is made between the basic categories of legal, economic and communicative steering measures, as well as organization (also called structuring, that is, e.g. the provision of infrastructure). These categories differ in terms of the type of incentives used to influence behavior (see in general e.g. Gunningham & Grabosky, 1998; Böcher, 2012; Glasbergen, 1992). Mees et al. (2013, p. 805) argue that within hierarchical governance, all instrument forms can be found, although there is a preference for legal measures. Non-hierarchical arrangements, in turn, mostly rely on communicative instruments. Apart from these basic classifications, certain specific aspects can be distinguished with regard to steering instruments (e.g. the presence versus absence of sanctions, a substantive or procedural focus, as well as fixed versus malleable norms). Against this backdrop, steering instruments can be analyzed via multiple dimensions. Treib et al. (2007, p. 5 ff.) suggest combining the instrument form with the approach of implementation. This results in the four types of coercion (legally binding followed by rigid implementation), voluntarism (non-binding and flexible), targeting (non-binding and rigid) and framework regulation (binding and flexible). Similarly, Tollefson et al. (2012, p. 14) categorize the form of instruments in governance according to its precision (how closely it con-strains private action), its bindingness (soft or hard law) and its delegation (the extent to which adjudication and enforcement is retained by a regulator or delegated to an independent third party) (cf. also Doelle et al., 2012, 49 ff.)

With regard to all the mentioned components of governance, there are finally certain general characteristics that influence the appearance of overall policy settings; and thus help to understand how governance works in substantive terms. First of all, policy settings reflect a more or less pronounced pursuit of *integrating contents*. This incorporates both the extent of horizontal integration across multiple sectors and vertical integration across multiple levels (see in general e.g. Lafferty & Hovden, 2003; Runhaar et al., 2014; Bornemann, 2013; Jordan & Lenschow, 2010). Scholars argue that there is frequently a greater striving for integration in non-hierarchical governance arrangements than in hierarchical ones (cf. e.g. Baker, 2009; p. 6 ff.; Driessen et al., 2012, p. 146).

Furthermore, the characters of governance processes influence the appearance of substantive settings in such a way that there is a greater or lesser quest for *learning* during policy development and implementation. This feature is embodied by readjustment and experimentalism as well as adaptive policy solutions and innovation in terms of contents. Compared to hierarchical arrangements, where policy-making approaches are frequently more routinized, scholars argue that there is a stronger pursuit of innovative policies and learning with ongoing evaluation and flexible readjustment in non-hierarchical arrangements (for instance Van der Wal et al., 2014; Van der Heijden, 2013; Reed et al., 2010). Such arrangements aim to cope with complexity and uncertainty with experimental characteristics, as well as by fostering adaptive capacities and knowledge sharing among multiple actors. Policies in this context are frequently viewed as experiments, which require modification as novel knowledge is gained (see in general McNutt & Rayner, 2014; Folke et al., 2005; Armitage et al., 2009; Pahl-Wostl, 2009).

This leads us to a final important aspect helpful to understand the workings of governance in different arrangements: the type of *knowledge use*. Different types thereby correspond with the overall character of processes outlined above, accompanied by varying types of knowledge production (see generally Rich, 1997; Bäckstrand, 2004; Guston, 2001; Miller & Edwards, 2001). This aspect refers to perceptions of what kind of knowledge is relevant and legitimate in predominant policy-science interfaces (see also Carrozza, 2015; Buizer et al., 2011), and touches upon more general shifts in the nature and role of expertise in society (see more generally Gibbons et al., 1994; cf. also the notion of the 'democratization of expertise', e.g. Funtowicz & Ravetz, 1992). Driessen et al. (2012, p. 146), for instance, point to the tendency for policy settings in hierarchical arrangements to rely mainly on universal scientific knowledge, while non-hierarchical settings make more frequent use of context-sensitive expertise (see also van Assche et al., 2014b). Van Bommel (2008, p. 40 ff.) argues that in hierarchical arrangements, knowledge rather takes the form of data, as scientists have the role of problem solvers. In this case, knowledge production and usage are treated separately; experts produce knowledge and policy makers use it. In contrast, scholars argue that non-hierarchical governance in general exhibits a greater emphasis on the co-production of knowledge and knowledge integration (e.g. Shiroyama et al., 2012). It is argued that instead of separating processes of production and usage, the knowledge required is gained interactively through dynamic policy-science interfaces. In these contexts, there is an emphasis on lay knowledge as well as multi- and transdisciplinary perspectives. Such knowledge is usually gained in deliberative approaches that incorporate citizens and experts (see in general Turnhout et al., 2007).

(iv.) The interplay of the dimensions

As mentioned above and further indicated by the previous elaborations, I regard the three dimensions of governance structures, processes and contents as inextricably interwoven. The most obvious basic logic of mutual influence among the dimensions would be that structures determine the way of processes (by providing a frame), which in turn shape the type of contents (as processes are supposed to yield substantive results). This also follows the assumption that structures are most stable.

However, notwithstanding such general tendencies, the discussion above indicates that multifaceted dynamics occur in different directions among the dimensions. Against this backdrop, the various structural, procedural and substantive characteristics exhibit interdependencies both within each dimension and across them. Governance is characterized by many different combinations of the aforementioned interdependent elements. Certain shapes or positions with regard to the elements (i.e. the status they can take) thereby fit together more naturally than others - resulting in certain complementarities of positions (cf. also the basic principle of complementarities explored e.g. by Milgrom & Roberts, 1990, or van Assche et al., 2014b, cf. also Bartolini, 2011, 12f.). This means that the shape of a certain element is always to be seen in reference to the position of other characteristics. Due to the highly interconnected nature of the dimensions, changes in one of them almost certainly result in alterations within the other two (through certain chain reactions).

This also makes clear that governance arrangements are not necessarily fixed in terms of the dimensions and their characteristics. During the evolution of an arrangement, variations of differing magnitudes and directions occurring within the dimensions might alter their form of appearance.

I strive to take the diversity of interdependencies into account by means of three two-sided linkages among the dimensions. This approach enables the analysis of the dimensional interplay in detail (for similar considerations on the interactions among certain governance facets cf. e.g. Van Leeuwen & Van Tatenhove, 2010; Bressers & Kuks, 2003; Tollefson et al., 2012; van Assche et al., 2014a and 2014b).

First of all, with respect to the *structures-processes interplay* of governance, I refer to the interconnected nature of the institutional architecture and the interaction processes. The two-sided linkage plays out as follows. On the one hand, the decision-making and implementation processes are largely shaped by the institutional framing conditions. For instance, regulative rules or social norms in place influence the number and nature of actors, the way interests can be articulated and on which basis legitimacy is founded. Likewise, institutions e.g. define the degree of influence that actors can exert through shaping their relations and interaction patterns -

as well as by distributing resources and power (such as regulatory power). On the other hand, the appearance of the processes and the accompanying political arena shape the embedding institutional set-up. For example, participating actors in any form of governance are actively involved in influencing existing value systems. The entry and exit of certain actors as well as changes in their interests and combinations of coalitions can provoke alterations in the rules of exchange and interaction. Also, the particular exercise of power shapes the degree of institutional formality, as well as the specific roles that actors assume.

Second, the *processes-contents interplay* refers to the dynamics of interaction processes with the substantive components. For one thing, the way processes unfold obviously determines the appearance of material products. For example, varying influences of state and societal actors during different stages of governance directly affect the manifestation of problem definitions and objectives. They also define the way decisions can be made, which issues are raised and which problem solving approaches are considered appropriate. Similarly, alterations in the interests of actors or in the mobilization and exchange of resources might shape the substantive setting in a different direction. Also, a process character with e.g. a focus on reciprocity, cooperation and exchange of information may increase the degree of integrating contents. On the other hand, substantive components shape predominant procedures. One example is that knowledge and power are intrinsically entwined. Knowledge use and production in governance regularly impact the exercise of power. Similarly, altered problem definitions may lead to variations in actor configurations. Also, substantive characteristics determine processes since the coalitions into which actors come together are bound by shared ideas and discourses.

Finally, the *structures-contents interplay* points to the interdependence between the institutional surrounding and the substantive setting. Again, there is a two-sided relationship. By defining the context through which policy formulation and implementation take place, the institutional architecture determines the appearance of substantive issues. For instance, the question if a legally binding instrument form and a rigid approach of implementation come into play is largely conditioned by the predominant degree of institutional formality and the relationships among actors. Similarly, the form of cultural-cognitive institutions (what is thinkable and what is unthinkable) clearly has an influence on the manner of policy-science interfaces. In turn, the substance of governance can also shape its institutional properties. For example, the kind of problems addressed and their delineation determine the appropriate institutional level on which action is required. Also, new rules of the game, both formal and informal, might be discussed and successively institutionalized through changes in knowledge use or in acceptable problem solving approaches (such as in the specific design and use of steering instruments). Likewise, a greater demand for innovation and learning in view of new unstructured problems can, for instance, shape the division of power and relations among actors.

Taking everything into account, these elaborations underscore the importance of considering not only the multiple facets of governance but also their interrelations. Based on dynamic relations among the dimensions, governance can then be interpreted as the (combinatorial) consequence of configurations among certain structural, procedural and substantive characteristics. The specific constellation of these characteristics then gives a certain governance arrangement its particular character.

In sum, I argue that only a multi-dimensional conceptualization (that gives consideration to all three dimensions of the political) adequately serves the variety and interdependence of governance facets. By exploring this interplay, the workings of different governance arrangements can be revealed, while covering the inherent complexity of collective action. In so doing, a systematic understanding of the multifaceted phenomenon of governance can be reached. Figure 3 gives an overview of the governance conceptualization.

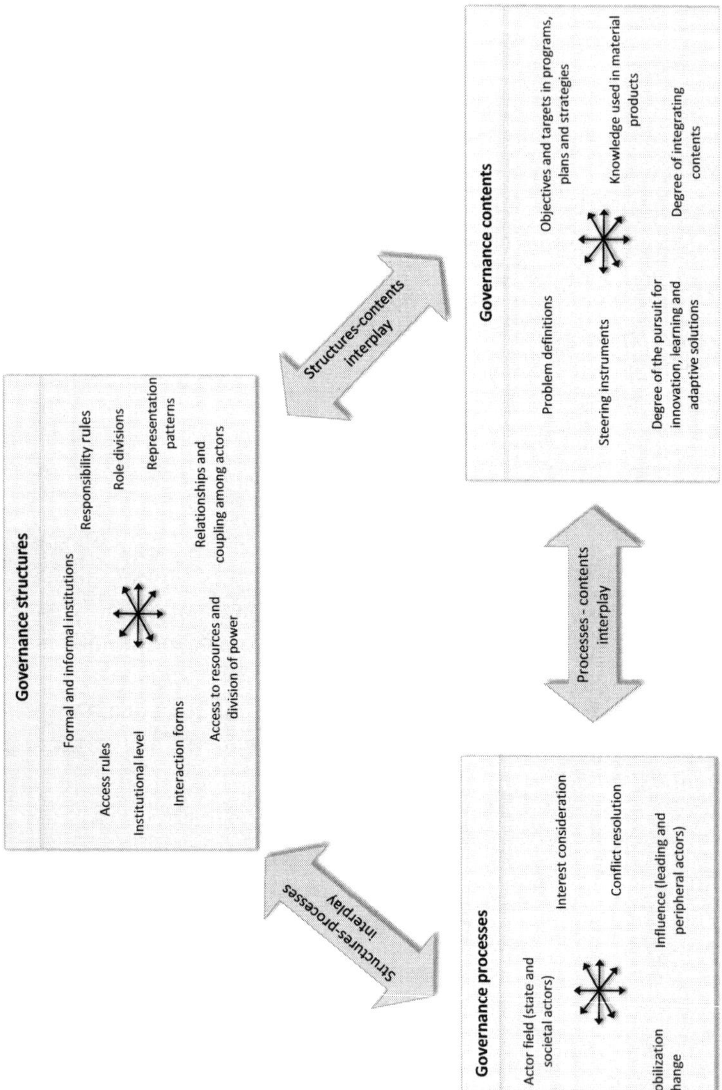

Figure 3: Summary of the conceptualization of governance (own illustration)

With this governance conceptualization, I am now equipped with a nuanced picture that can offer deepened insights into the way different real-world arrangements work. It thus serves as a sound conceptual basis to empirically retrace and understand the governance arrangements in my case study research - together with the ways through which governance induces societal changes. The next step which the research objective is calling for is to find a way for distinguishing among modes of governance.

3.2 Differentiating governance modes

As introduced in chapter 2.2, this study basically conceives of governance modes as forms of realizing collective goals by means of coordinated action. Based on the conceptualization of governance, this general understanding can now be specified. A *mode of governance* is understood as an encompassing governance arrangement that is characterized by a certain constellation of features - grouped along the three different dimensions of structures, processes and contents. A mode is thus a cluster that covers a specific configuration of different components of governing, which gives an arrangement its particular appearance. This appearance, however, is not fixed and can potentially shift over time. In each dimension, changes are possible during the proceeding of an arrangement (this will be considered in the empirical case study research).

Against the backdrop of this understanding, I am now looking for an appropriate frame that makes it possible to meaningfully differentiate among governance modes. The purpose of this frame in light of the research perspective of this study is as follows. It shall enable the allocation of real-world arrangements - as represented by the cases studies - to specific modes (from traditional hierarchical to non-hierarchical new modes). In so doing, the cases can be classified, which is a necessary fulfillment for answering the research question.

It is important at this stage to understand the relationship and difference between the governance conceptualization and the frame for modes. In general, the two schemes should be basically compatible with each other. Accordingly, all three dimensions of structures, processes and contents should be covered in the frame for modes - as these together form the understanding of governance in this study. However, as regards the specific aspects within the dimensions, the picture looks different, because the frame for modes has a different function than the governance conceptualization. The aspects within the conceptualization were worked out in order to understand the inner way of functioning of governance and its inherent complexity, i.e. how governance works in different arrangements and how it can induce change. For this purpose, it was shown above how governing evolves through the interplay of governance facets. In contrast, the formal frame for modes shall enable the classification of arrangements and their allocation to governance modes (and thus to explore the overall research question that is targeted at different modes). Not all of the aspects illustrated in the conceptualization are useful for this. And other aspects that were not included may instead be appropriate to do so.

Apart from that, the frame for governance modes should additionally meet the following basic requirements. First of all, it should include key aspects that to a large extent differ among the range of governance arrangements - and are thus well suited for the endeavor to meaningfully distinguish modes. Second, in order to do justice to the inherent complexity of governance, it should also add sufficient nuance within each dimension. Finally, it ought to provide a way for easily allocating real-world arrangements to ideal-typical modes, while covering the whole range from state intervention to societal autonomy.

Since I basically aim to rely on established material if it is suited for my research perspectives, it is promising to screen the (SD) governance literature for appropriate modes of governance classifications. As already introduced in chapter 2.2, indeed, several such classifications can be found in the literature (cf. e.g. Kooiman, 2003; Fenger & Bekkers, 2007; Bell & Hindmoor, 2009; Benz & Dose, 2010; Blatter, 2007; Howlett & Ramesh, 2015; Pierre & Peters, 2005). However, not all of these proposals satisfy the requirements mentioned above. The complexity of governance especially, as depicted above, is frequently not adequately captured.

In contrast, some scholars have made recent efforts to handle this complexity in their analyses (Tollefson et al., 2008; Howlett et al., 2009; Pahl-Wostl, 2009; Van de Meene et al., 2011; Van Leeuwen & Van Tatenhove, 2010; Weber et al., 2011). Among these contributions, there are three proposals that are particularly promising with respect to the afore-mentioned demands (Arnouts et al., 2011; Hysing, 2009; Driessen et al., 2012). These authors aim at meaningfully differentiating among modes of governance - as they are understood in this study[10] - by means of juxtaposed key features. In the following, I have a closer look at these proposals in order to reveal the one most suited for my purpose. After presenting the key elements of the approaches (i.-iii., chapter 3.2.1), I will highlight the similarities and differences and provide a reasoning for the choice of the formal frame (chapter 3.2.2) (cf. in the following also Lange et al., 2013).

3.2.1 Three proposals for meaningfully distinguishing among governance modes

(i.) The first promising proposal is provided by *Arnouts et al.* (2011). These authors follow Kooiman's (2003) basic distinction among hierarchical, co- and self-governance. These three ideal-typical governance modes differ from each other in the extent to which state and societal actors are involved. Referring to the variety of ways in which these actors can cooperate, the authors further elaborate the mode of co-governance into a 'closed' and an 'open' mode (the former describing a more restricted, structured and fixed form and the latter a more flexible and autonomous form of co-governing). This results in a differentiation of four governance modes. Arnouts et al. then refine these modes by means of the 'policy arrangement approach' (see e.g. Arts et al., 2006; Van Tatenhove et al., 2000). This leads to an operationalization in terms of an actor, a power and a rule dimension (figure 4).

10 As argued above, the understanding of governance modes is not consistent in the literature. Frameworks that apply an understanding that differs from the perception of modes in this study are not taken into account.

	Hierarchical governance	Closed co-governance	Open co-governance	Self-governance
Actors	Mainly governmental actors	Select mixed group of actors	Large mixed group of actors	Mainly non-governmental actors
Power	With government	Pooled	Diffused	With non-government
Rules	Governmental coercion	Restricted cooperation	Flexible collaboration	Non-governmental forerunning

Figure 4: First proposal for meaningfully distinguishing governance modes (adapted from Arnouts et al., 2011, p. 46)

Within the actor dimension, the authors differentiate between state and non-state actors and highlight the coalitions that are visible among such actors. Within the power dimension, they focus on the key feature of the relative power of state and non-state actors vis-à-vis each other. The authors propose exploring the means that constitute the capacity of actors, as well as the extent to which the actors use this potential (cf. also Arnouts, 2010). Within the rule dimension, which sketches a certain role division among the actors, the proposed aspects to be investigated are two types of interaction rules: access rules (determining which actors are allowed to take part in a governance arrangement) and responsibility rules (referring to the division of responsibilities among the involved actors).

(ii.) The second proposal has been developed by *Hysing* (2009). He makes use of the intensity of state involvement as the distinguishing factor to position different modes on a range from government to governance (cf. also Hysing, 2010, note that since Hysing juxtaposes government and governance, he uses the term governance in a narrow sense to depict non-hierarchal steering, cf. chapter 2.2). The modes are further differentiated by means of three dimensions that the author deduced by distilling the broader governance literature (figure 5).

Dimensions	Government			Governance	
Public-private relationships	Hierarchic relationship	Institutionalized public-private relations (state domination)	Facilitation and enabling of networks	Mutual dependency of networks between private and public actors	Private self-governing
Policy levels	National state governing	Delegation of authority and responsibility to other levels	Gatekeeping (governing in implementation)	Multilevel governance (circumventing the national level)	Governing by a global civil society
Governing instruments and styles	Command and control (legal sanctions)	Incentive-based instruments (taxes and grants)	Delegated public functions	Information instruments	Voluntary instruments (agreements and labeling)

Figure 5: Second proposal for meaningfully distinguishing governance modes (adapted from Hysing, 2009, p. 650)

The first dimension deals with the relationship between state and societal actors. Modes of governance closer to the state-centered side of government are characterized by mono-centric, hierarchically organized political institutions as the prime governors of society. In turn, modes near to the society-centered side feature networks of self-governing private and voluntary actors. The second dimension is concerned with the relations between policy levels. Here, governance modes where the level of nation state is the central locus of authority are distinguished from modes that are characterized by actors and institutions operating autonomously on multiple levels. Finally, the third dimension highlights governing instruments and styles, ranging from the exercise of sovereign rule by central governments as the primary mechanism to soft steering tools (such as information and voluntary instruments).

(iii.) The last proposal under scrutiny is offered by *Driessen et al.* (2012). Within this approach, five ideal-typical modes of governance are mapped, based on the relations among state, market and civil society actors. The frame differentiates forms where state actors are the main protagonists (subdivided in a centralized and decentralized mode), forms of public–private interactions ('public–private governance' and 'interactive governance'), as well as arrangements where primarily societal actors participate ('self-governance'). These five ideal-types are further refined by a distinction of the three dimensions of actor base, institutional features and features concerning content (figure 6).

		Centralized governance	Decentralized governance	Public-private governance	Interactive governance	Self-governance
		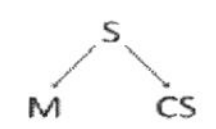	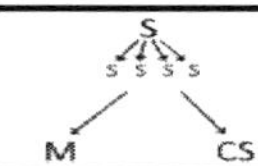		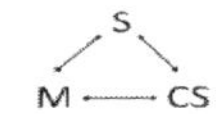	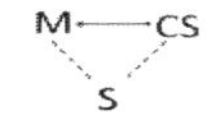
Actor features	**Initiating actors**	Central gov´t agencies (or supra national bodies)	Gov´t at its various levels of aggregation (subsidiarity)	Central gov´t agencies; private sector is granted a preconditioned role also	Multiple actors: gov´t, private sector and civil society	Private sector and/or civil society
	Stakeholder position	Stakeholder autonomy determined by principal agency	High likelihood of stakeholder involvement	Autonomy of market stakeholders within predetermined boundaries	Equal roles for all network partners	Self governing entities determine the involvement of other stakeholders
	Policy level	(Supra) national level	Lower levels of gov´t	Local to international level	Multiple levels	Local to international level
	Power base	Coercion; Authority; Legitimacy (democratic representation at the national level)	Coercion; Authority; Legitimacy (democratic representation at lower levels)	Competitiveness (prices); Contracts and legal recourse; Legitimacy (agreement on relations and procedures)	Legitimacy (agreement on roles, positions, procedures and process); Trust; Knowledge	Autonomy; Leadership; Group size; Social capital; Legitimacy (agreement on relations and procedures)
Institutional features	**Model of representation**	Pluralist (popular (supra) national election and lobbying	Pluralist (popular local election and lobbying)	Corporatist (formalized public-private governing arrangements)	Partnership (Participatory public-private governing arrangements)	Partnership (Participatory private-private governing arrangements)
	Rules of interaction	Formal rules (rule of law; fixed and clear procedures)	Formal rules (rule of law; fixed and clear procedures)	Formal and informal exchange rules	Institutions in its broadest form (Formal and informal rules)	Informal rules (norms; culture); Self-crafted (non-imposed) formal rules
	Mechanisms of social interaction	Top-down; command-and-control	Sub-national governments decide autonomously about collaborations within top-down determined boundaries	Private actors decide autonomously about collaborations within top-down determined boundaries	Interactive: social learning, deliberations, and negotiations	Bottom-up: social learning, deliberations and negotiations
Features concerning content	**Goals and targets**	Uniform goals and targets	Uniform and level specific goals and targets	Uniform goals; targets actor specific	Tailor-made and integrated goals and targets	Tailor-made goals and targets
	Instruments	Legislations, permits, norms and standards	Public covenants and performance contracts	Incentive based instruments like taxes and grants; performance contracts	Negotiated agreements; trading mechanisms; covenants; entitlements	Voluntary instruments; private contracts; entitlements; labeling and reporting
	Policy Integration	Sectorial (policy sectors and levels separated)	Sectorial (policy sectors separated)	Sectorial (branches and industries separated)	Integrated (policy sectors and policy levels integrated)	Sectorial to integrated (depends on problem framing by communities of interest)
	Policy-science interface	Primacy of generic, expert knowledge	Primacy of generic expert knowledge. Room for issue and time-and-place specific knowledge	Dominance of issue and time-and-place specific knowledge; expert and lay (procedures and consumers)	Transdisciplinarity: expert and lay knowledge in networks. Emphasis on integrated and time-and-place specific knowledge	Dominance of issue and time-and-place specific: expert and lay (citizens)

Figure 6: Third proposal for meaningfully distinguishing governance modes (adapted from Driessen et al., 2012, p. 146)

Within the actor dimension, the following key features are proposed by Driessen et al.: the key actors that initiate action, the position of other stakeholders, the predominant policy level[11], as well as the power base of the key actors. Within the institutional dimension, the model of representation, the rules of exchange and interaction, as well as the mechanisms of social interaction are studied. Finally, with regard to content, the following features are explored: the types of goals that are pursued, the policy instruments used, the extent to which policies are integrated or not, as well as the type of knowledge used for policy-making. The authors have deduced these key features together with their framing dimensions by distilling governance literature in general (cf. Driessen et al., 2012).

3.2.2 Reasoning for the choice of the formal frame

In the following, I will scrutinize the three proposals in light of the requirements mentioned above. As argued, I am looking for a frame that adequately considers the three dimensions of structures, processes and contents and adds sufficient nuance to each dimension. The frame should furthermore cover key aspects greatly differing among arrangements and enable their easy allocation to ideal-typical modes (ranging from state intervention to societal autonomy).

Generally speaking, all three proposals share the same point of departure: the degree of state and societal actors' participation in governing.[12] Basically, governance modes where state actors are predominant are dif-

11 Note that in the governance conceptualization in chapter 3.1, I conceive this aspect more generally as the institutional level of arrangements and thus allocate it to the dimension of governance structures.

12 Instead of choosing the degree of state and societal actor involvement as a leading distinguishing factor (which could be assigned to the dimension of governance processes), it would also be conceivable to basically arrange governance modes by means of features from the structures or contents dimension (e.g. according to policy instruments used). In principle, aspects within any of the three dimensions could serve as a starting point for classifying modes of governance. However, the aspect of actor involvement is most common in the literature.

ferentiated from modes characterized by actor interactions and societal-actor dominated modes. All proposals consider the whole range from state intervention to societal autonomy. Within this range, different ideal-typical governance modes are located (in comparison, Hysing's scheme is less appropriate for easily allocating real-world arrangements to modes, since it does not label ideal-types).

Furthermore, all authors highlight that a nuanced picture is needed to capture the variety of phenomena that governance is concerned with. Accordingly, they all operationalize governance modes with the help of distinct dimensions and key features. All proposals use key aspects that largely differ among governance arrangements and are thus suited for meaningfully distinguishing among modes. Looking at the three dimensions of structures, processes and contents, it becomes apparent that elements from all dimensions can be found among the proposals. However, the authors make different emphases. Arnouts et al. focus on the processes and structures dimension and neglect the contents dimension, arguing that governance is mainly an organizational matter (cf. also Arnouts, 2010). However, this does not fit with my governance conceptualization, as I hold the contents of governance as vital for grasping the whole phenomenon of collective action. In line with this, both Hysing and Driessen et al. incorporate this dimension in their approaches. Within Hysing's scheme, however, the processes dimension is neglected. Only within the proposal of Driessen et al. are all three dimensions considered equally.

In terms of key features used to distinguish among governance modes in detail, both Arnouts et al. and Hysing use a single feature per dimension. Driessen et al., in contrast, use a range of features inside each of the dimensions. Moreover, all the features used by Arnouts et al. and Hysing are basically covered in Driessen et al.´s scheme. These authors also add features that are hitherto discussed to a lesser extent within (SD) governance literature (such as the policy-science interface), but are useful for meaningfully differentiating among modes. Accordingly, the scheme allows for the equal consideration of the three dimensions and covers a broad range of relevant key features. With the help of the detailed differentiation, it is also possible to clearly demarcate the dimensions and to identify hybrids of governance modes. Overall, the authors do succeed in providing a differentiated picture to do justice to the complexity of real-world arrangements.

Taking everything into account, I thus conclude that the proposal of Driessen et al. is best suited as a frame for my research purposes. For meaningfully distinguishing among modes of governance in empirical research, the degree of differentiation is a crucial criterion. Driessen et al.´s approach represents one of the most detailed and nuanced conceptual lenses on governance modes within (SD) governance literature. I will thus rely on this heuristic as the theoretical background for the empirical part. Accordingly, within this study, five ideal-typical modes of governance are differentiated:

- a hierarchical governance mode in which central governments take the lead and the market and civil society are the recipients of government`s incentives (*centralized governance*),
- a hierarchical mode where regional or local governments are predominant, with market and civil society actors as mainly being recipients (*decentralized governance*),
- a non-hierarchical mode that exhibits cooperation between government agencies and market actors (*public-private governance*),
- a non-hierarchical mode that includes collaboration in equal terms between public authorities, market and civil society actors (*interactive governance*),
- a non-hierarchical mode in which actors from the market and/or civil society with far-reaching autonomy are able to initiate new approaches themselves (*self-governance*).

These modes can be arranged on a continuum from state intervention to societal autonomy. Referring to the understanding of the term new governance modes (non-hierarchical governing forms that incorporate societal actors, either exclusively or together with state actors; chapter 2.2), the latter three can be regarded as new modes. In contrast, the first two governance modes can be considered as traditional modes (cf. figure 7).

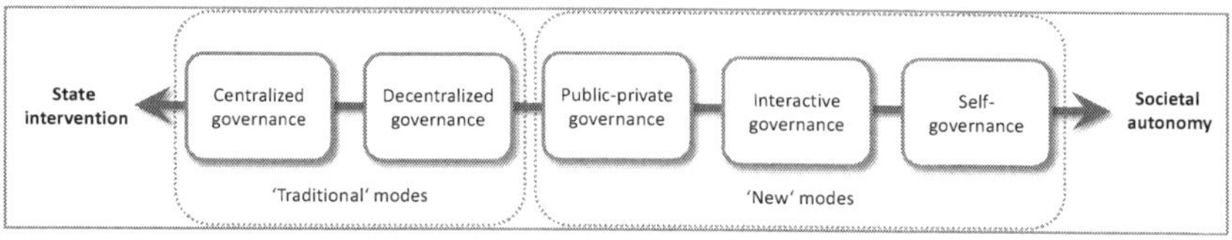

Figure 7: Continuum of governance modes (own illustration)

To avoid confusion, it should be noted here that - from a broader perspective as a general development - rescaling in the sense of transferring power from central to regional governments (cf. e.g. Cowell et al., 2015) can be interpreted as a change towards new modes. Indeed, such vertical shifts are mentioned by some scholars who refer to the storyline 'from government to governance' (cf. above). However, when addressing the mode itself, decentralized governance is clearly hierarchical - only on a lower level of government - and does not explicitly incorporate societal actors (since regional governments are predominant with the market and civil society as recipients).

Furthermore, in view of the empirical research part, the following consideration is important. While the grouping of theoretical ideal-typical modes has the virtue of providing a standard against which real-world systems can be compared, it is possible that empirical arrangements do not completely match these types. Thus, a clear distinction must be made between ideal types and complex real-world arrangements. Real-world governance may present hybrids of different archetypical modes, combining features (cf. also Wan & Bramwell, 2015). Moreover, as argued, governance may also change over time. Real-world arrangements are occasionally not fixed and may evolve over time. In line with this, Driessen et al. (2012) highlight that they provide a differentiated frame in order to be explicitly able to deal with shifts among modes (cf. also Weber et al., 2011).

Against this background, in empirical research, an *a priori* fixed connection between key features from different dimensions within a certain governance mode should be approached with caution. Some features might go hand-in-hand as they are functionally related to each other. For instance, governance arrangements that depend on the exercise of sovereign authority by states are likely to involve vertical relations and a formal governing structure, based on institutionalized and hierarchical interactions. Conversely, arrangements where governments play a minor role tend to be characterized by politics across state-market-civil society domains, in which horizontal relations among the actors (who share power and act in a more cooperative way) are predominant. This relationship likely rests on an informal polity and a network structure that is based on resource interdependency and trust.

However, even in terms of these key features, a simple generalization might not do justice to the variety and complexity of real-world arrangements. This becomes more apparent with regard to the clustering of features that are not as closely connected. For instance, it is not as clear that a specific actor model necessarily entails a certain set of steering tools (see in this regard also Hillman et al., 2011). Also, hierarchical arrangements might not exclusively rely on state actors, while non-hierarchical arrangements in turn might indeed include such actors at a distance. Hence, I conclude that a certain governance arrangement classified to a certain mode - e.g. at one point in time or to a certain degree - might contain key features that are usually associated with another mode.

As a consequence, in the empirical part of the study, the ideal-typical modes are used as a conceptual benchmark; however, they are not seen as necessarily fixed. The possibility of governance hybrids and their dynamic evolution in real-world settings over time is taken into account.

Overall, I am now equipped with a deepened conceptualization of governance in order to understand the workings of real-world arrangements and the possible ways to induce change - as well as a formal frame for allocating these arrangements to certain modes. The next required theoretical step is to find a way for exploring the results of governance. I will address this challenge in the following chapter.

3.3 Grasping the impacts of governance

In order to investigate the potential of governance modes to promote SD, I aim to focus on the interface between governance and its outcomes - i.e. the entirety of societal changes occurring in between governance workings and their end results on the ground (cf. chapter 1). Hitherto, this intermediate linkage (when understood in such an encompassing way) represents a ′black box′ within (SD) governance research. In the following, I aim at developing a heuristic device for grasping this linkage. Therefore, I will first clarify the elusive field of governance results (chapter 3.3.1). Subsequently, I will present my conceptualization of impacts (chapter 3.3.2).

3.3.1 A clarification of the results of governance

Within the literature, there frequently exists confusion about the accumulated results of governance. Relevant research strands in this respect are, for instance, the classical performance measurement of government programs (cf. e.g. Hatry, 2006), the ex-post evaluation of policy effects (cf. e.g. Hill & Hupe, 2014; Young & Zürn, 2006) or their ex-ante assessments (cf. e.g. George & Kirkpatrick, 2007), as well as attempts to evaluate the performance of certain governance forms (cf. chapter 2.4). Thus far, there is no consistent understanding of terms within the different streams of literature. In the words of Emerson et al. (2012, p. 18), there is an overall »*confusion in the literature about the impacts, effects, outputs, and/or outcomes*« of governance. A general theoretical desideratum is thus to provide greater conceptual clarity on the results of governance.

As a first step towards this clarity, I differentiate three forms of governance results: outputs, impacts and outcomes. *Outputs* are the direct products of governance that are introduced to solve the collective problem addressed - such as policy programs, laws, administrative acts, steering instruments, means and activities, as well as informal plans, visions or strategy papers. Following my understanding of governance, I perceive outputs as part of the contents dimension of governance, which includes both goals and means to realize such goals. I then conceive *impacts* in general terms as intermediate results induced by governance. These can be described as events, behaviors or occurrences within society that appear outside the actual workings of governance. The impacts lead to *outcomes,* understood as the end results on the level of the overall system, i.e. changes in environmental and socio-economic conditions.

This understanding of outcomes as end results is prevalent in general (SD) governance literature and thus adopted here (cf. e.g. Adger & Jordan, 2009; Koontz & Thomas, 2006; Rauschmayer et al., 2009). To avoid confusion, it should be noted that there is a prominent contrary use in combination with the term impacts - especially within (anglo-american) evaluation literature - where outcomes are perceived as intermediate effects and impacts as end effects (cf. e.g. Rossi et al., 2003; Gysen et al., 2006).

Accordingly, I generally conceive impacts as changes within society, which are initiated by governance and ultimately lead to outcomes. However, the crucial question here is: where exactly do such changes within society occur and how can these impacts be grasped? On which levels can governance potentially induce change?

Within classical policy research, the dominant understanding of policy impacts is reduced to the behavioral change of target groups (addressees) of a public policy (cf. e.g. Knoepfel et al., 2011; Bussmann et al., 1997). Following the prominent model of the policy cycle (e.g. Parsons, 1995) and the simplified model of the political system (Easton, 1965), behavioral change of target groups is regarded as a direct reaction to formal policy outputs (tangible end products of political-administrative processes). However, following this conception of impacts for my purpose would not do justice to the broader perspective of the governance concept (for instance, in view of self-governing modes, as Vermeulen and Kok (2012, p. 185) put it clearly, »*the general approach in policy analysis must be adjusted, in which governments are initiators of collective action and policy instruments are aimed at changing private actors behavior in line with public goals, and where businesses and citizens are the 'recipients' of government activity.*«).

First of all, since the governance perspective takes into account the blurring of boundaries between steering subjects and objects (cf. e.g. Mayntz, 2003), it is possible that there are more relevant products of governance that initiate change than just formal tangible outputs, such as laws. As non-hierarchical governance modes are concerned, the outputs also frequently include intangible results, such as joint future visions, values and plans among participants (cf. e.g. Sørensen & Torfing, 2009). Outputs may also not be the only interface between governance and society. Taking these considerations into account, I basically look upon all our three interdependent dimensions of governance structures, processes and contents as potential factors for initiating changes within society.

Furthermore, and more importantly, only considering behavioral change of target groups does not suffice for my research perspective. Target groups might not be the sole relevant actors that need to be considered for analyzing changes stimulated by governance. This is again especially true in light of blurred lines among steering subjects and objects.

Apart from this, only looking at behavioral change of target groups would especially not do justice to the field of promoting sustainable transformation processes. Particularly in this field, although behavioral change is important, there is more to be achieved. Promoting SD, for instance, requires transformative action and fundamental structural societal changes that get implemented through institutionalization processes. This is also especially relevant with regard to the realm of new governance modes that do not rely on established political systems and their prevalent structures. Also, the long-term goal of sustainability e.g. calls for changes in societal discourses. From this broad understanding, it follows that there is a multitude of relevant categories of change to be considered. In the next chapter, I will elaborate a heuristic that covers this diversity.

3.3.2 Conceptualizing governance impacts

When impacts are understood as the entirety of societal changes induced by governance, there are various realms in society that need to be taken into account. As a basic assumption, I hold that it is first and foremost through actors that alterations within the real world materialize. Taken together, actors shape the society they are living in. However, it is not sufficient to only explore the actual actions of actors. There are other important categories of change that need to be considered. For instance, as indicated above, governance might provoke alterations within societal discourses or changes within institutional rules that determine the actions of actors. I am thus looking for a perspective that considers both structure and agency and grasps the dyadic relationship between the actions of actors and institutions. This follows the line of reasoning of approaches in connection with governance like the actor-centered institutionalism (Scharpf, 1997), or the dialectic model of policy networks (Marsh & Smith, 2000). It should also incorporate the role of discourses and belief systems in accordance with approaches like the policy arrangement approach (e.g. Arts et al., 2006; Dang et al., 2015) or advocacy coalitions (e.g. Sabatier, 1998).

Since transformations within society get materialized through actors, I hold that it is possible to capture all these categories by means of an openly conceptualized actor-centered approach, more specifically an approach that focuses on *action strategies*. As I will argue, by means of the broad notion of strategies of actors affected by governance, it is possible to meet the above demanded openness for a range of analytical categories of change. It is not only possible to capture behavioral change of all kind of different affected actors (also including e.g. their goals and resources) but also broader induced institutionalization processes and the changing context of the actors (i.e. alterations in societal action conditions). This e.g. includes alterations in societal discourses and actor constellations or in the general political agenda (covering changes in agenda setting and problem awareness, or alterations in other affected governance arrangements, e.g. in their results - or the initiation of entire new arrangements).

Before elaborating in more detail on the notion of action strategies, I have to address two challenges, namely clarifying the demarcation of and the relationship between governance workings and impacts. The first question is *how to demarcate governance from governance impacts*, i.e. the actual workings of an arrangement from its impacts? From a traditional steering perspective, one might be tempted to do so by means of the type of involved actors. However, due to the blurring lines between subjects and objects, both the realm of governance workings and impacts potentially include state and societal actors. There is thus a need for a different heuristic of demarcation. As argued in chapter 2.2, I look upon governance from the perspective of regulating public issues and goods in light of collective problems. Along this line, non-hierarchical modes such as self-governance are also regarded as coordinative 'public' actions. From an analytical point of view, I follow the perspective of 'those who are steering and those who are steered'; yet, the focus is not on actors but on their strategies. I then distinguish the actual workings of governance from impacts by means of the character of strategies (and resulting actions). Within the realm of governance workings, strategies and actions are coordinated according to a common goal of public interest (collective decision making) and aim to solve a collective problem (*coordinated action of public nature*). In contrast, within the realm of impacts, strategies and actions are individualized and can be attributed to the private domain (*individualized action of private* nature - however, this does not mean that I only consider individual actors, but also collective actors, cf. below). Individualized strategies can indeed influence each other and relationships among them can be established, for instance, through discourses or institutional rules. However, they are not characterized by coordinated interactions in pursuit of collectively shaping societies.

Second, the *relationship between governance and its impacts* has to be addressed carefully. In each case it has to be scrutinized if changes on the level of impacts can in fact be attributed to the governance workings in question - as opposed to other potential influencing factors, such as interfering governance modes or contextual aspects (cf. more generally e.g. Hill & Hupe, 2014; Wolff & Schönherr, 2011; in the empirical research part, this will be e.g. addressed by asking experts what exactly was responsible for changing their action strategies, cf. chapter 6.3). Moreover, it has to be considered that governance evolves over time and includes various practices at multiple levels. A governance arrangement starts with its initiation by certain actors. At this stage there is not yet an impact. While the arrangement evolves over time and first practices are conducted, there might already be an identifiable impact due to these impulses. This stage might then be followed by other practices that also provoke impacts (in the empirical part, the considered timeframe will thus range from the initiation of governance to the present, cf. chapter 6.3). Taking this into account, I basically consider different temporal orders of governance and impacts in order to cope with the complex nature of this dynamic sequence (in terms of governance, these orders might also correspond to different levels; from the national to the local level). In order to understand this sequence, a deepened understanding of both governance and its impacts is required. With regard to governance, this is reached by the conceptualization presented in chapter 3.1 (that discloses its inherent complexity as dynamic interactions among structures, processes and contents). Regarding governance impacts, I in turn aim to reveal in detail the strategic reactions and responses of affected actors as changes within society.

In the following, I will clarify my central analytic categories for this endeavor. Figure 8 provides a corresponding overview of the synthesized model that includes governance, its impacts and outcomes. The model thus clarifies the 'system' in question by highlighting its boundaries and the linkage to governance workings and outcomes, and defines its structure, i.e. the covered elements and their relationships.

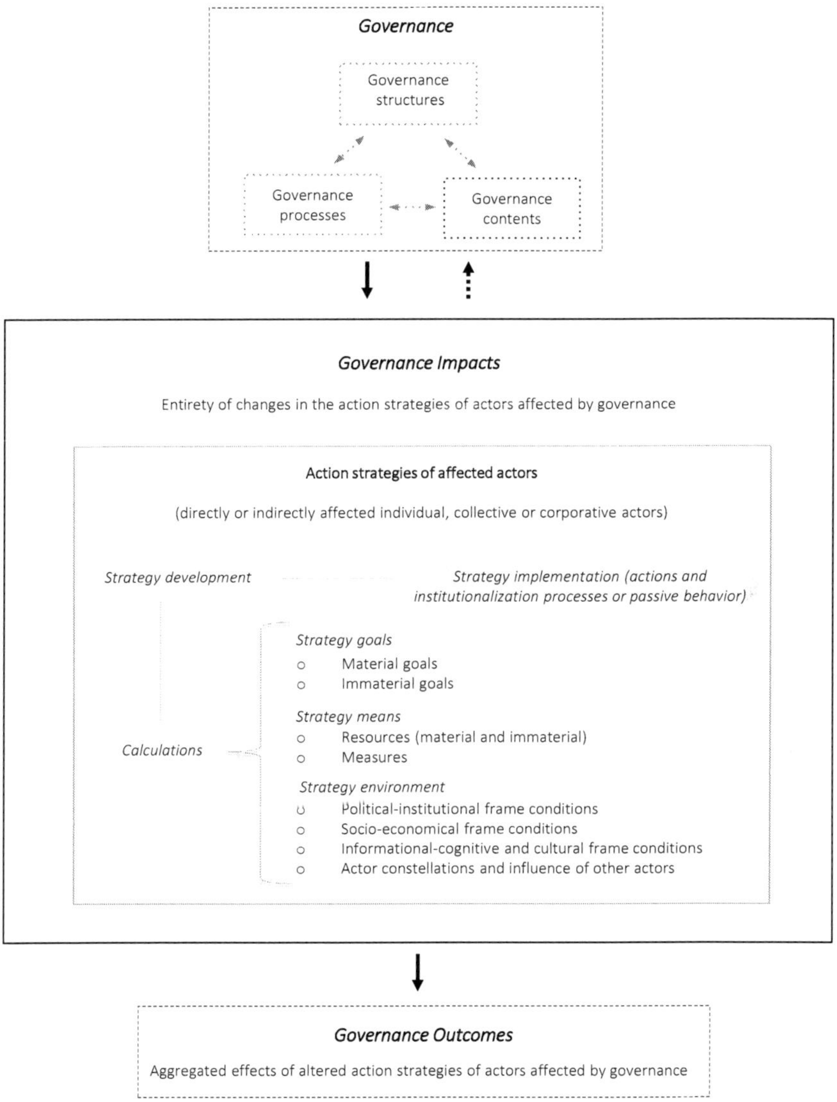

Figure 8: Governance impacts (own illustration)

I define governance impacts as the *entirety of changes in the action strategies of actors affected by governance*. This definition requires a clarification of the strategy term and of the relevant actor arena. As introduced in chapter 3.1, *actors* are basically understood in this study as any social unit possessing agency or power of action. I then aim to overcome the classical restriction on target groups as the only relevant affected actors by governance. Accordingly, I regard all actors within society to be potentially affected. This includes individuals (respectively groups of individuals) and collective or corporative actors (cf. e.g. Scharpf, 1997, p. 51 ff.) - as long as their action strategies are individualized and not coordinated. I furthermore include both directly and indirectly affected actors. This first of all covers target groups (i.e. actors whose behavior is seen as the (in)direct cause of a collective problem that a given governance arrangement addresses, or who are able to take action to deal with it). Moreover, end beneficiaries are included (i.e. actors who experience negative effects of a collective problem at hand and whose e.g. economic, social, or ecological circumstances should be improved once the results of governance occur). Apart from this, third party groups are addressed (i.e. actors who - without being directly targeted by governance - are affected indirectly, either positively or negatively) (cf. e.g. Knoepfel et al., 2011; Sauer, 2006). However, this is only to be seen as an orientation since, for instance, not all real-world arrangements may have end beneficiaries.

Taken together, directly and indirectly affected individual, collective and corporative actors span the actor field with regard to governance impacts. With these broad categories, I aim to cover the full range of potential impacts, while taking into account the blurring of boundaries between steering subjects and objects. Yet, the actor field addresses all potentially affected actors - and the question of which actors are ultimately considered is case-sensitive and needs to be addressed in empirical research.

Having clarified the actor field, I can now focus on the *strategy term*. With regard to the notion of strategy, there is thus far no common understanding or even a ′strategy-theory′. Yet, among different approaches, recurring elements can be identified. This includes the objectives addressed within strategies, the ways to achieve these objectives as well as the embedding context that determines the realm of action (for a recent overview of ′strategy′ conceptualizations, cf. e.g. Sohre, 2014).

Against this backdrop, I follow the idea of Tils (2005; cf. also Raschke & Tils, 2007) to conceive of strategies as building on dynamic, transsituational and success-oriented ′goals-means-environment-calculations′. Adapted to my context, I conceptualize action strategies as constructs, which rest on strategy calculations composed of the following items:

- *Strategy goals*, which I divide into material goals (e.g. economic or political interests) and immaterial goals (e.g. normative ideas and belief systems) of an actor,
- *Strategy means,* including material resources (quantifiable goods such as money and available personal) and immaterial resources (e.g. knowledge, capabilities or power) of an actor as well as the measures to realize the strategic goals; and finally the
- *Strategy environment*, which I distinguish into four types of frame conditions characterizing the specific strategy context (these conditions can be either stable, i.e. systemic, or instable, i.e. situational):
  - Political-institutional frame conditions (broader political-institutional structures shaping the action strategies of actors),
  - Socio-economical frame conditions (the constraints and consequences of the social, technical and economic conditions within a society),
  - Informational-cognitive cultural frame conditions (the prevailing knowledge base as well as long-term belief systems concerned with forms of behavior that are shared by the majority of a society); and finally the
  - Actor constellations and the influence of other actors.

By means of considering all these items within calculations, each actor referred to above pursues an individual action strategy - with regard to a certain policy field or collective problem (that a specific governance arrangement addresses). Action strategies can be formally divided into the two phases of *strategy development* and *strategy implementation*. Yet, in reality, the lines between these dynamic phases are frequently not clear cut, and implemented strategies are often readjusted by altered calculations. Action strategies are to be seen as general courses of action: the implementation of strategies can consist of several actions and institutionalization processes, however it may also lead to non-actions, i.e. remaining passive or omitting certain actions. The term of action strategies accordingly not only covers the calculations but also actual actions (respectively the omission of certain actions).

My focus of interest then lies on the changes in the action strategies induced by governance. Impulses coming from governance can affect only one or a range of the above items within strategy calculations. Examples are changes in the knowledge of a certain actor about a problem or in the socio-economic surrounding that frames the actions of actors. The items can also have an influence on each other, eventually affecting the overall calculations - for instance, changed institutional frame conditions might lead to alterations in terms of goals or power of a specific actor. Changes within strategy calculations may then ultimately lead to alterations in the phase of strategy implementation and thus lead to actual actions.

Accordingly, the *chain of governance and action strategies* can be illustrated as follows (cf. figure 9). The workings of governance - including the three dimensions of structures, processes and contents - stimulate changes in the action strategies of affected actors. This can occur by means of several governance interventions over time, which can be understood as impulses. The entirety of these changes is perceived as governance impacts. Once the action strategies have changed, in principle governance practices might be potentially readjusted due to these changes. The aggregated effects of altered action strategies are finally conceived as governance outcomes.

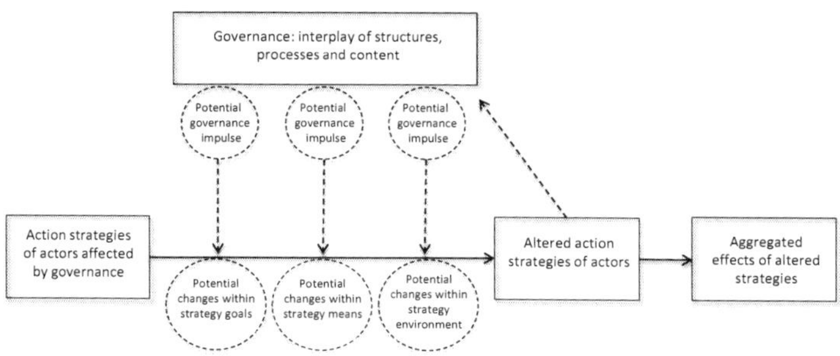

Figure 9: Chain of governance practices and action strategies (own illustration)

In sum, the perspective of action strategies is a promising approach to capture the multiple areas where governance impacts can emerge. It spans the range of possible changes that can be induced by governance. The specific strength of conceptualizing impacts as changes in action strategies consists in the openness of the approach (it is thus not only differentiated and clear but also comprehensive). The strategic momentum connects the goals of actors with their means and the broader strategy environment that influences the corridor of action. Relying on these systematic calculations, action strategies cover a broad range of change factors that can be stimulated through governance.

As argued above, the perspective of action strategies is especially illuminating and fertile in the field of promoting sustainability. It covers the plethora of areas where change is necessary for steps in the direction of SD (which calls for transformation processes that e.g. include structural changes or alterations in societal discourses). In so doing, it is able to grasp the general inherent dynamics within societies.

Moreover, the consideration of not only behavioral change and actual actions but also the 'meso-context' of actors is important - since certain impulses from governance may e.g. not lead to actual actions at first, but nevertheless induce changes that might provoke actions at a later time.

Furthermore, the approach can be applied not only to the courses of action of (groups of) individuals but also collective actors. This is crucial in view of impacts in general and in the field of SD in particular (as societal institutionalization processes are frequently induced by collective actors).

Overall, together with the conceptualization of governance, I hold that the heuristic device for governance impacts offers a promising way for exploring the complex sequence of governance workings and its results.

3.4 Sustainability appraisal

Having disclosed a way for grasping the impacts of governance, the last theoretical task called for by the research question of this study is to find adequate sustainability appraisal criteria. These shall guide the interpretation of the changes in action strategies in light of SD.

3.4.1 In search for sustainability criteria

As pointed out in chapter 2.1, SD is far from being a well-characterized concept. Despite its widespread support, there is a discrepancy between the general mission statement of SD and its theoretical conceptualization and operationalization. Apart from this, SD is per se a normative concept that has to be interpreted. The regulative ideal has to be filled with substance to arrive at comprehensible differentiations between 'sustainable or more sustainable' and 'un- or less sustainable' in specific contexts.

The context of the case studies addressed in the empirical part of this study is the field of Swiss energy policy. Accordingly, for my purpose, I am searching for sustainability criteria that are able to appraise whether the action strategies of actors within the field of the energy sector are on a sustainable path. This includes both content criteria that constitute a sustainable energy system (i.), as well as procedural criteria of sustainable action strategies (ii.) (note that in the strict sense, I hold that an energy system cannot be sustainable itself but only contribute to a sustainable development of a society).

(i.) In the past decades, the literature on sustainability assessment has grown (for an overview of the state of the art cf. e.g. Bond et al., 2012). In accordance with my understanding of sustainability introduced in chapter 2.1, the normative frame for sustainability appraisal should display three pertinent key features: orientation on justice, no reduction to 'environmental sustainability' and a certain identification of minimal necessary conditions. Although a resource conservation perspective is an important component within the sustainability understanding, the central intrinsic value is ensuring human well-being (including an obligation of mankind to interact cautiously with the environment out of a well-understood self-interest). This perspective could be characterized as 'enlightened anthropocentrism' (cf. e.g. Schultz et al., 2013). Apart from this, the frame should be oriented towards an established way of sustainability assessment that has already proven its value in several empirical work and policy informing processes.

To meet these demands, I choose as a basic orientation for the normative frame the well-established integrative sustainability approach by Kopfmüller et al. (2001; see also Grunwald & Rösch, 2011; Schultz et al., 2008; Kopfmüller, 2006). The approach has been developed from the early 2000s onwards and applied to several different objects and contexts. Accordingly, I follow the idea of an integrative sustainability understanding in contrast to a dimensional perspective (see also Gibson, 2006). The approach starts with three constitutive elements of sustainability: inter- and intragenerational justice, a global focus, and an enlightened anthropocentric perspective. These elements are 'translated' into three general goals: securing human existence, maintaining society's productive potential (including natural, man-made, human and knowledge capital) and preserving society's options for development and action. The three goals are in turn operationalized by fifteen substantive sustainability rules understood as minimum standards, i.e. stating what a sustainable society necessarily has to satisfy to sustain its action potential (table 4). The rules are universal, whereas the level of implementation allows for negotiation and differentiation. Conflicts between different rules are addressed by specific weighting principles (in addition to the substantive rules, instrumental rules describe how to fulfill the minimum conditions for SD, cf. in more detail Kopfmüller et al., 2001).

Table 4: General substantive sustainability rules for a society (adapted from Kopfmüller et al., 2001)

Goals	**1. Securing human existence**	**2. Maintaining society's productive potential**	**3. Preserving society's options for development and action**
Rules	*1.1 Protection of human health*	*2.1 Sustainable use of renewable resources*	*3.1 Equal access to education, information and an occupation*
	1.2 Securing the satisfaction of basic needs	*2.2 Sustainable use of non-renewable resources*	*3.2 Participation in societal decision-making processes*
	1.3 Autonomous self-support	*2.3 Sustainable use of the environment as a sink*	*3.3 Conservation of the cultural heritage and of cultural diversity*
	1.4 Just distribution of chances for using natural resources	*2.4 Avoidance of unacceptable technical risks*	*3.4 Conservation of nature's cultural functions*
	1.5 Compensation of extreme differences in income and wealth	*2.5 Sustainable development of real, human and knowledge capital*	*3.5 Conservation of 'social resources'*

The approach by Kopfmüller et al. (2001) paves the way for a non-arbitrary sustainability appraisal and brings distinctiveness in the form of test criteria to identify sustainable and unsustainable conditions. Applied in many case studies and co-determining the German sustainability discourse, it represents an established benchmark (although there remain several critical points to be taken into account; see for this in more detail e.g. Schultz et al., 2008; Burger & Christen, 2010; Kopfmüller, 2006). It thus serves as a sound basis for my endeavor.

However, the approach is aimed at a general sustainability assessment referring to the development of a society as a whole. Yet, societies exhibit differentiated functional systems. For the purpose of this study, the approach has to be adapted to the energy sector. Some substantive minimum requirements need to be left out since they are not relevant in the energy context (e.g. the compensation of extreme differences in income and wealth), others can be taken together and certain new requirements have to be added. My basic orientation for the more specific goals of a sustainable energy system are five general criteria as postulated by the Swiss Academies of Arts and Sciences (2012) for the evaluation of sustainability in the energy sector: human well-being, ecological compatibility, supply security, economic efficiency and the prevention of system endangering risks. Apart from this, two further demands are named in the study: upholding both the flexibility and diversity of the energy system. In my normative frame, I will include these two demands under the heading of upholding adaptation options.

Taken together, the basic orientation of the integrative approach and the more specific goals for the energy sector build a sound fundament for the normative frame with regard to substantive criteria. This fundament was cross-checked and supplemented by a literature review regarding contributions that outline criteria for a sustainable energy system (cf. especially Vera & Langlois, 2007; Patlitzianas et al., 2008; IAEA, 2005; Walter et al., 2001; Grunwald & Rösch, 2011; Kopfmüller et al., 2000; Brodmann et al., 2001; Streimikiene & Šivickas, 2008; Afgan et al., 2000; cf. also in general Schneider et al., 2014; Wiek & Larson, 2014). Against this backdrop, I have deduced fourteen *content criteria* that display minimum requirements constituting a sustainable development of the energy system.

(ii.) Apart from substantive criteria, procedural aspects are important for the endeavor of appraising action strategies, since these represent courses of actions. Against this backdrop, I have deduced three *procedural criteria* as general requirements for sustainable action strategies. The basis for this was a synthesis of a literature review regarding relevant procedural-institutional criteria for actions guided towards sustainability (especially Shiroyama et al., 2012; Huh, 2011; Steurer, 2010; Meadowcroft, 2007; Baker, 2009; Newig et al., 2008; Kemp et al., 2005; Voss et al., 2006; Rist et al., 2007; Lockwood et al., 2010; Biermann, 2007; Loorbach, 2010; Meuleman & In 't Veld, 2010; Den Uyl & Driessen, 2015; Pahl-Wostl, 2009; Folke et al., 2005; Bäckstrand et al., 2010).

These requirements arise from coping with three general challenges that can be basically associated with the pursuit of sustainability: coping with the future orientation and intergenerational scope, doing justice to the complexity of cross-sectoral and multi-scale sustainability challenges, and finally handling uncertainty of system dynamics and the resulting ambivalence of goals.

Since the procedural requirements arise from the particular challenges associated with the pursuit of SD, they are explicitly connected to the idea of sustainability. Other more general procedural criteria for actions (cf. also e.g. the above mentioned procedural criteria within the ′good governance′ discourse), can be functional to achieve these requirements. However, they are not explicitly dealt with here as criteria on their own, since I follow an explicit sustainability perspective.

3.4.2 Normative frame for sustainability appraisal

Taken together, the content and procedural criteria form the normative frame for sustainability appraisal (figure 10). They provide a differentiated picture from which to appraise action strategies of actors affected by governance in the energy sector with respect to SD. Accordingly, they provide a way for determining whether contributions are made towards a more sustainable development.

Note that this study does not aim to make a contribution to the literature on sustainability assessment criteria and their derivation on a transparent conceptual basis. This part of the study is instrumental. Also, the chosen criteria remain on a rather broad level since they are meant to provide an orientation for interpreting governance impacts, i.e. changes in action strategies, in light of overall sustainability goals. I do not aim at an encompassing and detailed sustainability assessment (e.g. on the level of outcomes) but rather at a general interpretive appraisal of the empirical findings. Accordingly, no further specific indicators were developed that operationalize the criteria in more detail (see in comparison indicators in conjunction with the Sustainable Development Goals, SDGs; cf. also Kopfmüller et al., 2001 and in relation to governance e.g. McNeill et al., 2014). My general guiding question is if there are good reasons to regard the respective changes induced by governance as a contribution to sustainability (as depicted by the overall guiding question and sub-questions in figure 10).

<table>
<tr><th colspan="7">Sustainability appraisal of governance impacts in the energy sector
(Guiding question: Do the changes in action strategies of actors affected by governance, i.e. governance impacts, contribute to a sustainable development of the energy system?)</th></tr>
<tr><td rowspan="3">Substantive criteria</td><td colspan="6">Goals and substantive minimum requirements of a sustainable energy system
(Guiding sub-question: Do the changes contribute to meeting the substantial minimum requirements of a sustainable energy system?)</td></tr>
<tr><td>Ecological compatibility</td><td>Human well-being</td><td>Supply security</td><td>Risk handling</td><td>Economic efficiency</td><td>Upholding adaptation options</td></tr>
<tr><td>• Preservation of resources (sustainable use of renewable and non-renewable resources)
• Protection of ecosystems and the climate system (sustainable use of the environment as a sink and conservation of nature's cultural functions)</td><td>• Protection of human health
• Provision of equal access to energy resources and services
• Safeguarding of social compatibility while facilitating autonomous self-support and conserving social resources
• Ensuring of participation in decision-making processes regarding the energy system</td><td>• Guarantee of the lasting and sufficient provision of energy resources
• Provision of an adequate energy supply infrastructure</td><td>• Prevention of system-endangering risks
• Minimization and just intergenerational distribution of unavoidable risks</td><td>• Ensuring of a justifiable cost design of the energy system in relation to other economic activities while internalizing external costs
• Strengthening of real, human and knowledge capital to sustain economic productivity</td><td>• Securing of flexibility to adapt the energy system
• Safeguarding of diversity of the energy system</td></tr>
<tr><td rowspan="3">Procedural criteria</td><td colspan="6">Challenges and procedural requirements of sustainable action strategies
(Guiding sub-question: Do the changes contribute to meeting the procedural requirements of sustainable action strategies?)</td></tr>
<tr><td colspan="2">Coping with the future orientation and intergenerational scope of sustainability</td><td colspan="2">Doing justice to the complexity of cross-sectoral and multi-scale sustainability challenges</td><td colspan="2">Handling uncertainty of system dynamics and the resulting ambivalence of sustainability goals</td></tr>
<tr><td colspan="2">• Strengthening reflexivity in courses of actions while preserving options for development and (re-)action</td><td colspan="2">• Expanding an integrative perspective in terms of thematic scope and spatial scales of action while coping with distributed power</td><td colspan="2">• Supporting social learning processes by means of deliberative characteristics in courses of actions</td></tr>
</table>

Figure 10: Normative frame for sustainability appraisal of governance impacts in the energy sector (own illustration)

Part III: Empirical case studies

4 Research methodology

Taken together, the four elements developed in the previous chapters (3.1-3.4) build the theoretical framework of this study. This framework serves as the foundational basis for the upcoming empirical part. In this chapter, I will first elaborate in more detail on the research methodology used. After describing the general approach of qualitative case study research (chapter 4.1), I will go into more detail with regard to the data collection (chapter 4.2) and data analysis techniques (chapter 4.3) employed in this study.

4.1 Comparative case study approach of a qualitative nature

The field of sustainability governance is contextual and varies among countries and policy sectors. Therefore, context-specific research on how SD is put into effect is required. To understand and improve governance towards SD, one must learn from real-world arrangements, requiring in-depth studies of specific situational settings. The overall research interest of this study - investigating the relation between governance modes and SD - represents a thus far sparsely explored topic. Taking this into account, I basically follow a *qualitative approach* to research (cf. e.g. Ritchie & Lewis, 2003; Flick, 2009).

Since exploring new fields and depth are strengths of case studies, I furthermore consider a *case study approach* as well suited for my objectives. Such an approach allows for the obtainment of a nuanced understanding of complex and dynamic processes and social phenomena (cf. e.g. Gerring, 2007; Stake, 2000; Verschuren, 2003). It is thus able to shed light on governance workings and their results. According to Yin (2009), the need for case studies arises out of the goal to grasp complex social phenomena. A case study is understood as an empirical inquiry that explores a phenomenon in depth within its real-life context.

I choose to investigate five different cases within the field of Swiss energy policy. Accordingly, I apply a *comparative research strategy* (cf. e.g.

George & Bennett, 2005). The choice of this case study approach follows the line of reasoning that the research objective calls for a setting that compares multiple arrangements (in order to shed light on the range of different governance modes). Apart from that a »*detailed comparative perspective is the best way to understand how governance really works*« (Capano et al., 2015b, p. 312). In each case study, complex governance workings and results shall be analyzed. As this requires an in-depth analysis, only a few cases are explored, which allows a detailed focus.

The function of the case studies is to illuminate the research question and to enable the formulation of hypotheses. Thus, they do not serve to explicitly validate the theoretical framework (however, I principally considered the possibility of an inductive alteration of the theoretical frames after some experience with the case study research if necessary, cf. also chapter 8.2). Also, the cases are to be seen as exemplary cases that were selected in light of the overall research desideratum (cf. in more detail below). They were thus not selected due to a specific interest in the content of the cases.

The rationale for choosing the field of *energy policy* is that it is one of the most relevant domains with regard to SD. The transformation of energy systems is widely acknowledged as one of the crucial challenges to lead societies towards more sustainable trajectories (cf. e.g. Robertson, 2014). While availability of energy services is essential for the well-being of societies, at the same time, the energy sector is responsible for problems with respect to endangered ecosystems, resource scarcity or human health. A decisive number of societal problems of unsustainability are directly or indirectly linked to this sector (cf. ibid.). It is thus increasingly under pressure to undergo fundamental change processes (e.g. towards renewable energy sources), and accordingly collective action is highly demanded. Apart from this, the field of energy policy is an illustrative choice in light of the fact that the promotion of SD requires institutionalization processes induced by governance. The transformation of energy systems is largely dependent on such processes due to the need for building new structures, e.g. of decentralized systems. It is thus a suitable example to illustrate how transformation processes can be achieved.

For studying the sector of energy policy, the context of *Switzerland* is well suited, since the country exhibits a high variability of different approaches in governing (cf. also chapter 5.1). The field of Swiss energy policy is generally characterized by a large heterogeneity of governance modes (hierarchical modes as well as non-hierarchical ones). Apart from this, the choice of Swiss case studies is also particularly useful in view of the goal to shed light especially on new modes. Due to established Swiss instruments of direct democracy (cf. chapter 5.1), even studying hierarchical arrangements can shed some light on aspects associated with new modes (for instance, Swiss hierarchical modes entail more participatory procedures than hierarchical modes in other countries).

In the following, I will explain the choice of the five particular case studies. Within the qualitative research literature, several strategies for case selection are proposed (cf. e.g. Flick, 2009). In general, I followed a *case selection strategy* with purposive strategic sampling, while striving for a representative sample with useful variation in the dimensions of theoretical interest (cf. e.g. Seawright & Gerring, 2008). Accordingly, I selected the cases through a multistage process that was based on several rational criteria. I will introduce these criteria in the following.

The primary general criterion for case selection was the relevance to the research objective (cf. e.g. George & Bennett, 2005). Accordingly, my goal was to choose cases that illuminate the overall research question. As a consequence, the following specific selection criteria were incorporated:

- As an intuitive heuristic, the cases ought to display the full range of existing ways of steering. As introduced in chapter 2.2, these ways basically range from top-down arrangements at different levels of government, to formalized public-private partnerships and deliberative networks, up to societal autonomy expressed in bottom-up arrangements. Generally speaking, the cases should thus exhibit relevant differences while together including all relevant sample characteristics. This strategy resembles the so-called diverse case method, i.e. achieving a maximum variance along relevant dimensions (e.g. Seawright & Gerring, 2008; Flick, 2009).
- Each case was then supposed to represent some sort of a key example and paradigm for a certain way of steering, i.e. exhibiting typical characteristics identified within governance literature and thus serving as a prototypical value. This goal follows the course of a paradigmatic case selection strategy (e.g. Flyvbjerg, 2006).
- Moreover, since certain governance impacts evolve over a longer time period, the initiation phase of the governance arrangements within the cases should date back at least a couple of years to ensure that all pre-

dominant impacts are covered. The time frame for each case thus spans from the initiation of the governance arrangement up to the present.

Apart from these criteria considered in light of the general research objective, I kept in mind the following supplementary criteria:

- I preferred cases that exhibit a high relevance within the field of Swiss energy policy (as well as Swiss and international policy in general). For instance, the cases should be regarded as being a crucial contribution to the field, being a prototypical or prominent and much debated approach or a role-model. The cases should also cover various areas within the field of energy policy (such as the electricity, transport and building sector that covers the aspect of heating; as well as the transcending issue of CO_2 emissions) in order to shed light on the multiple facets of this decisive sector for SD.
- Finally, for a pragmatic approach to research, the cases ought to facilitate access to relevant data. Accordingly, cases were preferred that already exhibit some existing research and that facilitate the access to the empirical field in terms of location (which is relevant for approaching the experts for interviews) (cf. also Yin, 2009).

The consideration of all these criteria together resulted in choosing the following *five cases*:

Case study 1: The first case study can be seen as a paradigm for top-down steering on a central, national level. It addresses governing in connection with the CO_2 levy in Switzerland that came into effect in 2008. The levy represents the central instrument of the Swiss CO_2 law - one of the most important pillars of energy policy in Switzerland (cf. chapter 5.2).

Case study 2: The second case represents a key example for top-down steering at (more or less autonomous) lower levels of government. It deals with the governance arrangement around the electricity saving fund Basel, implemented in 1999 in the canton Basel-City (consisting of a regulatory levy on power consumption and a refunding system). With international pioneer character, the arrangement has served as a role model for transfers to other places and contexts (cf. chapter 5.3).

Case study 3: The third case represents a paradigm for a typical collaboration between state and societal actors (formalized public-private partnership). It is concerned with governance for reducing motor fuel consumption - by a target agreement on new passenger cars between the Swiss Federal Office of Energy (SFOE) and the Association of Swiss Automobile Importers (ASIA). This represents the first target agreement implemented in 2002 by the Swiss Energy program, a major pillar within Swiss energy policy. The transport sector plays a central role since it accounts for around one third of overall CO_2 emissions in Switzerland (cf. chapter 5.4; cf. also e.g. IEA, 2012).

Case study 4: The fourth case study can be seen as typical network governance with deliberative rationalities and multi-level characteristics. It explores the 'Energy-Trialogue Switzerland', a stakeholder discussion process initiated in 2007. The goal of this process was to bring together representatives from science, economy and society to discuss the future of Swiss energy policy. The Energy-Trialogue has gained strong attention among the public, media and actors from the energy sector in Switzerland (cf. chapter 5.5).

Case study 5: The final case deals with an illustrative example for a governance arrangement that basically features a bottom-up logic. It is concerned with governing related to the Swiss Minergie label for buildings. Launched in 1998, the energy label has not only become an important driving force in Swiss energy policy (the building sector accounts for about half of the Swiss gross energy consumption), but represents one of the most successfully implemented labels in the realm of SD worldwide (cf. chapter 5.6). Moreover, space heating plays a decisive role with regard to overall CO_2 emissions in Switzerland (cf. e.g. IEA, 2012).

Taking everything into account, I look at very specific case studies (e.g. I do not explore the implementation of energy labels within the energy sector in general, but rather focus on a specific energy label). This follows the line of reasoning that I aim to assign each case to a particular mode of governance and to identify its specific impacts (e.g. the implementation of energy labels in general might exhibit several simultaneously co-existing modes that induce different impacts).

The general procedure of case study research was geared towards the methodologically linear but iterative process as described by Yin (2009), which includes the following steps: planning and preparing the case studies as well as collecting, analyzing and interpreting the data. A particular strength of case study research is its ability to deal with a large variety of empirical evidence, including multiple methods (cf. e.g. Hartley, 2004). In the following, the methods for data collection and analysis will be elaborated in more detail.

4.2 Data collection

The case study approach generally allows different kinds of data collection techniques (cf. e.g. Ritchie & Lewis, 2003). Against this background, I made use of a procedure of triangulation in terms of methods and sources. Different primary techniques were combined, bringing together multiple sources of evidence for each case. This procedure converges lines of inquiry, while the specific weaknesses of a certain method or source are compensated by the counter-balancing strengths of another one (cf. e.g. Yin, 2009; the theoretical framework provided orientation in the preliminary phases of data collection, cf. also e.g. Miles & Huberman, 1994).

First of all, *existing research* on the cases was studied. This included first and foremost scientific studies and partly publications by public bodies or societal initiatives. Apart from that, *official documents* were investigated. On the one hand, this included documents of political-administrative bodies participating in respective governance workings (such as laws, ordinances or programs as well as official evaluations). On the other hand, documents from participating societal bodies such as firms and other initiatives (e.g. published strategy papers and plans) were explored. The findings from existing research and official documents together provided a preliminary nuanced insight into the individual cases.

Based on this, qualitative in-depth *expert-interviews* were conducted. While the analysis of existing research and documents ought to provide insights regarding the official picture with respect to the cases (e.g. in terms of objectives and their achievement), the interviews should enable going beyond this. They ought to shed light on the actual workings of governance arrangements and their results in more detail. The goal was to arrive at in-depth and background knowledge, allowing a deeper understanding of the case studies (this type of knowledge can be best produced by the interview type of expert interviews). Experts can be generally considered as persons representing a group of a particular field of action, who possess special knowledge of the social phenomenon in question (cf. e.g. Bogner et al., 2014). The expert interview is a technique to make this knowledge accessible in order to allow the reconstruction of social situations (cf. e.g. Gläser & Laudel, 2010; Bogner et al., 2009).

The interviews were semi-structured and based on *interview guides* (cf. e.g. Brinkmann, 2013; Arthur & Nazroo, 2003). Such topic guides generally enhance the consistency of data collection, while combining structure with flexibility. In so doing, they ensure that relevant issues are covered systematically and with some uniformity, yet allowing a flexible adjustment to the specific interview partner. The guides were structured according to the theoretical frames for governance and impacts and their specific categories. Based on two basic interview guides (one directed at exploring governance and one for investigating impacts), for each expert interview, an individual topic guide was compiled. Accordingly, on the one hand questions were asked directed at exploring governance structures, processes and contents, as well as the characteristics of governance modes and their role for inducing impacts. On the other hand, the different elements composing the action strategies of affected actors were explored (in this regard, the focus was put on reported key changes in action strategies of different actor groups, cf. also chapter 8.2). Overall, themes were broken down into subtopics, including several open guiding questions. For operationalizing the theoretical frames, abstract notions had to be translated into questions adapted to the cultural and communicational context of the interview partners. The specific questions varied among the individual guides, e.g. depending on the particular expert addressed. In general, within each interview guide, platform questions to generate impulses for narrating were supplemented by specific further inquiries (an example of an individualized interview guide is provided in the appendix of this study). Overall, the structure of the interview schedules was made sufficiently flexible, permitting questions to be asked most suited to the interviewee (in order to safeguard the basic suitability of the interview guides, two pretest were conducted).

For the *selection of the interviewees*, I followed a theoretical-construct sampling design. Experts were chosen with regard to meeting certain characteristics against the backdrop of the theoretical framework (cf. for this procedure e.g. Tracy, 2013). Moreover, I followed four general guiding questions as formulated by Gläser & Laudel (2010, p. 117): who has the relevant information, who is most likely to provide the required data, who is most likely to share this data and finally who is available for an interview? (cf. also Bogner et al., 2014). This represents a purposive sampling approach (apart from this, in some instances, a snowballing technique was used, i.e. asking interviewees to identify potential interview partners).

Table 5 provides an overview of the *conducted interviews* on governance and impacts related to the cases. The actors are classified according to the distinction of being either key representatives stemming from political-administrative public bodies, the market sector or the field of civil society[13]. For the reconstruction of governance within the cases, expert interviews were held with key participating actors in the arrangement in question (e.g. a representative of an administration). For the identification of impacts, interviews were held with key actors either being affected by the respective arrangement (representatives for an affected collective actor), or general experts on its results (this also included actors that could give information on different action strategies, e.g. a representative of a trade association, providing insights on the strategies of various firms). Some of the actors hold a double role in terms of being both a key participating actor in governance and an expert for results. These actors were thus interviewed in both respects, i.e. two separate interviews were conducted each according to the different role (regarding this procedure cf. e.g. Gläser & Laudel, 2010). Accordingly, in total 24 interviews were held, including 17 key actors (for the fourth case, two short written statements were additionally requested, since a specific question - i.e. if the arrangement had an influence on politics - had to be explored). The number of interviews was based on the criterion that a certain thematic saturation had been reached (cf. e.g. Morse, 1995; Seidman, 2006; meaning that no further large variance among answers is recognized). In this regard, it was essential that all interview partners were central key actors with regard to

13 Note that the field of civil society here denotes representatives for groups of individuals, or of scientific and other societal bodies.

the cases from different backgrounds that could give representative insights. All interviews were held face-to-face between December 2014 and November 2015, with an average duration of one hour (cf. the interview list in the appendix for an overview). After asking for permission, all interviews were audio recorded (anonymity was assured to each interview partner). Subsequently, I transcribed each interview, following general transcription rules (see for these in detail, Kuckartz, 2007). Additionally, a post-script was developed that noted important background information of the interview (for an overview on general techniques of qualitative interviewing cf. e.g. Gubrium & Holstein, 2001; Helfferich, 2011).

Table 5: Overview of interviews conducted
(with interview numbers, the first digit indicates the case) (own illustration)

	Interviews on governance (with key participating actors in the governance arrangement)	**Interviews on impacts** (either with a representative of an affected collective actor or with a general expert in terms of the results of the arrangement)
Case 01: CO_2 levy	• Interview 01-01 (administration) • Interview 01-02 (politics)	• Interview 01-03 (market) • Interview 01-04 (civil society) • Interview 01-05 (administration)
Case 02: Electricity saving fund	• Interview 02-01 (politics) • Interview 02-02 (administration)	• Interview 02-03 (market) • Interview 02-04 (administration) • Interview 02-05 (politics)
Case 03: Fuel consumption covenant	• Interview 03-01 (market) • Interview 03-02 (administration)	• Interview 03-03 (administration) • Interview 03-04 (market) • Interview 03-05 (market)
Case 04: Energy Trialogue	• Interview 04-01 (civil society) • Interview 04-02 (administration)	• Interview 04-03 (administration) • Interview 04-04 (civil society) (in addition: two written statements from politics: short statements 04-01 and 04-02)
Case 05: Minergie label	• Interview 05-01 (civil society) • Interview 05-02 (civil society)	• Interview 05-03 (market) • Interview 05-04 (administration) • Interview 05-05 (civil society)

4.3 Data analysis

In terms of data analysis, I relied on the technique of qualitative content analysis, i.e. category guided text analysis (cf. e.g. Krippendorff, 2004; Mayring, 2015; Gläser & Laudel, 2010; for different processes of data analysis in qualitative research cf. e.g. Green et al., 2007; Flick, 2009). The strength of qualitative content analysis is that it is methodologically controlled by using a step-by-step approach. It follows a systematic and rule based proceeding through the use of category systems, i.e. a theory-driven elaboration of text material. Mayring (2000, p. 5) defines qualitative content analysis as an approach of »*empirical, methodological controlled analysis of texts within their context of communication, following content analytical rules and step-by-step models*«. Such a method of systematic data interpretation accordingly combines qualitative analysis with quantitative structuring elements - such as rules and steps - to systematize and verify it.

The data analysis applied in this study should enable to filter out particular aspects of the data material and follow a deductive category application based on a theoretical framework (also known as directed content analysis, cf. e.g. Hsieh & Shannon, 2005; Potter & Levine-Donnerstein, 1999). Against this backdrop, I followed the so-called content structuring technique[14] (cf. Mayring, 2000, 2010 and 2015). This technique basically combines two aspects. First, it filters and structures the material against a theoretically deduced set of categories. Second, it summarizes the culled contents per category. It thus allows a methodologically controlled assignment of certain text components to categories.

I principally followed the operational sequencing model of structured qualitative content analysis provided by Mayring (2010; cf. figure 11). The decisive aspect within this sequence is to formulate definitions and coding rules for each category; determining the circumstances under

---

14 Apart from the content structuring technique, Mayring (2000, 2010 and 2015) highlights two other techniques of analysis: summarizing content analysis with an inductive development of categories as well as explication, where text passages are isolated and explicated with other material in order to exemplify the meaning of the passage.

which a text passage is coded. Categories, definitions and coding rules are then put together within a category system.[15]

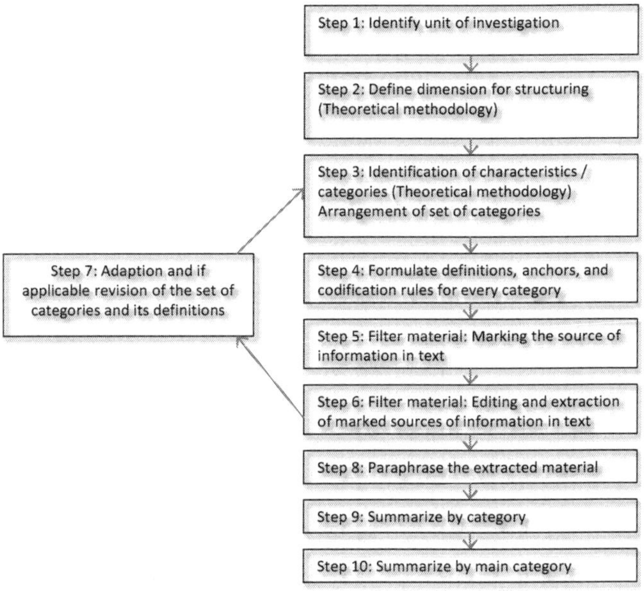

Figure 11: Structured qualitative content analysis (adapted from Mayring, 2010, p. 99)[16]

---

15 As introduced, the content structuring technique is embedded in the general procedure of qualitative content analysis. Mayring (2000, 2010 and 2015) in this regard defines four steps to be conducted before going through the steps illustrated in figure 11. This first of all includes a determination of the text material, an analysis of the situation in which the material originated, and a formal characterization of the material. This information has already been sketched out in chapter 4.2. The material includes texts from existing research, official documents as well as transcripts from the interviews. The background situation of the material is provided by the description of the cases in chapter 5, respectively by describing the interview sampling above. A final step that precedes the content structuring technique is to determine the direction of the analysis. In this regard, the focus was on the particular contents of the material itself - in view of the research objective and the theoretical framework.

Overall, the analysis is thus based on systematically extracting text components according to category systems developed in advance. The categories shall be derived from the research question and theoretically justified (cf. Mayring, 2000). Accordingly, as introduced in chapter 1.3, the first three components of the theoretical framework, i.e. the governance conceptualization, the frame for modes and the scheme for impacts were each translated into category systems (cf. table 1 in chapter 1.3). Table 6 provides an overview of the three deduced systems. Each part shows the main and sub-categories, the definition of variables (i.e. which text material falls under a certain category) as well as the coding rules (facilitating the allocation of material to a certain category and its demarcation).

---

16 As highlighted in figure 11, the first step of the content structuring technique is to define the unit of investigation. In this regard, the smallest component of material being part of the analysis (coding unit) was defined as composing single sentences. The largest component (context unit) in turn was a coherent paragraph. The succession of analysis was determined by the case studies and the theoretical framework.
Steps 2-4 are illustrated by the category systems. The illustration of the categories by anchor examples, i.e. citations from the interviews, was omitted due to the specific character of the theoretical frames. The deduced categories only span a potential realm, i.e. not all categories were supposed to be found in the texts. Illustrating each category by a citation would in this case have largely anticipated the analysis, especially with regard to the frame for governance modes (with five case studies that each represent one mode, each specific characteristic of the frame, e.g. civil society actors as initiating actors, appeared about only a single time).

Table 6: Category systems for content analysis
Part I: Governance conceptualization (own illustration)

Main Category	*Definition of variables*	*Coding rule*
Governance structures	*Any characteristic that refers to the framing conditions of governance, i.e. to the institutional architecture and the resulting roles, relations and mechanisms of social interaction among actors on different institutional levels: formal and informal institutions, structure and degree of institutionalization, access and responsibility rules, role divisions, models of representation, relationships among actors, access to resources and division of power, interaction patterns, institutional levels*	*References to the institutional embedding of a governance arrangement and the roles, relations and mechanisms of interaction among actors acting on institutional levels*
Governance processes	*Any characteristic that refers to the decision-making and implementation processes of interaction taking place within governance that are revealing how the interests of different state and/or societal actors with varying resources, power and influence are transformed into coordinated action: actor field during initiation and coordination, actor coalitions, consideration of interests, mobilization and exchange or resources, usage of power, basis for legitimacy, amount of influence of actors, general character of processes*	*References to the interaction processes inherent in a governance arrangement, revealing how interests of actors are transformed into coordinated action*
Governance contents	*Any characteristic that refers to the substantive policy setting of governance (with different material products): appearance of problem definitions, nature and type of formulated policy problems and their definitions, decisions and objectives made within programs, plans or strategies, approaches of problem solving, nature of steering instruments, policy integration, learning and innovation for adaptive policy solutions, type of knowledge use and production*	*References to the appearance of the substantive policy setting of a governance arrangement*
Interplay of structures, processes and contents	*Any characteristic that refers to the interplay of and interlinkages between governance structures, governance processes and governance contents as well as to their interdependent nature: structures-processes interplay, processes-contents interplay and structures-contents interplay*	*References to the interplay of governance structures, processes and contents*

Table 6: Category systems for content analysis
Part II: Frame for governance modes, actor features (own illustration)

Main Category	Sub-Category	Definition of variables	Coding rule
Actor features	*Initiating actors*	***Centralized governance:*** *Central government agencies (or supra national bodies)*	*References to central government agencies as initiating actors of a governance arrangement*
		Decentralized governance: *Governments at its various levels of aggregation (subsidiarity)*	*References to governments at its various levels of aggregation as initiating actors of a governance arrangement*
		Public-private governance: *Central gov't agencies; private sector and/or civil society are granted a preconditioned role also*	*References to central government agencies as initiating actors of a governance arrangement with a preconditioned role for the market and/or civil society*
		Interactive governance: *Multiple actors: gov't, private sector and civil society*	*References to government agencies, the market and civil society as joint initiating actors of a governance arrangement*
		Self-governance: *Private sector and/or civil society*	*References to market actors and/or civil society as initiating actors of a governance arrangement*
	Stakeholder position	***Centralized governance:*** *Stakeholder autonomy determined by principal agency*	*References to central government agencies as the dominant authority to decide on the involvement of other actors.*
		Decentralized governance: *High likelihood of stakeholder involvement*	*References to an involvement of actors others than the central government.*
		Public-private governance: *Autonomy of stakeholders within predetermined boundaries*	*References to autonomous decisions of actors within predetermined boundaries of central governments*
		Interactive governance: *Equal roles for all network partners*	*References to equal roles for all the actors involved in decision-making processes*
		Self-governance: *Self-governing entities determine the involvement of other stakeholders*	*References to decisions made by self-governing bodies of market actors and/or civil society about involving other actors*
	Policy level	***Centralized governance:*** *(Supra) national level*	*References to supranational or national levels of government*
		Decentralized governance: *Lower levels of gov't*	*References to lower administration levels (e.g. cantonal or municipal level)*
		Public-private governance: *Local to international level*	*References to local up to international policy levels*
		Interactive governance: *Multiple levels*	*References to multiple simultaneously coexisting policy levels.*
		Self-governance: *Local to international level*	*References pointing to local up to international policy levels*
	Power base	***Centralized governance:*** *Coercion; Authority; Legitimacy (democratic representation at the national level)*	*References to actions guided by coercive power, authority and/or democratic legitimacy of central government agencies*
		Decentralized governance: *Coercion; Authority; Legitimacy (democratic representation at lower levels)*	*References to actions guided by coercive power, authority and/or democratic legitimacy of government agencies at lower levels (cantonal or municipal)*
		Public-private governance: *Competitiveness (prices); Contracts and legal recourse; Legitimacy (agreement on relations and procedures)*	*References to actions guided by economic competitiveness, contracts and/or negotiated agreements on relations and procedures*
		Interactive governance: *Legitimacy (agreement on roles, positions, procedures and process); Trust; Knowledge*	*References to actions guided by negotiated agreements on roles, positions and procedures and/or to trust and knowledge*
		Self-governance: *Autonomy; Leadership; Group size; Social capital; Legitimacy (agreement on relations and procedures)*	*References to actions guided by the autonomy of a stakeholder, the need for leadership, social capital (e.g. social affiliation) and/or negotiated agreements on relations and procedures*

Table 6: Category systems for content analysis
Part II: Frame for governance modes, institutional features (own illustration)

Institutional features	***Model of representation***	***Centralized governance:*** *Pluralist (popular (supra) national election and lobbying)*	*References to a pluralist model of representation at the national or supranational level*
		Decentralized governance: *Pluralist (popular local election and lobbying)*	*References to a pluralist model of representation at lower governmental levels (cantonal or municipal level)*
		Public-private governance: *Corporatist (formalized public-private governing arrangements)*	*References to a formalized governance arrangement between public and private actors*
		Interactive governance: *Partnership (Participatory public-private governing arrangements)*	*References to a participatory partnership between public and private actors*
		Self-governance: *Partnership (Participatory private-private governing arrangements)*	*References to a participatory partnership between private actors*
	Rules of interaction	***Centralized governance:*** *Formal rules (rule of law; fixed and clear procedures)*	*References to formal interaction rules defined in regulatory frames and official legally binding documents for national levels*
		Decentralized governance: *Formal rules (rule of law; fixed and clear procedures)*	*References to formal interaction rules defined in regulatory frames and official legally binding documents for sub-national levels*
		Public-private governance: *Formal and informal exchange rules*	*References to formalized and / or informalized rules of interaction within partnerships between public and private actors*
		Interactive governance: *Institutions in its broadest form (formal and informal rules)*	*References to rules of interaction derived from institutions in a broader sense, for instance socio-cultural norms and belief systems*
		Self-governance: *Informal rules (norms; culture); Self-crafted (non-imposed) formal rules*	*References to informal rules of interaction (e.g. implicit social norms and cultural belief systems) or self-crafted formal rules of private actors*
	Mechanisms of social interaction	***Centralized governance:*** *Top-down; command-and-control*	*References to hierarchical interaction patterns and command-and-control interaction mechanism*
		Decentralized governance: *Sub-national governments decide autonomously about collaborations within top-down determined boundaries*	*References to autonomous collaboration decisions of lower government levels (cantonal or municipal) in the presence of directives from national governments*
		Public-private governance: *Private actors decide autonomously about collaborations within top-down determined boundaries*	*References to autonomous collaboration decisions of private actors in the presence of directives from governments*
		Interactive governance: *Interactive: social learning, deliberations, and negotiations*	*References to interactive interaction mechanisms between state, market and/or civil society such as deliberations*
		Self-governance: *Bottom-up: social learning, deliberations and negotiations*	*References to mechanism of social interaction that exhibit a bottom-up character originating from private actors (social learning, deliberations and negotiations)*

Table 6: Category systems for content analysis
Part II: Frame for governance modes, content features (own illustration)

Features concerning content	***Goals and targets***	***Centralized governance:*** *Uniform goals and targets*	*References to objectives and targets that are uniformly defined by central governments*
		Decentralized governance: *Uniform and level specific goals and targets*	*References to uniform objectives and targets specified in terms of the addressed level of administration*
		Public-private governance: *Uniform goals; targets actor specific*	*References to uniform goals but at the same time to specified targets in terms of addressed actors*
		Interactive governance: *Tailor-made and integrated goals and targets*	*References to goals and targets specifically adapted to their context exhibiting an integrated character*
		Self-governance: *Tailor-made goals and targets*	*References to goals and targets adapted to their context*
	Instruments	***Centralized governance:*** *Legislations, permits, norms and standards*	*References to regulatory steering instruments such as standards*
		Decentralized governance: *Public covenants and performance contracts*	*References to public covenants and performance contracts of different administration levels*
		Public-private governance: *Incentive based instruments like taxes and grants; performance contracts*	*References to economic steering instruments such as taxes*
		Interactive governance: *Negotiated agreements; trading mechanisms; covenants; entitlements*	*References to steering instruments of public-private cooperation like negotiated agreements, trading mechanisms, covenants and entitlements*
		Self-governance: *Voluntary instruments; private contracts; entitlements; labeling and reporting*	*References to communicative and/or voluntary steering instruments as well as private contracts*
	Policy-science interface	***Centralized governance:*** *Primacy of generic, expert knowledge*	*References to generic knowledge that is provided by experts with regard to the collective problem in question*
		Decentralized governance: *Primacy of generic expert knowledge. Room for issue and time-and-place specific knowledge*	*References to generic expert knowledge as primary source for action that simultaneously consider tailor-made knowledge*
		Public-private governance: *Dominance of issue and time-and-place specific knowledge; expert and lay (producers and consumers)*	*References to tailor-made knowledge production from experts and/or producers and consumers*
		Interactive governance: *Transdisciplinarity: experts and lay knowledge in networks. Emphasis on integrated and time-and-place specific knowledge*	*References to knowledge production from experts and/or producers and consumers that exhibits a transdisciplinary network character.*
		Self-governance: *Dominance of issue and time-and-place specific: expert and lay (citizens)*	*References to a predominant use of tailor-made knowledge from experts and to a participation of citizens in knowledge production*

Table 6: Category systems for content analysis
Part III: Scheme for governance impacts (own illustration)

Main Category	*Sub-Category*	*Definition of variables*	*Coding rule*
Changes in strategy goals induced by governance	***Material goals***	*Economic or political interests of a certain actor*	*References to changes in material goals of an actor due to governance practices*
	Immaterial goals	*Normative ideas and belief systems of a certain actor*	*References to changes in immaterial goals of an actor due to governance practices*
Changes in strategy means induced by governance	***Measures***	*Measures that are implemented to realize specific strategy goals of an actor*	*References to changes in measures of an actor due to governance practices*
	Material resources	*Objective and quantifiable goods of an actor (e.g. money and available personal)*	*References to changes in material resources of an actor due to governance practices*
	Immaterial resources	*Knowledge base, capabilities or power of an actor*	*References to changes in the immaterial resources of an actor due to governance practices*
Changes in the strategy environment induced by governance	***Political-institutional frame conditions***	*Political and institutional structures within society shaping the actions of actors*	*References to changes in political-institutional frame conditions due to governance practices*
	Socio-economical frame conditions	*Constraints and consequences of the social and economic level of development within society*	*References to changes in socio-economical frame conditions due to governance practices*
	Informational-cognitive and cultural and frame conditions	*The prevailing knowledge base as well as long-term belief systems concerned with forms of behavior that are shared by the majority of a society*	*References to changes in cultural and cognitive-informational frame conditions due to governance practices*
	Actor constellations and influence of other action strategies	*Constellations of actors that are affected by the governance mode in question and the influences of other individualized action strategies*	*References to changes in actor constellations and the influence of other action strategies due to governance practices*
Actions and institutionalization processes resulting from changes in strategy goals, means or environment		*Actions of actors and institutionalization processes that can be traced back to changes in strategy goals, means or environment induced by governance practices*	*References to actions of actors and institutionalization processes linked with changes in strategy calculations due to governance practices*
Passive behavior, i.e. the omission of actions resulting from changes in strategy goals, means or environment		*Passive behavior of actors that can be traced back to changes in strategy goals, means or environment induced by governance practices*	*References to passive behavior of actors linked with changes in strategy calculations due to governance practices*

The analysis was conducted by means of the computer program Maxqda, a software for qualitative data analysis. On the basis of the category systems, I identified and extracted relevant text passages, classified them according to the categories and summarized the culled contents per category. Figure 12 gives an example for illustrating the analysis. Eventually, the data analysis resulted in a structured information basis.[17]

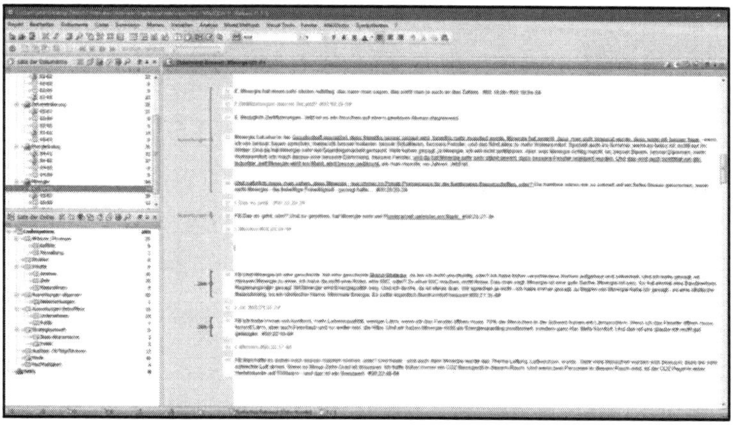

Figure 12: Illustration of data analysis by means of Maxqda
(own illustration)

Taking everything into account, the systematic research methodology as presented in this chapter supports the overall quality of the research. Generally speaking, providing transparency with regard to data collection and analysis - i.e. explaining in detail the steps taken to reach results - can be regarded as one of the main commonly acknowledged strategies to ensure quality in qualitative research (cf. e.g. Steinke, 2004; Bogner et al., 2014). This transparency has been provided above. Limitations with regard to gained results in this study are reflected in chapter 8.2 (cf. in this regard also the discussion on the transfer of quality criteria such as validity and reliability - e.g. Whittemore et al., 2001; Yin, 2009 - to the realm of quali-

17 An overview of interview transcripts and analyses was provided on an attached separate data medium.

tative research, and other criteria explicitly focused on a qualitative approaches in social research designs, e.g. Flyvbjerg, 2006; Gläser & Laudel, 2010; for an overview of different positions on quality criteria in qualitative research cf. e.g. Steinke, 2004).

5 Overview of the cases

In the following, I will give an introductory overview of the five case studies. I will first provide a general introduction by setting the cases in the context of Swiss energy policy (chapter 5.1; the goal of transforming energy systems is in turn seen in the wider context of SD). This framing serves as an embedding background orientation for the five case studies, which co-exist in the policy sector. Afterwards, each case is introduced individually in more detail. The chapters covering the cases (5.2-5.6) are ordered according to the different intuitive ways of governing (from top-down steering at the national and regional level, to a formalized public-private partnership, up to multi-level network and societal bottom-up governing). In contrast, in the following overview chapter, the cases are included in thematic order.

5.1 The case studies in the context of Swiss energy policy

Switzerland has a federal structure including the three political levels of the Confederation, the cantons and the municipalities. Energy policy is a split responsibility between the federal state and the twenty-six cantons (all aspects not assigned to the federal level are the responsibility of the cantons, cf. IEA, 2012). The foundations of Swiss energy policy are anchored in the Swiss Federal Constitution with a particular energy article - mandating the federal government and the cantons to ensure a sufficient, broad-based, secure, economic and environmentally benign energy supply, as well as the economic and efficient use of energy (article 89, paragraph 1, Swiss Confederation, 1999a).

As a consequence of this mandate, in 1999, the federal energy law was enacted, together with its according energy ordinance (cf. Swiss Confederation, 1998). Apart from the energy law, the second established legal basis for Swiss energy policy is the related CO_2 law, which came into force in the year 2000 (cf. Swiss Confederation, 1999b). The first case study (*Case 1: The Swiss CO_2 levy*) is to be seen in this context, since the CO_2 levy, implemented in 2008, is the major instrument for achieving the goals of this law (cf. ibid.).

In addition to legal foundations, Switzerland has implemented a nationwide Swiss Energy program from 2001 onwards (the successor of a program called ′Energy 2000′). It is conducted under the direction of the Swiss Federal Office of Energy (the SFOE, which belongs to the Department of the Environment, Transport, Energy and Communications, DETEC, the lead ministry in charge of Switzerland's energy policy). Established on the basis of the energy law and the CO_2 law, the Swiss Energy program sets up a general framework for voluntary measures promoting energy efficiency and renewable energies (cf. SFOE, 2011). Because energy-related CO_2 emissions in Switzerland stem mostly from oil use in transport and space heating, action is first and foremost needed in these areas (cf. IEA, 2012). One of the most important voluntary measures is the measure of target agreements between the Swiss government and the economy. The first target agreement made within the context of the Swiss Energy program is represented by the third case study (*Case 3 - The fuel consumption covenant in Switzerland)*. Based on the legal basis of the federal energy law and the CO_2 law, a voluntary covenant on motor fuel efficiency was established in 2002 (cf. SFOE, 2011).

A major pillar within the Swiss Energy program today is furthermore the voluntary building label Minergie (*Case 5: The Swiss energy label Minergie*; yet, the label originally evolved from 1994 onwards independently of the program through a bottom-up movement). The label is also to be seen in conjunction with the cantonal building regulations - the most important responsibility of the cantons to contribute to a more sustainable energy system (cf. EnDK, 2015). As stated in the Swiss Federal Constitution, the cantons are the responsible authorities for measures in the building sector.

In 2011, the Federal Council and Parliament decided for a newly oriented long-term national energy policy - the 'Energy Strategy 2050' - which aims at a successive restructuring of the energy system in the upcoming decades. The background and major impulse for this strategy came from the Swiss government's decisions to withdraw from the use of nuclear energy on a step-by-step basis (after the incident at the Fukushima nuclear power plant in spring 2011) (cf. DETEC, 2013).

In 2012, a pre-parliamentary consultation phase regarding the Energy Strategy took place. It is important in this regard and in view of the first two case studies to have background knowledge on Switzerland's strong tradition of *direct democracy* (cf. in the following e.g. Vatter, 2014). In Switzerland, voters have extensive rights of participation at each of the three policy levels (the Confederation, canton and communes). They are able to institute popular initiatives on their own to request an amendment to the constitution and legislation. Initiatives in turn must be submitted to a vote by the people, who have the final say. If voters do not agree with a new law, or changes in a law, they can force a referendum. A further important element with regard to the legislation procedure in Switzerland is the formal pre-parliamentary consultation phase, which is mandatory when drafting amendments to the constitution or to legislation. The Federal Constitution requires such changes to be submitted for public consultation. As stated in the Federal Act on the Consultation Procedure (Swiss Confederation, 2005), the purpose of the consultation phase on a federal level is to allow cantons, political parties and interest groups to participate in shaping the decision-making processes of the Confederation. In so doing, it shall guarantee the feasibility of implementation and public acceptance. The Federal Council invites all participants to give inputs. These are evaluated before the Parliament makes a decision.

After the consultation phase of the Energy Strategy, a first package of measures (targeted at the period until 2020) was developed in 2013. In this initial stage, the focus of the strategy lies on the exploitation of existing energy efficiency potentials and on the balanced utilization of the potentials of hydropower and new renewable energy sources. From 2020 onwards, the Federal Council aims to replace the existing promotion system with an incentive mechanism in the sense of an ecological tax reform (with a steering effect on energy demand) (cf. DETEC, 2013). For this change, the second case study (*Case 2: The electricity saving fund in the canton Basel)* can serve as a role model, since Basel-City is the only Swiss canton with a regulatory levy on electricity.

The fourth case study can also be seen in conjunction with the 'Energy Strategy 2050' (*Case 4: The Energy Trialogue Switzerland).* The Energy Trialogue, a multi-stakeholder discussion process initiated in 2007, aimed at developing a sustainable and competitive strategy for the Swiss energy sector. A further goal from 2012 onwards was to analyze the plausibility of the Energy Strategy 2050 (cf. Beyeler & Kaiser, 2012).

5.2 Case 1 - The Swiss CO_2 levy

The first case study deals with the governance arrangement around the Swiss CO_2 levy. The origins of the levy go back to Switzerland's Federal Law on the Reduction of CO_2 (CO_2 law). The law came into force in the year 2000 and nationally implemented the Swiss commitments in the Kyoto Protocol of the first commitment period from 2008-2012. Accordingly, it set the goal to reduce energy-related CO_2 emissions by 10% until 2010 compared to 1990. The relevant figures for the achievement of this target were the average values for the years 2008 to 2012. The overall goal corresponded with a reduction goal for fossil combustible fuels of 15% (and for motor fuels of 8%) (cf. article 2, CO_2 law, Swiss Confederation, 1999).

The CO_2 law counted first and foremost on voluntary measures (cf. also interview 01-01; Baranzini et al., 2004, Thalmann, 2013). However, the law also mandated the introduction of a levy on fossil fuels in case these voluntary efforts were deemed insufficient to meet the proclaimed targets (article 6, paragraph 1, CO_2 law). In the following years, several studies, partly commissioned by the Federal administration, revealed that additional measures were in fact needed (cf. e.g. Prognos, 2004; cf. also DETEC, 2004; IEA, 2007). Against this backdrop, the CO_2 levy was approved by the Federal Council in 2007 and came into effect in January 2008. It is imposed on all fossil combustible fuels, such as heating oil and natural gas, when used as a source of energy (to generate heat or light, produce electricity in thermal plants or operate combined heat and power). Motor fuels - petrol and diesel - are not affected by the levy (article 29 ff.; CO_2 law, cf. also FOEN, 2012). Designed as an incentive fee by making fossil combustible fuels more expensive, the levy aims to promote a switch to carbon-free energy sources and a reduction of energy consumption. Energy-intensive companies can make a request to be exempted from the levy, if they make a commitment to reduce their emissions (so-called reduction commitments) (cf. FOEN, 2013; SFOE, 2009). Large energy-intensive companies participate in the accompanying Swiss cap-and-trade emissions trading scheme and are also exempt from the levy (cf. article 9, CO_2 law). The exemption was established in order to cushion the burden on Swiss economy and to sustain international competitiveness (cf. FOEN, 2013; IEA, 2012; interview 01-02).

The responsible authority for implementation up to present is the Swiss Federal Office for the Environment. Collection is carried out by the Swiss

Federal Customs Administration (e.g. at border crossing). The levy is indicated on invoices for purchases of thermal fuels (cf. FOEN, 2012; Swiss Federal Council, 2015). The initial levy rate in the year 2008 was set at CHF 12 per ton of CO_2. The Federal Council has the competence to increase the levy rate in case proclaimed intermediate emission reduction goals are not met (cf. CO_2 ordinance, article 94, paragraph 1; Swiss Confederation, 2005). Since emissions in 2010 and 2014 were above the threshold triggering an increase, the levy was adjusted to CHF 36 per ton of CO_2 and to CHF 60 accordingly. A further increase is made in 2016 to CHF 84, which equals around 22 cents per liter of heating oil (cf. Thalmann, 2013). According to the CO_2 law, the rate can be increased up to CHF 120 per ton CO_2 (cf. article 29).

The levy was initially introduced on a revenue-neutral basis, i.e. redistributing the revenue proportionally to the Swiss population and economy independently of consumption. Until 2010, all revenues paid by households were reallocated per capita through health insurance companies. The redistribution to firms occurred relative to their social security payments through a compensation fund (Federal Old Age and Survivor's Insurance) in proportion to their declared payroll (cf. Niederberger, 2005; IEA, 2012). Since 2011, a third of the annual revenue is invested in the building refurbishment program of the federal and cantonal governments. Another CHF 25 is allocated in a technology fund (cf. article 34ff., revised CO_2 law) (cf. Elbeze & de Perthuis, 2011; FOEN, 2012).

In 2013, a revision of the CO_2 law came into force that implements the Swiss commitments for the second period of the Kyoto Protocol from 2012 to 2020. It sets out the target to reduce domestically emitted greenhouse gases until 2020 by 20% compared to 1990 (article 3, paragraph 1, Swiss Confederation, 2011). The revised law highlights the role of the CO_2 levy to achieve this target (article 29ff.). In line with this, the Federal Council states that »*the CO_2 levy is the most important measure to reach Swiss climate reduction goals*« (Swiss Federal Council, 2015, p. 52).

5.3 Case 2 - The electricity saving fund in the canton Basel

The second case study deals with the governance arrangement around the electricity saving fund Basel ('Stromsparfonds Basel'). In 1999, the canton Basel-City was the first Swiss canton that implemented a measure of this kind. The arrangement thus had a pioneer character. As a greening of the tax system, it was also the first of its sort in the German-speaking countries (cf. AUE, 2002a; interview 02-02). The canton stated that with the measure, it aimed to support the cantonal and federal goals of energy policy in connection with other means, such as the Swiss Energy program (cf. AUE, 2002b; Great Council of the Canton of Basel-City, 1998). The measure basically represents an allocation of costs for the main purpose of steering electricity consumption. Its two major instruments are a regulatory levy and a refunding system, the so-called electricity tariff bonus (cf. Governing Council of the Canton of Basel-City, 1999). Simultaneously with the implementation of the levy, the standard electricity costs were lowered in advance, so that the average costs for consumers have not been increased (cf. SFOE, 2003). The measure is furthermore neutral with regard to the public expenditure quota. This means on the one hand that no additional expenditures arise, since all administration costs are completely covered by interest earnings from the bonus system. On the other hand, all of the collected revenue from the levy is paid back to consumers and accordingly not used for public expenditures (cf. interview 02-01; IWB, 2004; Suna et al., 2013).

The origins for the electricity saving fund go back to a cantonal popular initiative called 'Energy canton 2000' (in line with the instruments of direct democracy in Switzerland - cf. chapter 5.1 - voters in Basel-City can institute such an initiative to request an amendment to legislation). The initiative was launched in 1992 by the so-called Northwestern Switzerland committee against nuclear power plants. Its core demand was the introduction of an uncommitted levy (cf. interview 02-02). Against this backdrop, a cantonal energy law was worked out in 1998 that built the legal basis for implementing the measure (cf. Great Council of the Canton of Basel-City, 1998). The executive administration up to the present is the Department for Environment and Energy of the canton Basel-City, which has established an ad hoc agency for managing the measure (cf. AUE, 2015).

As mandated by the energy law (paragraph 26), the regulatory levy is collected by the public utility company for energy and water in the region of Basel, the Industrial Works Basel (IWB). It is imposed in conjunction with the electricity bill, where it is shown separately. It concerns the two consumer groups of households and firms - while large-scale consumers were exempted, and energy-intensive firms were given specific attention so that no disadvantages arise for them (cf. energy law Basel, paragraph

17 to 18; IWB, 2015). The amount of the levy - per kWh between 3,1 and 6 centime - is linked to power consumption while considering external costs. In average, over the past years it equaled to an increase of 20 to 30 per cent of the electricity tariffs (cf. AUE, 2002b; interview 02-02). The revenue of the levy, about CHF 44 million per year, is transferred by the IWB to the electricity saving fund agency (cf. energy law, paragraph 19; AUE, 2007; cf. also interview 02-01). The total revenue collected within one year is paid back to households (per capita) and firms (per workspace according to the wage bills) in the subsequent year (households are thus rewarded to be located in the canton Basel-City and firms are rewarded to provide jobs in the canton) (cf. AUE, 2000; Great Council of the Canton Basel-City, 2015). The redistribution was for the first time paid out in 1999. The bonus system is, in contrast to the levy, irrespective of the amount of power consumption. Thus, the incentive mechanism for lower consumption plays out in the sense that consumers, who use less electricity pay a lower levy, while the refund is equal for all consumers (cf. SFOE, 2009; Statistical office of the canton Basel-City, 2015; interview 02-01).

5.4 Case 3 - The fuel consumption covenant in Switzerland

Case study three deals with governance for reducing motor fuel consumption based on a voluntary covenant between the Swiss Federal Department of the Environment, Transport, Energy and Communications (DETEC) and the Association of Swiss car importers (ASIA). The basis for the covenant was established by the Swiss energy law from 1998 (cf. Swiss Confederation, 1998a). It enabled the Swiss Federal Council to assign the DETEC with establishing covenants for reducing energy consumption. Specifically, it calls for target agreements made by the Swiss government with motor vehicle producers and importers (cf. ibid., article 8, paragraph 2; cf. also interviews 03-01 and 03-02).

This case study is to be seen in the context that Switzerland has committed to reduce its CO_2 emissions in the Kyoto protocol - and that around one third of the overall emissions in Switzerland come from the transport sector (with increasing emissions over the past decades). The energy consumption and emissions from new passenger cars in Switzerland are well above the European average and the reduction potential is particularly high (cf. e.g. Alberini et al., 2014; DETEC, 2013). In order to achieve the overall reduction goals of the first commitment period of the Kyoto protocol from 2008 to 2012, the Swiss CO_2 law specifically called for a reduction target of 8% for transport emissions compared to 1990 (cf. article 2, CO_2 law, Swiss Confederation, 1999). The law initially aimed to realize this goal by using voluntary instruments, such as the covenant (with the option of a subsidiary levy on motor fuels, if the measures turn out to be insufficient; cf. ibid.; cf. also interview 03-02).

Based on the legal basis of the Swiss energy law and the CO_2 law, representatives of the DETEC and the ASIA signed the voluntary covenant on fuel efficiency in February 2002 (cf. ASIA 2002-2012). The covenant represented the first target agreement made within the context of the Swiss Energy program, i.e. the general framework for Swiss voluntary measures in the field of energy policy (cf. chapter 5.1; cf. SFOE, 2011a). It also represented the only policy measure existing at that time for tackling emissions from the transport sector (cf. interview 03-02; DETEC, 2003).

The covenant demanded a step-wise reduction of average fuel consumption of newly registered passenger cars from 8.4 l per 100 km in the basis year 2000 to 6.4 l in 2008. This equaled a reduction of 24%. Accordingly, a yearly reduction rate of 3% was required to match the target in 2008, which equaled an annual reduction of 0.25 l per 100 km (SFOE, 2005; Börner, 2010; interviews 03-01 and 03-02). The DETEC reserved the right to abandon the agreement from 2005 onwards in case the yearly reduction rate was missed by a large margin. In return, the DETEC committed to support ASIA in their efforts to reach the goals. The responsible authority in this regard was the Swiss Federal Office of Energy that belongs to the DETEC (cf. e.g. SFOE, 2011b; Spielmann & Althaus, 2007; Volken, 2010). Precise means for reaching the agreement were not defined. The most important means that was implemented was an energy label system for passenger cars, introduced in 2003 within the context of the Swiss Energy program - alongside other information and marketing campaigns by the ASIA (cf. e.g. SFOE, 2007; DETEC, 2003; De Haan, 2007; ASIA, 2002-2012).

According to the Swiss energy ordinance from 1998, which complemented the Swiss energy law, an annual reporting of overall energy reduction results is required (cf. Swiss Confederation, 1998b, annex 3.6, cf. interview 03-02). On this basis, the DETEC has ordered the ASIA to record, assess and publish the achievements made in terms of reducing fuel consumption of new passenger cars every year - from 2002 until 2012. The data were transferred annually by Swiss car importing firms to the ASIA (Switzerland's car market depends entirely on imports and there is no domestic car manufacturing) (cf. ASIA, 2002-2012; Quandt, 2010; interview 03-01).

5.5 Case 4 - The Energy Trialogue Switzerland

The fourth case study is concerned with the Energy Trialogue Switzerland, a multi-stakeholder discussion process held on the future of Swiss energy policy. The approach brought together representatives from the three pillars of science, economy and society (also including public authorities) and covered one of the largest energy summits that ever took place in Switzerland (cf. interview 04-01). The Trialogue was affiliated to a private-law association, which was named after the project ('Energy-Trialogue Switzerland') and existed from 2007 to 2014. The first initiation of the project was made by the Swiss canton Aargau (a so-called energy-canton since it is responsible for about a third of the Swiss electricity production) (cf. interview 04-02; Energie Trialog Schweiz, 2007). The Trialogue was supposed to enable an objectified discussion within a protected area, preferably unaffected by self-serving political interests and the media. This procedure was intended to ensure a broadly accepted alliance, while taking into account existing knowledge and demands. Against this background, the moderated discussions ought to be scientifically sound and goal-oriented. The results of the project should in turn induce impulses for energy politics. The Trialogue was conducted under the patronage of the respective Federal Councilor, head of the DETEC (cf. Büsser, 2010; interviews 04-01 and 04-02; Energie Trialog Schweiz, 2007).

The Trialogue took place in two phases. The first project took place from 2007 to 2009, and was aimed at developing a sustainable and competitive strategy plan for the Swiss energy sector. It consisted of ten expert workshops, which made use of knowledge from several basic research studies commissioned on behalf of the Trialogue, and two larger discussion events. In these events, about 200 representatives from science (national and international experts), economy (firms and associations), society (such as NGOs) and public authorities participated (cf. interviews 04-01 and 04-02; PSI, 2008; Weidmann, 2013). The final output, a common strategy paper published in 2009 (Energie Trialog Schweiz, 2009), was worked out by a core group consisting of about 30 stakeholders from different backgrounds (cf. Studerus, 2011; cf. also Meier, 2010). The core group therein agreed on certain goals as guidelines for the future energy policy as well as strategies and measures for realizing these goals. These goals focus on different target years of fulfillment (2020, 2035 and 2050) and consist of eight core objectives: higher life quality, increased energy efficiency, impulses for economic growth, security of supply, protection of environmental resources, reduction of CO_2 emissions, stabilizing the financial burden and a society capable of making decisions (cf. Energie Trialog Schweiz, 2009; Energieforum Schweiz, 2009; Metrobasel, 2010).

After the completion of the first discussion process, a second project phase called 'New Energy policy' was conducted from 2012 to 2013. The project was initiated together by the Swiss Business Federation economiesuisse, the environmental NGO WWF Switzerland and the canton Aargau. Its goal was to discuss the 'Energy Strategy 2050' of the Swiss Federal Council that evolved from 2011 onwards (cf. chapter 5.1). On behalf of a steering group, twelve economic and environmental associations and organizations were invited to discuss the issues in a moderated dialogue (cf. Kaiser, 2012; Energie Trialog Schweiz, 2013). The project aimed at analyzing the plausibility of the strategy and increasing the knowledge among the participants. In so doing, a contribution was sought that would make the debate on energy policy more objectified. A final report of the steering group, which was published in 2013, summarized the core results of the discussion process. It assesses the Energy Strategy to be realizable from a technical point of view but refers to potential problems for its implementation. It also discloses possible conflicts of goals as well as approaches to solve these conflicts (cf. Beyeler & Kaiser, 2012; Energie Trialog Schweiz, 2013; Kaiser & Schips, 2013).

5.6 Case 5 - The Swiss building label Minergie

Case study five is concerned with the governance arrangement around the Swiss energy label Minergie. Minergie is a voluntary building standard for new and refurbished buildings owned by a non-profit private association. As a registered trademark, it sets performance criteria targeted at three main goals: i.) energy efficiency, ii.) better comfort and thus a higher quality of life for users living or working in buildings, as well as iii.) long-range real estate value retention through an increase in the buildings life cycle value (cf. Minergie, 2015).[18] Building clients, architects, and planners are thereby free in the design and the choice of materials as well as in the internal and external structure of their building. Apart from buildings, Minergie also certifies individual building components, such as ventilation systems (cf. Beyeler et al., 2009; Salvi & Syz, 2011).

Minergie has been launched in 1994 and until 1997 it was privately owned by its creator (Heinz Übersax). In 1997, the brand was taken over for one year by the cantons Zurich and Bern. In 1998, the Minergie association was founded and the usage rights were transferred (cf. interviews 05-01 and 05-02). Managing the label, the Minergie association presently counts over 500 members, including the federal government and all Swiss cantons. It includes a formal board, an executive strategy group, a technical agency, several competence centers and a network of licensed certifiers. It is financed by its members, sponsors and services (certification, education and information programs, consulting and coaching) and is linked to 900 local businesses (with experience in building according to the standard) as well as 1500 professional partners, such as architects and energy consultants (cf. Kriesi, 2009; Minergie, 2008 and 2015).

The label has been continually developed and comes in four different standards. All standards set an overall limit on energy use (for heating, hot water and ventilation), representing the main indicator to quantify the building quality (cf. SFOE, 2005; Minergie, 2011). This is achieved by means of several technical factors such as a compact building form and strong thermal insulation.[19] The basic standard sets a maximum annual

18 In a strict sense, Minergie, however, does not represent an all-encompassing sustainability label for buildings, since it focuses on the building quality and does not incorporate all relevant factors in this regard (e.g. the location of buildings).

19 On a technical level, the Minergie standard represents a combination of the following key elements: a compact building form, an airtight construction of the building shell, strong thermal insulation for walls and roof, windows with coated multiple glazing, an energy efficient, draft-free ventilation system, water-based heating and cooling, integration of renewable forms of energy, use of waste heat, careful selection of materials as well as efficient household appliances and lighting (cf. Beyeler et al., 2009; Minergie, 2015).

weighted energy consumption for new buildings of 38 kilowatt-hours per square meter heated gross floor area (equating 3,8 liters heating-oil equivalents) (cf. Salvi & Syz, 2011; IEA, 2007). Certified buildings thus have an energy demand of 20% of an average old building (standard new build from 1975). Apart from that, Minergie promotes the use of renewable energy as e.g. the basic standard requires that fossil-fuel consumption is not higher than 50% of the consumption of average conventional buildings (cf. Beyeler et al., 2009). Due to requirements such as a systematic ventilation system, Minergie moreover leads to higher levels of comfort for residents and employees (including higher thermal comfort, systematic air change, noise protection etc.). Overall, Minergie thus leads to an increase in the value retention of buildings (cf. interviews 05-01 and 05-02). To ensure economic competitiveness, construction costs for Minergie buildings must not exceed those for conventional buildings by more than 10% (cf. Carassus, 2007). The basic standard has been supplemented by the stricter versions of Minergie-P in 2003 (an equivalent to the German 'Passivhaus', with very low energy consumption), Minergie-eco in 2006 (a standard that includes health and ecological requirements such as noise protection, optimized daylight use, recyclability of materials and avoidance of scarce resources) and finally Minergie-A in 2011 (the Swiss standard for net zero energy buildings) (cf. Feige et al., 2011; Salvi & Syz, 2011).

Over the past decades, Minergie has achieved high brand awareness as well as a broad penetration within Switzerland in terms of the certification of new buildings of all type and size (cf. chapter 6.3.5). Against this backdrop, it is frequently argued that Minergie represents the most successful building standard world-wide, and one of the most successful labels in the realm of SD in general (see e.g. Salvi et al., 2010). However, in terms of the refurbishment of existing buildings, there is still a high potential (only 10% of Minergie certificates concern renovation). In the future, the association thus explicitly aims at pushing forward the modernization of the existing building stock (cf. Minergie, 2015; SFOE, 2011; interview 05-03).

6 Results of the case studies

Having introduced the cases, the empirical results are presented in the following (gained through the structured qualitative content analysis of the three data collection sources of existing research, official documents and expert interviews). The chapter is structured according to the four research steps as depicted in figure 1 in the introduction (chapter 1.3). First of all, I will provide a deepened understanding of governance workings in the empirical cases (chapter 6.1). Subsequently, I allocate each case to a particular governance mode (chapter 6.2), disclose the induced governance impacts (chapter 6.3), and appraise the impacts in terms of sustainability (chapter 6.4). Finally, an overview of the empirical findings is given (chapter 6.5) (interview quotes were anonymized and have been translated by the author).

6.1 Governance within the cases

In the following, I disclose the ways of internal functioning of the five governance arrangements in question (based on the analysis in view of the governance conceptualization translated into a category system, chapter 4.3). Each of the following chapters consists of three parts. I will first give a short general introduction to the respective case from a governance perspective. After that, I explore each of the three dimensions of governance structures (i.), processes (ii.), and contents (iii.). Based on this, I finally provide examples of the respective interplay of the dimensions by interpreting their linkages (iv.).

6.1.1 CO_2 levy

The basis for the governance arrangement around the Swiss CO_2 levy was provided by the adoption of the CO_2 law through the Swiss parliament in 1999. The CO_2 law came into force in 2000 and mandated the introduction of a levy on fossil heating fuels in case voluntary measures turn out to be insufficient to achieve Swiss emission reduction targets. When it became apparent that additional measures were needed, the government decided to implement the levy. After a formal pre-parliamentary consultation phase that took place from 2004 to 2005, the CO_2 ordinance came into force. Based on this, the CO_2 levy was approved by the Federal Council in 2007 and came into effect in January 2008 (cf. DETEC, 2005; FOEN, 2012; interviews 01-01 and 01-02).

(i.) In terms of *governance structures,* the formal institutional architecture of the governance arrangement gave rise to a well-established regulative, top-down approach (cf. interview 01-02). The binding frameworks of the CO_2 law (from 2000, revised in 2011) and the accompanying CO_2 ordinance (from 2005, revised in 2007 and 2012) led to clearly prescribed legal foundations with fixed procedures - however, this was softened by the pre-parliamentary consultation procedure (cf. below). Overall, the arrangement was characterized by a high degree of formal institutionalization that resulted in hierarchical and mono-centric governing structures at the central state level. Except from the participatory consultation phase, strict access rules provoked a closed governance arrangement (cf. interview 01-01). This was only accessible by representatives from the central political-administrative system (and actors that were explicitly involved by these actors, e.g. in the consultation phase). The existing domain rules in turn equipped these entities with an authoritative role (cf. Ingold & Varone, 2012; Sager et al., 2014). The Swiss Federal Council was accountable for implementing decisions made by the Swiss parliament, as well as for formally monitoring and reviewing results (cf. CO_2 law, articles 39 and 40, Swiss Confederation, 2011). Overall responsibility for implementation until present rests with the Federal Office for the Environment (FOEN), which belongs to the Federal Department of the Environment, Transport, Energy and Communications (DETEC). The Swiss Federal Office of Energy (SFOE) supports the FOEN in certain implementation tasks (for instance, with regard to the reduction commitments of firms to be exempted from the levy). The Federal customs administration is in charge of collecting and refunding the levy (cf. interview 01-01).

Accordingly, in terms of governance structures it can be concluded that tasks in the arrangement were formally allocated through official mandates. Apart from the consultation phase and active lobbying from the market sector (cf. below), actors from the market and civil society had the role of passive recipients with a dependent position. It can further be stated that representation of the arrangement followed the logic of the political - linked to official channels of government, with lobbying of societal actors. Vertical relationships between state and societal actors favored the federal state apparatus in terms of power and centric resource control. Reinforced by the command and control structures and the centralized locus of authority, the patterns of exchange and interaction were characterized by hierarchical direction. In the end, single governmental actors hold the power to make collectively binding decisions (cf. also interviews 01-01 and 01-02).

(ii.) As far as *governance processes* are concerned, the formal institutional setting of the arrangement led to an overall coercive appearance in terms of both decision-making and implementation, softened by the Swiss elements of direct democracy (cf. also chapter 5.1). The first efforts to implement a Swiss CO_2 levy go back to the 1990s, »*however, these failed due to high resistance in the consultation phase*« (interview 01-01, transl., cf. in more detail also Thalmann, 2013). The CO_2 law from 2000 finally mandated the introduction of a levy as a subsidiary instrument (cf. article 6, paragraph 1, Swiss Confederation, 1999). Several ex-ante assessments - partly commissioned by the Federal administration - in the subsequent years showed that additional measures were needed in order to reach the law's goals (cf. e.g. Prognos, 2004). As a consequence, work to develop the CO_2 levy began in the FOEN (cf. interview 01-01). At the same time, Swiss industry organizations such as the Swiss Fossil Fuels Association promoted the idea of a voluntary 'Climate Cent' in order to prevent a binding levy on motor fuels (cf. also chapter 6.3.1).

In 2004, a consultation phase with regard to the introduction of the levy was initiated by the Swiss Federal Council (cf. DETEC, 2005). As introduced in chapter 5.1, this pre-parliamentary consultation phase is mandatory in Switzerland when drafting amendments to legislation. During the consultation, different alternatives were discussed (cf. DETEC, 2004 and 2005): a levy on both combustible fuels and motor fuels, a levy only on combustible fuels with motor fuels subject to the voluntary Climate Cent; and finally the implementation of only the Climate Cent. While the CO_2 law from 2000 originally intended a levy on both combustible and motor fuels (article 7, paragraph 1), the private-sector initiative Climate Cent stood in contrast to this. The consultation phase displayed the conflicts among the different stakeholders in the field that was present from 2000 onwards. In a nutshell, two major competing coalitions argued against each other, while an intermediate group was mediating. A first coalition (composed amongst others of representatives from Swiss industry, transport, and right-leaning parties) argued for the implementation of only the voluntary Climate Cent. On the other hand, a second coalition aimed to implement the levy on both combustibles and motor fuels (containing e.g. the FOEN as well as representatives from left parties and environmental NGOs). In the mediating group, the most important actor was the SFOE that argued for the political compromise, i.e. the binding levy on combustibles and the Climate Cent on motor fuels (cf. Ingold, 2011; Sager et al., 2014). The Federal Council in the end followed this compromise solution. The levy on motor fuels was also disputed in the Federal Council since large earnings from the mineral oil tax - as an important source of income for the federal budget - would have decreased (cf. interview 01-01). Also, in the case of the announcement of implementing a levy on motor fuels, representatives of the first coalition most likely would have hampered its introduction in the subsequent parliamentary phase (cf. in more detail Ingold & Varone, 2012). Overall, lobbying actors (especially from the market) were thus able to actively influence political decisions (»*The lobby was strong enough to won out over other actors.*« interview 01-02, transl.).

To implement the compromise solution, the Federal council enacted the CO_2 ordinance in 2005 (Swiss Confederation, 2005). The official 'Message from the Federal Council to the Federal Assembly' then had to be approved by the Swiss Parliament with its two chambers: National Council and Council of States. After much controversy during parliamentary discussions on the modalities and the rate of the levy (»*In the end, it was a real close run that the levy could be implemented - the parliamentary debates lasted over two years.*«, interview 01-01, transl.), the two chambers decided in 2007 on a gradual introduction. The levy's rate was to be raised in the event that reduction goals were not met over the following years (cf. Elbeze & de Perthuis, 2011). Finally, the Federal Council approved the Parliament's proposals and amended the CO_2 ordinance accordingly. Based on this, the levy was implemented from 2008 onwards by the FOEN in cooperation with the SFOE and the Federal Customs Administration (for the refunding mechanism, the FOEN worked together with the health insurance companies and the Federal social insurance office, cf. FOEN, 2012; interview 01-02).

Overall, in terms of processes, it can be stated that the governance arrangement exhibited a tight actor field. This was dominated by political-administrative actors both during initiation and coordination, softened by the participatory consultation phase. Making use of the centralized resource control, the federal actors brought in resources of legislation accompanied by political support and force. The processes were thus marked by the exercise of sovereign authority; single actors exercised power through coercion as well as administrative and legal expertise. Corresponding to the relationship structures, these actors took the lead while interest groups from the market acted as influencing actors and successfully prevented a levy on motor fuels.

(iii.) With regard to *governance contents,* the described approach to decision-making and implementation resulted in a policy setting with a command-and-control character and fixed goals, formulated right at the beginning (cf. interviews 01-01 and 01-02). Standardized objectives in terms of emission reduction targets were set out within policy formulation against the backdrop of uniform goals in the Kyoto protocol. The original CO_2 law set an emission reduction goal of 10% by 2010 compared to 1990 (article 2). The according problem definitions in view of climate change mitigation were clear-cut and precisely delineated (e.g. in the official document on the consultation phase: DETEC, 2004 - or the explanatory report on the CO_2 ordinance: FOEN, 2012). The amount of the CO_2 levy was increased gradually in a flexible manner from 2010 to 2014 - from 12 up to CHF 60 per ton of CO_2, since proclaimed reduction goals over the years were not met (cf. IEA, 2012).

In terms of the approaches to problem solving, coercive frameworks were predominant within the governance arrangement. The CO_2 levy itself represented a state-initiated regulative and binding instrument that was enforced by a rigid form of implementation It followed an incentive-based approach by making fossil fuels more expensive. This incentive-based character was supported by the implementation of the supplementary Swiss emissions trading scheme (cf. interviews 01-01 and 01-02; Brönnimann et al., 2014). Overall, this led to a bilateral, 'contractual' link between the regulator and the regulated, i.e. the Federal government and council could make collectively binding decisions to the public with a centralized method of enforcement.

The approaches to problem solving were accompanied by rather separate processes of knowledge production and usage (apart from the consultation phase, in which the interests of diverse stakeholders were considered). For instance, policy makers took into account the scientific knowledge base produced by the Swiss Advisory Body on Climate Change (whose official role is to formulate strategic recommendations for

Swiss climate policy from a scientific point of view for politicians and the Federal administration, cf. Swiss Federal Council, 2015) - or the Intergovernmental Panel on Climate Change (cf. FOEN, 2012). Such general scientific knowledge provided the basis for policy preparation, decision-making, implementation and evaluation. Apart from that, the setting was determined by experiences with shortcomings of voluntary measures in the course of the Swiss Energy program, as well as inspiration taken from existing CO_2 taxes in other countries (cf. interview 01-02; for an overview in this regard cf. e.g. Sumner et al., 2011).

(iv.) Having elaborated the three dimensions individually, I will now have a closer look at their *linkages* by giving some interpretive examples of their close interplay. First of all, in terms of the *structures-processes interplay*, the regulative setting strongly determined the interaction processes of participating actors and vice versa. For instance, the pluralist representation of the arrangement with vertical relations explains why societal actors had only limited ways to influence the development (except from the formal consultation phase). The rule of law, materialized through binding documents, equipped federal actors with the necessary centralized power and resources of legal expertise. In turn, the dominance of these actors stabilized the high degree of institutional formality in the field.

Second, concerning the *processes-contents interplay,* there was a mutual exercise of influence between the statist forms of decision-making and implementation processes with the routinized substantive policy setting. For example, tight coalitions of political-administrative actors determined the evolution of the coercive character of policies and the 'contractual' link between the regulator and the regulated. This was in turn enabled by clearly delineated problem definitions at the beginning of the arrangement. Also, the rather strong separation between knowledge production and usage came along with the closed nature of the arrangement with regard to the participation of societal actors.

Finally, in terms of the *structures-contents interplay,* the well-established rule systems at the national level favored official channels of the federal government to stipulate a material setting with standardized objectives. On the other hand, the nature of policies with binding measures and a rigid form of implementation supported the strongly institutionalized structures with clear access and responsibility rules.

6.1.2 Electricity saving fund

The impulse for the initiation of the governance arrangement around the electricity saving fund was the popular initiative 'Energy canton 2000', launched in 1992. As a reaction, the parliament of the canton Basel-city, the great council, established a commission in order to work out a new cantonal energy law (cf. AUE, 2000; interview 02-01). The law was finally approved in 1998 and called for the implementation of a regulatory levy together with a refunding system (paragraph 17 to 33; energy law Basel; Great Council of the Canton of Basel-City, 1998). The cantonal regulation from 1999 further elaborated the functioning of the instruments. The executive administration, the Department for Environment and Energy of the canton Basel-City then established an ad hoc agency for implementing and managing the arrangement: the electricity saving fund agency (cf. AUE, 2002b). Up to the present, the levy is collected in conjunction with the electricity bill through the public utility company for energy and water (Industrial Works Basel, IWB). It is imposed separately in terms of the two consumer groups of households and firms. The revenue is transferred each year to the electricity saving fund agency, which pays it back to the consumers as a bonus (cf. interview 02-01; IWB, 2015).

(i.) With regard to *governance structures,* the binding documents of the cantonal energy law and the cantonal regulation, as the legal basis for the arrangement, paved the way for a rather high degree of institutional formality on a sub-national government level. This basis was further supplemented by an ordinance on the tariffs of electric energy from 2006 (cf. AUE, 2007). As reflected in the origin and nature of the institutional mandate, the governance arrangement exhibited a rule-based approach with legal cantonal foundations. Access to the governing setting was thus mostly restricted to actors from regional government and administration and to those that these actors chose to involve, leading to a relatively closed governance arrangement (cf. interviews 02-01 and 02-02; AUE, 2002a). However, due to the established instruments of direct democracy (see chapter 5.1), the arrangement exhibited a more open nature at the beginning - involving stakeholders from different backgrounds (see also the description of governance processes below). In the further course of the arrangement, the role divisions were then described in legislation through domain rules. Responsibility for governing finally rested with lower levels of government, following the principle of subsidiarity (cf. interview 02-

02; Great Council of the Canton of Basel-City, 1998). Specific tasks were formally allocated through official mandates. The canton Basel-City was in charge for formulating final problem definitions and objectives in the form of its executive administration (the Department for Environment and Energy) (cf. AUE, 2000). The authority for implementation, monitoring, evaluation and reporting was mandated to the electricity saving fund agency. The role of this managing collective actor was that of an organization controller (cf. interview 02-02; Governing Council of the Canton of Basel-City, 1999). Against this background, the model of representation was pluralist, based on democratic elections on the cantonal level. This resulted in a rather vertical relationship structure in which decentralized state levels exhibited a dominant role while households and firms were on the receiving end of governing. Due to this, the canton was in control of important resources of the arrangement, accompanied by hierarchical power relations (cf. interview 02-01; AUE, 2002b). Softened by the open character at the beginning, rather top-down forms of interaction, which came along with a central locus of authority for the regional actors, dominated the course of the arrangement (cf. interview 02-02; SFOE, 2003).

(ii.) In terms of *governance processes,* the well-established institutional set-up gave rise to rather hierarchical processes of decision-making and implementation - with participatory elements in the first phase of the arrangement in two respects: the initiation by a popular initiative and the consultation phase (cf. AUE, 2000). The initiation of the arrangement was a reaction to the popular initiative launched by the Northwestern Switzerland committee against nuclear power plants. The initiative was first met with disapproval in the parliament of the canton (the great council), especially from liberal party members (cf. interview 02-01). However, it brought the great council to establish a non-partisan commission to deal with the subject. The commission built trust above party lines and worked out a new energy law that included the implementation of the electricity saving fund (cf. interview 02-02). This law went through a consultation phase (see chapter 5.1), in which interest groups, i.e. stakeholders from a range of different backgrounds, were able to articulate their opinions. Important participants were the chamber of commerce, the trade association as well as representatives from large-scale consumers. Supported by the IWB, the chamber of commerce threatened to make the law subject of a referendum (see interview 02-01). However, the stakeholders declined to do so when the law was accepted overwhelmingly by the great council (crucial for the law to be politically accepted was that the measures were neutral with respect to the public expenditure quota, that the electricity tariffs were reduced simultaneously and that a refunding system was implemented; see interview 02-02). One interviewee stated in this regard: »*Since there was no referendum, the negotiation process was for the most part conducted between politicians and administration.*«, interview 02-01, transl.).

When it was foreseeable that the law would be approved, the Department for Environment and Energy of the canton Basel-City as the executive administration established the ad hoc agency for implementing the measures within one year. Due to the pioneer character of the arrangement, there were no role models that the actors could orient themselves to, and the whole implementation »*was under considerable strain from the political side*« (interview 02-02, transl.). The administrative core team responsible for implementation comprised a small coalition with people from different backgrounds working closely together - ranging from internal and external project leaders to specialized external advisers for statistics, software, economics and communication (cf. AUE, 2002a; interview 02-02). Up to present, the measures are conducted by the saving fund agency, while involving the IWB, which collects the levy in conjunction with the electricity bill (cf. IWB, 2015; Boogen, 2010).

Against the backdrop of this actor field, it can be said that the prevalent form of interest intermediation rested on a formal basis of power, based on a system of representative democracy with authority embedded in cantonal legislation. The interests of the popular initiative were put forward by the cantonal government. These did not stand in strong contrast to those of consumers from the market and civil society because coincident with the implementation of the levy, electricity costs were lowered so that average costs did not increase. The specific interests of market actors were considered especially at early phases. This led to the constraint that large-scale consumers (with an annual consumption of more than 40 gigawatt hours) were exempted from the levy (see energy law, paragraph 18). It was clear right from the beginning that it »*was politically unenforceable*« (interview 02-02, transl.) to include these firms. The exception can thus be regarded as a political compromise without which the instruments would not have been enforceable. It was argued that for large-scale firms drawbacks with regard to the location in Basel-City would have arisen, forcing firms to move away. This exception was supported by lobbying of market actors in early phases and the fact that the president of the commission that worked out the energy law, was simultaneously employed at a large-scale firm (cf. interviews 02-02 and 02-01). Yet, overall power of societal actors was exercised within the boundaries set by the regional government, who made use of its administrative expertise. Legitimacy was thereby founded on democratic representation. This went hand in hand with the predominant resources that were mobilized by the canton - namely, legal, financial, infrastructural and staff-related resources (cf. interview 02-01; AUE, 2002b; SFOE, 2003).

(iii.) With respect to *governance contents,* the character of processes supported a mostly routinized policy setting with a product orientation and fixed issues. Although the canton acted as a pioneer in terms of implementing an electricity saving fund, the setting exhibited standardized problem definitions with clear goals defined from the start (cf. AUE, 2000). The popular initiative aimed at pointing the way for a higher profitability of energy saving measures in the context of a popular movement against nuclear power plants (cf. interview 02-01). The main goal of the arrangement was then to lower power consumption, or at least hold it constant. As already indicated, the particular background situation at the beginning of the arrangement was that electricity consumers were getting a price reduction (17,5% for households, 27,5% for firms) due to large earnings of the IWB in previous years.[20] A lowering of the electricity tariffs to such an extent would have encouraged larger energy consumption. Thus, the arrangement was intended to prevent a drop in electricity tariffs. Simultaneously with the price reduction, the levy was implemented, so that average costs for consumers remained constant (cf. AUE, 2002a). The two target groups were households and firms, while energy-intensive firms were given special treatment to make sure that no competitive locational disadvantages arose for them[21] (cf. energy law Basel, para-

20 The electricity production costs in the canton were much below the Swiss average, as it relied in the past decades mostly on hydropower as opposed to more expensive nuclear power (cf. interview 02-01).

21 Drawbacks that come up are thus financially counterbalanced when firms make an application for a refunding of the levy. In this way, it is ensured that no firms are pushed to move abroad.

graph 18). The main goal was accompanied by two sub-goals: the whole arrangement should be neutral with regard to the public expenditure quota and external costs in conjunction with labor expenses should be internalized based on the model of greening taxes (cf. interview 02-02; SFOE, 2007).[22] These qualitative goals were embedded in the general purpose of the energy law to support an efficient, sustainable and profitable use of energy, assure supply security, promote renewable energy and minimize the dependence on energy imports (cf. Great Council of the Canton of Basel-City, 1998).

In terms of steering instruments, the basis was built by the binding regional documents of the energy law and the cantonal regulation, calling for the regulatory levy and the refunding system. The levy represents a legally binding regulative instrument followed by a rigid form of implementation that closely constrains private action. Its collection by the IWB was installed by means of performance mandates given by the canton Basel-City (IWB, 2004). This was accompanied by information measures to brief consumers about the goals, purpose and way of functioning of the arrangement - as ordered in the energy law (paragraph 26). The information measures comprised several approaches: external communication experts were commissioned to inform consumer groups, information events were organized for firms together with the chamber of commerce or the trade association; and an information line was established together with an internet platform providing background information for households (cf. interview 02-02; SFOE, 2003). Most importantly, an information brochure continues to be sent every year by post to consumers when the bonus is paid out. Information in the brochure on the levy and refund are complemented by a different topic with regard to electricity savings (cf. AUE, 2015).

---

22 In light of the pioneer character, the main internal aim within the administrative core team was not concentrated on results in terms of energy reductions but to »*demonstrate that such a system works, is easy to implement and harms nobody*« (interview 02-02, transl.). In light of this, the implementation team had to deal with several unknown factors, such as the amount of the bonus for consumers, especially for firms (cf. ibid.).

In terms of knowledge, the expertise considered during the evolution of the arrangement was rather universal (such as on electricity usage and the functioning of regulatory levies and refunding systems), while taking account of cantonal circumstances (cf. interview 02-01; AUE, 2002b). Knowledge use and production were thus somewhat separated in the sense that experts produced knowledge and political-administrative actors used it. This is illustrated by the fact that an external feasibility study was mandated by the commission in 1997. It assessed the practicability, economic tenability and operating expense of the measures to be implemented (cf. interview 02-02; AUE, 2000; Great Council of the Canton of Basel-City, 1998).

(iv.) Finally, in terms of the *interplay* of the three dimensions, there are several interdependencies that can be interpreted using the following examples. Concerning the *structures-processes interplay,* there is a strong interrelation between the official mandates on a sub-national government level and the rather hierarchical implementation processes. For instance, the responsibility rules favored political-administrative actors and enabled them to make decisions in an enforceable way, although considering societal stakeholders. The way the interests of these actors were considered, and the manner in which legal and infrastructural resources were mobilized, in turn buttressed the rather top-down interaction patterns.

With respect to the *processes-contents interplay,* the arrangement illustratively points out that the way processes play out shape the appearance of substantive products and vice versa. For example, there was obviously a mutual influence between the exercise of legislative and administrative power of regional state actors and the possibility for binding policy measures, followed by a rigid form of implementation. Moreover, the fact that interests of market actors were involved resulted in special permits for certain consumer groups.

In terms of the *structures-contents interplay*, the authoritative form of policy-making was fostered by the rule-based institutional framing (with formal regional documents and rather hierarchical relationships). Also, since the canton of Basel-City played a pioneer role in implementing the model of an electricity saving fund, the arrangement is a good example of how new institutional rules can be successively introduced through novel approaches of problem solving.

6.1.3 Fuel consumption covenant

The fundament for the governance arrangement around the fuel consumption covenant between the Swiss government and the Association of Swiss car importers (ASIA) was built in 1999 by the Swiss energy law, accompanied by the CO_2 law from 2000. In view of general emission reduction goals of Switzerland within the Kyoto protocol, a reduction target of 8 % for transport emissions between 1990 and 2010 was set in the CO_2 law. Switzerland aimed to realize this target by using voluntary measures. Against this backdrop, the Swiss energy law enabled the Federal Council to assign the Department of the Environment, Transport, Energy and Communications (DETEC) the task of establishing covenants with the private sector. It calls for specific target agreements made directly with motor vehicle producers and importers. The DETEC and the ASIA signed the covenant on fuel efficiency in 2002. It represented the first target agreement made within the context of the Swiss Energy program (cf. interviews 03-01 and 03-02, cf. also SFOE, 2011a; ASIA, 2002-2012).

(i.) In terms of *governance structures,* the governance arrangement exhibited a formally institutionalized partnership between the DETEC and the ASIA (»*There was a contract signed by the head of the DETEC and the president of the ASIA.*«, interview 03-01, transl.). The public-private structure rested on a formalized institutional architecture, as established by the regulative frameworks of the energy law and the CO_2 law (cf. interview 03-02). These laws were supplemented by the Swiss energy ordinance from 1998 that followed a specific ordinance for reducing fuel consumption of passenger cars, existing from 1996 to 2001 (cf. Swiss Confederation, 1998b; cf. interview 03-01). Access to the arrangement was granted to actors belonging to the two bodies of the DETEC and the ASIA. Conditions for changing or terminating the relationship were defined from the start. The Swiss government reserved the right to abandon the agreement from 2005 onwards in case the yearly reduction rate were missed by a substantial margin. In return, the DETEC committed to support ASIA in their efforts to reach the goals (cf. SFOE, 2011b; Spielmann & Althaus, 2007; interview 03-02). Apart from these formal rules of exchange, informal rules derived from market rule-systems played a role throughout the evolution of the partnership. These determined the internal interaction mechanisms among the actors from the transport industry (the ASIA, car importing firms and retailers). Such actors were acting autonomously within predetermined governmental directives (cf. ASIA, 2002-2012; interview 03-01; Quandt, 2010).

Overall, there was a division of responsibilities and authorities between the DETEC and the ASIA, resulting in a corporatist model of representation. The DETEC ordered the ASIA to conduct a recording, evaluation and reporting with regard to the achievements made every year (»*It was a real big effort to look after the data each year and check it; we recalculated each single car correct to each kilo.*«, interview 03-01, transl.; cf. also SFOE, 2005; ASIA, 2002-2012). The respective mandate originated from the Swiss energy ordinance from 1998, which calls for an annual monitoring of overall energy reduction results (cf. Swiss Confederation, 1998b, annex 3.6). The ASIA was thus responsible for notifying the extent to which the industry was successful in reaching the mutually agreed objectives. The DETEC in turn was in charge of verifying these results (cf. DETEC, 2003; interview 03-02). This makes clear that the two dominant entities were bound by an interdependency in terms of resources. The overall interaction patterns were thus determined by a shared control of these resources. Accordingly, it can be concluded in terms of structures that public actors, represented by the Swiss Federal Council and the DETEC, delegated power to private actors - leading to a situation where power was pooled between the two partners. The central government agencies and the market sector were thus exhibiting a basically equivalent horizontal relationship (with civil society actors, e.g. consumers of passenger cars, as passive recipients).

(ii.) With respect to *governance processes*, the formalized partnership structure yielded an actor field that was formed by representatives from the ASIA, the car industry and the DETEC. These actors built coalitions that were bound by the formal rule systems and shared goals and resources. As a representative of the ASIA argued: »*The association [ASIA] wanted to show that a voluntary approach is working; to find a solution that is reasonable for the economy [...] Energy efficiency is not a bad thing, there are no objections to it per se.*« (interview 03-01, transl.). The ways of interest intermediation went hand in hand with the corporatist model of representation. Both the DETEC and the ASIA were able to exercise a certain amount of influence and to bring in their interests (cf. Börner, 2010; SFOE 2011b). The federal government took the leading role for initiating the arrangement and defining its major conditions (»*Representatives of the Department of the Environment, Transport, Energy and*

Communications approached the association and it decided to agree on the terms.«, interview 03-01, transl.). The market actors enjoyed a certain amount of autonomy during coordination. Actors from the ASIA and the broader car industry were able to develop their own strategies in order to achieve the objectives of the arrangement. They could thus directly influence the evolution of processes (cf. ASIA, 2002-2012; SFOE, 2005). However, the private sector was constrained in this regard by the DETEC, which approved all monitoring reports and thus defined boundaries in which the ASIA had to operate (cf. interviews 03-01 and 03-02).

In view of resource interdependencies, the main base of power for actor groups came from legal resources and consensus arising from the covenant. Other resources that were mobilized and exchanged were knowledge regarding the transport sector and its internal conditions as well as respective infrastructure and organization. Actions were legitimatized by an agreement on roles and procedures as established by the covenant (cf. DETEC, 2003; SFOE, 2011a; interview 03-01). Altogether, the character of the processes was determined by the clear responsibility rules, resulting in an emphasis on cooperation and exchange of information.

(iii.) Regarding *governance contents,* the procedural conditions paved the way for a substantive setting that was fixed in terms of goals but flexible in its implementation, i.e. in reaching the objectives. The stakeholders were confronted with clear-cut problem definitions - with precise demarcations deduced from overall goals of reducing emissions in the transport sector by the CO_2 law (cf. Swiss Confederation, 1999). Targets at the beginning of the governance arrangement were commonly set by the federal government and the private bodies based on a market analysis (»*An analysis by the Swiss Dynamic Test Center scrutinized what is possible, what is the state of the art in technical terms. One took general European data of the last five year period and then tried to include Swiss peculiarities. Based on this, one came to the targets [...] However, the official targets that were finally set were a bit stricter, politics wanted to do the whole thing more ambitiously [...] You see, there the negotiation starts, there are of course particular interest.*«, interview 03-01, transl.). This resulted in a standardized step-wise reduction goal: the average fuel consumption of newly registered passenger cars should be reduced from 8.4 l per 100 km in the basis year 2000 to 6.4 l in 2008. This represented a total reduction target of 24% with yearly reduction rates of 3%, i.e. 0.25 l per 100 km per year (cf. ASIA, 2002-2012; SFOE, 2005; Börner, 2010; interview 03-02).

This goal setting was accompanied by ongoing review processes of policy setting by the DETEC (cf. SFOE, 2005).

In terms of policy instruments, the covenant itself represented a performance agreement. Precise means for reaching the goals of the covenant were not defined (»*Defined activities from the start would be counterproductive, the aim is that the industry has freedom to find reasonable solutions.*«, interview 03-01, transl.). During the evolution of the agreement, several information and marketing activities have been conducted by the SFOE and the ASIA, partly in collaboration and partly individually. The most important one was the energy label system for passenger cars, the so-called ′energy etiquette′. It was introduced by the SFOE in 2003 within the context of the Swiss Energy program. The implementation was supported by the Swiss Federal Roads Office and the ASIA (»*The ASIA was very involved in terms of promoting the energy etiquette. In partnership with the Federal Office, for instance, exhibitions and contests were organized.*«, interview 03-04, transl.; »*There was an active collaboration with the transport industry, for instance, for controlling the label.*«, interview 03-02, transl.). The etiquette made it required by law to declare the energy efficiency of newly sold passenger cars. The legal basis for this was built by the Swiss energy law (cf. Swiss Confederation, 1998a, article 8), and the energy ordinance from 1998, which explicitly calls for such a system in its annex (cf. Swiss Confederation, 1998b, annex 3.6). The etiquette informs prospective buyers of new passenger cars about the specific characteristics of a vehicle - by indicating its energy efficiency relative to its size in seven different categories (A to G). Specifically, it provides information about the fuel consumption (liters per 100 km) and the CO2 emissions (in grams per km), in relation to the unloaded weight of the vehicle (cf. interview 03-2; Alberini, 2014). The etiquette had to be displayed in a clearly visible manner directly on a vehicle at its selling point or in its immediate vicinity (cf. DETEC, 2003). The efficiency categories were adjusted each year (cf. interview 03-02). The second most important activity to help reach the goals of the covenant was an information and marketing campaign called ‘Smart Drive’. It was conducted by the ASIA from 2005 to 2008 (cf. ASIA, 2002-2012). Additionally, several smaller information and marketing means were realized (cf. in more detail chapter 6.3.4).

Finally, in terms of the predominant knowledge base, the policy setting was backed up by economic expertise such as state-of-the-art market assessments, e.g. by the market analysis of the Swiss Dynamic Test Center (cf. above). Partly, lay knowledge of car producers in terms of technological solutions played a role, providing information through dynamic interfaces (cf. interview 03-01; Börner, 2010).

(iv.) The *interplay* that took place among the three dimensions can be interpreted by highlighting some examples as follows. Concerning the *structures-processes interplay*, the formalized institutional partnership structure (with clear access and responsibility rules) reinforced the dominance of actors from the ASIA and the DETEC - and vice versa. The institutionalized public-private relationship resulted in a formal position of the industry in political processes with power to officially determine their evolution. In turn, through this direct engagement and the official allocation of resources to the market sector, informal channels of representation became rather insignificant in this field.

With respect to the *processes-contents interplay,* on the one hand, the substantive setting in terms of both policy formulation and implementation was clearly shaped simultaneously by actors from the central government and the market. On the other hand, the shared policy objectives between both actor groups in terms of reducing fuel consumption formed strong internal coalitions. These worked together on bringing forward the issues during the arrangement. The sharing of objectives was possible because both sides were benefiting from the partnership.

Finally, in terms of the *structures-contents interplay,* the commonly shared goals were formalized through official rule systems of the public-private cooperation. Informal market structures in turn determined the changing targets for the members of the ASIA. Moreover, the governance arrangement generally illustrates how the kind of problem definitions and their delineation clearly determines the institutional level where action is taken. Also, the degree of institutional formality went hand in hand with the chosen policy measure of a public-private target agreement.

6.1.4 Energy Trialogue

Initiated by the Swiss canton Aargau in 2007, the basic design of the Energy Trialogue was a multi-stakeholder discussion process. The idea was to bring together representatives from the three pillars of science, economy and society to contribute to a sustainable Swiss energy policy. Organization and control rested with the private-law association Energy-

Trialogue Switzerland (cf. interviews 04-01 and 04-02). In the first phase of the Trialogue from 2007 to 2009, about 200 representatives discussed the issues in protected areas to develop a sustainable and competitive strategy plan for the Swiss energy sector. The final output, a common strategy paper, was published in 2009 (cf. Energie Trialog Schweiz, 2009). The second project phase conducted from 2012 to 2013, was initiated by the Swiss Business Federation economiesuisse, the environmental NGO WWF Switzerland and the canton Aargau. Twelve economic and environmental associations and organizations were invited to discuss the 'Energy Strategy 2050' of the Swiss Federal Council. The final report of the steering group was published in 2013 (cf. Energie Trialog Schweiz, 2013).

(i.) In terms of *governance structures,* a tightly coupled network structure with a dispersed locus of authority resulted in a moderate degree of institutional formality. Only modest hallmarks of formal rules were in place (cf. interviews 04-01 and 04-02). This gave rise to more informal and experimental rule systems during roundtable discussions, workshops and presentations (although the organization of these events was formally designed). Deliberative norms played a decisive role and 'rules of the negotiation table' arose that were based on shared values and belief systems. Each participant had to sign a confidentiality agreement that the discussions are based on the so-called 'Chatham-House-Rules'. This means that participants were allowed to talk outside the discussions about their content but had to secure anonymity in this regard (cf. interview 04-01). Also, discussions took place in the absence of media and ought to be conducted without political interests. This was supposed to allow participants to bridge existing polarizations among the different groups. By analyzing the interests behind the positions and acknowledging diverging positions, the Trialogue aspired to common solutions. Accordingly, the participatory meeting places built on commonly shared rules of conduct (cf. interview 04-02; Kaiser, 2012).

With regard to general access rules to the arrangement, participation was selective under strategic considerations from the key players. The selection process was made by the Trialogue association based on the criteria of a balanced spectrum, thematic interest in the field and discussion skills. A central criterion in the first project phase of the Trialogue was that from all organization the chief executive officer participated (the assumption behind this was that only the CEOs of an organization are capable of changing the position of the respective organization) (»*The goal was that decision makers with influence, who are in the position to make changes in society, were on board.*«, interview 04-01, transl.; cf. also Büsser, 2010).

Overall, the setting was thus characterized by a partnership model of representation, with voluntary participation of actors from all different backgrounds, resulting in interactive structures. These structures arose out of the insight of resource interdependencies among actors with a stake in the Swiss energy sector and the pursuit of merging pooled competencies among them. The canton Aargau took a leading position as the host of the project. Responsibilities were then channeled through the independent private-law association Energy-Trialogue that operated on multiple levels of action. It included an executive board, composed of nine stakeholders from different backgrounds and a branch office (cf. Energie Trialog Schweiz, 2007; interview 04-01). The role divisions of the governance arrangement varied over time and so did the relations among the actors. During some phases, access was privileged to an exclusive group of key players. A core group of representatives then assumed control (e.g. on interim results and final strategy papers). While the results were discussed in the larger plenum sessions, they were adopted in the interaction pattern of almost unilateral action, with single actors possessing power and accesses to key resources. At other stages, the arrangement had a largely inclusive character, for instance at the large discussion events. Power and accesses to major resources were then pooled, accompanied by cooperative role divisions. Actors in this phases collaborated through interactive mechanisms of exchange and interaction (cf. interviews 04-01 and 04-02; Kaiser, 2012; Beyeler & Kaiser, 2012).

(ii.) With regard to *governance processes*, the network structure enabled a heterogeneous actor field consisting of a large spectrum of different stakeholders - from politics, society, economy and science. In the first project phase of the Trialogue, conducted from January 2007 to October 2009, ten expert workshops took place that reviewed the scientific basics - based on research studies. These results were then discussed in two larger moderated discussion events, with together about 200 representatives from science (national and international experts such as the Swiss Federal Institute of Technology, Zurich or the Paul Scherrer Institute), economy (firms and associations such as Shell or Axpo), society (such as NGOs like the WWF Switzerland or Greenpeace) and public authorities (e.g. from the canton Aargau and the city of Zurich or representatives from the Swiss Federal Office of Energy). The discussions were based on mediative elements (cf. interview 04-01; Energie Trialog Schweiz, 2007 and 2009). With regard to development of the final strategy, participants were reduced to the smaller core group of experts consisting of about 30 stakeholders from different backgrounds. Although the strategy was discussed at the larger plenum events and thus was »*an agreed output of all participants*« (interview 04-01, transl.), »*certain representatives felt excluded*« (interview 04-02, transl.). This especially concerned associations from the industry. Overall, this situation induced larger conflicts at the end of the first project phase in view of the unbalanced consideration of interests (cf. in this regard in more detail e.g. Studerus, 2011; Meier, 2010).

The second project phase of the Trialogue called 'New Energy policy' took place between October 2012 and March 2013 to discuss the 'Energy Strategy 2050' of the Federal Council. It was based on the experiences from the first project (cf. interview 04-04). Yet, in contrast to the first project, this phase was initiated by 'economiesuisse' and WWF Switzerland who asked the canton Aargau, if they could host a second project (cf. interview 04-03). Responsible for the project was a steering group that consisted of representatives of these three partners as well as a neutral leadership person and two moderators (cf. Energieforum Schweiz, 2009). On behalf of this group, twelve large Swiss economic and environmental associations and organizations were invited (such as the 'Agency for renewable energies and energy efficiency', the 'Conference of cantonal energy directors', 'Swisscleantech', the 'Association of Swiss electricity utilities', the 'Association of Swiss gas industry' or 'Greenpeace'). Criteria for this invitation were the political and economic importance, the know-how and the dependence on the developments in Swiss energy policy. In contrast to the first project, the CEOs of the organizations were not present (interview 04-01). The associations and organizations discussed the documents of the consultation phase to the first package of measures for implementing the 'Energy Strategy 2050'. The second phase started with a large plenum event that identified the topics with the greatest need for clarification. These topics (such as energy demand and efficiency or economic consequences of policy measures) were discussed in eight expert workshops by the associations and organizations in collaboration with scientists. The final results were published in a report that was presented at a media conference in August 2013 (cf. interviews 04-01 and 04-02; Beyeler & Kaiser, 2012).

Regarding the two project phases it can be said that actors from all different backgrounds could bring in their interests by putting forth their knowledge and opinions. However, as indicated, this consideration of interests varied during the different stages of the arrangement. Correspondingly, the amount of influence of actors differed. Yet, at most project phases, the varying actor groups were provided with the leverage to jointly take the initiative. Coordination among the groups was in most phases made easy to achieve. However, at some stages, decisions necessarily had to be mediated between competing sets of interests that were not easily reconcilable (cf. interviews 04-01 and 04-02). In terms of resources, the interdependencies resulted in a situation where knowledge, money and infrastructure were spread. Power was mostly exercised through cooperation and respect with an agreement on positions and procedures (apart from the end of the first project phase). Overall, it can be concluded that the Trialogue was characterized by deliberatively influenced negotiation processes that relied on communication and exchange of information. There was a common attempt to create a trust-worthy atmosphere. Cooperative attitudes founded on reciprocity were dominant at most times.

(iii.) With respect to *governance contents,* the actors came together against the backdrop of a commonly shared pursuit to discuss the future development of the Swiss energy system. The initial situation during the first project phase saw the energy debate characterized by hardened fronts - with emotionalized and polarizing discussions. Diverging positions among different stakeholders on the use of nuclear and renewable energy seemed to be unchangeable (cf. interview 04-01). Accordingly, society, economy and science were brought together in a protected area, unaffected by self-serving political interest in daily business and the media. By means of factual discussions that sought to be scientifically sound and goal-oriented, a sustainable and competitive road map for Swiss energy policy should be explored. The initial question was to what extent there is an overlapping consensus among the stakeholders (cf. interviews 04-01 and 04-02; Büsser, 2010).

The substantive output of the first project phase were ten basic research studies conducted on behalf of the Trialogue, summaries of meetings and the final strategy paper published in 2009. The report sets eight core objectives for the future Swiss energy system: higher life quality, increased energy efficiency, impulses for economic growth, security of supply, protection of environmental resources, reduction of CO_2 emissions, stabilizing the financial burden and a society capable of making decisions. The goals together are aimed at reducing energy demand by 2035 to about 20% and until 2050 to about 30%. For the main goal of reducing CO_2 emissions, concrete targets were formulated (a reduction until 2020 to 25%, until 2035 to 50% and until 2050 to 80% compared to 1990). Ten short and mid-term measures were proposed for realizing the goals (such as a uniform price for CO_2 emissions with regard to all energy sources, energetic targets for the building and transport sector, minimum requirements for electronic devices, expansion of the feed-in-compensation for renewable energies or the strengthening of innovation). One of the most important conclusions of the strategy is that domestic power supply will not be able cover the demand for electricity even if the measures are realized. Thus a power supply gap is estimated to emerge in the upcoming decades (under the assumption that no large-power plants are newly built) (cf. Energie Trialog Schweiz, 2009, interviews 04-01 and 04-02; Energieforum Schweiz, 2009).

The initial situation for the second project was that from 2011 onwards, the Swiss Federal Council developed the ‘Energy Strategy 2050‘. In view of existing controversies on the goals of the strategy among economic, societal and scientific groups, the stakeholders came together to discuss the official first package of measures. Making use of the experiences gained in the first project phase, the proclaimed goal of the second phase was to scrutinize the plausibility of the strategy and its underlying assumptions. Apart from that, the discussion was intended to increase the understanding of the participants on the strategy‘s goals and measures as well as on the potential effects of the first package of measures for the economy, society and the environment. In so doing, a contribution was sought to objectify the energy policy debate in society and politics (»*The goal was to reach at a better and broadly based basis of decision-making for the energy strategy.*«, interview 04-01, transl.; cf. also Beyeler & Kaiser, 2012). The final report of the steering group published in 2013 summarized the core results of the discussion process. It refers to potential problems for implementing the energy strategy and discloses possible conflicts of goals - as well as approaches to solve these conflicts. Also, it formulates open questions and concrete recommendations for Swiss federal politics. Apart from that, differences among the participating associations are highlighted. In the appendix, individual statements from the associations on the results and the process of the Trialogue are attached (cf. interviews 04-01 and 04-02; Kaiser & Schips, 2013).

Against the backdrop of the two phases, additional characteristics of the substantive policy setting can be summarized as follows. In terms of instruments, the prevalent approach was dominated by negotiated agreements. The consideration of multiple perspectives over time thereby led to a flexible character of problem definitions and a pursuit of integrating contents, successive learning and innovative solutions (cf. interviews 04-01 and 04-02). The two key outputs were based on the knowledge produced in several basic research studies conducted on behalf of the Trialogue, as well as the analysis of existing research (cf. Energie Trialog Schweiz, 2009 and 2013). Overall, the governance arrangement exhibited a dynamic science-policy interface. The round tables were composed of both stakeholders and scientists, with differing perspectives and expertise in the energy field. Scientific expertise accommodated the Trialogue by providing shared concepts that facilitate compromise, yet expertise was also used by stakeholders as a tool for gaining influence. Thus, on the one hand, a certain 'co-production of knowledge' took place in the search for consensus to arrive at conjointly supported decisions (cf. interviews 04-01 and 04-02). On the other hand, the struggle for power (among the multiple actors with conflicting views) also resulted in a discursive battle over which knowledge counts as relevant. Yet, overall, the discussions were regarded as constructive, based on mutual respect (cf. interviews 04-01 and 04-02; Kaiser, 2012).

(iv.) Regarding the *interplay* among the dimensions, first of all, the *structures-processes interplay* exhibited a mutual influence of the tightly knit network embedding with the deliberative character of the negotiation processes. For instance, the agreement on role positions went hand in hand with the pursuit of creating a trust-worthy atmosphere in the activities and vice versa. Likewise, the informal and experimental rule systems within formal boundaries strengthened the cooperative process characteristics and at the same time were supported by these. However, the high demand for coordination in a network structure also revealed the difficulties in terms of interest consideration and the need for conflict resolution.

With regard to the *processes-contents interplay,* there was a varying degree of influence exercised by different actors during the formulation of commonly agreed strategy papers. The exchange of information that was facilitated by the roundtable discussions resulted in an integrative character of mutual objectives. In turn, problem definitions and their delineation determined the composition of actors during the different stages of the Trialogue.

Finally, with respect to the *structures-contents interplay,* the dispersed locus of authority reinforced the evolution of commonly negotiated agreements and the other way around. Also, cognitive rule-systems with regard to the future development of the Swiss energy sector had a large influence on the co-productive policy-science interface and vice versa.

6.1.5 Minergie label

The Minergie label was created in 1994 by civil society actors in order to establish a Swiss building standard that combines the goals of energy-efficiency, comfort and value retention. As a private initiative, the label has been in individual property until the year 1997. However, to leverage it, the two cantons Zurich and Bern got involved and subsequently took over ownership (cf. interview 05-04; Minergie, 2008). In 1998, the non-profit private Minergie association was founded and the cantons transferred the usage rights to the association (»*The rights were transferred under the condition that they go back to the cantons in case the association dissolves.*«, interview 05-02, transl.). Up to the present, it is responsible for managing the label (cf. Minergie, 2015).

(i.) In terms of *governance structures,* the arrangement exhibited a low degree of institutional formality. The framing architecture included no formal legal mandate, resulting in informal, rather implicit and flexible institutions (cf. interviews 05-01 and 05-02). At the beginning of the arrangement in the early 1990s, self-governing actors with no formal authority played a dominant role. The patterns of interaction were thus characterized by unilateral action with non-governmental character. In this context, there were no formal rules, which vested the individuals with the liberty to take action. Because practices were not yet settled in the new problem domain of creating an energy label for buildings, strong bottom-up structures flourished (the individuals were building on their personal experience with a pilot project: a ′zero energy settlement′ established in Zurich; cf. Kriesi, 1995). This situation had a flexible and relatively unorganized character (cf. interview 05-02; Minergie, 2011). Since the whole arrangement thus held a pioneer role in the field, cultural-cognitive rules played an important part - in terms of mental models that influence the system understanding and the parameters for defining problems (cf. interview 05-01). When the civil society actors decided to transfer the label rights to the cantons Zurich and Bern, the structures became more formalized (cf. Carassus, 2007; interview 05-02).

When the Minergie association was institutionalized, the shared normative values as well as rules of good practice that dominated the context were not codified but gradually established: »*There was a partnership structure that was characterized by a shared common goal to try something new. The status of actors did not play a role in this regard.*« (interview 05-02, transl.). Accordingly, a rather loosely coupled network structure with shared authority and a partnership model of representation evolved with equal collaboration among state, market and civil society actors. Since no single actor was equipped with a hegemonic position, horizontal positions among actors vis-à-vis each other emerged, with a distributed locus of power. The actors were interrelated with little systematization and no hierarchical subordination (cf. interviews 05-01 and 05-02). The role of the key civil society actors were those of process managers, while the most important role of public actors was to bundle resources and offer infrastructure (»*The public sector was crucial for financing in the first bigger projects. Without this, the whole thing would not have leveraged.*«, interview 05-02, transl.).

Against this backdrop, patterns of interaction shifted between situations where decisions were made by majority vote and others with negotiated agreement (cf. interview 05-01). The dispersed locus of authority moreover resulted in multi-level characteristics in terms of the institutional level on which the governance arrangement was relying. The levels of action were mostly local but also national and - in the course of the further development - international (cf. Minergie, 2008).

(ii.) Concerning *governance processes,* the small group of leading individuals ('forerunners') shaped the actor field at the beginning of the arrangement with a high degree of autonomy. At this stage, governmental actors were kept at a distance (cf. interview 05-02). However, the self-governing entities began successively involving other stakeholders. Public authorities were approached to leverage the arrangement (cf. interviews 05-01 and 05-02). As soon as the key actors decided to start managing the label via a private association, actors from all different backgrounds were able to take action (cf. Minergie, 2008). Multiple coalitions acted alongside individually acting actors.

Up to the present, the association counts over 500 members (including the federal government, all 26 Swiss cantons, companies, associations, universities, schools and individuals). In terms of operational decisions, a head office (concerned with administration, marketing, communication, trademark protection and finances) is supported in technical issues by a building agency and three other competency centers dispersed across Switzerland. On the other hand, an executive committee (of nine people) is in charge of strategic decisions. The association is closely linked to (about 900) local businesses and (about 1500) professional partners - i.e. representatives from the building industry and construction work - such as architects, planners and energy consultants. The label certifications in turn are carried out by cantonal certification units located at administrations of all the Swiss cantons (alongside units in Liechtenstein and France) (cf. Beyeler et al., 2009; Kriesi, 2009; interview 05-04).

In view of this decentralized system of implementation, the overall processes of the governance arrangement strongly relied on the inputs of different actors, vesting several parties with influence (cf. interview 05-01). Also, there was an effort to consider the interests of consumers and the views of the public through strategic inclusion. In line with this, participants attempted to design the setting as transparently as possible (cf. interview 05-01). With regard to conflicts during the processes, there was some resistance from national public authorities (»*The Federal Office of Energy was kind of envious since Minergie is the most important player in the building sector - which is responsible for 50 % of the Swiss energy demand - and the office itself has little to say in this regard.*«, interview 05-2, transl.). Yet, the conflicts gradually dissolved since representatives were integrated in the executive committee of the association (cf. ibid.).

In terms of resources, the civil society forerunners mobilized their pioneering ideas and exclusive technical and marketing know-how with regard to introducing energy labels for dwellings. Other resources were also exchanged by stakeholders over time, such as infrastructure, organization and consensus (cf. interview 05-01; Minergie, 2011). Due to the high interdependence in terms of resources, power was exercised through trust, cooperation and respect - and actions were legitimatized by an agreement on roles and relations (cf. interview 05-02). Overall, the processes exhibited a self-regulating character, in which multiple actors interacted in ad-hoc decision-making. The procedures were based upon the idea of a bottom-up joining of forces and upon solidarity. Flexible collaboration among the actors was predominant with a focus on arguments, cooperation and unanimous decisions (»*The advantage was that - with the association - you could react flexibly to new circumstances.*«, interview 05-04, transl.).

(iii.) With regard to *governance contents,* a substantive setting evolved that was largely based on an innovative path for solutions - with flexible problem definitions and objectives. The rather new subject of energy labeling for buildings required both marketing and technical innovations with creative ideas. The innovative approach in order to promote the label was to strategically combine the goal of energy efficiency with the two aims of higher levels of comfort and value retention (»*The initiation of Minergie was to recognize that you cannot make a building label attractive by just focusing on the energy aspect.*«, interview 05-01, transl.). In so doing, the focus was put on the benefit for the consumer (this is also demonstrated by the limit on construction costs that must not exceed those for conventional buildings by more than 10%; cf. Carassus, 2007). Minergie was meant to reach the mainstream and transcend the image of a niche product for environmental friendly end users (cf. interview 05-03).

As a consequence, the label criteria were kept simple, following a pragmatic approach. Minergie thus focuses on the building quality and does not incorporate other relevant criteria in terms of sustainability such as the location of buildings: »*The label should be easy measurable, focusing on the building itself, where you can simply say, the building comes up to the requirement or not [...] Other labels have shown that with several other criteria, you frequently loose the main goal in energetic terms.*« (interview 05-02, transl.). The main indicator used to quantify the building quality is accordingly the overall limit on energy use (supplemented by more specific criteria, such as for systematic ventilation to ensure the high levels of indoor living environment). The specific targets in this regard have varied over time (cf. chapter 5.6 and 6.3.5). Broader goals also varied. For instance, in the beginning, Minergie was meant to gradually extend from the building sector to other branches, such as mobility and devices. However, because of capacity reasons and in order to not lose focus on the energy sector, these goals were abandoned later (cf. interviews 05-01 and 05-02). The setting was thus strongly characterized by a continuous flow of information that integrated different perspectives in order to facilitate innovation and flexible adaptation to changing circumstances (such as the legislative change of building regulations, cf. chapter 6.3.5).

The label was introduced on an experimental basis and based on ongoing evaluations it was shaped over time. Different versions evolved - from the basic standard in 1998 to the stricter version of Minergie-P, the Minergie-eco version that includes health and ecological requirements and finally the Minergie-A standard for net zero energy buildings (cf. Feige et al., 2011; Salvi & Syz, 2011). Due to the pioneering character, the participating actors regarded Minergie mainly as a challenge of communication and marketing. Accordingly, an elaborate brand strategy was established to boost the awareness of the label. The focus was a push-pull strategy: *»About 40 % of our communication activities were targeted at the building professionals, such as architects - plus investors and politics - and 60% at the end users such as residents and building owners.«* (interview 05-01, transl.). The different target groups were addressed by different themes. While for residents the main aspect was comfort, the focus for politics was energy-efficiency. Professionals were in turn presented with the arguments of competitiveness and technical feasibility, while for investors and building owners value retention was highlighted (cf. interview 05-02; Minergie, 2011). This target-group-specific approach was intended to address both demand and supply.

Up to present, all measures within the arrangement use the incentive of information to influence behavior, i.e. voluntarism as a non-binding instrument that follows a flexible approach to implementation. The most important communication instruments are events (such as trade and public fairs, exhibitions and congresses), information measures (such as publications for residents) and intensive media and public relations (cf. interview 05-01). Apart from this, the governance arrangement puts a specific emphasis on the mobilization of the construction actors' competencies and knowledge transfer. It has established an advanced vocational training system for planning and executive building professionals, i.e. architects, contractors and certification agencies (for instance offering training courses such as the ′Basic course sustainable building: healthy and ecological public builds′ alongside workshops, planning tools, seminars and conferences) (cf. Carassus, 2007; interview 05-05).

Through the close cooperation with stakeholders (for instance with professionals from the building sector), the association over the past years strove for a co-production of knowledge stemming from different cognitive communities. The key individual forerunners at the beginning strongly built on their own experience in the field, both in technical terms (e.g. with the established ′zero energy settlement′ established in Zurich) and with regard to communication (»*Two of the most decisive actors had long experience in marketing strategies, for instance with putting heat pumps on the market.*« interview 05-04, transl.; cf. also interview 05-01). Building up close network structures, there was a reliance on expert and local knowledge, with a pursuit for provisory goals and joint learning against the backdrop of the pioneering role (cf. interviews 05-01 and 05-02). In sum, the setting exhibited a relatively informal evolution and was flexible in terms of timelines and material products.

(iv.) An interpretative look at the *linkages* among the three dimensions reveals examples of their mutual influence. In terms of the *structures-processes interplay*, interdependencies between the bottom-up structure and the ad-hoc deliberative character of procedures can be observed. The agreement on relations facilitated joint decision-making and implementation, while the informal approach increased flexibility in the processes, allowing them to react to different directions in which the context of energy labeling developed. Awareness of interdependence and community among the actors encouraged the network, simultaneously increasing the effects of actors on each other. This in turn strengthened the coherence of the network and excluded the option of singular dominance. The large degree of shared normative values and norms as well as rules of good practice explains why power was exercised mostly through trust and respect.

Concerning the *processes-contents interplay*, there was a mutual influence between the participatory oriented interactions and the voluntarism form of goal attainment. The consensus in terms of the common discourse to promote the label facilitated a process in which actors were bound in ad-hoc coalitions. This in turn strengthened the shared objectives. The intense coordinative procedures of network steering made it possible for a substantive setting of constant experimentation to emerge.

Finally, with regard to the *structures-contents interplay*, the weak formal institutional configuration in place encouraged the capacity of civil society actors dealing with new ways of problem solving. This in turn maintained the low degree of institutional formality in the field. The horizontal relations among the actors also paved the way for a fast development of and reliance on co-productive forms of knowledge production, which in turn supported cooperative structures for decision-making.

6.2 Allocation to governance modes

Having reached a deepened understanding of governance within the cases, the arrangements will in the following be allocated to particular modes of governance. In light of the formal frame for differentiating modes translated into a category system, three broader groups of key features are scrutinized by exploring the respective sub-categories: *actor features* (including the initiating actors, the stakeholder position, the policy level and the power base), *institutional features* (covering the model of representation, the rules of interaction and the mechanisms of social interaction) and *features concerning content* (including goals and targets, instruments as well as the policy-science interface).[23]

6.2.1 CO_2 levy: Centralized governance

The governance arrangement around the CO_2 levy can be classified as the mode of *centralized governance*. In this mode, central governments take the lead and the market and civil society are the recipients of government`s incentives (yet, it has to be considered in this regard that hierarchical modes in Switzerland are more participatory in nature due to established instruments of direct democracy - cf. chapter 6.1.1 and 5.1). In accordance with the analysis of governance workings in chapter 6.1.1, the key features of the frame for governance modes that are associated with the centralized mode can be basically identified (cf. in the following interviews 01-01 and 01-02; FOEN, 2012 and 2013; DETEC, 2004 and 2005; Swiss Confederation, 1999, 2005 and 2011; Ingold & Varone, 2012; In-

---

23 Since I address specific governance arrangements, I do not incorporate the feature of policy integration, which in the form presented in the frame for governance modes rather concerns governance in terms of whole policy sectors.

gold, 2011; Sager et al., 2014; Thalmann, 2013; Elbeze & de Perthuis, 2011; Brönnimann et al., 2014; Sumner et al., 2011; Niederberger, 2005; IEA, 2012).

With respect to the actor features, central government agencies can be recorded as *initiating actors,* responsible for formulating policy objectives and legislation. Regarding the *stakeholder position*, there is strong stakeholder autonomy in which public authorities determine the position of other stakeholders. The predominant *policy level* at which key actors operate can be documented as the national level. With regard to the *power base* by which actors implement their interests, the legal coercive and authoritarian system is predominant.

Concerning the institutional features, a pluralist *model of representation* can be recognized. Roles of key actors are prescribed in legislation, determining the formal *rules of interaction* between the actors. The consequential *mechanisms of social interaction* are characterized by hierarchical top-down structures dominated by command and control mechanisms - softened by the instruments of direct democracy, such as the consultation phase at the beginning of the governance arrangement.

Finally, in terms of the features concerning policy content, there is a uniformity of *goals and targets*. Furthermore, legally binding instruments are predominant policy *instruments*. The circumstance that the character of these binding instruments is mainly incentive-based formally points towards the direction of the ideal-typical mode of public-private governance in the frame. However, as elaborated in chapter 3.1, in real-world governance arrangements, there are several examples of incentive-based policy measures within hierarchical governing settings. Eventually, in terms of the *policy-science interface*, a primacy of generic, expert knowledge can be identified.

6.2.2 Electricity saving fund: Decentralized governance

The governance arrangement around the electricity saving fund Basel can be allocated to the mode of *decentralized governance* (cf. in the following interviews 02-01 and 02-02; AUE, 2000; 2002a, 2002b and 2007; Great Council of the Canton of Basel-City, 1998; Governing Council of the Canton of Basel-City, 1999; SFOE, 2003, 2007 and 2009; Boogen, 2010; Suna et al., 2013; IWB, 2004). In this mode, regional governments are predominant, with market and civil society actors as mainly being recipients (again, instruments of direct democracy lead to a more participatory character).

With respect to actor features, lower levels of governmental actors, involving *stakeholders* from different backgrounds, can be registered as *initiating actors* (these actors formally started the arrangement that was a reaction to a popular initiative). The predominant *policy level* at which key actors operate is the regional level. Regarding the *power base*, the authorities are embedded in legislation, which results in coercive power.

In terms of the institutional features, a pluralist *model of representation*, determined by popular regional election can be documented. The predominant *rules of interaction* are of formal nature, such as the rule of law. Furthermore, *mechanisms of social interaction*, in which the regional government decides autonomously about collaborations within top-down determined boundaries can be noticed, softened by the consultation phase.

Finally, in terms of the features concerning content, there are uniform *goals and targets* that are adjusted to the regional policy level. Furthermore, the levy and the bonus system, which were implemented based on public covenants can be recorded as predominant policy *instruments*. Finally, in terms of the *policy-science interface*, generic expert knowledge paired with regional time-and-place specific knowledge is predominant.

6.2.3 Fuel consumption covenant: Public-private governance

The governance arrangement for reducing fuel consumption in Switzerland can be classified as *public-private governance*. This mode of governance exhibits equal cooperation between government agencies and market actors. The key features of the formal frame for governance modes that are associated with this mode can be identified (cf. in the following interviews 03-01 and 03-02; DETEC, 2003; ASIA, 2002-2012; SFOE, 2005, 2007, 2011a and 2011b; Swiss Confederation, 1999, 1998a and 1998b; Quandt, 2010; Börner, 2010; Alberini, 2014; Spielmann & Althaus, 2007; Volken, 2010; De Haan, 2007).

In terms of actor features, federal government agencies can be recorded as *initiating actors*, while the private sector is granted a preconditioned role. The *stakeholder position* is determined by autonomy of market actors within predetermined boundaries vested by the government. The according *policy level* can be identified as the national level. The *power base* is correspondingly based on contracts and legal recourse.

With respect to institutional features, the *model of representation* can be described as corporatist, as depicted by the formalized public-private arrangement. In terms of *rules of interaction*, there is a co-existence of formal rules of exchange and informal rule-systems. With regard to the *mechanisms of social interaction*, private actors from the market manage the collaboration within boundaries determined by the government.

Regarding features concerning content, uniform *goals* but actor specific targets prevail. Furthermore, a performance contract can be identified as the predominant policy *instrument*. Finally, in terms of the *policy-science interface,* issue and time-and-place specific knowledge involving the knowledge from producers predominates.

6.2.4 Energy Trialogue: Interactive governance

In line with the deepened understanding of governance workings reached in chapter 6.1.4, the case of the Energy-Trialogue can be characterized as the mode of *interactive governance* (cf. in the following interviews 04-01 and 04-02; Energie Trialog Schweiz, 2007, 2009 and 2013; Energieforum Schweiz, 2009; Kaiser, 2012; Büsser, 2010; Beyeler & Kaiser, 2012; Kaiser & Schips, 2013; Weidmann, 2013). This non-hierarchical mode includes collaboration between state, market and civil society actors.

In terms of actor features, multiple actors from different backgrounds act as *initiating actors*. This goes hand in hand with a *stakeholder position* of equal roles for all network partners. Furthermore, in terms of the *policy level*, multiple levels are actively incorporated. In terms of the pertinent *power base*, trust and knowledge as predominant aspects can be identified.

With regard to institutional features, there is a partnership *model of representation* between public actors and actors from both civil society and the market, who voluntarily participate. With respect to the *rules of interaction*, institutions in the broadest sense with both formal and informal rules simultaneously guiding the interaction processes prevail. The resulting *mechanisms of social interaction* can be labeled as interactive with deliberation and negotiation as important key elements.

With respect to features concerning content, context-specific and integrated *goals and targets* prevail. The corresponding predominant *instru-*

ments used are negotiated agreements. In terms of the *policy-science interface*, a key role for expert and lay knowledge in networks with an emphasis on integrated and time-and-place specific knowledge can be noted.

6.2.5 Minergie label: Self-governance shifting to interactive governance

Finally, the governance arrangement around the Minergie standard can be labeled as the mode of *self-governance* with a gradual shift to *interactive governance*. In this case, there are dynamics in the arrangement over time. While the mode of self-governance exhibits civil society actors with far-reaching autonomy, the interactive mode includes collaboration between state, market and civil society actors. The features associated with the two modes in the formal frame can be identified respectively (cf. in the following interviews 05-01 and 05-02; Minergie, 2008, 2011 and 2015; Beyeler et al., 2009; Kriesi, 2009; EnDK, 2004; SFOE, 2005, 2011a and 2011b; Carassus, 2007; Feige et al., 2011; Salvi & Syz, 2011; Salvi et al., 2010).

With respect to the actor features, actors from civil society act as *initiating actors* determining the *stakeholder position* of other actors. The *policy level* at which actors operate thereby varies from the local to the international level. With the shift towards interactive governance, multiple actors become involved. In terms of the corresponding *power base*, an evolution from autonomy of self-governing entities to an agreement on roles and processes among participating actors can be observed.

Regarding institutional features, there is a participatory partnership *model of representation* that gradually shifts from a private-private to a public-private governing arrangement. In terms of the *rules of interaction*, institutions in the broadest sense with informal rules are the predominant ones. The *mechanisms of social interaction* can be characterized as changing from primarily bottom-up to interactive - with deliberation and negotiations as key aspects in the governance arrangement.

In terms of features concerning content, context-specific *goals and targets* prevail - as well as voluntary policy *instruments* of labeling and reporting as key measures. Finally, in terms of the *policy-science interface*, a predominant use of issue and time-and-place specific expert and lay knowledge of citizens can be noted.

Table 7 provides an overview of the allocation of the cases to governance modes. The intuitive heuristic introduced in chapter 4.1 for choosing the five cases (which should display the full range of existing ways of steering) is rationally informed by this analysis.

Table 7: Allocation of the cases to governance modes (own illustration)

Case study	*Mode of governance*
Case 1: CO_2 levy	*Centralized governance*
Case 2: Electricity saving fund	*Decentralized governance*
Case 3: Fuel consumption covenant	*Public-private governance*
Case 4: Energy Trialogue	*Interactive governance*
Case 5: Minergie label	*Self-governance shifting to interactive governance*

6.3 Governance impacts

In the following, I will present the results from data analysis with regard to governance impacts in each case. The analysis was guided by the scheme for impacts translated into a category system (cf. chapter 4.2). As described in chapter 3.3, this theoretical scheme spans the entire possibility space of changes that can be induced by governance, making use of the broad lens of action strategies. The frame was thus used as a guide that points to the scope of possible areas where changes can occur. Yet, this does not mean that in each empirical case all these areas change. Accordingly, I refrain from going sequentially through all the strategy categories of the frame (and reconstructing entire action strategies of each individual actor affected). Instead, the 'storyline' of the text is structured according to the thematic scope and important cornerstones in the respective case. In relation to the theoretical frame, I each refer to the strategy categories when describing the empirical key changes, particularly in subheadings that structure the text. This includes both the phase of strategy implementation, i.e. realized actions and institutionalization processes, and strategy development, i.e. goals-means-environment calculations.

Since the considered timeline ranges from the point of the initiation of the governance arrangement up to the present, impacts can arise already due to first coordinated actions within governance workings. As the level of governance impacts can in some instances be illustrated and documented with developments on the outcome level, I will occasionally also refer to this level.

For each case, I will proceed as follows. First of all, I will introduce the main groups of affected actors, together with their respective interfaces to the governance arrangement in question (partly the groups are not mutually exclusive, meaning that some actors belong to more than one group). After that, I disclose the changes in action strategies that were induced by the arrangement (in this regard I will wherever appropriate cite statements of interview experts since I follow the explicit objective to 'let the people talk about their experiences').

6.3.1 CO_2 levy

The governance arrangement around the Swiss CO_2 levy mainly affected the following actor groups in their action strategies. The first group consisted of Swiss firms and households paying the levy and simultaneously receiving a refund from the reallocation system. A second group entailed energy-intensive firms that made a request to be exempted from the levy by making a binding commitment to reduce their emissions. Large energy-intensive companies are exempted from the levy when they participate in the Swiss emissions trading scheme. A further group was made of actors who took part in the consultation process in conjunction with the energy law. Finally, political-administrative actors from other governance arrangements, such as the building refurbishment program, were affected. In the following, the most important changes in the action strategies of these actor groups are pointed out.

Changes in energy usage of Swiss firms and households (realized actions and institutionalization processes; strategy goals of firms and households)

The most important impact of the governance arrangement was to make a contribution to reducing the Swiss domestic demand for fossil combustible fuels. The CO_2 levy changed the energy price structure by making fossil fuels more expensive in relation to other energies such as renewable ones (»*The levy had a strong signaling effect - especially firms had to adapt to the new circumstance that CO_2 now has a price.*«, interview 01-05, transl.). Rational changes in the action strategies of Swiss firms and households are thus a substitution of fossil fuels with less CO_2 intensive or carbon-free energy sources; and/or a reduction of energy consumption through higher efficiency or a more economical usage. The same incentive is set by the binding commitments and the emission trading scheme required for firms wishing to get exempted from the levy.

According to the CO_2 law, a regular review of the effectiveness of measures by the Federal Council is required (cf. Swiss Confederation, 1999, paragraph 40). In the year 2015, the Federal Office of the Environment (FOEN) has thus commissioned the research and consulting agency Ecoplan to conduct an official ex-post evaluation of the CO_2 levy. The assessment consists of three studies to be published in 2016 - which were provided in advance by the FOEN for this study: Ecoplan, EPFL & FHNW (*forthcoming*), Ecoplan (*forthcoming*) and EPFL (*forthcoming*).[24] The evaluation is based on two different economic models (time series analysis and general equilibrium model) and compares the actual development with the situation if no levy had been implemented.

The results show that the most important influence of the levy on both firms and households was a substitution effect in terms of energy sources. The evaluation differentiates between the four sources of heating oil, gas, electricity (e.g. heat pumps) and remainder-energy, which is for the most part CO_2 free (including 'timber', 'long-distance heating' and 'other renewable energies'). While the amount of energy consumed in the form of gas and electricity only changed a little, there was a major substitution effect among heating oil and remainder-energy. Figures 13 and 14 show this development with regard to households and firms respectively (for an analysis of different industrial branches see EPFL, *forthcoming*). The evaluation argues that the upward adjustments of the levy rate in 2010 and

24 For the evaluation, Ecoplan was supported by the two universities 'University of Applied Sciences and Arts Northwestern Switzerland' and 'Ecole polytechnique fédérale de Lausanne'.

2014 strengthened the substitution and that the raising in 2016 will do so, too. Considering that the rate in 2016 is seven times the rate of 2008 (cf. chapter 5.1), it is likely that the effect will strongly increase.

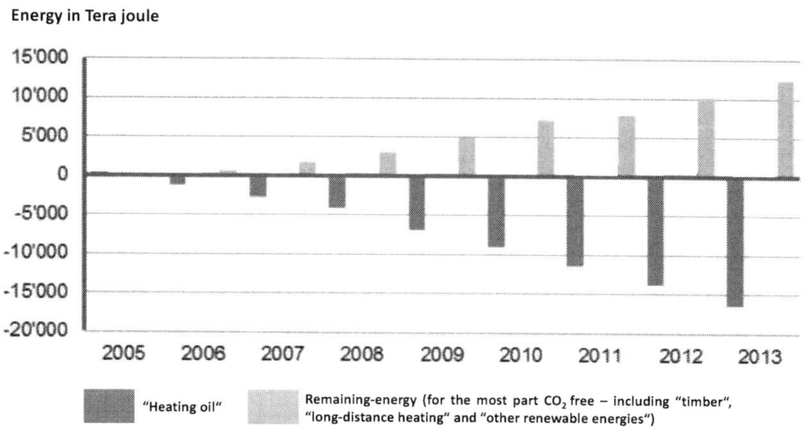

Figure 13: Development of energy demand of Swiss households for different energy sources. Difference between empirical values and a scenario without the levy. Own illustration based on data from Ecoplan, EPFL and FHNW (*forthcoming*), Ecoplan (*forthcoming*) and EPFL (*forthcoming*).

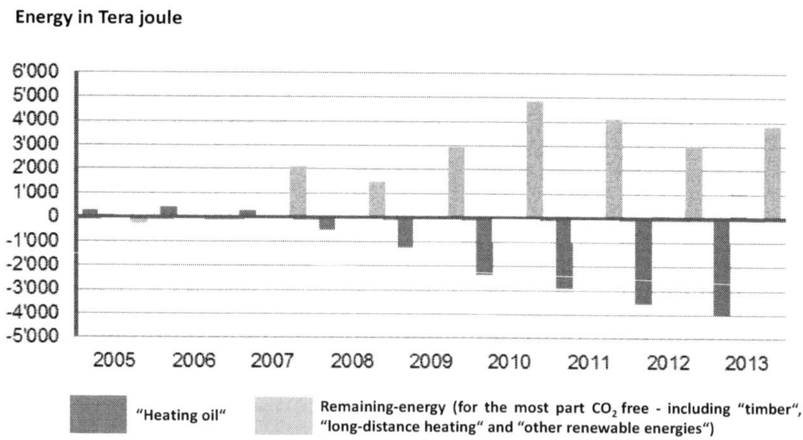

Figure 14: Development of energy demand of the Swiss industry for different energy sources. Difference between empirical values and a scenario without the levy. Own illustration based on data from Ecoplan, EPFL and FHNW (*forthcoming*), Ecoplan (*forthcoming*) and EPFL (*forthcoming*).

The figures reveal that the levy already changed the action strategies of firms and households before its actual implementation in the year 2008. The evaluation thus argues that the actors anticipated the levy (the Federal Council already decided in March 2005 on the implementation of the levy, cf. chapter 6.1.1). Figure 15 explicitly reveals this by showing the share of heating oil in overall energy consumption for the case of Swiss households, showing that the actual development and a scenario without the levy differ already from 2006 onwards (cf. Ecoplan, EPFL and FHNW (*forthcoming*), Ecoplan (*forthcoming*) and EPFL, *forthcoming*).

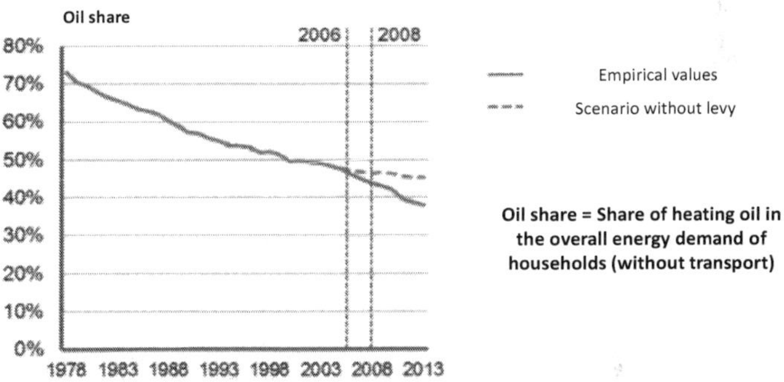

Figure 15: Share of heating oil in overall energy consumption of Swiss households
Own illustration based on data from Ecoplan, EPFL and FHNW (*forthcoming*), Ecoplan (*forthcoming*) and EPFL (*forthcoming*).

With regard to *Swiss firms*, an important part of the described reduction of fossil fuel demand was achieved by the energy-intensive firms that could make a request to be exempted from the levy (if they agree to make a commitment with the FOEN to reduce their emissions). A representative of the 'Energy Agency of the Economy' argued in an interview: »*One of the major effects of the levy was the possibility of firms to get exempted, which had a very strong and severe effect indeed [...] It induced an enormous dynamic within the industry.*« (interview 01-03, transl.). Within the commitments (officially called 'reduction commitments' or 'exemption without emission trading system', cf. article 9, CO_2 law, Swiss Confederation, 2011), the firms were obliged to achieve certain reduction targets - first and foremost for the commitment period from 2008 to 2012 (cf. DETEC, 2004). In the event the companies failed to achieve the agreed targets, they had to pay the levy ex post facto. To establish and achieve the commitments, the firms had to become members of the Energy Agency of the Economy (EnAW). The agency supervised the activities with a corresponding performance mandate made with the federal government (»*It was a large advantage that politics could work together with the agency as a connector and mediator to the economy.*«, interview 01-05, transl.). The firms included in the agency are responsible for about half of Swiss CO_2 emissions from the industry sector (»*There is no large CO_2 emitter that is not included.*«, interview 01-03, transl., cf. also EnAW, 2014). From 2004 onwards, when it was foreseeable that the levy will be implemented, about 1200 companies have gradually established reduction commitments and had to report the progress to the FOEN each year (cf. FOEN, 2014b) (»*The companies prepared for the levy in advance, so to speak [...] They reacted very quickly in order to increase planning security. Already before the levy was implemented, reduction commitments were established.*«, interview 01-04, transl.; »*There was also a reaction to the two increases of the levy rate - more and more companies wanted to get exempted over the years.*«, interview 01-05, transl.). The means used by the firms to fulfill their commitments were, apart from substituting energy sources, efficiency measures established within different management models of the EnAW (»*Apart from switching, for instance, from heating oil to timber, a lot was induced with regard to analyzing processes and according potentials for increasing efficiency.*«, interview 01-03, transl.). In a recent report, the EnAW concludes that efficiency of the firms taken together even increased to a larger extent than stipulated by respective target values in the reduction commitments - see figure 16 (cf. EnAW, 2014).

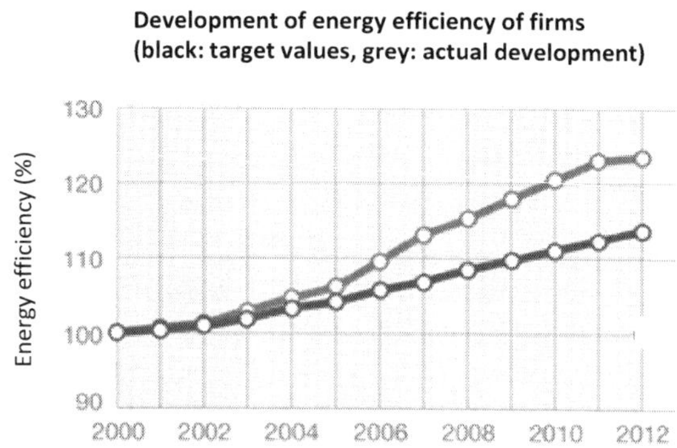

Figure 16: Development of energy efficiency of Swiss companies in the EnAW (EnAW, 2014, p. 15)

The EnAW furthermore demonstrates the developments in energy consumption with progress in the CO_2 intensity of the firms (a value that describes how much emission reductions have been made in comparison to overall emissions, excluding external parameters such as economic growth). While the official goal, set in an overall target agreement between the agency and the Federal government, was a reduction to 80% CO_2 intensity by the year 2012, an actual reduction to 65% was reached taking all firms together - see figure 17 (cf. EnAW, 2014). A representative from the Energy Agency argued as follows in an interview: »*The incentive worked since there was a binding target - but the economy had complete freedom in how to achieve it. According to the first CO_2 law, fossil fuel emissions should be reduced about 15% by 2012 compared to 1990. With regard to the companies in the Energy Agency a reduction of 25 % was reached by means of the reduction commitments.*« (interview 01-03, transl., for a detailed evaluation of the reduction commitments cf. also SFOE, 2009). Figure 17 shows that, already from 2004 onwards, when the first efforts were made due to the foreseeable implementation of the levy, the CO_2 intensity of the companies decreased.

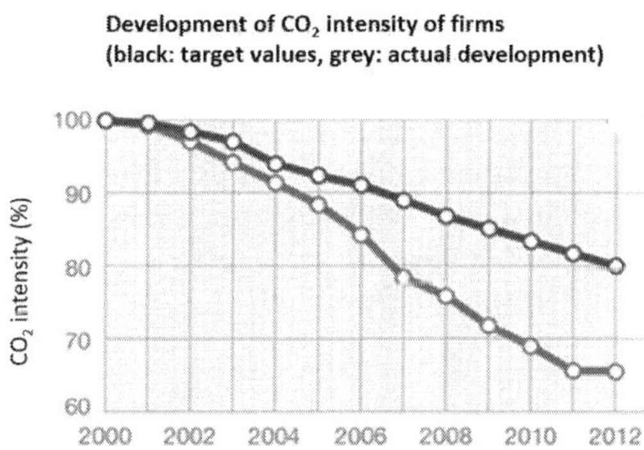

Figure 17: Development of CO_2 intensity of Swiss companies in the EnAW (EnAW, 2014, p. 15)

Thus, overall, the reduction commitments that came into force due to the levy had a large effect: »*I can tell you as an economic expert - the industry would have done massively less without the levy. So it is a nice example that the government should set long-term and binding framing conditions, also with punishment, but enable complete flexibility for the economy how to reach the targets [...] Economically justifiable and cost-efficient means could be realized [...] Unfortunately, for the second commitment period from 2013 to 2020, this flexibility is reduced. However, in the first period the industry showed that it can work.*« (interview 01-03, transl.).

Since the reduction commitments for large firms were transformed into registered emission rights (according to the CO_2 ordinance, paragraph 12; Swiss Confederation, 2005), a national market for the trading of emissions emerged (the so-called Swiss emission trading scheme, cf. article 15, revised CO_2 law,). The levy was the decisive element for this: »*With the help of the penal component of the levy, the emission trading system could be implemented.*« (interview 01-05, transl.). In the commitment period from 2008 to 2012, 440 companies participated in the scheme (cf. FOEN, 2014b). However, actual trading did not take place among the companies in this period (»*I have not recognized one single trade - one reason was that there was no overall limit of emission rights.*«, interview 01-03, transl.; cf. also in more detail Krysiak & Oberauner, 2010). Around 80% of the companies had a surplus of emission rights due to an excess allocation at the beginning and an overfulfillment of goals (cf. FOEN, 2014b).

Most of the emission rights - 1,3 million - were thus bought up by the so-called Climate Cent initiative (which could pay a higher price compared to the trading among firms; cf. interviews 01-04 and 01-03). This initiative was established by Swiss industry organizations, such as the Swiss Fossil Fuels Association, to prevent the implementation of a levy on motor fuels (cf. chapter 6.1.1). As introduced in chapter 6.1.1, the CO_2 law from 2000 originally intended the CO_2 levy to be raised both on combustibles and motor fuels (article 7, paragraph 1; Swiss Confederation, 1999; «*Of course, the climate cent on motor fuels would not have been established without the threat of the levy.*«, interview 01-05, transl.; cf. also in more detail Niederberger, 2005). After controversy during the consultation phase on the levy, the federal government decided in 2005 on the compromise solution of a levy on combustibles and a voluntary 'Climate Cent' surcharge on motor fuels (cf. chapter 6.1.1). The Climate Cent program ran from 2005 to 2013. It introduced a surcharge of CHF 0.015 per liter on gasoline and diesel, which generated an income of about CHF 100 million per year (cf. Climate Cent Foundation, 2014). This revenue was used to buy up the emission rights from Swiss companies (»*The effect of the Climate Cent in the industry worked through buying emission rights. In the motor fuel sector in turn almost nothing happened.*«, interview 01-03, transl.). The initiative made an agreement with the Federal Department of the Environment, Transport, Energy and Communications (DETEC) to meet an overall target of reducing 17 million tons CO_2 over the commitment period from 2008 to 2012 - while at least two million tons had to stem from domestic projects. The final report of the Climate Cent initiative revealed that the target was achieved (with emission reductions of 2,7 million tons CO_2 in Switzerland and 16 million tons abroad; cf. Climate Cent Foundation, 2014). This was confirmed by the DETEC in 2013 (cf. interview 01-05). From 2013 onwards, a new mandatory emissions trading scheme was launched with 55 firms in alignment with the rules of the European scheme (cf. interview 01-03). However, according to EPFL (*forthcoming*), so far the effect has been low (cf. also Betz et al., 2015).

Taking everything into account, the levy, together with its accompanying mechanisms for exemption, led to major changes in the action strategies of Swiss firms and households (i.e. in strategy goals, resulting in actions). Ultimately, the changes coming along with reduced fossil fuel consumption can also be documented by having a look on the level of outcomes: the reduction of Swiss domestic CO_2 emissions. The evaluation of Ecoplan, EPFL and FHNW (*forthcoming*) calculates the reductions induced by the levy (cumulatively up to 2013) to 2,5 – 5,4 million tons of CO_2. While the first number represents a lower bound calculated by the general equilibrium model, the second is an upper bound estimated by the time series analysis. With a reduction in 2013 of 0,5 to 1.2 million, the levy reduced Swiss emissions to 2,5 - 6% - measured against total emissions of 20 million tons (cf. Ecoplan, EPFL and FHNW, *forthcoming*).

Accordingly, a contribution was made to the general decreasing trend of Swiss CO_2 emissions over the past decade. In the official inventory of the FOEN, the CO_2 statistics show a decrease from 2004 onwards (cf. FOEN, 2015). Figure 18 displays this development. In 2014, the FOEN declared that Switzerland has achieved its overall goal in the Kyoto Protocol from the first commitment period 2008-2012 to reduce CO_2 emissions by 10 % compared to 1990 (cf. FOEN, 2014a). With regard to the sub-goal of reducing emissions from fossil combustible fuels, a decrease of 14,2% has been achieved, i.e. a slight breach of the goal of 15 % (cf. chapter 5.1, cf. interview 01-05). In general, a representative from politics, however, was partly critical on the statistics: *»Partially such numbers get enhanced, emissions get sourced out - allocated to upstream processes or abroad - however this a general problem, it does not affect or minimize the effect of the levy itself.«* (interview 01-2, transl.).

Figure 18: Energy-induced CO_2 emissions from fossil combustible fuels (from 1990 to 2014 in million tons, adapted from FOEN, 2015, p. 7)

Revenue of the levy (realized actions and institutionalization processes; socio-economic framing conditions)

As prescribed by the CO_2 law, Swiss households and firms get a refunding of their levy payments (cf. article 34 ff., revised CO_2 law, Swiss Confederation, 2011). With regard to households, the refunding so far had no further impact due to small amounts (*»The amount per capita so far is too low for the people to get recognized, they do not notice it on the bill of the health insurance companies. An information bulletin is attached but it gets lost in the general bill.«*, interview 01-04, transl.). According to a representative survey among the Swiss population (conducted by the research and consulting agency INFRAS on behalf of the FOEN), only 24% of respondents know that they get a refunding of the levy (Schwegler et al., 2015). 89% also argue that the revenue should be used instead to contribute to the expansion of renewable energies. Yet, the survey also reveals that 56% of respondents support the upward adjustment of the levy in case targets are not reached (while 38 % object it) (cf. ibid.). The impact of the refund on households might increase with higher levy rates and correspondingly higher revenues in the future (cf. OcCC, 2005 for a model calculation on the distributive impacts on households revealing that the refunding tends to favor low and medium income brackets, cf. also FOEN, 2010). In this case, the governance arrangement will also have slight effects on welfare aspects.

Yet, so far, impacts in economic terms of the levy with its refunding mechanism have been low (e.g. the creation of workplaces). This includes impacts resulting in changes on the outcome level such as in the gross domestic product, welfare and employment rates as well as distribution effects on Swiss industrial branches. There are ex-ante calculations with regard to such potential economic effects (for an overview on studies cf. e.g. Betz et al., 2015; cf. also Ecoplan, 2008; Jochem & Ott, 2005; FOEN, 2010). For instance, the DETEC (2004), highlights that a slight positive economic effect emerges, resulting in an increase of 0,1 % of the Swiss gross domestic product and of 0,2 % of employment rates. This comes along e.g. with a creation of at least 6000 jobs, a lowering of incidental wage costs and an innovation boost for efficient technologies. There is also a large amount of general scientific literature dealing with the diverse (potential) effects of carbon taxes in different countries (e.g. arguing that a double dividend effect might be obtained through economic effects; for an overview cf. e.g. Meng et al., 2013; Sumner et al., 2011). However, ex-post studies on the actual economic effects of the Swiss CO_2 levy and its refunding mechanism have not been conducted yet. Interviewees regard the effect as insignificant so far (»*I know there are studies suggesting that a levy with its refunding has economic effects - growth, employment gains, distribution effects among industries and the like - but from my point of view, we can rarely observe such effects.*«, interview 01-03, transl., »*I do not think that there were economic effects.*«, interview 01-05, transl.).

Yet, via the refunding of the levy for firms, there was an important impact with regard to the Swiss industry. As a consequence of the redistribution of the revenue to companies, the 'Swiss Climate Foundation' was founded in 2009 (»*The Climate Foundation was an additional success and unforeseen side-effect of the levy that strengthened its steering effect.*«, interview 01-03, transl.). Since the revenue is redistributed in proportion to declared wage bills, companies in the service sector (with comparatively high wage bills) receive essentially more refunding than they have paid. The non-profit foundation then enabled service enterprises to donate their net gains, i.e. their windfall profits (cf. interviews 01-05 and 01-03). The money was used for suitable emission reduction projects carried out by small and medium enterprises, i.e. reducing energy demand in production, promoting efficiency and supporting innovative products. Since 2009, the foundation supported about 1000 enterprises and invested about CHF 12 million in projects (in addition CHF 30 million were induced by start-up funding). This resulted in emission reductions of about 400 000 tons CO_2 (plus an indirect mitigation of emissions due to the boosting of innovative products) (cf. Swiss Climate Foundation, 2014).

Despite using the levy revenue for refunding, since 2011 a third of the annual revenue (at most CHF 300 million of totally about CHF 900 million per year) is invested in the building refurbishment program of the federal and cantonal governments (cf. article 34 ff., revised CO_2 law, Swiss Confederation, 2011). In order to increase the effect on the Swiss building sector, the program was established in 2010, resulting from a parliamentary initiative (»*A mechanism should be established that gets building owners to take sanitation measures. This resulted in the situation that the levy partly became a tax.*«, interview 01-05, transl.). The program includes a federal, nationwide program for the refurbishment of building shells to make them more energy-efficient. It also includes various cantonal programs for promoting renewable energy, the use of waste heat and the optimization of energy systems (cf. FOEN, 2012). As the revenue from the levy is the most important means for financing the program (in average about CHF 200 million come from the revenue, another CHF 80 million from cantonal investments, cf. FOEN, 2012), it could not exist without the levy (»*The building program could not be financed without the levy [...] If the revenue could not be used, the program would end since the federal and cantonal governments do not have the corresponding budget and politically it is not feasible to create extra budgets.*«, interview 01-04, transl.). Since 2010, the program invested about CHF one billion in the measures (cf. interview 01-05).

Apart from this, another CHF 25 million of the levy revenue is allocated each year in a technology fund (cf. article 34ff., revised CO_2 law), created by the federal government (again resulting from a parliamentary initiative). It aims to promote innovative technologies that reduce greenhouse gas emissions and the consumption of resources, to support the use of renewable energy and increase energy efficiency. It has been operative since the beginning of 2015. The government provides loan guarantees to lower the hurdle for innovative companies to get the necessary financing in place. The financing from the levy revenue is used to cover losses on the guarantee (cf. interview 01-03; FOEN, 2012).

Changes in discourses (informational-cognitive and political-institutional frame conditions; strategy goals of firms; actor constellations)

The governance arrangement induced some discourse changes, materialized by shifts in the informational-cognitive and political-institutional environment. First of all, a certain change among firms was recognized among interviewees. A representative of the FOEN argued that »*thanks to the levy, the energy and CO_2 issue generally rose on the priority list of companies. It has induced a shift in the perception of the issue, especially consumption of fossil fuels. So it indeed triggered change in this regard, a process could be initiated that companies increasingly consider the subject.*« (interview 01-05, transl.). Another interviewee argued: »*Companies now actually deal with the topic - thinking about their energy sources - I do not think this would have happened without the levy and the accompanying mechanisms.*« (interview 01-04, transl.). The shift was also confirmed by a representative of the EnAW, who argued from its internal point of view: »*I think the levy has indeed made a lasting effect in terms of getting production processes more sustainable - a more rational use of energy and a conscious move to less carbon-intensive fuels toward renewables and increasing energy efficiency. And this is not only in the short-run, but you change behavior of companies in the long-term, so you have alterations both in terms of technical aspects and in terms of thinking - in people's heads.*« (interview 01-03, transl.).

Apart from that, the governance arrangement marked an important shift in Swiss energy and climate policy and the debate on policy instruments. More specifically, it designated a reorientation from solely voluntary instruments - as intended initially by the CO_2 law and implemented in the context of the Swiss Energy program - towards more stringent, regulatory measures. As Brönnimann et al. (2014, p. 18) argue: »*The tax marked a turn in Swiss climate policy and reanimated discussions about the introduction of different CO_2 instruments.*« This also had an influence on the constellations of actors and their power in the field, for instance, during the consultation phase on the levy (see also chapter 6.1.1). A reorganization of actors took place - since arguing for solely voluntary measures was no longer reasonable, while in return the implementation of a levy became possible: »*Between the first phase of voluntary measures (1995-2000) and the second phase where the tax was negotiated (2002-2008), political parties, industry and transport representatives changed positions and strate-*

gies.« (ibid., p. 19; cf. also the final evaluation of the Swiss Energy program, SFOE, 2011; as well as Sager et al, 2014; Ingold, & Varone, 2012).

6.3.2 Electricity saving fund

Actors that were mainly affected by the governance arrangement around the electricity saving fund Basel - in the sense that changes in their action strategies were induced - pertained to three groups. The first group consisted of all electricity-consuming actors resident in the canton Basel-City, particularly households and firms (with the exception of large-scale firms). Actors belonging to this group were mostly affected through three interfaces to the governance arrangement: through the levy on power consumption collected in conjunction with the electricity bill, through the bonus refunding system that pays back the earned revenue each year (to households per capita and firms per workspace according to the wage bills), and finally through information measures (e.g. the information brochure sent yearly in conjunction with the bonus). The second group entailed actors, who participated in the consultation phase in conjunction with the new energy law. The interfaces in this case are all acts and procedures that stand in connection with the phase. The third group consisted of political-administrative actors from affected governance arrangements that are influenced in their development or results by the electricity saving fund arrangement (e.g. through formal and informal information exchange among the actors from the arrangements). This is especially the case since the arrangement attracted interest as a role model due to its pioneer character. In what follows, the most relevant changes in the action strategies of the three actor groups are presented.

Electricity consumption, efficiency measures and accompanying effects (realized actions and institutionalization processes; strategy goals of households and firms)

As introduced in chapter 6.1.2, the background situation at the beginning of the governance arrangement was characterized by strongly decreasing electricity tariffs in the canton Basel-City. By means of the regulatory levy, the arrangement held the tariffs constant through raising the relative prices of power consumption. From a macro-economic perspective, the levy raised the too low electricity tariffs when considering external costs (cf. SFOE, 2003 and 2004). According to the Swiss Federal Office of Energy (SFOE), the increase (per kWh between 3,1 and 6 centime) was able to internalize the external costs that arise in conjunction with electricity production. It quantifies this reduction of external costs about CHF five million per year (cf. ibid.). Basically, the arrangement thus provided incentives for firms and households to reduce electricity consumption.

Generally speaking, a change in the behavior of firms and households in this respect could be induced through different stimuli. On the one hand, behavior could be affected towards a more economical usage, e.g. through an alteration in material strategy goals (a change in economic interests through the higher price for consumption), or immaterial goals (a change in the attitude towards consumption, e.g. through higher environmental consciousness due to information measures). On the other hand, behavior could change in terms of promoting efficiency measures, e.g. induced by increased material resources (gained through the bonus with an impulse to use in in the same domain) or changes in immaterial resources (knowledge about efficient devices). In general, the arrangement set price signals towards more efficiency - making investments for devices that substitute energy-intensive ones more profitable, i.e. reducing financial barriers by shortening payback times (»*The disposition to buy in terms of efficiency measures increased crucially because of the levy.*«, interview 02-05, transl.).

In the year 2003, the SFOE published an official evaluation of the electricity saving fund. Within the evaluation, the SFOE quantifies an annual saving potential in terms of electricity between 33 and 100 gigawatt hours (GWh) (and of according electricity costs of about CHF ten million) (cf. SFOE, 2003). It is argued that - in light of the fact that the annual saving potential of the Swiss Energy program with regard to the electricity sector is about 125 gigawatt hours - this potential is significant (cf. ibid.).[25] Similarly, Rechsteiner (2002) estimates electricity savings between 114 and

25 Although the contribution could be higher if large-scale firms were included, which contribute around one third to the total electricity consumption.

200 gigawatt hours (and annual savings of CHF 15 to 26 million compared to executive costs under CHF 0,3 million).

Statistics about the actual development of electricity consumption show that compared to the overall development in Switzerland, the trend in Basel-City is pointing towards larger savings (see Statistical office of the canton Basel-City, 2015). While there was an overall increase of electricity use in Switzerland of 14,1% between 1999 and 2009, in the canton Basel-City there was only an increase of 8,2% (despite a high increase in the gross domestic product, cf. also interview 02-04). The newest energy statistics moreover reveal that compared to the year 2010, electricity consumption in Basel-City has decreased until 2012 about 5% (cf. Statistical office of the canton Basel-City, 2015; IWB, 2015).

Brutschin[26] (2012, p. 4, transl.) argues in view of the electricity saving fund that »*there are indeed indications for a change in the behavior of electricity consumers.*« In line with this, according to a representative of the trade association, efficiency measures among firms have increased: »*Change among the firms could indeed be recognized due to the shorter payback times - maybe not very systematically but a lot happened in this direction.*« (interview 02-03, transl.). It was further argued by interviewees that through the incentives for electricity savings, new internal energy commissioners were established among firms: »*Industries installed new positions that are in charge of environmental and energy issues when they realized that nobody was responsible for this so far.*« (interview 02-04, transl.). Moreover, the number of firms that made use of external energy-related advisory services increased: »*Gradually, more and more people thought `Well, let`s contract an energy specialist and see if he can give us some advice` [...] This also happened in other locations, when the firms had additional branch offices there - however, it needed people who took the reins.*« (cf. interview 02-03). The arrangement thus set incentives for market players to get informed about their power efficiency and electricity saving potential. Firms also aimed to understand in detail if they do or do not profit from the measures in the end (cf. interview 02-04).

---

26 The author is the principal of the department for economics, social policy and environment and a member of the governing council of the canton Basel-City.

However, the precise extent to which the electricity saving fund contributed to a lowering of electricity demand could only be quantified by means of a broadly based inquiry, which has not been conducted so far (cf. interview 02-04). Still, the saving potential mentioned above points to a contribution (for boosting the steering effect, an increase of the levy is recently being discussed among politicians - currently it equals a rise of 20 to 30% of the electricity tariffs; cf. e.g. Häne, 2015; interview 02-05). Also, the arrangement prevented an increase in electricity consumption - a situation that would have been likely without the arrangement due to the rapidly decreasing tariffs around the year 1999 (»*If it was not in place, the temptation for wasting energy would be high.*«, interview 02-05, transl.).

According to the SFOE, a relatively reduced electricity demand comes along with reduced power generation from fossil energy sources (cf. SFOE, 2003). This holds true although most electricity generation of the IWB stems from hydro energy. The SFOE argues that, due to low marginal costs of hydroelectric plants, it is profitable for power producers in Basel-City to sell electricity that is not used to other regions. Power producers in these regions using fossil energy sources with higher marginal costs are thus put out of the market (cf. ibid.). In line with this, Rechsteiner (2002, p. 10, transl.) argues that »*although Basel's electricity stems for the most part from hydro power, for the evaluation of the levy, the dynamic (marginal) observation is essential - if electricity consumption increases, the additional consumption can stem from nuclear or gas turbine power generation, so steering of consumption is needed.*«

An interviewee further argued that by maintaining the electricity tariffs, the arrangement enabled competing technologies to gain stronger currency - since they became more profitable in comparison: »*The IWB in particular could make long distance heating profitable area-wide in the canton Basel-City. Also solar panels for hot water generation and photovoltaic constructions for private use became more lucrative. In this sense, the intended mechanism worked perfectly.*« (interview 02-05, transl.). Following this perspective, the arrangement contributes to rational electricity usage by reducing incentives for substitutions in favor of electricity.

Overall, Rechsteiner (2002, p. 4, transl.) argues that »*the levy is an important milestone towards more sustainability. External costs of power generation are internalized, the levy sets market-based dynamic incentives for efficiency, operates with the polluter pays principle and is neutral regarding the public expenditure quota.*«

Reception, mood and awareness among households and firms (immaterial goals and immaterial resources; informational-cognitive cultural frame conditions)

A remarkable effect touching upon informational-cognitive and cultural frame conditions was created by shared goals among the governance administration, firms and the trade association while carrying out the bonus system. In light of these shared goals, different positions were softened and mutual trust emerged (cf. interview 02-03). Critical voices among related industries that were generally arguing against state-imposed instruments gradually became silent (except with regard to representatives from the chamber of commerce) (cf. interview 02-04). In this way, the arrangement reduced prejudices such as that the state 'always aims to constrain and thus harm the industry' (cf. ibid.). It changed the climate among industries and the trade association, making them more open to governmental measures directed at making the energy sector more sustainable: »*I think the soft factors were most essential - a certain political and societal climate towards sustainable energy measures could be furthered. In this regard, the setting was an important piece in the puzzle.*« (interview 02-03, transl.). The governance arrangement thus served to open the door to upcoming arrangements in similar areas (cf. below).

Apart from that, after implementing the levy and the bonus system, the electricity saving fund agency had lively discussions with electricity consumers about the advantages and drawbacks. Especially with energy-intensive companies the administrative board stood in close contact (cf. interview 02-04). Some industrial sectors had a rather wait-and-see attitude (»*Certain firms were slightly skeptical in the beginning, especially since large scale-consumers were exempted, although this did not cause a large outcry.*«, interview, 02-03, transl.). However, all in all, the agency had the impression that the system was received favorably by both consumer groups of households and firms (cf. interview 02-04). A representative of the trade association shared this opinion: »*The pioneer character brought about a feeling among firms that they have the opportunity to be part of an entirely new approach [...] and that they can actively co-create. This was really attractive. It was also important for the local acceptance in society as a whole.*« (interview 02-03, transl.). This is moreover backed up by a broad survey conducted in the context of the evaluation study of the SFOE (2003). A detailed understanding of the system was not prevalent - especially that the bonus is paid out irrespectively of the levy (as confirmed by an expert: »*I have the impression that firms do not understand the refunding mechanism in detail up to today.*«, cf. interview 02-03, transl.). However, the survey showed that the whole arrangement is well known and that the great majority of consumers welcomed it (correspondingly, the administration of the measures went relatively smoothly over the years[27], cf. interviews 02-03, 02-04 and 02-05). The general support in the public was documented in the year 2000 (touching upon ideas and belief systems, i.e. immaterial strategy goals and the informational-cognitive strategy environment): A nationwide referendum addressed the implementation of a regulatory levy on electricity consumption and »*the canton Basel-City was the only canton that voted for the implementation - that is remarkable*« (interview 02-04, transl.).

Furthermore, since it is possible that the sensitivity for questions of electricity among consumers would have declined without the arrangement (in the case of a strong reduction of electricity costs), »*the arrangement contributed to a stabilization in this regard*« (cf. SFOE, 2003, p. 115; interview 02-04).[28] Information activities (e.g. the annual information brochure also containing information on a different topic with regard to electricity savings) were meant to support this (cf. interview 02-04). In so doing, the arrangement in the whole conducted educational work with regard to the energy sector (the saving fund agency e.g. argued that many discussions about electricity were induced, cf. ibid.).

Firms and households and their financial net results (material resources)

Depending on their electricity consumption and due to the interplay of the levy and the bonus system, actors are financially either net beneficiaries of the arrangement or they receive a net loss. With regard to households, the

27 For instance, consumers had to make a postal application in the first year in order to get the bonus, which the vast majority did - 93% of households and 90% of firms (cf. SFOE, 2003).

28 An increase in public environmental and energy consciousness was not registered, which could be due to the fact that environmental awareness was already traditionally high in the canton Basel-City (cf. SFOE, 2003).

more energy-efficient an entity gets, the greater is the net benefit (e.g. a private person annually receives an amount of about CHF 70, cf. e.g. Häne, 2015). Since the refunding for households is based on a per capita mechanism, there is no further effect on the distribution of income. In terms of firms, generally speaking, net beneficiaries are mostly services and offices, while higher energy-consuming entities are confronted with net loss (cf. interview 02-04). The effect on the group of energy-intensive firms is relatively small since they receive a financial counterbalance. An interviewee argued that these were usually rather energy-efficient already before the implementation of the arrangement, due to economic calculus in terms of competitiveness (cf. interview 02-03).

Effects on labor costs and accompanying effects (socio-economical frame conditions)

One important impact of the governance arrangement was to contribute to reduced welfare loss in the employment market. By means of the bonus refunding for firms, which occurs proportional to the wage bills, the labor costs were reduced through a lowering of incidental wage cost (an amount of about 0,65%; cf. SFOE, 2003). The arrangement thus contributed to a relief in this regard and counteracts potential distortions on the employment market induced by wage costs (distortions that result from a high difference between gross and net pays) (cf. ibid.; cf. also Rechsteiner, 2008).

Reduced labor costs bring about two other effects. An interviewee argued that on the one hand, the offering of new job positions and employment figures gets slightly more attractive - and that the bonus system had a moderate impact in this regard: »*A firm will not provide a huge amount of job positions just because of the bonus system. However, one does indeed recognize change in this realm. It is a fixed amount that gets budgeted, people ask for it. And for a bigger company it is by now indeed a relevant value.*« (interview 02-04, transl.). On the other hand, the SFOE argues that there was also a slight increase in the location attractiveness for labor-intensive firms that profit from the electricity saving fund as net beneficiaries. Because of the refunding, the competitive position of these firms improves in comparison to firms from other regions. However, since electricity costs are only a minor location factor, this influence is small (cf. ibid.).

Consultation phase (material goals of actors and actor constellations in the field)

Further affected actors were interest groups involved in the consultation phase in conjunction with the approval of the energy law (which formed the legal basis for the arrangement). The most important actors involved were the chamber of commerce and the trade association. While the latter supported the arrangement and was a strong advocate, the former was a major opponent of the measure. It criticized amongst others the startup costs and the allocation formula for the bonus, arguing that it was a disadvantage to production firms compared to the service industry. The administrative board of the governance arrangement recognized that lobbying of both actors increased (cf. interview 02-04). Also, they increasingly tried to influence consumers in their opinions on the measures according to their positions (cf. ibid.).

Effects on other governance arrangements (political-institutional frame conditions; strategy goals of political-administrative actors)

Affected in their action strategies were also political-administrative actors from other governance arrangements, in the sense that the electricity saving fund attracted interest as a role model - due to the pioneering approach and unique characteristic in Switzerland. This especially concerns actors from the canton Basel and Switzerland, but also from abroad, due to the international pioneering character (as mentioned above, as a greening of the tax system, the measures were the first of their kind in the German-speaking countries). As the instrument of a regulatory levy in conjunction with a refunding system was a novel approach, the arrangement demonstrated the workings of such a measure (»*A system of this kind was a real exotic at these times. Thus, it was really important for the whole debate to show that such a system is actually possible and gets accepted.*«, interview 02-05, transl.). In this regard, there was an influence on the political agenda and other measures on a cantonal, national and international level.

First of all, on a cantonal level, there was a close personal exchange of information between the administrative core team and politicians from other cantons that planned to implement similar measures (for instance, with communes in Appenzell, Obwalde or the energy provider EWZ in Zurich) (»*There were politicians that appreciated our system and wanted to put forward a similar one. We then tried to present them in detail how the system works.*«, interview 02-04, transl.). Also, there were several attempts in different cantons, such as Bern, to implement a similar system (cf. e.g. Leimbacher, 2008; interview 02-04). In the canton Basel-City, there was an attempt to translate the system to the realm of renovating buildings. The arrangement furthermore induced discussions in the great council of the canton Basel-City to promote a regulatory levy on fuel oil and natural gas on the cantonal level (cf. interview 02-05). Moreover, there were attempts to further develop the electricity saving fund in the way that firms belonging to the heat sector are exempted from the levy. The aim in this case was to promote the use of heat accumulators in order to support the usage of renewable energy (which depends on energy storage), and uphold the competitiveness of electricity generated from renewables compared to oil and gas usage (»*The levy in this regard has the potential of making heat accumulators more profitable when it is designed as a percentage dynamic instrument.*«, interview 02-05, transl.).

On a national level, the electricity saving fund has served as a role model for the implementation and improvement of the Swiss CO_2 levy (»*The saving fund was clearly a precedent for the CO_2 levy and made a great impression in this regard. I was a member of the Swiss parliament and when we discussed the levy in Bern, we always looked at the system in Basel - for example, how the refunding is organized and how energy-intensive companies are dealt with.*«, interview 02-05, transl.). There was an exchange of information between the administration team and the Swiss parliament. In this way, the arrangement paved the way for solving some problems with the CO_2 levy (for instance, the electricity saving fund administration negotiated over eight years with the tax authorities regarding tax-relevant issues, i.e. that the system is not relevant in terms of the value-added tax, cf. interview 02-04). Apart from this, there were attempts to implement a Swiss national electricity saving fund based on the model of Basel (cf. the referendum in the year 2000 mentioned above, and a motion submitted to the Swiss Parliament in the year 2007 'Electricity Saving Fund according to the Basler model - Motion 07.3419'). As introduced in chapter 5.1, from 2020 onwards, the Swiss Federal Council aims to implement a nation-wide levy within the 'Energy Strategy 2050'. The system in Basel is frequently referred to as a role model (cf. e.g. Great Council of the Canton Basel-City, 2015, p. 5, transl.: »*The Confederation plans to implement a Swiss-wide levy on electricity and orients itself along the model of the canton Basel-City.*«)

Furthermore, with regard to the international level, the arrangement to a certain extent served as role model for the greening of the tax system e.g. in Germany that implemented a similar system shortly after (»*We held several lectures at congresses to German delegates and introduced the measures to give some advice as a role model.*«, interview 02-05, transl.).

6.3.3 Fuel consumption covenant

The main addressees targeted by the governance arrangement around the fuel consumption covenant were three groups: Swiss car importing firms belonging to the Association of Swiss car importers (ASIA), car retailers and manufacturers abroad (since in Switzerland, there is no domestic car manufacturing), and Swiss consumers of new passenger cars. The interface of the firms, retailers and manufactures to the arrangement were the resulting actions from the objectives of the covenant. The interface of car consumers were implemented information and marketing measures as a reaction to the covenant (such as the energy etiquette). Apart from that, political-administrative actors dealing with the transport sector were affected through the evolution of the field due to the arrangement.

Average fuel consumption of new passenger cars - failure of the covenant (actions and institutionalization processes; strategy goals of firms and car consumers)

As a reaction to the covenant, the Swiss Federal Department of the Environment, Transport, Energy and Communications (DETEC) assigned the ASIA from 2002 onwards to record, analyze and report the data of newly registered passenger cars every year. In so doing, progress with regard to the goals of the covenant should be revealed (cf. chapter 6.1.3). The ASIA thus commissioned its members, i.e. 42 Swiss passenger car import firms to annually convey their individual data. In average, data of about 98% of the newly sold cars could be annually recorded in this way (cf. ASIA, 2002-2012). The data included the fuel consumption per 100 km, the CO_2 emissions and the average net weight of newly registered passenger vehicles. They were controlled by the ASIA by plausibility check and random sampling (cf. ASIA, 2002-2012; interview 03-05). According to the covenant, a step-wise reduction of average fuel consumption from 8.4 l per 100 km (in the reference year 2000) to 6.4 l (in 2008) was required, i.e. a yearly reduction rate of 3% (cf. chapter 6.1.3).

Taking stock, average fuel consumption in Switzerland declined to 7.14 l per 100 km with yearly reduction rates of about 2% (ASIA, 2002-2012). Figure 19 displays this development in comparison to the target values of the covenant over the years. The reductions resulted in a decrease of total fuel consumption of about 6% in 2008 compared to 2000 (considering the cumulative share of newly registered cars relative to the total stock and the annual amount of fuel savings; cf. Börner, 2010). However, as it will be pointed out below, this reduction trend was furthered by other influencing factors, such as the general technical progress and the fuel price.

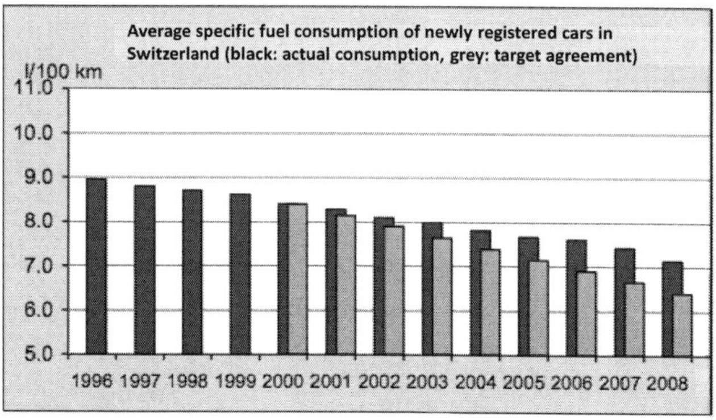

Figure 19: Covenant for fuel efficiency of new passenger cars and actual development (own illustration based on data from ASIA, 2012)

Both responsible partners acknowledged the fact that the reduction trend was influenced by other factors (cf. interviews 03-03; 03-04). Yet, they also pointed to a certain connection of the trend and the agreement. A representative from the ASIA argued in an interview: »*Yes, there was a relation between the target agreement and the reduction path [...] Well - you see, otherwise, all the measures to reach the goals would have been a waste of money. The activities were very expensive, both for the Swiss Federal Office of Energy and for the ASIA. So, all that was not to be had for nothing.*« (interview 03-04, transl.). The SFOE points out that »*Switzerland proclaims a strategy with which the agreement with the car importers are supported by better consumer information [...] These efforts take effect.*« (SFOE 2007, p. 7, transl.; cf. Spielmann & Althaus, 2007).

Despite this, there was still a considerable gap of 0.74 l per 100 km between the target value (6,4 l per 100 km) and the actual result (7,14 l per 100 km) in 2008. Accordingly, the overall goal of the covenant was missed. Besides the failure to reach the target value in average fuel consumption, the accompanying goal of the Swiss CO_2 law to reduce CO_2 emissions from the transport sector about 8% until 2010 compared to 1990 (article 2, CO_2 law, Swiss Confederation, 1999) was also missed. Emissions even increased until 2010 compared to 1990 about 13,3% (cf. SFOE, 2011a; although emissions relating to the average car were reduced from 197,5 g/km in 2002 to 161 g/km in 2008, emissions from overall transport increased due to an increasing car stock in Switzerland; cf. SFOE, 2007; ASIA, 2012).

The ASIA still regards the covenant as a success. As argued by an interviewee: »*You have to see, there was reduction in each and every year, so the whole thing was a success story, it worked [...] The automobile industry could show that we make efforts. The voluntary efforts that are made in the industry, without pressure, are underestimated. Our interest is to make reasonable efforts.*« (interview 03-04, transl.). However, a representative of the SFOE argues that it was a failure, »*since the goals of the voluntary covenant have been clearly missed*« (interview 03-03, transl.). In line with this, the final official evaluation of the Swiss Energy Program concludes that »*in the transport sector it became apparent that voluntary measures were insufficient within the scope of the Swiss Energy Program. It is an example for a policy failure*« (SFOE, 2011a, p. 129, transl.).

Impacts of information and marketing activities resulting from the covenant (realized actions and institutionalization processes; strategy goals of consumers and firms; informational-cognitive environment)

Despite the failure of the goals of the covenant, a reduction trend in average fuel consumption took place. In the following, the influencing factors behind this trend will be further investigated, i.e. exploring if it can be traced back to changes in action strategies of consumers, importing firms and / or manufacturers. Basically, the strategies of these groups could potentially be affected by the information and marketing activities that were realized by both the ASIA and the SFOE as a reaction to the covenant.

The most important activity was the energy label system for passenger cars (energy etiquette), implemented by the SFOE in 2003. The etiquette made it required by law to declare the energy efficiency of newly sold passenger cars (cf. chapter 6.1.3). It was officially launched in order to help the car industry reach the goals of the covenant (cf. DETEC, 2003). The ASIA and the Swiss Federal Roads Office supported the implementation (cf. interview 03-02). Apart from this, several other information activities in the context of the Swiss Energy Program were supported by the SFOE (such as an information catalogue on fuel consumption by the Touring Club Switzerland and an orientation manual on efficient passenger cars by the association of traffic participants in Switzerland) (cf. SFOE, 2005). Furthermore, the ASIA realized certain information and marketing activities on its own. Annual reports published by the ASIA from 2002 to the end of the covenant in 2008 state that the covenant induced certain activities (cf. ASIA, 2002-2012). Most importantly, the information and marketing campaign ′smart drive′ was launched that entailed different means to promote energy efficiency (such as promoting efficient cars on the ′Geneva International Motor Show′ and different campaigns like the ′environmental test′ with which consumers could calculate the emissions of cars; cf. interview 03-04). The campaign was supported with an annual budget of CHF 1.5 million between 2005 and 2008 (cf. Börner, 2010). Additional activities were the declaration of the specific fuel consumption of cars in price lists and the promotion of diesel vehicles (e.g. by demo models and information brochures), pushing the import firms to influence manufacturers to acquire more efficient cars (cf. ASIA, 2002-2012).

With regard to the *action strategies of consumers* of Swiss passenger cars, the energy etiquette increased the degree of transparency as an orientation guide. According to a representative of the SFOE, it *»served as a uniform benchmark to compare passenger cars [...] and led to a more rational decision to purchase«* (interview 03-02, transl.). In an evaluation of the SFOE that includes a survey among passenger car buyers, 70% of respondents declared familiarity with the etiquette (SFOE, 2005). A similar market analysis furthermore highlighted that the way the label functioned was well understood among about 75% of buyers (SFOE, 2003). According to data from the Touring Club Switzerland, about two thirds of consumers were interested in the etiquette (SFOE, 2005). The survey by the SFOE furthermore reveals that in terms of consumers of smaller cars, a car labeled with the highest efficiency category A increases the likelihood to be purchased by 6% compared to the lowest category G (for bigger cars, results are not significant) (SFOE, 2005). Moreover, the etiquette increases the market share of the highest efficiency categories A and B of about 2% (ibid.). However, the study also reveals that the etiquette overall is relevant for the decision to purchase for only a minority of 5 to 10 per cent of consumers, since energy demand is not a priority criterion in terms of purchase (ibid.). With regard to the energetic effect of the etiquette due to the cars sold to consumers, the SFOE states that it results in a reduction of the specific fuel consumption of about 0,4 per cent per year (40 terajoule, TJ), leading to an annual reduction of CO_2 emissions of 3000 t (cf. ibid.). The latest evaluation of the first period of the Swiss Energy Program in the year 2011 confirmed this energetic effect (SFOE, 2011b). Yet, compared to the project with the highest contribution to the Program, the Minergie label (cf. chapter 6.3.5) with an annual energetic effect of 1145 TJ per year, this number is comparatively low (cf. SFOE, 2011a). Due to the *»contribution of 0,4% to the annual reduction goal of 3% as formulated in the covenant, [the SFOE] evaluates the etiquette as positive [...] However it does not suffice for reaching the reduction goals of the agreement [between the DETEC and ASIA]«* (cf. SFOE, 2005, p. 8, transl.).

With regard to the effect of the several accompanying information activities supported in the context of the Swiss Energy Program (the information catalogue by the Touring Club Switzerland and the orientation manual by the association of traffic participants), the evaluation of the SFOE assesses the *»the effect of these activities as very low overall«* (SFOE, 2005, p. 78, transl.). Asked for the success of information and marketing activities by the ASIA, a representative argued: *»The marketing activities aimed at increasing the demand for efficient cars among consumers by placing special emphasis on efficiency instead on performance as it was long the case [...] In the end you need a buyer. You come up with new efficient technology but if you do not find a buyer, it is all for nothing [...] And development over time shows a reaction of the consumer, a change in consumer behavior [...] For instance, in the showroom, consumers increasingly asked for efficiency.«* (interview 03-04, transl.). This statement points to changes in the strategy goals of consumers. However, according to a study of De Haan (2007) that analyzes the buying criteria with regard to passenger cars, energy efficiency is relevant for the purchase decision of only a minority of consumers (in accordance with the evaluation of the SFOE). The most important influencing factors mentioned are utility (such as size), brand, price, design and security (cf. De Haan, 2007), *»with efficiency at the sixth position for buyers of small cars* *and at the tenth position for bigger ones*« (SFOE, 2005, p. 71, transl.). Additionally if energy demand is relevant, »*it is in most times due to financial reasons and not ecological ones.*« (ibid., p. 67).

Moreover, as already mentioned above, in the period of the covenant from 2002 to 2008, there was a strong trend among Swiss consumers towards heavy cars with higher performances - especially sport utility vehicles - with much higher average fuel consumption than smaller cars (during the period the net weight increased from 1380 to 1500 kg - per 100 kg additional weight, a passenger car consumes about 0,5 l more fuel per 100 km; cf. SFOE, 2015). The fact that the net weight increased does not mean that no sensitization among consumers towards more efficiency took place at all. Also in the same vehicle class, efficiency gains can be reached, e.g. though the switchover to smaller engines. Yet, a rethinking among consumers in the sense of a fundamental change towards driving efficient - and thus also smaller - cars did not take place. The increase of the average net weight of passenger cars was regarded by both the ASIA and the SFOE as a hindrance (»*The achievements would have been much higher if the net weight of the Swiss car stock had not increased.*«, interview 03-04, transl.; cf. also interview 03-03). This trend was accompanied with the mechanism of the energy etiquette to relate efficiency with vehicle weight. Heavy cars could thus be labeled with the highest efficiency category (cf. ASIA, 2002-2012; Börner, 2010, interview 03-03). Seen in relation to the goals of the covenant, this led to the situation that cars with higher average consumption than the target value addressed by the agreement (6.4 l per 100 km) could be labeled with the highest efficiency category (this was targeted by revisions of the etiquette in 2006 and 2011; cf. SFOE, 2011b).

With regard to the *action strategies of car manufactures*, the covenant had no influence: »*Switzerland at best matriculates 300 000 cars per year, this is what Germany does in one month. So no car manufacturer explicitly produces cars for the small market of Switzerland with a market share of 2% [...] Thus, there was no influence on car manufacturers, no, that would be unrealistic to say.*«, interview 03-04, transl.). Alberini et al. (2014) also argue that manufacturers are un-likely to modify their models just for the small Swiss market. Apart from this, the time frame of the covenant of six years is a short time span in view of the innovation cycle for designing new cars (cf. e.g. Quandt, 2010).

In terms of the *action strategies of the Swiss car importers and retailers*, the effect of the covenant must also be considered as low. A broad survey by Börner (2010) among the firms based on expert interviews with 15 directors in light of the covenant revealed the following results. First of all, knowledge at the firms about the covenant was rather poor, and few respondents could explain the contract. The majority referred to the ASIA for details (Börner 2010). While a representative of the ASIA argues »*that the agreement was heavily discussed among importers [...] and the members of an association have to agree when an association signs a contract*« (interview 03-01, transl.), the survey from Börner (2010 p. 14) points out that firms were »*badly informed about aims and measures of the agreement.*« These results are backed up by the final official evaluation of the Swiss Energy Program conducted on behalf of the SFOE, which also took a look at the covenant (SFOE, 2011a). The study argues that it was not clear who was responsible for implementing measures - the firms, the ASIA or the SFOE - and that firms passed along the responsibility. This was reinforced by the fact that the agreement addressed a whole sector and lacked individual targets for firms. Börner (2010) further argues that firms face an incentive to 'free ride' on other firms efforts, since no individual firm targets were set and achieving the overall target thus becomes a public good. Quandt (2010) states in this regard that the scope of activities to be taken by firms is limited - since they rely on the products of the car manufacturer (cf. also interview 03-05; cf. in this regard also e.g. Lienhard, 2006, for general risks of public-private partnerships, such as the asymmetrical dissemination of information, an opportunistic behavior of private enterprises, a lack of transparency as well as uncertainties in task fulfillment and control deficiencies).

When it comes specifically to the energy etiquette, the evaluation study by the SFOE concludes that the implementation by the industry is very good, however, the etiquette is scarcely used as a sales argument (SFOE, 2005). The correct application by the firms was controlled every year by the Touring Club Switzerland and corrected in case of shortcomings (cf. interview 03-01). Over the years, the number of new cars that were equipped with a complete correct application of the energy etiquette increased from 2003 to 2008 from about 70% to about 90% (cf. Touring Club Switzerland, 2008). Apart from this, the impact of the etiquette on firms - e.g. in the sense of changed strategy goals - was low (»*In case of explicitly efficient cars, the etiquette might be promoted, but regularly it has no effect on the firms.*«, interview 03-02, transl.; cf. interview 03-05).

Summing up the findings, the action strategies of manufacturers and firms did not change due to the governance arrangement. Those of consumers changed only to a small degree for certain groups. Against this background, it is likely that the most important factor for the reduction achievements was the autonomous technical progress. This would have occurred also without the covenant. A representative of the ASIA confirmed that »*the essential driver is the technical development - engineering achievements - that is for sure [...] Efficient technology is just state of the art and you cannot swim against the stream*« (interview 03-04, transl.). He also argued »*that the fuel prices also plays a role*« (ibid.).

Pointing to an increase of the average fuel price (Bleifrei-95) from about CHF 1,30 in the year 2002 to about CHF 1,80 in the year 2008, Börner (2010, p. 14) also argues that »*one of the most important factors explaining the reduction achievements was the rise of the oil price having the effect of an indirect fuel tax.*« She furthermore complains about considerable shortcomings in the covenant´s design since it provided neither financial incentives nor sanction mechanisms (cf. Börner, 2010). The SFOE also argues in this direction (SFOE, 2011a; interview 03-03). As it will be shown below, this provoked the SFOE to react to the failure of the covenant with more stringent measures some years later.

Reactions on the failure of the covenant (realized actions and institutionalization processes; political-institutional frame conditions; strategy goals of political-administrative actors)

Since the covenant did not include any sanction mechanisms in case of non-compliance, the failure to reach the formulated goals had no direct effect on the transport sector (cf. interview 03-02). Originally, as intended by the CO_2 law, a levy on motor fuels should have been introduced in the event that voluntary measures turn out to be insufficient (article 6, CO_2 law, Swiss Confederation, 1999). In fact, Börner (2010) argues, that firms in the survey argued from a strategic point of view that the voluntary covenant had been signed in order to avoid the introduction of a levy. However, this was the case only at the beginning of the arrangement. In the further development, the threat turned out to be not credible. As revealed in chapter 6.1.1, a levy on motor fuels had little chance to get implemented. This was due to active lobbying of market actors like the Swiss Fossil Fuels Association. Also, there were strong opponents in the Federal Council, referring to the loss of earnings from the mineral oil tax as an important source of income for the federal budget (cf. SFOE, 2011a). Accordingly, »*a levy on motor fuels certainly had no chance to be implemented due to a lack of majorities*« (interview 03-02, transl.).

Due to the failure of the voluntary covenant, the SFOE stated that - since the target agreement was based on a voluntary basis and the Federation cannot impose sanctions on the ASIA - it aims to make reduction targets legally binding in the future (cf. SFOE, 2009). Efforts made by the ASIA to implement a novel voluntary agreement instead of legal measures were met with resistance by politics: »*We really tried everything to make a new voluntary contract [...] We argued that we now have experience with such a means, that the covenant worked - although our opponents argue differently. But this is nonsense, we had a clear reduction development as shown by the measured data [...] Yet, a new covenant just did not work out politically.*« (interview 03-04, transl.). Against this background, the Swiss government implemented the first binding measure in the transport sector from 2012 onwards: legally binding CO_2 emission regulations for newly registered passenger cars (analogous to the European Union). The regulations apply to all Swiss importers of new cars. They are required to reduce the level of CO_2 emissions from cars registered in Switzerland to an average of 130 grams per kilometer by 2015 (cf. DETEC, 2013; cf. also interview 03-02). This corresponds to an average fuel consumption of about 5,3 l per 100 km (cf. SFOE, 2011a). The target is designated to be reduced to 95 grams by 2020. If the emissions per kilometer exceed the target level, a penalty applies (cf. interview 03-02).

The DETEC clearly states that the implementation was a result of the failure of the covenant: »*The ASIA and the DETEC had an agreement to reduce average fuel consumption to 6,4 l per 100 km until 2008. Although consumption declined, the goal was clearly missed, the decline was much slower than scheduled. Thus, it was clear that more stringent measures needed to be implemented.*« (cf. DETEC, 2013, p. 1, transl.). As a representative of the SFOE argued in an interview, »*for sure, the introduction of a sovereign regulatory measure by the government was absolutely a reaction to missing the goals of the voluntary covenant [...] We then used the window of opportunity due to the regulations on the European level*« (interview 03-02, transl.). While the information and marketing campaigns before were demand-oriented, to change the action strategies of consumers, the regulatory measure was targeted at the supply side. As an expert argued: »*I clearly want to highlight that to influence decisions to purchase of consumers is really difficult, that is a heavy challenge - so we now address the supply side.*« (interview 03-03, transl.).

In view of a comparison of the development of average fuel consumption before and after 2008 - i.e. a situation with a voluntary means in comparison to a situation with a binding one, cf. figure 20 - a representative from the SFOE argued: »*There is a sharp fall of the curves from 2007 and 2008 onwards, both regarding diesel and gasoline cars [...] This was the time where it was clear that the 130 g target will come - in 2009 the European ordinance was established and already in advance there was a reaction by manufactures [...] The decline until today can be traced back to this - the binding target has resulted in the fall. Up to now there have been few sanctions - so the measure functions well [...] Our evaluation reveals that it accelerated the reduction beyond the technical progress [...] So, a declining path is reachable by politics [...]. In comparison, the voluntary covenant did not have such an effect.*« (interview 03-03, transl.).

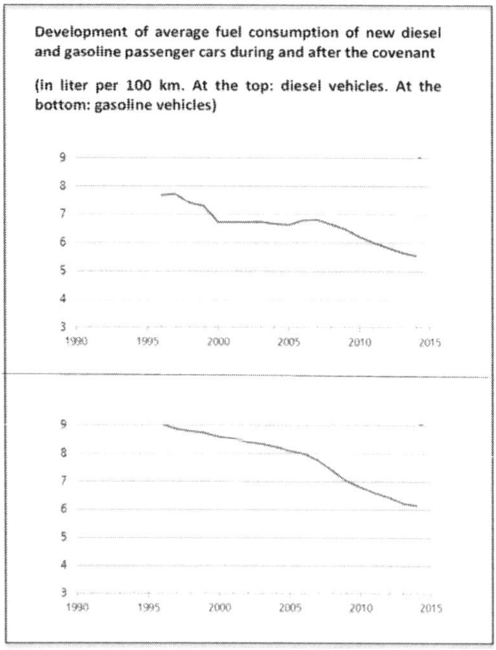

Figure 20: Average fuel consumption of new diesel and gasoline cars during and after the covenant (in liter per 100 km. Above: diesel vehicles. Below: gasoline vehicles. Own illustration based on data from SFOE, 2015)

6.3.4 Energy Trialogue

The main addressees targeted by the Energy Trialogue were federal and cantonal politicians. The outputs of the two project phases of the Trialogue (cf. chapter 6.1.4) both included recommendations for politics. However, as it will be pointed out below, the arrangement did not affect political-administrative actors in the sense that a change in their action strategies took place. The main actually affected actors were those groups that also participated in governance workings - including, public, market and civil society actors. These actors were affected through learning processes induced throughout the Trialogue, with a potential effect on these actors after the governance arrangement was terminated.

Failure of realized projects and influence on Swiss energy policy (actions and institutionalization processes)

Overall, the analysis of expert interviews, official documents and existing research on the case did not reveal changes in action strategies that included actual actions or institutionalization processes. First of all, actions could not be induced since there were no activities for realizing the goals and measures of the first Trialogue project - as proposed in the final strategy report from 2009. As a matter of fact, plans in this regard were proclaimed by the Energy Trialogue association, announced in the program for the year 2010 and upcoming years. On the one hand, results should be communicated to cantonal executives, representatives from economy and society as well as institutions abroad in order to discuss the proposed measures. Moreover, projects should be introduced to realize the measures, while participants of the Trialogue should be engaged in consulting activities in this regard. Finally, cantonal and communal concepts for transferring the measures on lower levels of government should be designed (since the goals of the Trialogue are targeted at the national and international level (cf. Büsser, 2010; cf. also the official webpage of the Trialogue). Yet, the only explicit further concept for realizing the measures was a study on the metropolitan region of Basel (cf. Metrobasel, 2010), which is - however - not referred to in the current energy strategy of Basel (cf. AUE, 2012). Since the canton Aargau was the host of the Trialogue, its results build a foundation for the energy policy of the canton Aargau (cf. interviews 04-03 and 04-04). Yet, concrete projects that explicitly promoted the goals from the Trialogue could not be found. Overall, it can be said that there were no actual activities for institutionalizing the goals and measures proclaimed by the Trialogue: »*There were no direct projects for implementation, no - there is also no study of whether the Trialogue was the actual trigger for a certain activity. This would also be very difficult since most people would sell such activities as being an initiative on their own. So it is in general very difficult to identify effects induced by the Trialogue at all.*« (interview 04-04, transl.).

Against this backdrop, one interviewee stressed that the Trialogue should mainly be seen as a preparation for politics, that it ought to »*induce impulses for politics, and not install a 'co-existing organization' to actual politics. I observed that politicians do not like such co-existing projects since they feel that they interfere with their competencies*«, interview 04-03, transl.). Accordingly, the main addressee of the Trialogue was federal politics. The Trialogue as an approach that brings together all different groups of society should function as a catalyst for politics with majority appeal, and the results should be incorporated into the legislative processes. After the publication of the two final reports in 2009 and 2013, the results were thus communicated to the energy commissions of the National Council and the Council of States, as well as to the Federal Department of the Environment, Transport, Energy and Communications (cf. interviews 04-04 and 04-03; the second report also included explicit recommendations for federal politics).

Yet, the analysis of expert interviews, existing research and documents did not reveal that actual changes in politics were induced. This holds true with regard to both project phases. First of all, the interviewees referred to fixed strategies of politicians from the federal level in this regard. As one interviewee pointed out: »*In both project phases, we presented the results in more than ten events with different audiences. With regard to politicians, presentations were given to the energy commission of the National Council and the Council of States. [...] However, the positions of the politicians were static in this regard. In general, it was difficult to achieve anything at all, to change opinions based on factual data [...] Politics function differently. Here it is important to have a strict opinion, find partners and build coalitions. Factual arguments are inferior.*« (interview 04-04, transl.; cf. also press releases by the Committee for Environment, Spatial Planning and Energy of the National Council and the Council of States during the years 2009 and 2013).

An analysis of the official documents from the Swiss Federal Council on energy policy backed up these statements. As introduced in chapter 5.1, from 2011 onwards, the Swiss Federal Council has promoted a new 'Energy Strategy 2050'. In the final report on the results of the consultation phase to the first package of measures for implementing the strategy, there is no reference at all to the report of the Trialogue, its goals or results (cf. DETEC, 2013). Moreover, there is also no reference within the official 'Message from the Federal Council' to the Federal Assembly of Switzerland concerning the Energy Strategy in the year 2013 (cf. Swiss Federal Council, 2013). Schips (2013, p. 62) argues in line with this that »*the Trialogue has pointed out important correlations for the success of the 'Swiss Energy Strategy 2050'. However, the 'Message from the Federal Council' from 2013 does not include these interdependencies.*« Naturally, there are indeed some statistics and targets that are similar to those in the Trialogue reports, for instance with regard to the topic of hydropower. However, as one interviewee argued in this regard: »*Politics had their own sources to develop the 'Energy Strategy 2050', for the most part the scientific consulting institute Prognos AG.*« (interview 04-04, transl.).

Finally, the analysis was backed up by two requests for short written statements sent to representatives of the Swiss Federal Office of Energy and the scientific consulting institute Prognos AG (which functioned as a major consulting institute for the Federal Office regarding energy policy). The received statements highlight that the Trialogue had no influence on the 'Energy Strategy 2050' and that a general influence on Swiss energy policy was not noticed (cf. short statements 04-01 and 04-02). Accordingly, it can be concluded that the action strategies of politicians responsible for Swiss energy policy did not change due to the Energy Trialogue.

Learning processes of participating actors, consensus building (strategy goals and immaterial resources of participants; informational-cognitive cultural environment; actor constellations)

The stakeholders participating in the Trialogue came from various backgrounds and exchanged information in a protected area. In the first project phase, the stakeholders increased their knowledge with regard to general Swiss energy policy and the core group reached a consensus in terms of certain - former controversial - topics, such as the existence of a future Swiss power supply gap (cf. interviews 04-03 and 04-04). The second project then contributed to increasing the knowledge of participants in terms of the 'Energy Strategy 2050' of the Federal Council.

Although the analysis did not reveal an influence on the Swiss energy discourse as a whole (cf. in this regard also the critics complaining about the consideration of interest and the according failure of penetration, e.g. Studerus, 2011; Meier, 2010), certain other effects occurred. First of all, the leadership of the Trialogue passed their gained knowledge for guiding organizations that host similar multi-stakeholder discussion processes (e.g. a project by the Federal Office of the Environment on Biodiversity, cf. interview 04-04). Moreover, in 2015 a further Trialogue was initiated by the canton Aargau on waste disposal with representatives from about twenty organizations (cf. interview 04-03 and 04-04).

Apart from that, the Trialogue provided the participants with a protected forum or interaction. Individual statements of the participating organizations in the appendix of the final report of the second project phase document evolved learning processes: »*polarizations could be bridged here and there*«; »*the participation in the Trialogue was beneficial*«; »*the understanding of the different stakeholders has increased*«; »*although there were thematic differences, the discussions exhibited a constructive and respectful character*« (Energie Trialog Schweiz, 2013, pp. 125; 127; 131; 137; transl.). One leader of the project confirmed this in an interview: »*Once a basis of trust was established, astonishing new solutions were discussed with an added value for all parties. A change of perspectives indeed happened from time to time - for example with regard to a discussion on the appropriate use of hydro power [...] People were astonished that they could argue with political opponents based on facts.*«, interview 04-03, transl.). Since the discussions were characterized by an atmosphere of mutual respect and took place on a factual basis, participants had the opportunity to understand and learn from each other's perspectives (cf. interview 04-03; 04-04). In so doing, a more complete picture with regard to energy policy could be acquired. Other learning processes concerned the acquisition of new skills of collaboration (»*I think the organizations learned that there is another way of promoting their goals, not by arguments based on positions but on factual and scientific data.*«, interview 04-04, transl.), and increased knowledge of the existing network structures in the field of energy policy. Also, new contacts among actors in terms of network building could be made in the field (cf. interview 04-03).

These effects pertain to the strategy goals and immaterial resources of actors as well as to the informational-cognitive cultural environment and actor constellations. However, one of the most important aspects of learning in such a context is that participants act as information transmitters. This means that participants transfer new information and opinions developed in the protected area out to their individual organizations (cf. Turcotte & Pasquero, 2001; Sharma & Kearins, 2011). It is debatable whether learning processes in the case of the Trialogue were also communicated out to the 'real world', and accordingly whether action strategies changed as a result: »*The Trialogue provided a learning opportunity like no other project in place. However, the danger is that a participant, who has learned something in the Trialogue and comes back to the individual organization, experiences pressure to represent again the official opinion of the organization. It is one thing to discuss in a protected atmosphere without media, but a completely different thing to bring this out into the rough world.*«, interview 04-04, transl.). A few positive examples were given by one interviewee - referring to initiatives by the electricity industry after participating in the Trialogue to explore the potential of geothermal energy in Switzerland; and plans by the city of Zurich to promote reducing the use of fossil fuels. However, whether there is a clear correlation with the Trialogue was considered as uncertain (cf. interview 04-03). A strong counterexample is related to one of the three initiators of the second phase of the Trialogue - the Swiss Business Federation economiesuisse. First of all, it pointed out in its individual statement in the final report that »*of course the different interests will stay controversial*« (Energie Trialog Schweiz, 2013, p. 129; transl.). Remarkably, the 'economiesuisse' then was one of the few groups that voted against the first package of measures for implementing the 'Energy strategy 2050' (while the goals of the strategy are similar to those of the Trialogue) (cf. DETEC, 2013). Overall, the fact that even the strategy goals of one of the initiators of the Trialogue did not change, renders the transmission of learning processes from the protected area out to individual organizations unlikely.

6.3.5 Minergie label

The governance arrangement around the Minergie label mainly affected the action strategies of four actor groups. The first group comprised all actors dealing with the building industry, who were thus directly in contact with all developments around Minergie. This includes architects, planners and engineers (especially the official professional partners in this regard), building contractors, manufactures and suppliers, as well as investors and financial institutions. The second group consisted of end users - that is, building owners and residents, respectively employees, living or working in Minergie certified buildings. The third group entailed all collective, corporate and individual members in the Minergie association and the corresponding network. Finally, cantonal and federal public authorities were affected, especially those responsible for designing building regulations or implementing these regulations in legislation. These actors were influenced by the general prevalence of the developments around Minergie in the building industry. In the following, the most important changes in the action strategies of these actor groups are presented.

Change of legislative building regulations (realized actions and institutionalization processes; political-institutional frame conditions; strategy goals of political-administrative actors)

One of the most significant impacts of the governance arrangement around the Minergie label has been a pulling effect on cantonal public authorities and their energy policy as well as corresponding legislative bodies. As introduced in chapter 5.1, in Switzerland, the cantons are the responsible authorities for measures in the building sector. Regulations are under the jurisdiction of cantonal administrations and federal regulations only function as guiding principles (Federal Constitution, article 89, paragraph 4; cf. also Bharathi & Nicol, 2013). Against this backdrop, the cantons have established cantonal building regulations (so-called model regulations) that set up minimal heat requirements for new buildings.

As a response to Minergie, these regulations have been gradually aligned. The correlation was approved by the responsible body for the model regulations itself (the Conference of Cantonal Energy Directors): »*The standard Minergie has induced a certain development in the market, so that the cantonal regulations have been brought close to the standard.*« (EnDK, 2015, p. 9, transl.; cf. also SFOE, 2013; interviews 05-03, 05-05).

In detail, the gradual adjustment took place as follows (cf. figure 21). The original Minergie standard from 1998 set the heat requirements for new buildings to 4,2 heating-oil equivalents (liters per square meters living space) - compared to a value of 22 for conventional buildings. In 2000, the cantons modified their original regulation from 1992 to a target value of 9 heating-oil equivalents. In 2008, there was a further alignment to a value of 4,8 (cf. EnDK, 2015). Model regulations are legally binding only once a canton adopts them into law (cf. IEA, 2007). By 2012, all cantons had implemented the 2008 regulation in their legislation with correspondent laws and ordinances (cf. Sager et al., 2014; Minergie, 2015).

As a reaction to this, Minergie then gradually set stricter standards. This demonstrates a mutual influence with legislation (»*The Minergie standards were adjusted in the course of the stricter legislative requirements.*«, SFOE, 2013, p. 23; transl.). First of all, there was an adjustment of the baseline model in 2009 with a value of 3,8 heating-oil equivalents: This was followed by the more comprehensive versions Minergie-P and A (cf. chapter 5.6; for gradually adjusting the label standards and act as a dynamic pioneer, flexible structures achieved by the choice to organize Minergie as an association were of importance, cf. interview 05-03).

In turn, as a reaction, there was a further revision of the cantonal regulations in 2014 to a value of 3,5. This revision finally corresponds with the heat requirements of the basic Minergie model (while other criteria of Minergie e.g. in terms of ventilation and quality assurance were not taken over). The final revision has been adopted in January 2015. At the latest in 2018, the cantons shall implement it in their legislations (cf. EnDK, 2015).

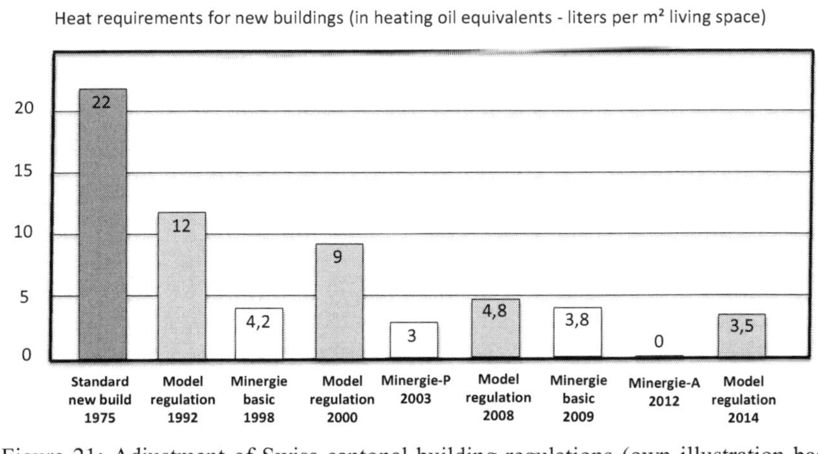

Figure 21: Adjustment of Swiss cantonal building regulations (own illustration based on data from EnDK, 2015; interview 05-04 and Beyeler et al., 2009)

Having this in mind, it can be stated that the governance arrangement around Minergie has led to major changes in political-institutional frame conditions. By means of its voluntary forerunner position, it induced a 'preparation of the field' and created the preconditions for the major increase in cantonal building requirements (and its harmonization among the cantons). This is true both with regard to the acceptance among the building industry and in terms of creating majorities among politicians. Minergie demonstrated that stricter standards are actually doable, as a large part of the building sector already built according to them. This was highlighted in an interview with a representative for a responsible political administration: »*The Minergie label as a marketing tool was a forerunner for the regulations, the field for testing where something can be tried. Once the tool worked, there was no opposition against the regulations.*« (interview 05-04, transl.). As a consequence of this change in the Swiss building discourse (cf. also below), there was no resistance against stricter cantonal regulations - since the 'field was already prepared'. Minergie is thus attributed a »*pulling effect on the legislative standards, further developing in the direction of Minergie*« (SFOE, 2005, p. 109, transl.). Before Minergie, at the time around 1990, a strengthening of the building laws would have been almost impossible due to both a lack of majority appeal among politics and acceptance in the building industry: »*The cantons could never have realized such strict building requirements without Minergie, showing that it is actually doable. It was a clear pioneering role.*« (interview 05-05, transl.).

Overall, the arrangement thus paved the way for a gradual change in legislation that would not have happened without its existence. Since the changes in political-institutional frame conditions furthermore led to an alteration in the common way of constructing conventional new buildings (cf. in more detail an evaluation of the effects of the cantonal building regulations; SFOE, 2014a), major institutionalization processes were induced in this regard by Minergie.

Certified buildings and accompanying effects (realized actions and institutionalization processes; strategy goals of end users)

Minergie had a considerable impact on the Swiss building sector and shaped it to a degree no voluntary instrument did before. Against this backdrop, the International Energy Agency argues that »*the Minergie standard sets a strong example for other countries«* (IEA 2007, p. 44). Up to the year 2016, about 40.000 new buildings of different types and sizes have been voluntarily certified by the different versions of the label (mostly single and multi-family homes as well as public buildings) (cf. interview 05-03; Minergie, 2015; cf. also data from the official webpage of Minergie). Minergie served as a ′communicative link′ between actors, i.e. as the connector between demand and supply in the property market. This communication function plays out in the way that end users (investors and financial institutions) can be sure of the building quality, as secured by architects, engineers, manufactures and suppliers.

The amount of buildings corresponds with a total amount of certified gross floor area of about 50 million square meters (cf. ibid.). The according overall market share in Switzerland in terms of the certification of new buildings has reached about 35% in the housing sector and about 25% on commercial buildings (with regional differences - for instance, in the canton Zurich, the market share is over 50%) (cf. Minergie, 2011 and 2015; Salvi & Syz, 2010). As a consequence, up to 2012, Minergie had the highest total penetration rates in the originating country among international building standards (cf. Sager et al., 2014). In view of this, Minergie represents the most successful building standard of Switzerland with »*a market penetration of sustainable buildings unmatched elsewhere in the world, showing that buildings can be both sustainable and economically competitive*« (Beyeler et al. 2009, p. 241).

With regard to the different versions of the label (see chapter 5.6), the largest part of the units is certified according to the original standard (about 36000), followed by the stricter standards of Minergie-P (about 3000), Minergie-eco (about 1400) and Minergie-A (about 350). In the past years, a slow but steady shift to the certification with the stricter versions is recognizable, with the rate in this regard increasing each year (cf. Minergie, 2015). Apart from this, with its international roll-out, there have been Minergie certifications in neighboring countries and an international transfer of gained know-how (for instance there is a license agreement with France with an established license agency, certified buildings in Liechtenstein, Italy, Germany and Austria, a Swiss village built according to the Minergie standard in Abu Dhabi as well as relations to countries such as Sweden, England, Japan, China, Korea, Russia and Chile) (cf. ibid.).

The annual reduction in energy consumption as a consequence of the certified buildings is reported to be around 200 million liters heating-oil equivalents (this equals about four times the impact of all Swiss solar energy panels and photovoltaic constructions together and corresponds to a decrease of CO_2 emission by about 400 tons per year) (cf. interview 05-03; EnDK, 2014; cf. also the evaluation study on the energy demand of Minergie buildings; EnDK, 2004). In line with this, the certification of the buildings also »*boosted the use of renewable energies since already the basic standard's energy conversion factor cannot be reached without their usage*« (interview 05-04, transl.).

Within the latest impact analysis of the Swiss Energy program (Minergie has become an important part of the program, cf. below), it is approved that with regard to energy savings, »*Minergie makes by far the largest contribution to the overall effect of the whole Swiss Energy program (23% which equals 1145 TJ per year) and has a proportion of about 50 percent of the whole energetic effect in the building sector [...] Within the duration of the whole Swiss Energy program, the contribution of Minergie has continuously increased: from the first assessment in 2002 to 2010 around 400%*« (SFOE, 2011b, p. 13 and 45; transl.). Within the final evaluation of the program covering the years from 2002 to 2010, the cumulative energetic effect of individual measures is summarized. Figure 22 shows that Minergie is the measure with the by far largest effect (cf. SFOE, 2011a, p. 81). In the latest impact analysis of the program it is furthermore pointed out that with regard to energy savings, »*Minergie has the best value in cost-effectiveness of all the measures within the program*« (SFOE 2011b, p. 5, transl.).

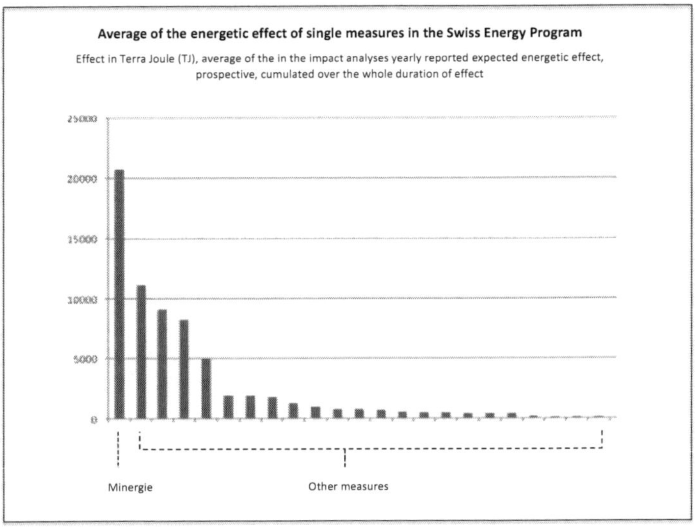

Figure 22: Average of the energetic effect of single measures in the Swiss Energy program (own illustration based on SFOE, 2011a)

Apart from energy savings, buildings certified with the Minergie-eco standard follow strict recyclability of materials plus avoidance of scarce resources and volatile organic compounds or formaldehyde (thus minimizing environmental and air pollution) (cf. Kriesi, 2009).

In terms of health aspects, residents and employees (about 400.000) attain a higher living or working comfort and thus a greater quality of life in residential or commercial buildings in Minergie certified buildings (cf. Minergie, 2015; interview 05-05). In detail, the people enjoy higher thermal comfort, heat gain protection, moisture control, reduction of dust, pollen and pests as well as a higher air quality through systematic air change (cf. interview 05-04; cf. also Hässig et al., 2003 - a study on the health effects of systematic ventilation systems, revealing a beneficial influence on room air quality). In Minergie-eco certified buildings, this is supplemented by optimized daylight conditions, low indoor air contaminant loads (in terms of hazardous substances, microbes and radiation), as well as strong noise protection (cf. Minergie, 2011). A survey among residents and employees on behalf of the Conference of Cantonal Energy Offices revealed that about 90% of the users are either satisfied or very satisfied with the living or working comfort (cf. EnDK, 2004).

In sum, the governance arrangement around Minergie has majorly changed the overall Swiss building environment with its certified buildings: »*That Switzerland builds in this energetic quality, like nobody else in Europe - this is definitely due to Minergie and a large success story.*« (interview 05-04, transl.).

Changes in the Swiss building sector through stimulated innovation and institutionalized network structures (realized actions and institutionalization processes; actor constellations)

The governance arrangement further paved the way for a large increase in the innovation of building technologies in different branches (such as ventilation systems, insulations, windows, electric heat pumps and solar thermal systems) (cf. interview 05-04). On the one hand, this is due to the fact that Minergie leaves it to the planners, architects and builders to decide on how to reach the certification requirements for certified buildings (»*If Minergie had prescribed how the houses shall be build - just as if the public sector tells the people how a sustainable building exactly looks like - this innovation would not have been possible. You have to set a general target and then certain developments and trends are induced that gradually get accepted.*«, interview 05-04, transl.). In so doing, a creative competitive struggle among developers of new technologies was induced.

On the other hand, Minergie boosted innovations by their certification system of building modules (cf. chapter 5.6). Such modules cover all kind of branches and mark the best products in its category (cf. Minergie, 2008). In so doing, they stimulate producers in terms of optimization. Minergie thus created new market segment for Swiss firms that sell these products (»*Most of these products are produced in Switzerland.*«, interview 05-05, transl.), leading to their expansion and consequently an increase in the domestic economic value (cf. below). The firms that are internationally active furthermore transfer the gained know-how to associated companies abroad (cf. Wallbaum, 2010). In turn, other companies were increasingly driven out of the market - for instance suppliers for central-heating boilers for gas and oil - due to the increasing use of heat insulation, ventilation systems and heating pumps (»*In the new builds sector, the oil and gas branches were gradually pushed aside, so there are winners and losers in the market.*«, interview 05-04, transl.; cf. also interview 05-03). Accordingly, Minergie has induced changes in the actor constellations in the building industry and in the mutual influence of actors. It has contributed to a standardization of more sustainable products and majorly shaped the general Swiss construction technique (in con-junction with a general change in the Swiss building discourse, cf. below).

Since the new technologies gradually became state of the art (i.e. accelerating the development and mainstreaming of best available technology and techniques), changes also took place in the ways for heating, venting and insulation in conventional new builds (»*Minergie had a major impact with regard to establish better technologies in general, for instance, that better windows were realized. Since Minergie is in place, the general insulation has become better.*«, interview 05-03, transl.). For instance, the usage of heat pumps in new single and multi-family houses that are not certified by Minergie »*increased to over 70% and that was undoubtedly influenced by the positive image in conjunction with the Minergie buildings*« (cf. Kriesi, 2009; p. 24, transl.). Against this backdrop, it is argued that additional to the certified Minergie buildings, »*there is roughly the same amount of buildings in Switzerland that come up to the building quality of Minergie but are not explicitly certified*« (interview 05-04, transl.). This is also due to the general improvement of knowledge in terms of more sustainable building of architects and manufactures by means of the Minergie vocational training system (cf. below).

Apart from that, Minergie has gradually institutionalized a broad Swiss network for sustainable building over the past decades, bringing together the important stakeholders in the field. In so doing, Minergie serves as the common meeting and reference point and the communication platform, from which joint action can emerge (»*Minergie has an important coupling and networking function, bringing the actors together.*«, interview 05-05, transl.). This is frequently regarded as one of the most important success factors of Minergie (cf. interview 05-05). Up to present, the network includes all stakeholders from the building industry (architects, planners, engineers, building contractors, suppliers and investors) and concerned public authorities (for instance, the steering committee of the association includes representatives from the cantonal government). It is held together by the association (which gradually increased its balance sheet total up to CHF five million, cf. interview 05-05), but also by adjacent structures, such as a vocational training system for professionals (cf. below). The network is supported by several events for professionals, building owners and end users, in line with the communication strategy of Minergie (cf.

chapter 6.1.5). The communication strategy of Minergie was awarded in 2007 with the so-called »Marketing Gold Trophy« by the Swiss Marketing Club (cf. interview 05-05; in this vein, it is argued that *»it was essential to gradually establish communication partnerships and that Minergie could be active together with the industry [...] You see, a law does not need communication, but the more voluntary a measure is, the more important communication is«*, interview 05-05, transl.).

Shaping the image and discourse of sustainable construction (informational-cognitive cultural environment; immaterial goals of actors dealing with the building industry)

The arrangement around Minergie largely shaped the image and perception of what constitutes sustainable construction, and in so doing made it socially acceptable. This impact is frequently regarded as the most important result of Minergie (cf. interviews 05-03 and 05-05, cf. also Minergie, 2011). Around the year 1990, the perception in this regard was frequently linked to narrow-minded, negative images associated with sacrifice, i.e. a spartan way of life, or highly expensive techniques. A sustainable way of building was regarded as uncomfortable, complicated in use, unreliable and difficult to sell. It was a niche only supported by ′eco-minded′ actors and forerunners, while facing strong resistance from the majority of actors in the building industry (cf. interview 05-05).

Minergie in contrast strategically connected the three primary communicated goals of comfort (and thus an increased quality of life), energy-efficiency and added value of buildings (i.e. a social, an environmental and an economic aim). In so doing, it could reach out to broader actor groups and achieve majority appeal (cf. Kriesi, 2009). With its pioneering role, the arrangement created a discourse in terms of more sustainable construction: »*Minergie virtually initiated the discussion about sustainable building single-handedly and created the preconditions for the gradual development of this discourse.*« (interview 05-05, transl.). This promoted a rethinking and the transformation of the image of sustainable construction into a more positive, modern and progressive one (cf. interview 05-03). In this regard, it was essential in the communication strategies for consumers, that a focus was put on the additional benefit through Minergie and its affordable and pragmatic approach (»*It was important that Minergie was a simple easy-to-use approach. If it is too complicated, peo-*

ple are not attracted [...] Also, Minergie changed the communicated aspects of sustainable building in contrast to regulations. Regulations frequently are reproachful in the sense of: 'you have to save energy'. Minergie in contrast put its focus on the resulting benefit.«, interview 05-05, transl.). The notion of Minergie served as an umbrella term to place these aspects on the market. In this way, aspects like energy efficiency and the use of renewable energy were revaluated (an important role for the change in perspective was the voluntary nature of the Minergie label: »*The voluntary form was essential, to achieve these changes. Building owners before 1995 [...] thought, if nobody builds sustainably voluntarily, it must be silly, so keep the hands off*«, interview 05-03, transl.; since the climate among the building industry was characterized by opposition among regulations, it was also important that Minergie started as a bottom-up movement to build trust; cf. interviews 05-03 and 05-05).

In sum, sustainable building became matter of course for new buildings of all type and size and for all social classes. As a consequence, it is also argued that Minergie contributed to a rising awareness of energy related topics as well as ecological and health aspects of building (»*The sensitization in the areas of sustainable construction is without doubt significantly due to Minergie*«, Wallbaum, 2010, p. 11; transl.). An interviewee argued that there was a large increase in terms of reporting about such topics in different media over the past decades (cf. interview 05-03).

A precondition for the discourse change was to reach high brand awareness. A study conducted on behalf of Minergie showed that already in the year 2001, 93% of architects knew the term Minergie (as quoted in Minergie, 2011). The broad acceptance among actors dealing with the building industry, end users and politics is also demonstrated by other factors. This includes the cooperation with professional partners and businesses, the cantonal application and certification - as well as the involvement of a diverse actor field in the association (the design as an association served the integration of key players, cf. interviews 05-03 and 05-05). Accordingly, Minergie has become a »*primary benchmarking tool for Swiss politics, financing mechanisms, cantons, communities and building owners*« (Bharathi & Nicol, 2013, p. 748).

Apart from this, Minergie also introduced new concepts to the discourse, such as the technical notion of a ´comfort ventilation system´. Also, it promoted the concept of a building as one coherent ´system´ to be optimized holistically by combining different technical components.

Minergie also helped reduce confusion about the meaning of several co-existent terms in the field (such as 'low energy-house' or 'eco-house'), by creating a clearly defined standard that was easy to comprehend (cf. interviews 05-03 and 05-04).

Overall, Minergie created a system of novel ideas and norms for more sustainable construction that is commonly shared by the relevant actors from the building sector and end users (»*Architects offer to build with Minergie quality, because otherwise they get fewer orders.*«, interview 05-04, transl.). Without the gradual shift in the informational-cognitive cultural environment, the cantonal regulations (cf. above) could not have been intensified to such a high degree. The sophisticated standards were mostly accepted and appreciated in the building industry already before the mandatory regulations were implemented. Due to its international pioneering role, Minergie moreover influenced the international discourse on sustain-able construction (cf. interview 05-05).

Increased know-how of building professionals through the vocational training system (realized actions and institutionalization processes; immaterial resources of professionals; informational-cognitive environment)

With the established advanced vocational training system for the planning and executive building professionals (such as architects, contractors and certification agencies, cf. chapter 6.1.5), the arrangement around Minergie has gradually institutionalized »*the largest Swiss training organization in the building industry*« (interview 05-05, transl.). This led to an increase in the know-how of the professionals in terms of more sustainable construction (the variety of upgrade training courses has about 5000 participants each year, cf. Minergie, 2015).

Trained professionals in this regard can distinguish themselves in the market with the trademarked designation of 'Minergie professional partner' (cf. ibid.). A side effect of the knowledge transfer was that »*Minergie led to a tightening of the SIA norms 3801/1 and 380/4*« (Wallbaum, 2010, p. 31; transl.), i.e. the building norms made by the Swiss Association of Architects and Engineers - Switzerland's leading association for construction, technology and environment specialists (cf. also interview 05-04).

The area-wide know-how among the actors dealing with the building industry was crucial for the general change in the Swiss building discourse and an important building block with regard to the legislative adjustments of the cantonal regulations (cf. above).

Certified buildings and their real estate value; additional investments; creation of new workplaces (socio-economic frame conditions; material resources)

The governance arrangement around Minergie moreover induced several changes in the building sector that are relevant in terms of socio-economic frame conditions. First of all, the certified buildings by the label show higher value retention compared to conventional buildings *(»It is rational for people to invest from an economic point of view due to the higher real estate value of Minergie buildings.«*, interview 01-03, transl.). This is documented by the fact that several of the largest Swiss banks assess Minergie buildings as more reliable and offer special mortgage conditions at reduced rates of interests (e.g. resulting in savings about CHF 10 0000 for single family homes) (cf. SFOE, 2011b, interview 05-04): *»This is economically reasonable. If a bank has to take back a house, it can sell it more easily if it is a Minergie building.«* (interview 05-05, transl.).

While technology development gradually devaluates buildings that do not display the latest state of the art, Minergie ensures that buildings come up to the latest standard and that risks are minimized (such as damages due to moisture) (cf. interview 05-05). Two different studies from the ′Center for Corporate Responsibility and Sustainability Zurich′ on the return on investment conclude that building owners are ready to pay 7% higher sale prices and tenants accept an additional charge of 6% on the net rent (e.g. due to the higher levels of comfort). The studies thus conclude that Minergie pays off in financial terms for investors, is honored by the market and that the buildings can be more easily retailed and rented. Additionally, the buildings have a longer life span resulting in more revenue years for building owners (cf. Salvi et al., 2008 and 2010). This is supported by the development *»that many building owners were sensitized to the need to invest more in the maintenance of the buildings as a side effect of Minergie«* (interview 05-05, transl.). Overall, the real estate value of the around 40.000 certified buildings is quantified to around CHF 100 billion (cf. Minergie, 2015; interview 05-03).

Generally speaking, Minergie has evolved as a relevant economic factor in the Swiss building industry. Approximately CHF four billon of additional investments were induced in conjunction with Minergie certified buildings (cf. interview 05-05; Kriesi, 2009), thus strengthening several innovative branches in the Swiss building sector (such as suppliers of comfort ventilation systems, thermal insulation, heat pumps, windows, solar panels etc.; cf. above). The increased know-how in sustainable building also strengthens the firms in these branches as exporters. Moreover, it is argued that savings resulting from less imported fossil energy per year due to the decreased energy demand of Minergie buildings come up to about CHF 200 million (cf. Wallbaum, 2010; interview 05-05). Accordingly, domestic investments are boosted while the net capital outflow is reduced.

Apart from saved energy costs, the result of Minergie on living and working conditions and thus on health (cf. above) leads to a saving of healthcare costs and increases the productivity of employees (»*The leverage effect in economic terms with regard to saved healthcare costs and increased productivity is much higher than saved energy costs*«, Minergie, 2008, p. 13). Moreover, it is argued that about 8500 new job positions in the Swiss building industry were created due to the development of novel market segments (corresponding to a share of about 3% in the total Swiss building industry, which accounts about 300.000 jobs, and an added value of CHF 30 billion per year) (cf. interview 05-03; Minergie, 2015; Salvi et al., 2010). Overall, Minergie has thus contributed to an increase in the domestic aggregate value added (cf. interview 05-05).

Driving force of Swiss energy policy; governments promoting Minergie; effects on other arrangements (political-institutional frame conditions; strategy goals of political-administrative actors)

Minergie also became one of the major driving forces in Swiss energy policy in general and an important pillar for Switzerland to achieve its climate targets (the building sector accounts for about 50% of the Swiss gross energy consumption, responsible for about 40% of CO_2 emissions, cf. EnDK, 2014): »*Minergie is the most important and most successful actor in the building sector [...] and became a major factor in Swiss energy policy.*« (interview 05-05, transl.). This is demonstrated within official strategy documents with regard to the 'Energy Strategy 2050' and the Swiss Energy program (cf. chapter 5.1), in which Minergie is mentioned as a crucial element. In fact, it is regarded as one of the most effective and cost-efficient measures for reducing Swiss energy demand (cf. SFOE, 2011 and 2015; cf. also above).

Minergie is accepted and promoted by all Swiss cantons and the Federation (cf. e.g. SFOE, 2005). This is demonstrated by their membership in the association and the offering of special subsidies. The majority of the cantons have defined Minergie as a prerequisite for receiving financial support for the construction of new and the refurbishment of existing buildings (the subsidies paid for a Minergie single-family home range from about CHF 1000 to 8000 including certification costs). Most cantons - 19 out of 26 - are opting to subsidize the stricter Minergie-P standard (with higher subsidies averaging around 11000 per new single-family home) (interview 05-05; Bharathi & Nicol, 2013). Apart from these financial incentives, there were also legal stimulations with regard to urban planning and building permits (such as the allowance of 10% more floor area for Minergie buildings in the Genève canton, cf. interview 05-04). On a national level, Minergie moreover represent an »*eligibility requirement to qualify for federal building subsidies*« (Bharathi & Nicol, 2013, p. 748). The subsidies stem from the 'Swiss building program' launched in 2010. Moreover, several cantons mandated the Minergie-eco standard for public buildings, which became the norm for all new Swiss public buildings and renovations (cf. SFOE, 2013; interview 05-04).

Finally, due to its pioneering role, Minergie influenced other similar governance arrangements in Switzerland and abroad. Nationally, it provided one the most important bases of decision-making with regard to the 'Sustainable Construction Network Switzerland'. This project of public authorities and stakeholders, in which Minergie was involved, was launched in 2013 and aimed at establishing a more comprehensive sustainability label for buildings, the 'standard sustainable construction Switzerland'. The standard shall be established by building on the Minergie label (cf. SFOE, 2014b). In a similar manner, Minergie influenced the development of the 'Energy performance certificate for buildings' launched by the Swiss cantons in 2009 (cf. SFOE, 2013).

With regard to the international level, Minergie is an important reference for international politics aimed at more sustainable building, such as the goal in the European Union that from 2020 on all new buildings shall be 'nearly zero energy buildings'. The SFOE (2015, p. 3, transl.) states that »*for the implementation of the EU directive 2010/31 'Nearly zero-energy Building', Minergie is path breaking*«. It also influenced the development of similar energy labels, such as the passive house in Germany (cf. Minergie, 2011; cf. also interview 05-05, transl.: »*The developments around Minergie were always carefully observed by actors abroad in similar fields such as the passive house.*«).

6.4 Sustainability appraisal

In the following, the impacts of the governance arrangements identified in the previous chapter are interpretively appraised via the normative frame for sustainability appraisal (chapter 3.4). The leading question in this regard is whether the described changes in the action strategies of affected actors make a contribution to a certain criterion of the frame. The appraisal is based on the characteristics of ´a contribution is made´, ´no contribution is made´ and ´a contribution is possible but not clearly determinable´. For each appraisal, a reasoning is provided (for the references in this regard, e.g. for statistics mentioned, cf. chapter 6.3).

6.4.1 CO_2 levy

Table 8: CO_2 levy - sustainability appraisal (own illustration)

Category	Criterion	Contribution	Reasoning
Ecological compatibility	*Preservation of resources (sustainable use of renewable and non-renewable resources)*	*Yes*	*The levy and its accompanying mechanisms to get exempted led to a substitution effect in favor of less CO_2 intensive energy sources - mostly renewable - and higher efficiency. In so doing, a contribution is made to reducing the Swiss domestic energy demand in terms of fossil combustible fuels. This is a direct contribution to the preservation of resources.*
	Protection of ecosystems and the climate system (sustainable use of the environment as a sink and conservation of nature's cultural functions)	*Yes*	*Due to reduced fossil fuel consumption, CO_2 emissions can be saved (for instance, emissions saved due to the levy alone are calculated cumulatively up to 2013 to 2,5 - 5,4 million tons of CO_2; with a reduction in 2013 of 0,5 to 1.2 million, the levy reduces overall Swiss emissions to 2,5 - 6%). This contributes to the sustainable use of the environment as a sink.*
Human well-being	*Protection of human health*	*Yes*	*Since reduced consumption of fossil fuels lowers exhaust emissions, a contribution to air quality is made, while harmful effects on health are lowered. This is a contribution to the protection of human health.*
	Provision of equal access to energy resources and services	*No*	*There is no obvious contribution to the provision of equal access to energy resources and services.*

	Safeguarding of social compatibility while facilitating autonomous self-support and conserving social resources	*Possible, but not clearly determinable*	*As the refunding system relies on a per capita mechanism through health insurance companies, social compatibility is assured. The refunding tends to favor low and medium income brackets. Moreover, as the refunding for firms occurs proportional to wage bills, labor costs can be reduced through a lowering of incidental wage cost - potentially generating a 'second dividend' and furthering economic activity.*
	Ensuring of participation in decision-making processes regarding the energy system	*Yes*	*The consultation phase at the beginning of the arrangement enabled stakeholders in the field to co-determine the development of energy policy.*
Supply security	*Guarantee of the lasting and sufficient provision of energy resources*	*Yes*	*An indirect contribution to supply security is made via reducing the domestic demand for fossil combustible fuels and thus the (potential) amount of imported energy. This decreases the dependence on the import of heating oil and natural gas from foreign countries.*
	Provision of an adequate energy supply infrastructure	*No*	*There is no obvious influence on the energy supply infrastructure.*
Risk handling	*Prevention of system-endangering risks*	*Possible, but not clearly determinable*	*The decrease in the dependence on the import of heating oil and natural gas from foreign countries principally lowers risks. A contribution might also be made to prevent the construction of riskier plants. Yet, a clear estimation in this regard is not possible.*
	Minimization and just intergenerational distribution of unavoidable risks	*Possible, but not clearly determinable*	*A contribution might be made due to the same reasons as for the prevention of system-endangering risks. However, this is also not clearly determinable.*
Economic efficiency	*Ensuring of a justifiable cost design of the energy system in relation to other economic activities while internalizing external costs*	*Yes*	*Since the arrangement represents elements of a greening of the tax system, there is a direct contribution to the internalization of external costs as regards the design of the energy system as a whole.*
	Strengthening of real, human and knowledge capital to sustain economic productivity	*Possible, but not clearly determinable*	*A positive influence on certain branches in the Swiss industry (and a contribution to increasing the gross domestic product, welfare and employment) might exist, but this is not clearly determinable. Competitiveness of energy-intensive firms is in principle secured through the exemption mechanism. Economic value added is also principally promoted through reducing the cash drain in terms of imported energy.*
Upholding adaptation options	*Securing of flexibility to adapt the energy system*	*Possible, but not clearly determinable*	*Certain factors might contribute to securing the flexibility of the energy system - such as induced innovation and technology boost due to increasing energy efficiency as well as the substitution effect in favor of less CO_2 intensive sources, which strengthens diversification. Yet, this is not clearly determinable.*
	Safeguarding of diversity of the energy system	*Yes*	*Through the substitution effect in favor of less CO_2 intensive energy sources, the domestic dependence on heating oil is reduced, while the usage of different renewable energy sources increases. This strengthens the diversification of used energy sources.*

Category	Criterion	Contribution	Reasoning
Coping with the future orientation and intergenerational scope of sustainability	*Strengthening reflexivity in courses of actions while preserving options for development and (re-) action*	*Yes*	*Through increasing the diversification of the Swiss energy mix, reflexivity in courses of actions is furthered - while preserving options for development and (re-) action.*
Doing justice to the complexity of cross-sectoral and multi-scale sustainability challenges	*Expanding an integrative perspective in terms of thematic scope and spatial scales of action while coping with distributed power*	*Possible, but not clearly determinable*	*The influence on the general political agenda, on the discourse of energy policy and other arrangements in the field might marginally contribute to harmonization in terms of thematic and spatial scales. Yet, this is not clearly determinable.*
Handling uncertainty of system dynamics and the resulting ambivalence of sustainability goals	*Supporting social learning processes by means of deliberative characteristics in courses of actions*	*Yes*	*Through the effects of the consultation phase, a contribution to deliberative characteristics in courses of actions is made.*

6.4.2 Electricity saving fund

Table 9: Electricity saving fund - sustainability appraisal (own illustration)

Category	Criterion	Contribution	Reasoning
Ecological compatibility	*Preservation of resources (sustainable use of renewable and non-renewable resources)*	*Possible, but not clearly determinable*	*The trend in the canton Basel-City is pointing towards larger electricity savings, and a contribution of the arrangement in this regard is likely. This supports the preservation of resources due to lowering potential power generation from non-renewable sources (the potential savings are linked to consumption reduction, stimulating investments for efficient devices, a larger amount of advisory services, and rational electricity use - due to reducing incentives for substitutions in favor of electricity, e.g. for the heat market).*
	Protection of ecosystems and the climate system (sustainable use of the environment as a sink and conservation of nature's cultural functions)	*Possible, but not clearly determinable*	*Via electricity savings, potential power generation from non-renewable energy sources can be lowered. The result of reduced potential emissions can be a contribution to the protection of ecosystems and the climate system.*
Human well-being	*Protection of human health*	*Possible, but not clearly determinable*	*Via protecting ecosystems and the climate system, a positive indirect influence on human health might exist, but this is not clearly determinable.*
	Provision of equal access to energy resources and services	*No*	*There is no obvious direct or indirect contribution to the provision of equal access to energy resources and services.*
	Safeguarding of social compatibility while facilitating autonomous self-support and conserving social resources	*Yes*	*Since the bonus system for households is based on a per capita mechanism, social compatibility is assured. The effect on income distribution does not come at the expense of low-wage earners. Furthermore, as the bonus refunding for firms occurs proportional to wage bills, labor costs are reduced through a lowering of incidental wage cost. This contributes to a relief in this regard and counteracts potential distortions on the employment market potentially induced by wage. The bonus system might slightly support the provision of new job positions.*
	Ensuring of participation in decision-making processes regarding the energy system	*Yes*	*Through the consultation phase at the beginning of the arrangement (and possibilities of continuous feedback, e.g. via the information measures) a contribution to participatory characteristics is made.*
Supply security	*Guarantee of the lasting and sufficient provision of energy resources*	*Possible, but not clearly determinable*	*A marginal contribution to supply security might be made by means of reduced electricity demand.*

	Provision of an adequate energy supply infrastructure	*No*	*There is no obvious influence on the energy supply infrastructure.*
Risk handling	*Prevention of system-endangering risks*	*Possible, but not clearly determinable*	*A marginal contribution might be made to prevent the new construction of riskier plants, but a clear estimation is not possible.*
	Minimization and just intergenerational distribution of unavoidable risks	*Possible, but not clearly determinable*	*A contribution might be made due to the same reasons as for the prevention of system-endangering risks, but this is not determinable.*
Economic efficiency	*Ensuring of a justifiable cost design of the energy system in relation to other economic activities while internalizing external costs*	*Yes*	*Since the arrangement includes elements of a greening of the tax system, external costs are internalized. Moreover, the efficiency of the measure (the relation between costs and potential electricity savings) is high, (costs are completely covered by interest earnings). This especially holds true in comparison with other measures in the realm of electricity: based on a calculation of the SFOE (2003 p. 69), the administrative costs per saved kWh are much lower - about 1 to 4 centime per kWh - in comparison to e.g. the funding of photovoltaic power plants in the context of the Swiss Energy program.*
	Strengthening of real, human and knowledge capital to sustain economic productivity	*Possible, but not clearly determinable*	*A positive influence on location attractiveness for firms might exist, which could attract existing companies or support start-ups. This would strengthen the real and human capital with regard to economic productivity. Also, the arrangement does not strain the industry since it lowers incidental wage cost. Accordingly, there are no location drawbacks for firms.*
Upholding adaptation options	*Securing of flexibility to adapt the energy system*	*No*	*There is no influence on the flexibility to adapt the energy system.*
	Safeguarding of diversity of the energy system	*Possible, but not clearly determinable*	*The pioneering character of the arrangement had an influence on the general political agenda, the energy policy discourse, and other arrangements on a cantonal and national level (implementation of similar measures like the national CO_2 levy or translation to other realms, e.g. renovating buildings). This might marginally contribute to diversity, but this is not determinable.*

Category	**Criterion**	**Contribution**	**Reasoning**
Coping with the future orientation and intergenerational scope of sustainability	*Strengthening reflexivity in courses of actions while preserving options for development and (re-) action*	*No*	*There is no obvious influence on reflexivity and adaptability in courses of actions.*
Doing justice to the complexity of cross-sectoral and multi-scale sustainability challenges	*Expanding an integrative perspective in terms of thematic scope and spatial scales of action while coping with distributed power*	*Possible, but not clearly determinable*	*The influence on the general political agenda, the energy discourse and other arrangements might marginally contribute to harmonization. Yet, this influence is not clearly determinable.*
Handling uncertainty of system dynamics and the resulting ambivalence of sustainability goals	*Supporting social learning processes by means of deliberative characteristics in courses of actions*	*Yes*	*The shared goals between administration and firms while carrying out the bonus system contributed to harmonize different positions and to generate mutual trust, while reducing prejudices. In so doing, social learning processes were supported.* *Moreover, through the consultation phase and the feedback possibilities, a contribution to deliberative characteristics in courses of actions is made. Also, there might be a contribution to learning processes in light of energy consciousness in the public through continuous information means.*

6.4.3 Fuel consumption covenant

Table 10: Fuel consumption covenant - sustainability appraisal (own illustration)

Category	Criterion	Contribution	Reasoning
Ecological compatibility	*Preservation of resources (sustainable use of renewable and non-renewable resources)*	*Possible, but not clearly determinable*	*It might be possible that the covenant on motor fuel efficiency and its accompanying information and marketing means (such as the energy etiquette) have slightly contributed to a decline in average fuel consumption of new passenger cars. In so doing, a contribution to the preservation of resources would be made. Yet, this influence is not clearly determinable.*
	Protection of ecosystems and the climate system (sustainable use of the environment as a sink and conservation of nature's cultural functions)	*Possible, but not clearly determinable*	*Due to potential fuel consumption savings, emissions would be reduced. This would result in the contribution to the protection of ecosystems and the climate system.*
Human well-being	*Protection of human health*	*Possible, but not clearly determinable*	*Via the potential protection of ecosystems and the climate system, a positive indirect influence on human health might exist, but this is not determinable.*
	Provision of equal access to energy resources and services	*No*	*There is no obvious direct or indirect contribution to the access to energy resources.*
	Safeguarding of social compatibility while facilitating autonomous self-support and conserving social resources	*No*	*There is no obvious influence on the safeguarding of social compatibility in view of the energy system.*
	Ensuring of participation in decision-making processes regarding the energy system	*Yes*	*The model of a public private partnership and the specific design of the target agreement provided the market sector with the decisive power to co-create the development. The transport industry could determine the goals for fuel consumption together with the government and enjoyed complete freedom in terms of means to reach the goals.*
Supply security	*Guarantee of the lasting and sufficient provision of energy resources*	*Possible, but not clearly determinable*	*A potential reduction in fuel consumption would contribute to the sufficient provision of energy resources, but this is not determinable.*
	Provision of an adequate energy supply infrastructure	*No*	*There is no obvious direct or indirect influence on the energy supply infrastructure.*
Risk handling	*Prevention of system-endangering risks*	*No*	*There is no obvious influence in terms of preventing risks.*
	Minimization and just intergenerational distribution of unavoidable risks	*No*	*No obvious contribution is made with regard to the minimization or distribution of risks.*
Economic efficiency	*Ensuring of a justifiable cost design of the energy system in relation to other economic activities while internalizing external costs*	*No*	*There is no obvious influence with regard to a justifiable cost design of the energy system.*
	Strengthening of real, human and knowledge capital to sustain economic productivity	*No*	*There is no obvious contribution to real, human or knowledge capital within the sector.*
Upholding adaptation options	*Securing of flexibility to adapt the energy system*	*No*	*There is no obvious influence on the flexibility to adapt the energy system as a whole.*
	Safeguarding of diversity of the energy system	*No*	*No obvious contribution is made with regard to safeguarding diversity of the energy system.*

Category	Criterion	Contribution	Reasoning
Coping with the future orientation and intergenerational scope of sustainability	*Strengthening reflexivity in courses of actions while preserving options for development and (re-) action*	*No*	*There is no obvious influence on the reflexivity and adaptability in courses of actions.*
Doing justice to the complexity of cross-sectoral and multi-scale sustainability challenges	*Expanding an integrative perspective in terms of thematic scope and spatial scales of action while coping with distributed power*	*No*	*There is no obvious influence on furthering the integrative perspective in terms of thematic scope and spatial scales of action.*
Handling uncertainty of system dynamics and the resulting ambivalence of sustainability goals	*Supporting social learning processes by means of deliberative characteristics in courses of actions*	*Yes*	*The public-private partnership and the according collaboration among political-administrative and market actors furthered mutual insights. It thus increased the understanding of the workings of each other. In so doing, social learning by means of deliberative characteristics was furthered.* *The specific design of the target agreement provided the market sector with power to co-create the development of the sector - and with complete freedom in terms of measures taken to reach the proclaimed goals.*

6.4.4 Energy Trialogue

With regard to the case of the Energy Trialogue, a sustainability appraisal in terms of content criteria would make no sense. Crucial contributions to meeting the substantive minimum requirements of a sustainable energy system (as highlighted by the guiding sub-question for the content criteria of the sustainability appraisal framework, cf. chapter 3.4) can only be made if societal changes in terms of actions or institutionalization processes are induced. However, the Trialogue did not change action strategies of actors in terms of leading to actual actions, e.g. via projects to realize the proclaimed goals or through influencing politics. Thus, no contribution in terms of substantive criteria was made - except from contributing to participation in decision-making processes regarding the energy system. Accordingly, only an appraisal with regard to procedural requirements is conducted in the following.

Table 11: Energy Trialogue - sustainability appraisal (own illustration)

Category	Criterion	Contribution	Reasoning
Coping with the future orientation and intergenerational scope of sustainability	*Strengthening reflexivity in courses of actions while preserving options for development and (re-) action*	*Possible, but not clearly determinable*	*The Energy Trialogue induced learning processes of different kind within a protected network area. This includes strengthening the understanding of different perspectives among stakeholders in the energy sector - and forming a more complete picture in this regard. It also covers the acquisition of new skills of collaboration, as well as increasing knowledge of the existing actor constellations and structures.* *These learning processes are able to strengthen reflexivity in courses of actions.* *However, it is not clearly determinable if learning was also transferred from the protected network area out to the 'real world', e.g. to the individual organizations of the participants.* *If actual strategy changes, for instance in terms of changed strategy goals, were actually induced, is not clearly determinable.*
Doing justice to the complexity of cross-sectoral and multi-scale sustainability challenges	*Expanding an integrative perspective in terms of thematic scope and spatial scales of action while coping with distributed power*	*Possible, but not clearly determinable*	*Learning processes as described above principally contribute to expanding an integrative perspective in terms of thematic scope and spatial scales of action - while coping with distributed power. However, again it is not clearly determinable if actual changes within action strategies took place.*
Handling uncertainty of system dynamics and the resulting ambivalence of sustainability goals	*Supporting social learning processes by means of deliberative characteristics in courses of actions*	*Yes*	*The Energy Trialogue highly enlarged deliberative characteristics in the field of energy policy by bringing together a decisive amount of stakeholders over a long period. The participants stemmed from various backgrounds covering the realms of society, politics, economy and science.* *In so doing, it enabled stakeholders in the field to determine the development of energy policy.*

6.4.5 Minergie label

Table 12: Minergie label - sustainability appraisal (own illustration)

Category	Criterion	Contribution	Reasoning
Ecological compatibility	*Preservation of resources (sustainable use of renewable and non-renewable resources)*	*Yes*	*The building sector is responsible for about half of the Swiss gross energy demand. The governance arrangement around Minergie has significantly shaped the way of constructing new buildings towards energy savings. This contributes to a reduction of energy demand.* *The annual reduction from Minergie certified buildings is estimated to around 200 million liters heating-oil equivalents. This is supplemented by the effects of non-certified buildings with Minergie standard, e.g. through the change in legislation. It is also supplemented by the changes in the building sector through stimulated innovation, the shaping of the image and discourse of sustainable construction as well as the increased know-how of building professionals.* *Due to the resulting energy savings - as well as the strengthening of energy usage from renewables (especially also through the Minergie-A label) - a direct contribution to the preservation of resources is made.*
	Protection of ecosystems and the climate system (sustainable use of the environment as a sink and conservation of nature's	*Yes*	*The building sector accounts for about 40% of Swiss CO_2 emissions. Due to the reduced energy demand of non-renewable energy sources, a contribution to the lowering of emissions is made (corresponding to an estimated decrease of CO_2 emission of about 400 tons per year - plus the effects*

	cultural functions)		*of non-certified buildings with Minergie standard). Buildings certified with the Minergie-eco standard moreover minimize environmental and air pollution due to recyclability of materials - plus avoidance of scarce resources and volatile organic compounds or formaldehyde. This directly contributes to the protection of ecosystems and the climate system.*
Human well-being	*Protection of human health*	*Yes*	*A direct contribution to the protection of human health is made since residents and employees in Minergie buildings attain a higher living or working comfort (through increased indoor quality) and thus a greater quality of life (people enjoy higher thermal comfort, heat gain protection, moisture control, reduction of dust, pollen and pests as well as a higher air quality through systematic air change). In Minergie-eco certified buildings, this is supplemented by optimized daylight conditions, low indoor air contaminant loads (in terms of hazardous substances, microbes and radiation), as well as strong noise protection.*
	Provision of equal access to energy resources and services	*No*	*There is no obvious contribution to the equal access to energy resources and services.*
	Safeguarding of social compatibility while facilitating autonomous self-support and conserving social resources	*No*	*There is no obvious contribution to the safeguarding of social compatibility in view of the energy system.*
	Ensuring of participation in decision-making processes regarding the energy system	*Yes*	*The broad institutionalized Swiss network for sustainable building, the vocational training system for professionals and the possible membership in the association enables participation of stakeholders in the field. With this coupling and networking function, a common meeting point and communication platform is in place, from which joint action can emerge. The network is supported by the range of organized events for professionals, building owners and end users, which also contribute to participatory decision-making structures.*
Supply security	*Guarantee of the lasting and sufficient provision of energy resources*	*Yes*	*A contribution to supply security is made via reduced domestic energy consumption in the building sector. The decreased energy demand reduces dependence on foreign countries (this is demonstrated e.g. in economic terms since savings resulting from less imported fossil energy per year are estimated to about CHF 200 million).*
	Provision of an adequate energy supply infrastructure	*No*	*There is no direct or indirect contribution to the provision of an adequate energy supply infrastructure*
Risk handling	*Prevention of system-endangering risks*	*Possible, but not clearly determinable*	*A contribution might be made to prevent the construction of riskier plants. A decrease of the energy dependence on foreign countries also reduces risks. However, these influence are not clearly determinable.*
	Minimization and just intergenerational distribution of unavoidable risks	*Possible, but not clearly determinable*	*A contribution might be made due to the same reasons as for the prevention of system-endangering risks, yet this is not clearly determinable.*
Economic efficiency	*Ensuring of a justifiable cost design of the energy system in relation to other economic activities while internalizing external costs*	*No*	*There is no obvious influence on the cost design of the energy system as a whole in relation to other economic activities.*
	Strengthening of real, human and knowledge capital to sustain economic productivity	*Yes*	*With regard to real capital, Minergie has evolved as an important factor in the Swiss building industry. Additional investments (around CHF four billion) were induced in conjunction with certified buildings. This increases the domestic economic value added and strengthens innovative branches in the Swiss building industry. Moreover, the higher real estate value of the around 40.000 certified buildings is quantified to around CHF 100 billion. Economic value added is also promoted through the use of regional products and reducing the cash drain in terms of imported energy.*

			Furthermore, the induced knowledge transfer by the advanced vocational training system for the planning and executive building professionals contributes to an increase in knowledge capital. With the largest Swiss training organization in the building industry in place, there is a strengthening of know-how of professionals in terms of sustainable construction (which also contributes to future economic productivity and thus strengthens real capital).
Upholding adaptation options	*Securing of flexibility to adapt the energy system*	*Yes*	*Minergie contributes to stimulating innovation of building technologies in different branches (such as ventilation systems, insulations, windows, electric heat pumps and solar thermal systems). It thus creates new market segments for producing firms in this respect.* *It also leads to a creative competitive struggle among the developers of new technologies and entails a stimulation effect in terms of optimization. This accelerates the development and mainstreaming of the respective best available technology and techniques over time (i.e. new technologies gradually become state of the art). Overall, this contributes to the flexible adaption of the building sector to new developments. Since the sector is highly important in terms of domestic energy demand, this contributes to the securing of flexibility of the energy system as a whole.*
	Safeguarding of diversity of the energy system	*No*	*There is no obvious direct or indirect influence on the diversity of the energy system as a whole.*

Category	**Criterion**	**Contribution**	**Reasoning**
Coping with the future orientation and intergenerational scope of sustainability	*Strengthening reflexivity in courses of actions while preserving options for development and (re-) action*	*Yes*	*The acceleration of the development and mainstreaming of the respective best available building techniques (through the stimulation of innovation) - and the resulting contribution to the flexible adaption of the building sector to new developments - strengthens reflexivity in courses of actions.*
Doing justice to the complexity of cross-sectoral and multi-scale sustainability challenges	*Expanding an integrative perspective in terms of thematic scope and spatial scales of action while coping with distributed power*	*Yes*	*With regard to the building sector, an integrative perspective in terms of thematic scope is furthered by integrating environmental, social and economic goals (energy efficiency, living quality and value retention). The Minergie-eco standard furthermore includes health and ecological criteria. Also, Minergie served as the most important basis for the establishment of the more comprehensive sustainability label for buildings, the 'standard sustainable construction Switzerland'.* *In terms of the integrative perspective of spatial scales, Minergie moreover serves as a common reference point among the federal, cantonal and local level (and partly internationally).*
Handling uncertainty of system dynamics and the resulting ambivalence of sustainability goals	*Supporting social learning processes by means of deliberative characteristics in courses of actions*	*Yes*	*By means of the institutionalized network structures in the building industry, as well as the induced knowledge transfer through the training system for building professionals, deliberative processes are stimulated.*

6.5 Overview of findings

In the following, a summary of key empirical results is given. Each of the five cases (i.-v.) will be looked at from an encompassing perspective that includes the understanding of governance workings, the allocation to modes, the identification of impacts and their sustainability appraisal.

(i.) First of all, the governance arrangement around the Swiss CO2 levy exhibited hierarchical governance workings on a national level. Legal foundations of the CO_2 law and ordinance promoted a formal institutional structure, softened by the Swiss instruments of direct democracy. Clear responsibilities and vertical relationships vested the Federal Council and the parliament, as well as the Federal Office for the Environment and the Swiss Federal Office of Energy with legal and administrative power and resources. As a consequence, top-down decision-making and implementation evolved (apart from the consultation phase during which market actors prevented a levy on motor fuels). This gave rise to a policy setting with a command-and-control character and fixed emission reduction goals, leading to a coercive and incentive based approach to problem solving.

In accordance with this understanding of governance workings, the arrangement was then classified as the mode of centralized governance - a mode that is characterized by the national government taking the lead, while market and civil society actors act as recipients.

The arrangement induced several changes in the action strategies of affected actors, namely Swiss firms and households. First and foremost, it made a contribution to reducing the domestic demand for fossil fuels, mostly through the substitution of heating oil. A major factor in this regard were the reduction commitments of energy-intensive firms in order to get exempted from the levy. Furthermore, due to the refunding mechanism, projects were established or supported, such as the Swiss Climate Foundation and the building refurbishment program.

The induced impacts contributed to the sustainable development of the energy sector in several areas. Most notably, a contribution was made to the protection of resources and ecosystems as well as for ensuring the provision of energy while internalizing external costs. Also reflexivity in courses of actions was furthered through reduced dependence on heating oil, while contributing to the diversification of the energy mix.

(ii.) The second case study, the arrangement around the electricity saving fund in the canton Basel, showed hierarchical governance workings on a regional level. The basis was a new cantonal energy law established by the great council of Basel. This paved the way for a rather formal institutional structure, with the cantonal political-administrative actors (such as the established agency) in control of power and resources and vertical relationships to consumers. Yet, again, the resulting process character of the arrangement was 'opened' by the consultation phase and the fact that the initiation was a reaction to a popular initiative. The resulting policies then included problem definitions and goals defined right from the start - with the levy and the refunding mechanism as incentives for electricity savings.

In line with this perception of governance workings, the arrangement was then allocated to the mode of decentralized governance, with regional government actors mostly providing incentives for societal actors.

In terms of impacts, the arrangement most likely contributed to the trend in the canton Basel-City towards larger electricity savings. The majority of consumers also welcomed the system. The shared goals among administration, firms and the trade association while conducting the bonus system reduced prejudices and increased the openness among industries for governmental measures. The bonus system also counteracted distortions in the employment market induced by wage costs. Finally, due to its pioneering and unique nature, the electricity saving fund attracted interest

Against this background, the arrangement contributed to a justifiable cost design of the energy system by internalizing external costs. The bonus system also contributed to safeguarding social compatibility through the lowering of wage bills. The shared goals among administration and the economy harmonized different positions and supported learning processes.

(iii.) The third case, the fuel consumption covenant, exhibited an officially institutionalized partnership between the Department of the Environment, Transport, Energy and Communications (DETEC) and the Association of Swiss car importers. The Swiss energy law enabled the Federal Council to empower the DETEC to establish covenants with the private sector. Shared responsibilities came along with a horizontal relationship among the partners. This provoked a process with emphasis on cooperation and exchange of information. The resulting substantive setting was fixed in terms of step-wise targets to reduce fuel consumption of new passenger cars - but completely flexible in reaching those targets.

The arrangement was characterized as the mode of public-private governance - a mode that exhibits equal cooperation between political-administrative agencies and market actors.

In terms of impacts, the overall goals of the covenant were missed. The arrangement did not lead to major changes in the action strategies of consumers, car manufactures or importers. The Swiss Federal Office of Energy thus regards it as a policy failure.

In view of SD, the arrangement increased the participation in decision-making processes. The specific design of the target agreement provided the market sector with power to co-create the development, offering freedom with regard to conducted means. Social learning via deliberative characteristics was furthered since collaboration among state and market actors increased the understanding of each other´s activities.

(iv.) The fourth case, the Energy Trialogue Switzerland, was built on a network structure to enable a multi-stakeholder discussion process on the future of Swiss energy policy. Organization rested with a private-law association, giving rise to rather informal and experimental rule systems. This led to deliberatively influenced negotiation processes that relied on communication and exchange of information. The access rules varied during the evolution of the arrangement. This provoked a heterogeneous actor field of different stakeholders from society, economy, politics and science, in which the amount of influence changed over time. The consideration of different perspectives led to a flexible character of problem definitions and a pursuit of integrating contents, successive learning and innovative solutions. A dynamic science-policy interface came along with a discursive struggle over which knowledge counts as relevant.

Against this backdrop, the arrangement was classified as the mode of interactive governance, which includes collaboration in equal terms between government agencies, market actors and civil society.

The main addressees targeted by the arrangement were federal and cantonal politicians. However, a change in the action strategies of these actors did not take place - the arrangement did not induce actual actions or institutionalization processes. There were no projects to institutionalize the goals and measures proclaimed by the Trialogue and changes within overall Swiss energy policy were not induced. The main actually affected actors were those groups that also participated in the process. Participants had the opportunity to understand each other’s perspectives, polarizations could be bridged and new solutions were discussed.

In terms of the procedural requirements of sustainable action strategies, the arrangement thus contributed to supporting social learning processes by means of furthering deliberative characteristics in courses of actions.

(v.) The last case study, the governance arrangement around the Swiss building label Minergie, was in its beginning dominated by bottom-up structures with individuals taking the lead as forerunners. When these actors decided to include public authorities to leverage the arrangement, the structures became more formalized. The Minergie association with members from all parts of society was then responsible for running the label. Shared authorities led to flexible cooperation among stakeholders and actions were legitimatized by an agreement on roles and relations. Accordingly, the arrangement strongly relied on the inputs of actors with different backgrounds. This provoked a policy setting largely based on an innovative path for solutions with changing problem definitions and objectives. The label was introduced on an experimental basis and based on ongoing evaluations it was shaped over time. In this regard, there was a reliance on expert knowledge with a pursuit for provisory goals against the backdrop of the pioneering character of the arrangement.

In accordance with this understanding of governance workings, the arrangement was allocated to the mode of self-governance (in which actors from civil society with far-reaching autonomy are able to initiate new approaches themselves), gradually shifting to interactive governance.

The arrangement induced a range of changes in the action strategies of affected actors (i.e. actors dealing with the building industry, end users and cantonal and federal public authorities). First of all, it led to a change of legislative cantonal building regulations, which were gradually adjusted to the stricter versions of the Minergie label. The arrangement thus led to major changes in political-institutional frame conditions and the regular way of constructing conventional new buildings. Apart from this, a large number of buildings have been certified by the standard, making it the measure with the greatest energetic effect in the Swiss Energy program. Moreover, the building sector was largely altered by the arrangement due to stimulated innovation and institutionalized network structures, with increased know-how of building professionals. Also, Minergie largely shaped the image of sustainable construction by making it socially acceptable.

Overall, the arrangement thus contributed to the protection of resources, ecosystems and human health. It also strengthened the real, human and knowledge capital in the energy sector and increased its flexibility while supporting an integrative perspective in terms of thematic scope and spatial scales.

Part IV: Discussion

7 Implications

In light of the case study results presented in the previous chapter, implications of the findings are discussed in the following. The first chapter paves the way for answering the overall research question, by concluding if the governance mode makes a difference when it comes to promoting SD. In this regard, I will also derive conclusions from the case study results in light of claims in the literature regarding the merits of new modes. Furthermore, other factors determining the potential of governance to promote SD are discussed. In general, the presentation of implications is supplemented by references to respective similar research findings in the literature (chapter 7.1). Following the implications, hypotheses to be tested in future research are formulated (chapter 7.2). In the final synthesis chapter, the implications are brought together into a concluding argument in view of further research and practice of SD governance (chapter 7.3).

7.1 Does the mode make a difference?

The overall research question of this study asked, if there are differences among governance modes supporting an assumption that certain modes are per se better suited to promote SD than others. The research was especially driven by the influential normative claim in mainstream SD governance literature that new modes are superior to traditional ones.

As formulated in the introduction, a governance arrangement must fulfill two requirements in order to effectively promote SD. First, it has to induce societal changes, i.e. changes in the action strategies of affected actors. And second, these changes must be in line with the goals associated with SD. When these two requirements are fulfilled, an arrangement leads action strategies in a sustainable direction.

Against this backdrop, the research question could be answered positively in the following situation: specific differences among modes were found, indicating that certain modes are per se superior for steering action strategies in a more sustainable direction. However, the findings did not reveal such differences. There are no indications that the specific characteristics of certain modes make them a priori superior to others: neither are there indications that certain modes are better suited for inducing changes in action strategies, nor that certain modes are more able to induce changes in line with sustainability goals.

Accordingly, the normative claim that new modes perform better than traditional ones cannot be supported in light of the findings. In contrast, the findings do question and relativize the claim. The most extensive changes in the action strategies of affected actors were induced by the governance arrangement around the CO_2 levy (a traditional hierarchical mode) and the arrangement around the Minergie label (a non-hierarchical, new mode). This especially concerns the potential of inducing actual actions and institutionalization processes, which is highly relevant for promoting SD. On the continuum of governance modes from the two opposing ends of state intervention to societal autonomy (cf. figure 7, chapter 3.2.2), these are the leftmost and rightmost modes respectively. The two other new modes explored - the arrangement around the fuel consumption covenant and the Energy Trialogue - failed to induce crucial changes in action strategies at all. The findings also do not indicate that new modes lead to changes that per se fulfill a broader range of SD goals. Taking everything into account, this clearly contradicts the assumption that the specific characteristics of new modes (i.e. modes closer to the right end on the continuum) make them generally more suited to promote SD than traditional ones (modes closer to the left end).

In the following, the specific insights gained from the individual five case studies are discussed. I will first present the most striking insights, gained from the cases of the Energy Trialogue (i.), and the Minergie label (ii.). Subsequently, I discuss the most important implications of the cases of the fuel consumption covenant (iii.), the CO_2 levy (iv.), and the electricity saving fund (v.). Finally, I will present important results that the cases revealed with regard to other influencing factors for promoting SD (vi.).

(i.) The case of the Energy Trialogue: interactive governance modes can easily fail to induce societal changes

First of all, the case study of the arrangement around the Energy Trialogue revealed that interactive modes of governance can easily fail to induce any actual changes in society towards SD at all. As introduced in chapters 5.5 and 6.1.4, the Trialogue started with high expectations and received a lot of attention from actors within the field of Swiss energy policy (both project phases were also conducted under the patronage of the respective Federal Councilor). As an approach that brings together all relevant stakeholders in a protected area, it should function as a catalyst for politics with majority appeal (it also included one of the largest energy summits that ever took place in Switzerland). While the first phase aimed at developing a sustainable and competitive strategy plan for the Swiss energy sector, the second phase analyzed the official 'Energy Strategy 2050' of the Federal Council. As regards the first project, there were several plans how to realize the proposed goals and measures on both a national and cantonal levels. The second phase also aimed at delivering new impulses for federal and cantonal politics. After the publication of the two final reports, the results were thus e.g. communicated to the energy commissions of the National Council and the Council of States, as well as to the Federal Department of the Environment, Transport, Energy and Communications.

However, the governance arrangement did not affect political-administrative actors in the sense that a change in action strategies took place. Interviewees referred to fixed strategies of politicians in this regard: »*When it came to communicating the results, we realized that politicians already formed their opinions.*« (interview 04-04, transl.). Apart from this, it was argued that politicians had their own sources to develop the 'Energy Strategy 2050' such as scientific consulting institutes. Accordingly, there were no activities for realizing the goals and measures of the Trialogue and no apparent influence on Swiss energy policy at large. Eventually, a leading participant of the Trialogue remarkably concluded that »*the challenge is clearly to reach actual political decision-making processes and to feed in the results. And such classical steering processes are definitely needed in the end. Ultimately, these processes are that which steer our societies.*« (interview 04-04, transl.).

The only recognized effect of the arrangement was the development of different kinds of learning processes among the participating actors. However, indications for the crucial aspect of learning in such a context, i.e. that participants transferred the newly gained knowledge from the protected area out to the 'real world' could not be found. This indicates that no actual societal changes outside of the governance arrangement were induced.

Apart from this, the case revealed difficulties coming up in multi-stakeholder discussion processes and thus network governing in general. The first project phase provoked large critiques with regard to adequately including stakeholders. This was due to the fact that the final strategy paper was worked out by only a small core group. Other participants felt excluded in view of the unbalanced consideration. This suggests that participation by a large group of actors can hinder reaching commonly agreed project outputs.

Accordingly, this indicates that considering multiple viewpoints of stakeholders does not necessarily ensure that the outputs of a governance arrangement are aligned with sustainability goals - let alone that these outputs generate some form of actions and institutionalization processes to promote SD. The substantial critiques in terms of the adequate consideration of multiple stakeholders may have contributed to the situation that the outputs had no societal effect. This also demonstrates the risk of multi-actor governance that responsibilities are not clearly fixed and accepted among all participants. Overall, participation may also hinder reaching sustainable results.

These findings are in line with general governance literature pointing to flaws of multi-actor governing - such as inadequate stakeholder representation, output paucity, a lack of efficiency and clashes between knowledge types (see e.g. the overview in Arts et al., 2014). They also correspond with the conclusion drawn by Arnouts & Arts, (2009, p. 225) reached in an in-depth case study that »*multi-actor governance [is] not necessarily 'good governance', in the sense that effective and legitimate policies are its result. This bias, so often found in the governance literature, should be put into perspective.*« The authors speak of potential actor overloads in multi-stakeholder arrangements as well as of power struggles, conflicting discourses and unclear rules. This leads to potential governance failures in terms of both effectiveness and legitimacy (cf. ibid.).

The findings are also in accordance with research pointing to drawbacks of network forms of governance: for instance, Meuleman (2014, p. 893) argues on the basis of a case study on network governing that dialogues resulted in endless talks with no results. They are furthermore backed up by studies from the governance and political science literature, analyzing the challenges and success factors of governing in networks and the effectiveness thereof (cf. e.g. Klijn et al., 2012; Börzel & Panke, 2007; Wurster, 2013). The ambition to integrate different perspectives from various stakeholders, generate trust and reach joint solutions might e.g. restrict the success of such governing to areas where all participants expect advantages for themselves (cf. on the downside of participation in such contexts also e.g. Böhling & Arzberger, 2014).

Taking everything into account, it can be deduced from the findings that a certain form of meta-governing (i.e. co-ordination from a higher level) may have been beneficial in this case - in order to harmonize the Energy Trialogue with general energy politics by public authorities (e.g. the development of the 'Energy Strategy 2050'). The aspect of meta-governance will be further explored in chapter 7.3.

(ii.) The case of the Minergie label: a 'shadow of hierarchy' in self-governing can be required as leverage

The case of the arrangement around the Minergie label on the one hand remarkably disclosed that a new mode of governance can indeed be very potent in contributing to SD. It is a paradigm case for a largely successful bottom-up movement and interactive governing form. The arrangement induced a range of impacts, especially institutionalization processes (including an enormous market penetration, the alteration of the conventional building sector and the change of the image of sustainable construction). It also contributed in several ways to a sustainable development of the energy sector, since induced changes in action strategies were in line with sustainability goals (e.g. in terms of protecting resources, ecosystems and human health, strengthening real, human and knowledge capital or increasing reflexivity and integration).

Notably, the case has shown that self-governing can lead to major changes in legislation. In this case, a bottom-up movement from civil society with a pioneering idea gradually changed the informational-cognitive cultural environment. These changes were then adopted in building regulations. This finding backs up research highlighting that new modes of governance can pave the way for future regulation (e.g. Van der Heijden, 2015). Accordingly, new modes can be a 'testing ground' for more stringent governance.

However, on the other hand, a crucial point in this case is how governance processes evolved - as the analysis in chapter 6.1.5 revealed. At the beginning, the Minergie label was in private property and a small group of individuals from civil society (acting as forerunners) was completely autonomous. At this stage, state actors were kept at distance. However as one of the individuals clearly stated in an interview: »*As a private initiative the whole thing would most certainly have remained a niche product.*« (interview 05-04, transl.). As a consequence, the civil society forerunners first of all transferred the usage rights to cantonal authorities to boost the label's awareness, reach trust and lend credence by adding an official character. This inclusion of authorities catalyzed the penetration of the label. Partly, Minergie was even seen in the public as an official measure of national and cantonal energy policy. With the transfer of the label rights to cantonal authorities, the structures became much more formalized: »*We knew that if we want to make a difference in the Swiss building sector, we explicitly have to involve the cantons - responsible for the building sector in Switzerland - so that the whole thing gets an official character and to increase legitimacy [...] So you can say, although it was a private launch, the public actors played a major role.*« (interview 05-01, transl.).

As a second step, to manage the label, the Minergie association was founded - with the federal government and all Swiss cantons as key members (»*In the executive board, there are also cantonal representatives.*«, ibid.). The association is not only supported (e.g. in financial terms) and promoted by public authorities through subsidies for buildings according to Minergie, but the certifications are also carried out by cantonal certification units located at the respective administrations. In view of this, one of the forerunning individuals concluded that »*without the support of the public sector the whole thing would not have worked, that is for sure*« (interview 05-02, transl.). Accordingly, the success of Minergie was largely dependent on the support from public authorities (while it was in turn stressed by an interviewee that careful communication was needed - since public authorities can also hamper the development of self-governing at its beginning stage due to a form of 'jealousy', cf. interview 05-05). The case thus suggests that a 'shadow of hierarchy' in self-governing might be required to leverage such arrangements.

This is backed up by general governance literature arguing that non-hierarchical governance is frequently embedded in hierarchical structures and operates with public support in the background (cf. e.g. Héritier & Lehmkuhl, 2008; Börzel & Risse, 2010; Lynn, 2011; Buzogány, 2015; Goetz, 2008 - for the interaction of self-governing with governments, cf. also Bell & Hindmoor, 2012). In light of an empirical case study, Van der Heijden (2013) refers to a need for governmental regulation as a backdrop for new environmental arrangements (cf. also Bäckstrand et al., 2010). Some scholars even argue that new modes do not have an effect unless they are linked to traditional governance (see e.g. in Héritier & Rhodes, 2011; in favor of hierarchical governance one interviewee also further argued that »*hierarchical regulation provides predictability, it is easy comprehensible for affected actors once in place [...] Bottom-up steering alone is not really controllable.*«, interview 01-04, transl.). From these perspectives, it follows that to a certain degree, governments play a role within all governance arrangements, although in different forms (cf. also further Capano et al., 2015a). This also contradicts the hypothesis that the power of the state has declined due to the evolution of new modes (cf. chapter 2.2).

Self-governance in the shadow of hierarchy moreover represents a form of hybridity. This seems to be so common in real-world governance that theoretical frameworks differing among governance modes (cf. chapter 3.2) might benefit from supplementing common ideal-types with such hybrid ideal-types in their own right (cf. further also chapter 8.2).

At the same time, the arrangement around Minergie would have most certainly not had such a strong effect if it had been solely a public initiative. The inclusion of all relevant stakeholders in the association was vital for the gradual change in the building discourse (»*Minergie as a sole initiative of the federal government, such as from the Swiss Federal Office of Energy or by the cantons, this would have had much less success. You need to integrate the whole environment that surrounds such a thing like a label - this is possible through network structures, you need to integrate all players.*«, interview 05-04, transl.) Apart from this, it needs to be considered that the self-governing characteristics were also essential for the success. By means of its voluntary forerunner position - individuals could experiment in a new area - the arrangement induced a ′preparation of the field′ and created the preconditions for major changes (»*The advantage of Minergie was that you could react quickly to changes. It represented a testing field to try new things - to build the basis for later regulation [...] With such voluntary developments you have a basis for showing what is possible in the field [...] The voluntary aspect was essential to go beyond the present regulations and to gradually evolve.*«, ibid.). Thus, the steady and fast innovative development of the standard towards stricter versions and including new topics of SD could not have happened without the flexible bottom-up characteristics (cf. interview 05-05).

Overall, these considerations suggest that a combination of governance modes may be superior to a single mode when it comes to effectively promoting SD. This implication will be further discussed in chapter 7.3.

Apart from this, since the Minergie case gradually evolved from the mode of self-governance to interactive governance, it is a paradigm example that governance arrangements are not static and fixed entities but can continuously evolve over time. This finding is in line with research explicitly pointing to the dynamics of governance arrangements (e.g. Driessen et al., 2012; Capano et al., 2015a). Since the development of cantonal building regulations, representing hierarchical governing, have evolved due to Minergie, it is also a nice example that co-existing modes mutually influence each other - and that one mode can provoke the introduction of another.

(iii.) The case of the fuel consumption covenant: public-private modes can easily fail when there is no threat of a more stringent mode

The case of the arrangement around the fuel consumption covenant disclosed that public-private governance modes can easily fail without a threat of a more stringent mode. The covenant was the first target agreement made within the Swiss Energy program, aimed at a reduction of average fuel consumption of newly registered passenger cars. However, the arrangement did not induce a major change in the action strategies of affected actors, namely consumers, car manufactures or importers. As a consequence, the overall goals were not met. This is in line with one interviewee arguing that »*when it comes to voluntary partnerships between politics and economy, I think, the economy always strives for finding loopholes. In my view, this is often a strategy of avoiding radical changes*« (interview 01-04, transl.).

The interesting point in this regard is a comparative look at the first case study, the CO_2 levy. As presented in chapter 6.1.1, energy-intensive firms could get exempted from the levy when making a commitment with the Swiss Federal Office of the Environment to reduce their emissions. When it was foreseeable that the levy will be implemented, a high number of companies gradually established such reduction commitments. The firms had to become members of the Energy Agency of the Economy that supervised the activities with a corresponding performance mandate made with the federal government. The agency accordingly functioned as a connector between politics and the economy. Overall, the commitments represented the same approach as the target agreement on fuel consumption. In both cases, there was a public and a private partner while setting reduction targets over a certain time period. The private partner had to report the reduction achievements, which were controlled by the public partner.

However, while the fuel consumption covenant failed, the reduction commitments were a success that made an important contribution to reducing fossil fuel demand. The difference between the two was the threat of a stringent reaction in case of missed overall goals (i.e. in case of failure). With regard to the CO_2 levy, the firms would have to pay the levy ex post facto if they failed to achieve the emission goals. There was thus a legal framing environment. This represented a clear threat: »*Cumulated over the years, this was indeed a lot of money - when you suddenly recognize in the year 2013 that you have to pay a major fee, this was a real threatening punishment.*« (interview 01-05, transl.). In contrast, with regard to the fuel consumption covenant, there was no threat in case of a failure. Actually, this was intended in the first place. As defined in the CO_2 law, a levy on motor fuels should have been introduced if the overall targets in the sector were not reached. In the first place, the Association of Swiss car importers and certain firms indeed signed the covenant for strategic reasons to avoid the introduction of a levy. However - in contrast to the case study of the CO_2 levy - in the further course of the development the threat turned out to be not credible. It was obvious that a levy on motor fuels had no chance to get implemented due to a lack of majorities. Accordingly, the Swiss Federal office of Energy clearly points to the non-credibility of the threat: »*As legally fixed, the Federal Council could implement legal measures when reduction goals for fuel consumption are not met, but does not have to. There was no pressure on the car industry to meet the agreement [...] So it was a toothless tiger with no credible incentives.*« (SFOE, 2011, p. 128).

This finding connects with the more specific literature on the effectiveness of voluntary (environmental) agreements (e.g. Koehler, 2007; Segerson & Miceli, 1999). This literature e.g. points out that two basic mechanisms are thought to motivate participation in voluntary agreements: positive incentives (e.g. cost-sharing and subsidies) and the threat of legislation, i.e. a background threat of subsequent mandatory instruments (in other words sanction mechanisms in case of non-compliance). The finding moreover corresponds with studies from (SD) governance literature questioning the view that market-based governance can be self-managing and promoting sustainable results without being embedded in regulatory frameworks (e.g. Bell & Park, 2006; Martin & Gunningham, 2014).

This is in line with interviewees arguing for the state to set long-term regulatory conditions. As one expert stated: »*From an economic perspective, I think the best steering mechanisms is when the state sets clear long-term, stable and reliable regulatory framing conditions, at least for ten years - and then leaves it up to the economy how to get there [...] You see, the state does not know the firms and how optimization is possible in an efficient way [...] So the state needs to set framing conditions and a punishment needs to be introduced in case of non-compliance.*« (interview 01-03, transl.). Another interviewee argued: »*The state should set clear framing conditions and we as the economy then see how to realize them.*« (interview 03-04, transl. - cf. also interview 01-01, transl.: »*Top-down steering is crucial for setting conditions to provide a long time horizon.*«).

As a reaction to the failure of the covenant, the Swiss government eventually implemented legally binding emission regulations for newly registered passenger cars some years later. The Swiss Federal office of Energy argues that this more binding way of governing turns out to be more effective than the voluntary arrangement (cf. chapter 6.3.3). This is a further example that a mode of governance (especially in case of its failure) can provoke the introduction of another mode (e.g. a more stringent one).

Overall, again it follows that the arrangement could have benefitted from a form of meta-governance. Such meta-governing could have matched the endeavor of a public-private mode with a more stringent mode of governance (either already in place or to be introduced) to uphold a threat in case of failure. The advantage of the public-private mode - that the market has a certain freedom to reach targets set by state actors (and thus the possibility »*that the economic optimum can be reached in the most efficient way*«, interview 03-04, transl.) - could in so doing be exhausted (with a potential higher goal achievement and without the elapsing of several years before a more stringent mode is introduced).

(iv.) The case of the CO_2 levy: participatory elements can also hinder faster and more sustainable results

The case study of the CO_2 levy first of all showed that ´traditional´ hierarchical modes can be capable of promoting SD. A range of impacts was induced (such as the reduction of the domestic demand for fossil fuels as well as the support of other projects as the Swiss Climate Foundation and the building refurbishment program). Also, these impacts supported the SD of the energy sector in different areas (e.g. through the protection of resources and ecosystems or promoting diversification).

Yet, just as in the case of Minergie, insights into the evolution of processes revealed further interesting results. The case disclosed some potential drawbacks of the Swiss instruments of direct democracy (cf. chapter 5.1) and thus of participatory elements in general.

As described in chapter 6.1.1, there were efforts to implement a Swiss CO_2 levy already in the 1990s. The Federal Council aimed to implement a levy in 1996 with a subsequent rising of the levy rate. However, this attempt met high resistance in the consultation phase. As a consequence, the Federal Council revised its proposal and counted on voluntary measures in the first place. As these measures in the course of the Swiss Energy program failed to reach emission goals, the implementation of a levy gained more prominence. The CO_2 law from 2000 then intended a levy on both combustible and motor fuels. In 2004, the Swiss Federal Council initiated a consultation phase. During the consultation, different alternatives were discussed (a levy on both combustible and motor fuels; a compromise with the levy only on combustible fuels with motor fuels subject to the voluntary Climate Cent, and finally the implementation of only the Climate Cent). Two major coalitions argued against each other for the first and latter solution, while an intermediate group tried to mediate with the compromise. Although the CO_2 law contemplated a levy on motor fuels, the Federal Council in the end followed the compromise solution. If the implementation of a levy on motor fuels had been announced, representatives of the first coalition would have most likely blocked it in the subsequent phase. For implementing the compromise, the Federal Council enacted the CO_2 ordinance in 2005. The official 'Message from the Federal Council to the Federal Assembly' then had to be approved by the Swiss Parliament with its two chambers. After much controversy during parliamentary discussions, the chambers decided in 2007 on a gradual introduction. Finally, the Federal Council approved the Parliament's proposals and amended the CO_2 ordinance accordingly.

Accordingly, the levy was only implemented from 2008 onwards. In comparison to the stated period required by law, the opponents of the levy were able to postpone its implementation for another four years. Moreover, until today, the levy rate was increased several times. Thalmann

(2013, p. 38) argues that »*it is clear that a better stepped increase would have been possible if the levy had been introduced earlier.*« An interviewee with direct insights into the procedures stated that »*there are of course disadvantages of our democratic participatory system. It has advantages, such as transparency; processes get induced through initiatives, but there also drawbacks [...] The whole system generates a large amount of loopholes [...] and the lobby often works successfully [...] All these are difficult processes that are not really controllable. Frequently, in the end you do not get a coherent package due to the many changes that are made to come up to the interests of diverse people.*« (interview 01-04, transl.).

Overall, it can be argued that the instruments of direct democracy - such as the consultation phase and the possibility of forcing or threatening a referendum - delayed the introduction of the levy and have hampered a potentially 'more sustainable' solution with a levy also on motor fuels: »*With the opportunity of the facultative referendum, a levy on motor fuels is really difficult to realize. The transport lobby is really powerful and influential in Switzerland.*«, interview 03-03, transl.). Thus, just as in the case of the Energy Trialogue, this implies that participatory elements can also hinder reaching faster and more sustainable results.

This is in line with authors that critically scrutinize such elements in light of SD. Lafferty (2004) in this regard points to potential tensions between dominant democratic norms found in governance principles, such as participation, and the objectives of SD. Also, for instance, the inclusion of actors can increase conflict potential and hamper decision making; learning may be a wishful thinking when actors strive for decisions in their self-interest (e.g. Dupuis & Knoepfel, 2015). Some authors thus also speak of a substance-procedure divide (e.g. Huh, 2011). In a more specific case study on stakeholder involvement and environmental outcomes, Young et al. (2013, p. 369) remarkably highlight that »*our findings emphasize the risks associated with the assumption that good processes are more likely to lead to good outcomes.*«

(v.) The case of the electricity saving fund: certain aspects thought responsible for the supposed superiority of new modes can also occur through hierarchical governance

The case study of the electricity saving fund to a certain degree supported the insights from the case of the CO_2 levy that hierarchical modes can succeed in contributing to SD (albeit societal changes were not as present as in the case of the CO_2 levy). The arrangement induced certain impacts (such as supporting a trend towards electricity savings or counteracting distortions on the employment market), that contribute to SD (such as promoting a justifiable cost design and safeguarding social compatibility).

Apart from this, the case showed that certain aspects associated with new modes of governance - and thought responsible for their supposed superiority - can occur through hierarchical modes, too. As introduced in chapter 6.3.2, in light of the bonus system, governance administration, the trade association and firms had shared goals. Due to this, learning processes among actors with different positions and an atmosphere of mutual confidence and gradual trust evolved. Also, there was a strengthening of solidarity. As a representative from administration argued: »*Our goal was to get in close contact with the industry, so that the stakeholder`s trust in the government is increased when they make good experiences with us. When they see, the government is not only the 'big regulator' but there are also agencies that help the people. So prejudices are cut down, I think that is very important.*« (interview 02-02; transl.). In this course, critical voices among industries, generally arguing against state-imposed instruments, gradually became less. Prejudices were reduced towards governmental measures. Remarkably, all this was also highlighted by an interviewee from the side of the market, i.e. by a representative of the trade association: »*The trade association and the canton had shared goals since it was good for both sides [...] People with formerly quite different positions started to talk to each other, contributing to a climate of solidarity in which mutual learning was furthered [...] Reciprocal invitation to assemblies led to a local network of mutual confidence, where comprehension on both sides was cultivated. I think this was of major importance. It helped to reduce prejudices towards administration, resulted in short distances and put down objections.*« (interview 02-03, transl.).

This finding corresponds to literature arguing that hierarchical modes are in many cases affected by deliberative rationalities (cf. e.g. Héritier & Lehmkuhl, 2008; Kronsell & Bäckstrand, 2010). In turn, this tempers normative claims in the (SD) governance literature that put emphasis on new modes due to their ability to promote deliberative characteristics.

(vi.) Other influencing factors with regard to the potential of governance to promote SD

Apart from the insights regarding the specific characteristics of governance modes and their role for promoting SD, the cases revealed important results with regard to other influencing factors. It became apparent that there are alternative aspects that may in some instances be more influential, and thus more crucial for the potential of governance to promote SD than the mode itself. Most notably, this concerns the particularities of the actors involved in governance and the nature of the embedding context, e.g. the political-cultural embedding of an arrangement.

First of all, it can be crucial to 'have the right people on board' during governance workings, especially in terms of leadership. This, for instance, relates to particular skills and preferences or the willingness to cooperate. The case of the Minergie label revealed that the specific skills and positions of actors involved in governance - especially at the beginning of an arrangement - can be of high importance. Both the development of the innovative label and its high market penetration were largely dependent on the particular competences of single actors. In the case, especially two forerunning individuals were important. The first one had both technical experience in the field of sustainable construction in terms of engineering and held a key position in the field of cantonal energy policy: »*Decisive was my beneficial and visible position as the head of the energy office of [a Swiss canton] in the formation phase of Minergie. Apart from that, as the person in charge and resident of a successful zero-energy residential estate, I had both the technical knowledge and was credible.*« (interview 05-03, transl.). The other individual was a marketing and communication expert that also had long experience in the field of sustainable building components: »*On the one hand it was important that I had experience with construction. I am a business economist but worked in the building industry, in Switzerland and abroad. Apart from that I also worked in a consultation agency [...] I was mostly responsible for the success of heat pumps in Switzerland. And all the things needed for Minergie - development, launching, penetration and the like - I had already done with the heat pumps. So I could largely rely on previous experience. The two things were congruent until the end, although the challenge with Minergie was of course more complex [...] And from my marketing experience I knew that it was central for communication to highlight the comfort aspect of sustainable building.*« (interview 05-05, transl.).

This puts emphasis on the role of individual pioneers that can make a significant difference in governance. It suggests that particularly the success of bottom-up structures can depend to a large extent on the agency of a few key change agents. The individual qualities and interests of the key players and their relation to other actors can be of central importance.

Other cases also indicated that the ′right involvement′ of actors within governance can be vital: »*The question of whether people like or dislike each other is important for the reception and effects of a policy. I remember a situation where two people in influential positions were always of a different opinion as a matter of principle. Regardless of the content, these two would never agree.*«, interview 02-03, transl.; »*If you do not have the right grouping of actors that works for bringing forward a certain idea, then it is doomed to failure.*«, interview 02-02; transl.). An interviewee with insights in political-administrative procedures further pointed out: »*What is most important in the end with regard to the question of whether goals are reached is what kind of different people are involved in politics and administration.*« (interview 02-05, transl.).

Overall, these findings are in line with research highlighting the role of the specific type of participating actors - e.g. involving the 'right people', such as key individuals and policy entrepreneurs - in light of the success of governance (cf. e.g. Gailing & Röhring, 2016; Timmermans et al., 2014). For instance, Newig and Fritsch (2009) argue in view of a meta-analysis of case studies that more than any other variable, specific preferences of involved actors determine the results of governance.

Second, the case of the electricity saving fund disclosed that the embedding context - e.g. in the form of the political-cultural environment of an arrangement - can be of vital importance for the potential of governance to promote SD. This first of all concerns the specific background situation at the beginning of a governance arrangement. Examples are the general attitude of the public and the existing dominant cultural discourse according to the topic in question. As an expert for the governance workings from administration pointed out: »*In the canton Basel-City we had very favorable external preconditions [...] Both the public and the politicians were already comparatively sensitive to sustainability topics due to environmental catastrophes in the past, so both the general politics and the public mostly supported such measures [...] So we did not have to position the lever in this regard since the general discourse was so supportive.*« (interview 02-02, transl.). This was confirmed by an interviewee from the market: »*In the canton Basel-City, the conditions were good to make such an approach a success. In contrast, in the canton Basel-Country, the general mood is totally different, not so open and much more conservative. People are not so much interested in such `green stuff` as it does not lead to anything in their opinion.*« (interview 02-03, transl.). Also, the existing power relations in the field or sector addressed by governance can make a tremendous difference with regard to the workings of an arrangement and thus ultimately to its success (cf. interview 02-02). Similarly, the influence of specific circumstances in the field can be of importance: »*I think for a commune, such as Appenzell, an arrangement with a levy would not be the right choice. There the effort would be too high in comparison to the earnings [...] In contrast, on a national level I think such a measure would be very efficient. For instance, the bonus can be paid back through the compensation office. At the federal level, the earnings would be much higher than the effort.*« (interview 02-04, transl.).

In general, this finding is in line with governance research that points to the role of certain contextual factors. Governance workings, e.g. interactions among actors and with institutions, are largely dependent on their embedding context, e.g. in terms of the larger natural, political-administrative, socio-economic or cultural embeddedness (e.g. Lejano et al., 2007; Sinha, 2012; Emerson et al. 2012; Ostrom, 2010; Newig & Fritsch, 2009; Van der Heijden, 2012; Gollagher & Hartz-Karp, 2013; Ansell & Gash, 2008; cf. also the more specific established literature on the influence of contextual factors on policy instrument success). The surrounding context creates opportunities and constraints that shape governance workings at the beginning and over time (this is also linked to issues of scale, cf. for the importance of scales in light of governance e.g. Padt et al., 2014; Bressers & Rosenbaum, 2003; Mauerhofer, 2013). Delli Carpini et al. (2004, p. 336), for instance argue in light of an overview of empirical case studies on participation and deliberation that »*most important, the impact of deliberation [...] is highly context dependent [...] Although the research summarized in this essay demonstrates numerous positive benefits of deliberation, it also suggests that deliberation, under less optimal circumstances, can be ineffective at best and counterproductive at worst.*« A further example of such contextual factors are socio-materialities, i.e. the mutual constitution of social and physical spaces, e.g. highlighting regional differences in terms of socio-economic trajectories or physical landscapes (cf. Gailing & Röhring, 2016; cf. also the evolutionary governance theory with its focus on object formations and their role in the discursive realities of governance paths, van Assche et al., 2014a).

Overall, it can be summed up that no indications for a general superiority of a certain mode of governance for bringing about sustainable results could be found. Specific promises with regard to the merits of new modes should thus be approached with caution.

The findings correspond with conclusions in empirical studies from both the more specific literature on the environmental effectiveness of new modes and the more general research on their performance - as introduced in chapter 2.4. These literature strands point out that there is no straightforward answer to the question whether new modes increase general or environmental effectiveness compared to traditional ones.

This is not to say that new modes are not needed for governing societies towards more sustainable tracks. The findings indicate that just as hierarchical modes, they have both drawbacks and advantages. Accordingly, they have their place in the endeavor to induce transformation processes towards SD - as the complexity of unstructured and persistent problems calls for approaches with different strengths (cf. further chapter 7.3). This generally implies that a mix of governance modes might be more successful in promoting SD than a single mode. The discussion also already pointed to the importance of a certain form of meta-governing. These two aspects will be further elaborated in chapter 7.3.

7.2 Hypotheses to be tested in future research

Based on the insights from the previous chapters, hypotheses to be tested in further sustainability governance research are formulated in the following. The hypotheses can on the one hand guide quantitative studies that aim at exploring governance arrangements with a larger number of cases (which might also touch upon causal relations). On the other hand, qualitative studies that explore a particular hypothesis in more detail are possible. Supposing that certain findings are of structural and procedural nature in terms of the mode of governance - and thus not specific to sustainability governance and its content - some hypotheses can also guide more general studies in the broader field of governance research.

H1a: *Interactive modes of governance easily fail to induce any changes in society towards SD at all (especially actual actions and institutionalization processes).*

H1b: *Interactive governance modes fail more easily than hierarchical modes to induce actual actions and institutionalization processes.*

H2: *A 'shadow of hierarchy' in self-governance modes, i.e. support by public authorities in the background (especially at early phases), is required to leverage the arrangement and thus to promote SD.*

H3: *Public-private modes of governance fail to promote SD when there is no threat of a more stringent mode (either already existing or to be implemented in case of failure).*

H 4: *Certain aspects associated with 'new' modes of governance - and made responsible for their assumed superiority to 'traditional' modes in light of SD - can also occur through hierarchical modes (such as learning, the increase of trust among actors with different positions in an atmosphere of mutual confidence, and the strengthening of solidarity).*

H 5: *Participatory elements in governance arrangements can hinder reaching faster and more sustainable results.*

H 6: *The nature of the embedding context, e.g. the political-cultural environment of a governance arrangement, can be more influential for the potential of governance to promote SD than the mode itself.*

H 7: *The particularities of actors involved in governance (e.g. their skills, preferences, origin and commitment or the positioning to other actors) can be more influential for the potential of governance to promote SD than the mode itself.*

H 8: *The potential of governance modes to promote SD differs according to variation in the nature of the embedding context and the particularities of the actors involved.*

7.3 Sustainability governance as a meta-governed interplay of modes

Against the background of the findings and implications presented above, this study aims to bring forward a shift in the focus of the current sustainability governance discourse. More specifically, I will argue that the debate should shift its focus - from currently concentrating on new modes of governance - to two aspects: the interplay of governance modes in different contexts (i.), and the meta-governing of this interplay (ii.).

(i.) The situational interplay of governance modes

A general insight from the findings of this study is the indication that there is no 'one-fits-all-solution' when it comes to governing towards SD. Some interviewees also explicitly argued that there is no single best way of steering and that an approach must fit its particular purpose (»*Depending on what you want to achieve, you must find a different way of steering.*«, interview 02-04, transl.; »*There are several mechanisms of steering, and I think all make sense according to different target groups and situations.*«, interview 01-03, transl.; »*I mean, a certain arrangement is not the all-in-one device suitable for every purpose.*«, interview 02-02, transl.).

This indicates that the choice of a particular mode of governance for a given situation necessarily requires the consideration of both the goals addressed and the embedding context. For instance, experts argued that in certain areas change can best or even only be achieved through hierarchical steering by governments with legal power. As one interviewee pointed out: »*If you have a situation where the prices of goods are not right and you want to internalize external costs, only the government has the resources and legitimacy to increase prices in a distributional way and decide upon the usage of the money.*« (interview 01-02, transl.). In turn, another interviewee argued, for instance, that the success of the arrangement around the Minergie label is linked to the specific circumstance that the building sector is close to affected people with a direct stake: »*Minergie is a nice example that a completely voluntary movement can work [...] But you have to see, the building sector is really close to the people that are affected. People thus have a direct stake. This is crucial in this regard.*« (interview 01-03, transl.). Similarly, an expert argued that the purpose and environment for bottom-up steering has to fit: »*In the mobility sector, if you want to change something, these are systemic radical changes with regard to overall established infrastructures and so on. This is a difficult environment for bottom-up steering and grassroots movements. So - this is an argument to regulate top-down with science-based and long-term politics.«* (interview 03-03, transl.).

Following these perspectives, the general challenge then turns out as finding tailored solutions for specific situations, i.e. a best fit - an approach that works best in a particular problem frame. The variety of problems associated with the pursuit of SD calls for a flexible repertoire of responses, i.e. 'requisite variety' (e.g. Jessop, 2002). The importance of governance solutions tailored to the particular context is highlighted by several authors (cf. the references to contextual influence above, cf. more specifically Bornemann et al., *forthcoming*; cf. also Gritsenko, 2014; van de Meene et al., 2011). An overall crucial question is what works where, when, how and why in terms of promoting SD (cf. Lafferty, 2004).

The results of this study indicate that new governance modes are no panacea in this regard - the findings do not point to a general superiority of certain modes to bring about sustainable results. Against this backdrop, it is reasonable to argue that the future debate should overcome its particular focus on new modes. The findings do not indicate generic differences among governance modes that would make such a focus promising.

This is not to say that research on new modes should not be conducted. Quite the contrary, empirical scrutiny of the merits of such modes is highly required. A deeper understanding of new governance arrangements in light of SD will substantially advance both sustainability governance research and practice. In line with this, the hypotheses in the previous chapter do explicitly call for further inquiry and can guide future research. However, a too focused perspective on new modes could be counterproductive as other important questions are neglected. On the one hand, there is a danger of losing sight of the role of hierarchical governance. The assumption that traditional governance is ill-equipped to handle SD problems contributes to reproducing normative claims and pushes research on hierarchical governance into the background (cf. e.g. Meuleman, 2008, p. 121: »*Much research seems to have adopted a 'network is everything' paradigm and in general neglects the study of contemporary hierarchical governance.*«). On the other hand, and even more importantly, the interaction of modes is neglected. The assumption that with certain modes there is a superior solution might hinder the exploration of the question of which mix of modes is appropriate in certain situations.

The in-depth case studies of this study indicate that each governance mode has its specific strengths and weaknesses, especially in view of addressing sustainability challenges. Jessop (1998; cf. also Howlett & Ramesh, 2015) argues that failure is central to all social relations and thus to all governance forms. Governance failure can be concerned with both procedural (e.g. touching legitimacy issues) and result issues (e.g. effectiveness in problem solving and achieving objectives) - which influence each other (cf. in this regard also general literature on the advantages and drawbacks of the institutions of hierarchies, markets and networks[29]; e.g. Meuleman, 2008; Jessop, 2009; Evans, 2012). Following this perspective, the challenge in governance practices is to bring together the respective advantages of different existing modes and to counter their drawbacks.

Accordingly, arguing for a focus shift in the discourse does also not say that new modes do not play a vital part in promoting SD in practice. The case study results indicate that while in certain situations, hierarchical steering can be appropriate, in other contexts, new modes may be indeed more promising (in the case of Minergie, the network structure to include all relevant stakeholders, and the flexible self-governing characteristics to enable an innovative forerunner position were vital for the success of the arrangement). Yet, hierarchical governance should not be played off against new modes or the other way around. The findings indicate that all modes of governance have their role to play for promoting SD. In this regard, the potential of governing already existing in the form of several coexisting modes can be used, making the best of today`s variety to govern.

To exploit this potential, investigating the interplay of governance modes in different contexts becomes important. An advanced understand-

29 While networks e.g. might have the advantage of being high in trust and inclusion, they may on the other hand have weak democratic legitimation and might result in long talks without reaching results. Markets may value efficiency and individual responsibility but risk producing market failures. In comparison to hierarchies, networks and markets may suffer from structure, reliability and accountability. Hierarchies may have advantages with regard to control, lines of command, clarity of responsibility, and elaborated planning systems. Potential weaknesses include inflexibility, bureaucratic procedures or a lesser focus on innovation (cf. in more detail e.g. Meuleman, 2008; Jessop, 2009; Evans, 2012).

ing is needed of which mix of modes functions best in certain circumstances to bring about sustainable results (which is ultimately an empirical question). The sustainability governance discourse should thus not only explore isolated modes and their performances but also their interplay and the situational appropriate mix of modes. In this sense, the practice of sustainable governance in turn can evolve as the contextually best combination of modes (from state steering to public-private partnerships, to interactive and self-governing forms), without making one mode a panacea, or denying a certain one a role in the mixture. The findings of this study indicate that this way of governing might be better suited to handle the complex challenges associated with sustainability. Treating modes as alternatives, rather than complementary approaches, unnecessarily narrows options for promoting SD. The task in practice is then to improve the performance of an encompassing governance system, composed of different modes (cf. also illustrations by Martin & Gunningham, 2014).

The endeavor of combining modes has explicit relevance in view of the integration challenge due to cross-sectoral problems of unsustainability. It may be the case that a certain mode of governance would be very successful in isolation, but - in combination with others - no sustainable results are induced, due to undermining interdependencies. In line with this, authors argue that steering societies towards SD can be seen as an overall integrated endeavor, e.g. crossing the borders of policy areas (cf. e.g. Bornemann, 2013; Steurer, 2010; Cristopolous et al., 2012). Such authors highlight that sustainability governance is more than the sum of its parts. The single parts have to be seen in one common context, while sustainability governance takes effect in many ways that are geared to each other. Larger governance systems by a mix of modes would in this regard entail the virtue that the failure of a certain mode does not necessarily mean a failure of the whole system - since another mode can step in.

The implication of the findings - putting emphasis on the situational mix of governance modes to promote SD - is not necessarily surprising. However, it does stand in a certain contrast to (partly implicit and partly normative) prominent thinking in SD governance literature and adjacent discourses. Several studies regard hierarchical governance as ineffective in dealing with sustainability problems and set high expectations for new governance modes (cf. chapters 1.1 and 2.4). There are indeed scholars who also explicitly argue for new modes but do not juxtapose them with hierarchical ones - and see an important role for traditional governing, too.

For instance, Meadowcroft (2011, p. 5) states that »*while one can't make progress towards sustainability without new governance mechanisms, there is also a critical place for good old-fashioned [...] state action*« (cf. also below). However, a high focus on new modes and a respective domination of studies in the general discourse is clearly observable. The strongly concentrated evolution might be one of the reasons why parts of the discourse hold new modes as generally superior. When more and more studies get published that focus on new modes - without the hint that such modes are not supposed to replace but only supplement traditional hierarchical ones - the whole discourse risks to turn in this direction. Researchers then reduce the pool of possible governing alternatives by 'being stuck' with certain modes and in some way 'wearing new modes glasses' - entailing the danger that new modes are seen without question as the 'Holy Grail'. This can not only be problematic in terms of their (assumed) performance in promoting SD, but also raises other critical questions, for instance, with regard to their implementation in deeply hierarchical or non-democratic states, or in terms of legitimacy and accountability.

Yet, there are also authors in the sustainability governance literature, who explicitly point to the importance of combining state, market and network oriented governance in view of dealing with sustainability (e.g. Baker, 2009; Hysing, 2015; Meadowcroft, 2011; Huh, 2011; Meuleman & In 't Veld, 2010). The shift in the focus that I argue for is in line with these contributions. For instance, Huh (2011) speaks of a configuration among state, market and civil society that is indispensable for the realization of SD (cf. also Webb, 2005). Driessen et al. (2013, p. 7) argue: »*Although mainstream literature emphasizes the need for collaborative and deliberative modes [...] there is still a special role to play for the state.*« Other authors more generally argue for a mix of the broader styles of hierarchies, markets and networks, leading to hybrid arrangements (e.g. van de Meene et al., 2011; as well as Hoppe, 2010, who state that complex problems cannot be successfully tackled by hierarchies, markets or networks alone). From this perspective, it follows that state steering is not (to be) replaced by new modes but supplemented, and that the state remains a central actor amongst others (cf. also chapter 2.2 and 3.1.1). Baker (2009) argues in view of SD that hierarchically oriented governance may be especially appropriate for initiating action and ensuring transparency, accountability and legitimacy. Governance oriented rather on the market, such as partnerships, may be able to rouse entrepreneurship and self-regulatory responsibility. More network and interactively oriented governance in turn might be better suited to laying the basis for consent and long-term support and supplying innovative insights (cf. Meuleman & In 't Veld, 2010).

The focus shift towards exploring appropriate mixes of modes would in a way correspond with the development of the more specific research on policy instrument choice (cf. e.g. Howlett & Rayner, 2007). Research in this regard »*tended to focus on single instruments, albeit acknowledging that others are present [...] Third generation thinking has now recognized the need to develop optimal policy instrument designs in complex multi-instrument settings.*« (Taylor et al., 2012, p. 282). Givoni et al. (2013), for instance, speak of policy packages, i.e. considering the full range of instruments available and employing a carefully designed mix to create positive interactions - and to respond to context-dependent features (cf. also Gunningham & Grabosky, 1998). I hold that general research on sustainability governance should similarly break out in this direction. In this regard, it can learn from and make use of the experiences gained in the more specialized field of policy instrument choice to find appropriate mixes (cf. e.g. Howlett & Rayner, 2007, for a summary of problems and challenges in this regard). This entails the endeavor of finding ways to bring governance modes into packages, leading to more sustainable results when compared to single modes deployed in isolation. However, even in the narrow field of policy instruments (given that a mode of governance can pursue a range of instruments), the scientific evaluation of the effectiveness of instrument mixes and their interactions is only beginning to grow (cf. e.g. Weber et al., 2014).

The shift in the discourse focus would also correspond with a certain existing trend in broader governance research. Rayner (2015) retraces the past and future of governance studies and the evolution of governance literature by identifying certain patterns. In his view, early contributions had a focus on governing change, being restricted to an understanding of the governance concept as new governance. Over an increasing identification of general forms (hierarchies, markets, networks), highlighting the importance of hybrid modes of coordination and their failures became more important, as well as acknowledging governance dynamics.

From the experience gained in the empirical part of this study, it furthermore appears that sustainability governance practice stands in a certain contrast to research. Among practitioners, the normative assumption putting emphasis on new modes is not as present as in science. In practice, it seems more natural to rely on a mix of approaches (in this sense it might even be argued that research in a certain way lags behind actual practices of sustainability governance). Several interview experts specifically highlighted the importance of the interaction of modes in a certain policy field (»*I think it is important to regard the different existing ways of steering not in juxtaposition. If you want to change something, action in several different ways is necessary [...] One approach in a policy field can only be one element of many others. Also, one should not expect things that a single arrangement can simply not provide.*«, interview 02-05, transl.; »*Bottom-up and top-down steering - one needs both [...] You need diversity.*«, interview 02-03, transl.; »*To address a problem from different sides, an interaction of approaches is decisive.*«, interview 05-04, transl.). Moreover, even practitioners in self-governing and interactive arrangements explicitly stressed the importance of governmental steering (cf. chapter 7.1). The strong focus on new modes in research thus in part slightly seems to be a development in an ′ivory tower′. In line with this, critiques are raised on new approaches such as transition management. In practice, such approaches frequently take place in areas protected from established policy-making systems and thus stand partly in contrast to real-world politics. This raises the question of the transfer - and according functionality - from the experimental test fields to a co-existence with incumbent governance regimes (cf. e.g. Shove & Walker, 2007; Voss & Bornemann, 2011).

(ii.) The meta-governance of an appropriate mix of modes in different contexts

Combining governance modes and choosing the right mix for specific situations clearly presents a challenge. An interplay of different modes is of course not successful per se. Governing by a mix of modes necessarily provokes the confrontation of various aspects; for instance in terms of thematic scope, spatial and temporal scales, levels, sectors and the cooperation of multiple actors. This entails the challenge of integrating potentially competing aspects, to coordinate the activities of actors and to find a coherent approach. This can lead to tension and unsatisfactory results.

The interplay of modes can be especially problematic since modes can not only enable but also interfere with and preclude each other. A certain mode can undermine another one and combinations may lead to conflicts due to competition. Certain modes may be incompatible with others in a specific situation (for a description of the tensions between the broader governance styles of hierarchies, markets and networks cf. e.g. Torfing & Triantafillou, 2013; Meuleman, 2014; for an empirical analysis of tensions between participative and hierarchical modes cf. e.g. Brownill, 2009).

Overall, the possible failure of governance mixes thus has to be explicitly taken into account. Finding a workable relationship among modes, i.e. a balance so that one mode e.g. does not crowd out another, is no easy task. Accordingly, an understanding of how to harness productive relationships among modes and of dealing with trade-offs is needed (for an analysis of synergies cf. e.g. Meuleman, 2008; cf. also insights from the more specific research on policy instrument mixes and packages, e.g. Taylor et al., 2012). Knowledge is required to increase the likelihood that modes cross-fertilize each other, i.e. being mutually supportive, and that a situational mix of different modes is working smoothly. Therefore, the modes′ synergetic and contradictory interrelationships have to be carefully explored (in this regard, the embedding context of a larger governance system also plays a decisive role).

Accordingly, in order to be able to choose an appropriate combination for a given situation, it is necessary to go one step beyond respectively above governance. A 'smart' fusion of modes requires an advanced understanding of where different modes succeed or fail - as well as of when and how modes can complement or hamper each other. Therefore, some sort of a 'bird's eye perspective' is needed to harmonize the different aspects; periodic monitoring and evaluation is required. This calls for explicitly coordinating the broader conditions under which governance takes place, in other words, a certain form of meta-governance.

The concept of meta-governance has increasingly gained momentum over the past two decades. It is basically understood as the 'governance of governance' (cf. e.g. Kooiman & Jentoft, 2009; Torfing et al., 2012; Jessop, 2011), i.e. steering attempts from a level above. Referring to some form of higher-order governance, it thus concerned with the »*organization of the conditions for governance*« (Jessop, 2002, p. 48; cf. also Rayner, 2015; Torfing & Triantafillou, 2013; Kickert et al., 1997). It addresses designing, shaping or managing governance and entails both institutional and strategic aspects as well as norms and ideas about how to govern. Yet, beyond the broader basic understanding, the concept of meta-governance is ill-defined and has been interpreted in several different ways.

The approach has become particularly prominent in light of failures of different governance mechanisms - especially network failures. The predominant understanding restricts the notion to the steering of networks only, i.e. the regulation of self-regulation. Most authors thus perceive meta-governance in the form of network management, by influencing the conditions under which networks operate (e.g. in light of interdependency, governability, integration or governmentality theories; e.g. Sørensen & Torfing, 2009; Larsson, 2015). Similarly, meta-governance is conceived as a way for supervising or regaining state control over networks and markets (e.g. Whitehead, 2003; Bell & Park, 2006; Kelly, 2006). However, there are also authors, who perceive meta-governance in a broader sense - as an approach for coordinating a mix of the broader governance styles of hierarchies, markets and networks (e.g. Jessop, 2002; Meuleman, 2008; Cristopoulos et al., 2012). Accordingly, in most basic terms, meta-governance understandings can be distinguished regarding whether they are concerned with one style of governance or a combination thereof. Jessop (2011) accordingly differentiates between a tinkering kind of meta-governance (seeking to make a particular set of governance arrangements more effective) and an architectural kind (aiming to address the weaknesses of one governance arrangement with the strengths of another).

I hold that the approach can unfold its full potential when it does not prescribe a certain mode of governance and when it is used in a broad sense that is not reduced to e.g. institutional mechanisms. In this way, it is concerned with all practices, structures, strategies and ideas that affect the way in which governance workings are designed and managed. Used in this manner, it in principle provides a promising 'tool' for the challenge of adequately integrating different modes to achieve sustainable results in different context. This includes the choice of modes as well as managing the links between them. A meta-governance perspective may enable one to explore how modes interact and how an appropriate mix of modes in certain situations could look like. Accordingly, it can prevent the selection of a certain mode a priori. Instead, encompassing governance systems may be developed that include the best combination of modes for a given situation. Besides combining governance modes, meta-governance also implies the ability to switch between modes when the situation requires or maintain a successful governance mode mixture. Such a perspective principally provides the space for recognizing strength and weaknesses of specific modes and to find a productive equilibrium between them. It may also increase the understanding of failures of modes and mixtures. Approaches for dealing with failures can then be gradually strengthened. Scholars highlight in this regard that standardized recipes should be handled with caution and argue for a learning from working situations, i.e. 'good practices' (cf. e.g. Meuleman, 2008; Meuleman & Niestroy, 2015).

A meta-governance perspective might further entail the potential to be better equipped to govern in a context-sensitive way (cf. also Cristopoulos et al., 2012; Meuleman, 2008). Since different combinations are possible, a flexible repertoire of responses may be at hand to find tailor-made answers - in light of the cross-sectoral and multi-dimensional challenges associated with SD. By taking a situational 'bird's eye view', meta-governance in principle enables the identification of the best solution for a given situation, while taking into account different influencing factors - such as the nature of the embedding context or the particularities of actors involved (cf. chapter 7.1). On the basis of a thorough context analysis, an appropriate mix of modes can then be developed and managed.[30]

The question is then what a concrete meta-governance approach for SD can look like in practice. Within the literature, practical guides and analyses have emerged that aim to show how arrangements are or should be meta-governed. Meta-governance forms are thereby usually summarized under the headings of 'hands-off and hands-on meta-governance', which usage depends upon the context and the intended objectives (cf. e.g. Torfing & Triantafillou, 2013; Larsson, 2015; Torfing et al., 2012). In hands-off meta-governance, steering is exercised at a distance and without direct interaction with the governing actors, by providing e.g. institutional design and structuring of processes or allocation of resources. Hands-on meta-governance in turn is exercised in closer proximity and involves direct interaction with the actors participating in governance.

However, in general, research on the concrete problems and merits of meta-governance is pretty much in its infancy and only beginning to grow. There is thus a need for more studies that systematically investigate the

30 This is also relevant in light of the question of transferring 'western' governance models to 'non-western' countries. The meta-perspective entails the potential to take cultural aspects into account (cf. e.g. Meuleman, 2008).

specific conditions under which (and the mechanisms by which) meta-governance produces certain results. Since meta-governance entails challenges and limitations, failures need to be explicitly considered and learned from (cf. in more detail e.g. Jessop, 2011). Most work so far deals with the approach on a rather abstract level, neglecting more specific practical questions. There are some case studies of meta-governing in action (e.g. Whitehead, 2003; Kelly, 2006; Bell & Park, 2006; cf. also empirical contributions in Torfing & Triantafillou, 2013). However, most empirical studies are reduced to the realm of governmental steering of networks.

Apart from this, there is some more general research on forms of meta-governing in the field of SD. For instance, Haughton et al. (2008) deal with the potential of meta-governance to provide coherence between fragmented landscapes of governance. Engberg and Larsen (2010) are concerned with meta-governing as a form of providing context-oriented solutions and enabling public authorities to solve governance dilemmas by using a second-order perspective. Lund et al. (2012) in turn highlight that meta-governance might stimulate cross-sectoral collaboration, while Parkins (2008) elaborate on institutional adaptation. Finally, Cristopoulos et al. (2012) take a broad perspective by comparing certain SD related cases. The authors conclude that »*incorporating a meta-governance approach in the design and implementation phases of interventions for SD holds the promise of increasing their success rate*«, and generally speak of a »*coordination potential of meta-governance that can make it valuable for addressing the complexity of SD [...] Meta-governance has the potential to cast light on what is the right patchwork of governance elements in order to develop the right cross-sectoral mix of policies.*« (ibid., p. 306-307).

Against this backdrop, future research and practice ought to increasingly elaborate on how an appropriate meta-governing of a mix of modes to promote SD could look like. The so far rather abstract notion of meta-governance needs to be specified in the sense of how it concretely unfolds in real-world settings. Alongside exploring the merits of meta-governance, this also includes investigating its problems and potential failures. Yet, with regard to practices, Meuleman (2008) also demonstrated by a comparison of five case studies on public-sector policy projects that responsible actors already used aspects of meta-governance (combining, switching and maintaining governance styles of hierarchies, markets and networks) although they had never heard of the term (again, this might suggest that governance practices in a certain way may be 'ahead of science').

One of the central questions in view of concrete meta-governing is who may adequately act as a 'meta-governor', and how the mechanisms that allocate responsibilities unfold. Most contributions in the pertinent literature point to public authorities as the subjects of meta-governance (for discussion on the 'manager of meta-governance', cf. e.g. Sørensen, 2006; Meuleman & Niestroy, 2015; Meuleman, 2008; Larsson, 2015). Some authors even exclusively understand meta-governance as the role of the state in the oversight, coordination and resourcing of governance arrangements (e.g. Whitehead, 2003; Bell & Park, 2006; cf. also Kelly, 2006; Bell & Hindmoor, 2009). In light of their capacity and legitimacy, such authorities may be able to take leadership in the tasks of analyzing situations, as well as developing and managing an appropriative governance mode mix. Governments can thereby either act as a regulator, a coordinator or as an authority to create enabling environments for other actors. Accordingly, for the larger system of meta-governed modes, public authorities might play a key role. In line with this, interviewees pointed to the necessity that the state sets long-term framing conditions (cf. above). Yet, there are also critical studies on public authorities as meta-governors, pointing to limitations (e.g. because of the need to keep sufficient public support). Authors in this regard argue that publications on meta-governance frequently take a perspective of the central steering role of governments (neglecting the ways through which societal actors could play this role), and that societal actors can indeed develop meta-governance capacities (e.g. In't Veld, 2013; Glasbergen, 2011; Koppenjan et al., 2013; for a more specific elaboration on the roles and functions of state authorities and societal actors in meta-governing, cf. Cristopoulos et al., 2012, p. 309).

Basically, meta-governance entails a struggle between meta-governors and meta-governed actors. It can also fail due to rivalry between governors or due to either too little or too much meta-governing. In general, the question of who should perform meta-governance in which way would thus be one of the central questions if research 'head out' to increasingly explore the appropriate meta-governance of a combination of modes.

Taking everything into account, by illustrating general potentials, I argued in this chapter for a focus shift in the sustainability governance discourse: from an 'overconcentration' on new modes to the meta-governing of a situational mixture of modes. However, several questions in this regard stand out and new research fields to be addressed in future research arise (cf. also chapter 8.3).

Part V: Conclusion

8 Summary, reflection, outlook

In this final part of the study, I will - in a backward looking manner - first give a summary on the key theoretical and empirical results (chapter 8.1), and then reflect on the strengths and limitations of the research (chapter 8.2). Finally, in a forward looking manner, I will sketch out research desiderata for the field of sustainability governance (chapter 8.3).

8.1 Summary

This study has taken up the growing scientific and political discourse on how to govern societies towards more sustainable tracks. The lively debate in this regard reflects the quest for adequate governance in pursuit of sustainability in general, and for understanding the relation between modes and SD more specifically. Against the backdrop of an influential normative claim in the literature that SD calls for new governance modes, this study explored the potential of the range of different modes to promote SD. In so doing, it contributes to filling the knowledge gap concerning whether certain modes are in fact generally superior to others when it comes to inducing societal transformation processes towards SD.

The study adds to the discourse in both theoretical and empirical respects. In theoretical terms, it shed light on governance, its modes and impacts in light of sustainability by providing conceptual clarification to each of these aspects. Particularly, the following contributions were made. First of all, the study unraveled the elusive field of governance by developing a sound conceptualization, which covers the inherent complexity of real-world arrangements. The multi-dimensional approach explicitly considers the interdependencies of institutional structures, interaction processes and substantive settings. In so doing, it facilitates a systematic understanding of how governance works in different arrangements. Second, the study shed light on approaches to meaningfully distinguish among modes of governance. Apart from that, it contributed to clarifying the chain of governance and its results. It elaborated a scheme for grasping governance impacts as strategic reactions of affected actors. This enables one to capture the multiple areas in society where governance can induce change and provides the link between governance modes and end results. Finally, the study illustrated a way for appraising impacts in terms of sustainability by developing sound situational appraisal criteria.

In empirical terms, the study offers insights on the merits of governance modes in terms of SD. Guided by the theoretical framework, the study applied a comparative case study approach of a qualitative nature to empirically explore five real-world arrangements in Swiss energy policy. The arrangements were first of all analyzed by means of the governance conceptualization, in order to arrive at a deepened understanding of their workings. Subsequently, each arrangement was allocated to a certain mode of governance - from hierarchically centralized and decentralized governance, to public-private and interactive modes up to self-governance. Finally, the impacts of the arrangements were identified and appraised in terms of SD. Overall, this led to a differentiated picture of the workings of different arrangements that cover the range of modes, and their triggering of societal changes towards SD.

The results of the empirical case studies revealed no differences among modes of governance indicating that certain modes are generally better suited to promoting SD than others. In contrast, the superiority of new to traditional modes - as proclaimed in mainstream sustainability governance literature - is put into perspective. The results neither indicate that new modes are per se better suited to induce changes in action strategies of affected actors - nor that induced changes are more in line with sustainability goals. Instead, findings indicate that interactive governance can easily fail to trigger actions towards SD at all. The results also show that self-governing can be very successful in promoting SD, yet a ′shadow of hierarchy′ may be required as leverage. Moreover, public-private modes can easily fail when there is no threat of a more stringent mode, and participatory elements can also hinder faster and more sustainable results. Finally, traditional hierarchical modes can be potent in contributing to SD and certain aspects held responsible for the supposed superiority of new modes can also occur through hierarchical modes. Apart from this, findings also indicate that other factors - such as the particularities of involved actors or the nature of the embedding context - can occasionally be more influential for the potential of governance to promote SD than the mode itself. Against this backdrop, it can be concluded that the mode does not determine the potential of governance to promote SD in such a way as assumed in the literature. Thus, new modes are no panacea for sustainability governance. Based on the results, a set of hypotheses to be tested in future research was formulated.

Taking everything into account, the study contributes to the search for suitable sustainability governance by shedding light on the potential of governance modes to promote SD. In so doing, it serves as a basis for discussing claims on the merits of modes and informs normative literature strands with empirical evidence. In view of the findings, future sustainability governance research should shift its focus from concentrating on new modes to the interplay of modes, and the meta-governing of a tailored mix of modes in different contexts.

As the study fosters a deepened understanding of governance in pursuit of SD, it also provides valuable information to societal practitioners in the field. It produced an information basis for better understanding both actual workings of governance and their results in light of SD. In view of the findings, some advice for 'governance planners and makers' can be formulated. Apart from thoroughly reflecting on the complex field of governance results, practitioners should increasingly conceive of sustainability governance as a meta-governed situational interplay of different modes. In this way, the best of today`s variety to govern can be made, putting forward the quest for steering societies towards SD.

8.2 Reflection on the research

In the following, a critical reflection on the research of this study is given. It highlights both the insights gained and merits of the study, as well as problems and limitations that have arisen. I will first have a look at how the theoretical framework proved itself as a benchmark for the empirical research - and reflect on the difficulties that came up in the empirical part in light of the framework (although the goal of the case studies was not to explicitly validate the framework, but to illuminate the research question and enable the formulation of hypotheses, cf. chapter 4.1). This includes experiences with the governance conceptualization (i.), the frame for modes (ii.), the scheme for impacts (iii.), and the normative frame for sustainability appraisal (iv.). Afterwards, I reflect on the research methodology (v.), and respective limitations in terms of gained results (vi.).

The four elaborated elements of the theoretical framework generally turned out to be useful heuristic devices for the empirical part, and thus for illuminating the research questions (since they covered the relevant aspects in view of the research objectives, the frames were not altered in view of some experience with the case studies - cf. in this regard also chapter 4.1).

(i.) First of all, it can be noted that the *governance conceptualization* successfully enabled the empirical analysis of governance arrangements. The three interdependent dimensions of structures, processes and contents, together with their interplay, provided an appropriate lens to shed light on the complexity of real-world arrangements. For each case study, the workings of governance, and thus the ways through which change could be induced, were disclosed. This built the basis to understand the chain of governance and results.

However, as expected (cf. chapter 3.1), it became apparent in empirical research that it is partly difficult to clearly distinguish among the dimensions and their covered aspects. The division lines in real-world arrangements are in fact blurred, resulting in a nested character. The empirical case studies thus emphasized the interdependence and overlap of the dimensions. Separating them for analytical reasons was frequently not an easy task - leading also to some repetitions in the presentation of results and the referral to certain aspects from one dimension in another one.

Apart from this, it was sometimes difficult to draw the demarcation lines of a governance arrangement. For instance, in the case of the CO_2 levy it became apparent that the mechanism to get exempted from the levy and thus the reduction commitments must be seen as a part of the arrangement (this mechanism was also of major concern for certain induced impacts). The Climate Cent instrument in turn stood in close connection to the arrangement but it was clearly not a part of it. Overall, this indicates that analyses of governance arrangements should not focus on the official policy instrument without noticing the aspects connected to it - since an instrument can frequently not be regarded as completely isolated. Moreover, the boundaries of a governance arrangement in relation to other arrangements have to be carefully drawn.

Furthermore, when designing and conducting the expert interviews, it became apparent that the translation of a complex conceptualization to the real-world environment of actors is not an easy task. This was even more complicated due to the nested fashion of the dimensions. Also, it turned out that the experience of 'governance planners and makers' is frequently focused on the used policy instruments of an arrangement. Since the perspective of interview experts was often reduced to this aspect, it was difficult to talk about other aspects that governance is also about. Yet, once an appropriate reduction of complexity and translation to the real-world environment was found, the dimensions and their interplay together formed an in-depth picture of the empirical cases.

In this regard, insights could be produced to a desideratum several authors call for: that further empirical knowledge is required to understand how sustainability governance exactly works in different real-world settings (e.g. Van Zeijl-Rozema et al., 2008; Adger & Jordan, 2009). Analyses of governance arrangements that include multiple dimensions, while considering their interplay, are only beginning to grow. This study has shown that the approach of analyzing governance via several key features among different dimensions enables one to reach a deep understanding of real-world workings.

As it has proven its usefulness, it can be said that the conceptualization with its lens on governance facets and their interdependencies represents a contribution to (SD) governance research. A more general version of the conceptualization, i.e. its basic structure, has been published in Lange et al. (2013). Its merits have been shown on the one hand by subsequent empirical studies that explicitly take it as a theoretical basis and apply it in their research (e.g. Wan & Bramwell, 2015 - or Dai, 2015). On the other hand, certain theoretical contributions explicitly refer to its virtue. For instance, Pisano et al. (2014, p. 13) state that »*an extremely useful viewpoint on governance for sustainable development is offered by Lange et al.*« Yet, further empirical scrutiny, e.g. by quantitative studies, is required. While the basic structure seems reasonable (cf. justifications in chapter 3.1), the aspects considered within the dimensions to shed light on the workings of different arrangements may be debatable and should be further scrutinized.

In general, the conceptualization furthermore supplements the 'form-follows-function' consideration, as introduced in chapter 2.4, by providing analytic clarification. It allows for developing a more differentiated picture of suitable forms of sustainability governance, by drawing attention to the three constitutive and interdependent dimensions of governance. More specific questions regarding the concrete design of structures, processes and contents, including their relationships, can then be explored (i.e. which designs of key features among the dimensions are detrimental to SD and how the dimensions ought to look in order to best foster SD). While the procedural dimension touches on issues such as the appropriate representation of interests, the structural dimension e.g. raises questions of a suitable form of democracy for SD. Finally, the contents dimension relates to issues of appropriate policy integration and the proper use of knowledge. In principle, the pursuit of SD plays a role in all three different dimensions (for a similar consideration cf. also Wydra & Pülzl, 2013). Transcending issues, such as reflexivity and adaptability, can also be analyzed from a new angle by exploring them in light of the three individual dimensions. Hence, the conceptualization allows for explicating adequate sustainability governance in both a more differentiated and comprehensive manner.

(ii.) Second, the chosen frame for *governance modes* turned out to be a suitable way for meaningfully distinguishing among modes - and allocating the empirical cases accordingly. A general analogy of the ideal-typical governance modes and the explored real-world arrangements could be found. It was also possible to identify shifts in modes of governance over time (a shift from self-governance to interactive governance in the Minergie case study). However, in some cases, certain key features were mixed up compared to the ideal-typical frame. An example is the case of the CO_2 levy. It was clearly assignable to the centralized mode (since most key features of the ideal-type could be observed in the case). Yet, with regard to the key feature of policy instruments, the case showed an instrument associated with a different ideal-type: incentive-based measures like taxes are in the frame associated with the public-private mode. However, generally speaking, especially hierarchical governing arrangements make use of different policy instruments. This confirmed that the modes in the framework clearly have to be seen as ideal-types (cf. also chapter 3.2.2, cf. also Driessen et al., 2012). It also directs attention to the demand that future work dedicated to developing frameworks on governance modes should strive for justifying why specific dimensions are considered in a certain way (revealing the respective potential and limitations). The rationale for the choice could, for example, based on the research interest and thus on theoretical and/or empirical grounds. Thus, while the theoretical perspective from which research is undertaken can determine the selection, empirical fertility and context adequacy can also function as a touchstone.

While the frame used in this study has proven its value for analyzing governance arrangements, further empirical scrutiny is also required in this regard (cf. also Driessen et al., 2012). An expansion, as well as a reduction in terms of features might be suitable, e.g. if further empirical testing should reveal that certain aspects are underrepresented or negligible.

The case studies of this study disclosed that it might be explicitly promising to complement the frame with hybrid modes in their own right. Possible supplements are an ideal-typical 'self-governance mode in the shadow of hierarchy' or a 'centralized mode with deliberative rationalities'. Such hybrid modes seem to appear frequently enough in real-world governing that a specific consideration is particularly useful.

(iii.) The scheme for *governance impacts* in turn has proven itself as a suitable lens for covering the broad range of possible societal changes induced by governance. The open perspective of action strategies allowed the recognition of several important areas. It not only shed light on actions and institutionalization processes but also e.g. on structural changes and alterations in discourses. With regard to the field of promoting SD, it is particularly illuminating since it is able to grasp the general inherent dynamics within societies.

Since the linkage between governance workings and end results - when understood in an encompassing sense as the entirety of societal change - so far represented a 'black box' within (SD) governance research, the frame is a contribution to the debate. In general, it adds to research in the pursuit of reaching a better understanding of the spheres where governance can trigger change. In turn, the insights gained via the frame in the empirical part contribute to the understanding of the societal changes induced by different governance modes. However, this field of research, when considered holistically, can be regarded to be in its beginning. Again, further empirical scrutiny is required to validate the frame (e.g. in terms of its specific considered categories of action strategies).

The empirical part further revealed that (just as in terms of the governance conceptualization) it was difficult to translate a complex theoretical frame for analysis, e.g. to the real-world environment of actors approached for expert interviews. The perspective of action strategies turned out to be a highly abstract one that had to be carefully broken down to the concrete experiences of the actors. Moreover, it was frequently difficult to talk about a range of governance results, respectively the effects of an arrangement on the different relevant areas in view of affected actors. The experience of interviewees was often completely reduced to the results of the policy instrument used in the arrangement. Also, it turned out that affected actors frequently do not perceive the influence of a specific arrangement to a detailed degree. The experience of politics and governing for real-world actors is much broader. Questions about the influence of specific aspects of a governance arrangement were thus in part too much to ask of interview experts in light of their real-world perception.

A complete reconstruction of action strategies (and their change) of all the different actors in the field was then not appropriate in light of the research objectives. Originally, at the beginning of the research, I aimed at doing so (together with a larger amount of interviews for displaying entire action strategies of all affected actors). Yet, the structuring according to important thematic cornerstones turned out to be more suitable - especially since the theoretical frame 'only' spans the realm of potential changes induced by governance; and not all the categories were relevant in every case. A complete reconstruction of action strategies of all affected actors turned out to be hardly practicable and would have reduced clarity with regard to the presentation of induced impacts (in comparison with the more graspable structuring according to thematic cornerstones).

In general, it moreover became apparent in the empirical part that governance practitioners frequently do not reflect thoroughly on governance results. For instance, an expert from an administration stated: »*If only I would know, but unfortunately I have no idea what is induced [...] I have no clue about how and why consumers react in detail. [...] It is difficult to prove effects and hardly possible to find out which actions were induced [...] The arrangement has an impact in terms of energy-consumption, you can see this, but nobody knows the exact mechanism [...] It is difficult to verify and quantify the effects.*« (interview 02-02, transl.; cf. also interview 01-01). Also, for instance, in the case of the Energy Trialogue, induced results did not play a high role for actors involved (cf. interviews 04-01 and 04-02). Generally speaking, the different levels on which governance can induce change were frequently not given any thought by practitioners (let alone that changes were reflected in light of the respective mode of governance). If impacts were reflected, they were reduced to effects of the policy instrument on the explicitly chosen target group. In view of this, difficulties of result assessment were mentioned by interview experts, e.g. that in a counter-factual manner, it always has to be considered what would have happened if the governance arrangement had not been in place. Also, it was argued that there are a lot of other influencing factors and these are not easy to isolate (cf. e.g. interviews 01-01 and 02-04). It was further stated that at the time the results of evaluations are out, governance arrangement is more or less fixed or finished (cf. e.g. the second case in chapter 6.3.2). Practitioners are then occupied with other things and do not care about the results of arrangements they were dealing with some time ago (cf. ibid.). It thus became apparent that, in practice, results are frequently only addressed in evaluation studies - if such studies are even conducted. Overall, it seems that the link between governance workings and the evaluation of governance results in practice is rather weak and that practitioners do not thoroughly reflect on the range of levels through which governance can induce change (cf. also problems of performance measurement in public policy and governance, e.g. Kuhlmann et al., 2004; Sanders, 2002; Paleo, 2014).

(iv.) The normative frame for *sustainability appraisal* turned out to be a useful device for a general evaluation of the impacts induced by governance in light of SD. It revealed a way to explore action strategies in the energy sector in terms of both substantive and procedural terms. However, I did not provide an encompassing and detailed sustainability assessment but only a broad interpretive appraisal of the findings. I only aimed at exploring if there are good reasons to regard the respective changes induced by governance as a contribution to SD. As the evaluation was meant in such a general way, the criteria remained on a rather broad level, and no further specific sustainability indicators were deduced. Also I did not distinguish between different orders of effects (e.g. first, second and third order effects), or the degree of the contribution (e.g. a high or low contribution). I furthermore did not make an additional assessment in terms of goal attainment, i.e. the effectiveness of the arrangements.

Future research dealing with the assessment of governance results could be oriented towards the frame and supplement it with concrete indicators that would make a more detailed assessment possible. A comprehensive sustainability assessment of different governance arrangements would have to consider the particular purpose and goals of the arrangements, in order to enable a 'fair' comparison. I did not include this aspect, since I only aimed at a general interpretive appraisal, e.g. in light of normative claims in the literature (indicating that new modes induce changes that are better aligned with sustainability goals).

(v.) With regard to *research methodology*, the comparative case study approach of a qualitative nature has in principle proven to be instrumental for illuminating the research objectives. The case study perspective provided a nuanced understanding of complex, dynamic social phenomena - and enabled an in-depth analysis of real-world governance and results. The five cases were generally appropriate to shed light on the range of different ways of steering.

Yet, with regard to the selection of the cases, potential critical questions in terms of circularity might arise. As the five cases more or less exactly displayed the five modes of governance of the formal frame, it may be asked if the modes were apparent beforehand - and why an allocation by means of the frame was actually necessary. However, although - as an intuitive heuristic - the cases were selected in light of displaying the full range of existing ways of steering (intuitively I considered top-down arrangements, public-private partnerships, deliberative networks and bottom-up arrangements), a differentiated analysis was needed to allocate the cases to clearly delimitable modes. This also revealed dynamics of governance - especially in terms of the last case study with a shift from self- to interactive governing.

With respect to the methods for data generation and analysis, it can be recorded that they were overall suitable for the research purposes. The triangulation of sources contributed to reaching in-depth insights of the respective case studies. The content structuring technique proved to be a suited way for extracting relevant information in a transparent way - while the software of Maxqda was a particular helpful device in this regard.

With regard to preparing the expert interviews, a difficulty partly came up to actually trace the key actors. This was due to a trade-off. Case studies had to be chosen that date back enough years, so that the time frame for capturing impacts was sufficient. Yet, this meant that for the most part, people that were responsible for governing in the cases were not in the same positions or role anymore (some people were also retired). When asking these actors for an interview, they frequently referred to the current practitioners at charge. This partly hampered a larger consideration of interview experts. Apart from this, in view of governance impacts, it turned out that people are in general less motivated to talk about a situation when it dates back a longer time horizon. These trade-offs had to be dealt with. Yet, once key actors were identified and were found willing to give an interview, a detailed overview with regard to governance workings and results could be achieved. Since only central key actors were chosen that were able to give core insights, a sufficient thematic saturation was reached in each case after some conducted interviews (backed up by the analysis of existing research and official documents).

(vi.) Naturally, the chosen research design inevitably leads to *limitations in terms of results* and the reach of conclusions drawn. The research approach was qualitative and exploratory in nature and focused on an in-depth analysis of a small number of case studies. Accordingly, there are clear limits with regard to the reach of gained findings - and in view of generalizing from particular cases drawn from specific contexts (cf. also Payne & Williams, 2005, referring instead to the term of moderatum generalization in qualitative research). The goal of this study was to reconstruct in detail the workings of specific arrangements and their triggering of societal changes. It was directed at providing a differentiated picture of the basic way of functioning of different steering forms towards SD. Modes of governance should be investigated in terms of their characteristics, i.e. to explore if indications can be found that certain modes perform better. The general purpose was then to formulate hypotheses for future work. Accordingly, I did not arrive at generalizable conclusions with regard to the merits of governance modes in terms of SD or at causal correlations between certain modes and sustainable results (i.e. which mode is generally most suited for steering societies towards more sustainable tracks).

For reasons of feasibility, the case studies were furthermore reduced to the field of energy policy in a single country. A comparative perspective both in terms of different policy fields and countries would have given additional insights. In light of the research perspective, the choice of Switzerland can also be seen critical - since hierarchical governance is more participatory in nature than in other countries. Although this enabled to derive additional insights with regard to new modes, in view of the research goal to comparatively explore hierarchical and non-hierarchical modes, this is partly problematic. Compared to a country with even larger variation in terms of the characteristics of existing traditional and new modes, this reduces the reach of conclusions drawn in terms of hierarchical modes. Thus, the consideration of a second country would have been beneficial.[31] However, apart from the consultation phase, the cases addressed where clearly hierarchical and the instruments of direct democracy did not affect the mechanism of action itself with regard to induced results.

Considerations of feasibility were also responsible for reducing the research design to exploring the realm of societal changes (refraining from considering the field of outcomes, which would have allowed to make valuable statements about the actual end effects in terms of SD) - and to a general interpretative sustainability appraisal.

However, at an early state in the evolution of the addressed research field (i.e. exploring the relation between governance modes and SD), this study provided in-depth insights that can be elaborated further in upcoming research. The findings can thus be seen as propositions to orient future work and to be scrutinized in next rounds of empirical studies (cf. also Yin, 2009). In general, quantitative research in this research field is highly required (cf. below). Studies on different policy sectors and countries would be desirable to supplement the reach of the conclusions drawn in this study.

Generally speaking, the theoretical foundations established in this study together with the empirical part contribute to *linking different research fields*. On the one hand, sustainability governance literature was considered alongside general governance research and the broader political science literature. On the other hand, an effort was made to further the dialogue between normative and empirical strands (by clearly elaborating the existing normative assumptions and informing them with empirical insights). This contributes to addressing research desiderata as e.g. pointed out by Jordan (2008). He complains that the exchange between the norma-

31 Originally, the design of this research project was directed at including two countries (Switzerland and the Netherlands) and two policy sectors (energy and food policy) - to enable a comparative perspective. However, with a reference to feasibility, funding of this project was only granted for the presented research design.

tive and empirical-analytical SD governance literature in terms of learning processes has been rather limited and should be increased. In his view, this ought to lead to a more dedicated theory of sustainability governance. Adger and Jordan (2009) further explicitly argue that it would be mutually beneficial, if the emerging literature of sustainability governance engaged in a deeper manner with broader governance and political science literature. This study made a contribution in both respects.

8.3 Outlook on further research

Looking forward, there remain several desiderata in the field of sustainability governance research. Overall, a better understanding of which forms of steering work where, how and why in terms of promoting SD is needed.

In the vein of this study, future studies should increasingly explore the relation between governance modes and SD - in comparative settings and various sectors - while considering the whole range of different modes. In general, research in this regard ought to be unbiased in terms of normative claims, especially in view of new modes. It should approach existing claims on modes with caution and be careful with regard to implicit normative assumptions.

Although research on procedural aspects of governance has a virtue on its own, I argued that the result side of governance is most crucial for scrutinizing the merits of modes in terms of SD. While the exploration of actual end effects is highly demanding in view of data availability, it is largely desirable. Especially, empirical research designs with a large number of case studies (large N-studies), thus enabling inquiry of correlations between governance arrangements and sustainable results, would give essential insights. This would allow generalizable statements about the merits of different modes (if data for such research are not at hand, the insights from this study can guide research to derive conclusions on (un)sustainable end effects).

Overall, the theoretical contributions (the four elements of the framework) and the empirical findings of this study can orient future work in this regard. They provide a foundation to arrive at more conceptual clarity and empirical scrutiny. Experience with the elements of the framework point to certain aspects that should be considered when exploring the relation between governance modes and SD. First of all, the inherent complexity of the real-world phenomenon of governance must be acknowledged. For instance, governing should not be reduced to a certain policy instrument used in an arrangement. Apart from that, the aspect of hybrid modes of governance (e.g. non-hierarchical modes in a 'shadow of hierarchy' or hierarchical modes with deliberative rationalities) should explicitly be considered. Moreover, the complex chain of governance results has to be carefully addressed, while results should not be reduced to behavioral change of target groups. The findings of this study clearly disclose that there is more to be considered when exploring collective action and its induced changes - especially in the field of SD. Finally, research in this regard should strive for holistic sustainability evaluations (instead of e.g. a reduction to environmental effectiveness). In this regard, the range of results should be evaluated - by adopting a broad view on governance and its possible ways to induce change (this e.g. means to go beyond assessing the effects of policy instruments).

The hypotheses formulated in light of the findings particularly suggest the exploration of the following aspects in further research. First and foremost, the possibility that new modes fail to induce societal changes at all, especially actual actions and institutionalization processes towards SD, should be scrutinized. This aspect should also be explored in comparison with traditional modes. Furthermore, the risk that participatory elements impede faster and more sustainable results ought to be investigated in more depth. Apart from that, the role of hierarchical governance in light of the performance of new modes is a constant remaining research desideratum. In turn, it should be increasingly studied to what extent certain aspects made responsible for the supposed superiority of new modes can also occur through hierarchical governance. Finally, the influence of other factors on the potential of governance to promote SD than the mode itself needs further inquiry. Examples are the nature of the embedding context and the particularities of involved actors. The formulated hypotheses can be tested by studies of a quantitative nature that aim at (comparatively) investigating a larger number of governance arrangements, supplemented by qualitative studies that explore a certain hypothesis in more depth.

Overall, the findings of this study have shown that exploring the relation between governance modes and SD is a complex field. As there is more to be considered than 'just' the mode, research in this regard should generally strive for a holistic approach and avoid hasty conclusions regarding the performance of certain modes. This includes being aware of external influencing factors and taking into account other explanatory patterns that determine the sustainability potential of governance. An illustrative example for research in such terms is the recent empirical study by Gailing and Röhring (2016). The authors question the assumption that the success of energy transitions depends to a large extent on collaborative network-based governance and take into consideration critical governance literature. Apart from the role of the mode of collaborative governance, they explore the importance of three factors (as the authors argue, 'blind' spots in previous governance research): socio-material conditions, power relations and individual key persons. The authors conclude that these factors play a crucial role when it comes to the performance of governance.

In general, studies in this regard should increasingly rely on insights from other research strands to further 'thinking outside the box', and to not lose sight of alternative influencing factors. One promising complementary strand is the established implementation research in general political sciences. Also, with regard to particular influencing factors, more specialized research strands that can enlighten the analysis should be considered. For instance, as regards the role of the particularities of involved actors, research on policy or institutional entrepreneurship (e.g. Timmermans et al., 2014; Kingdon, 1995; Hardy & Maguire, 2008) might provide an added source for insights.

Last but not least, this study suggested that future sustainability governance research should increasingly explore the interplay of governance modes and the meta-governing thereof. In light of the findings, it must be concluded that part of the discourse, with its particular high focus on new governance modes, evolves in an unpromising direction. The focus on specific questions regarding new modes might hamper exploring the full picture of today's variety to govern and thus neglect other important questions. Apart from the comparative exploration of modes, the appropriate mix in different contexts should be increasingly kept in mind.

Addressing the interplay of governance modes raises several new research questions, for instance, in terms of which modes in a certain situation cross-fertilize or undermine each other to promote SD. Of particular interest in this regard is how tensions between modes can be mitigated and synergetic relationships be supported.

Furthermore, since for harmonizing a mix of modes some form of metagovernance is necessary, research in this direction is sorely needed. Several questions arise in this research field. For instance, how can broader governance systems of different modes be generally steered? What does appropriate meta-governing look like in certain contexts and which changes in incumbent structures would be needed to enable such second-order governing? Which state or societal bodies should conduct meta-governance in which way and how can meta-governing capacities of different actors be supported? Important questions in this regard also touch upon issues like if there is always the possibility to actually choose a certain governance mode in a given context - or under which circumstances a mix of modes is working smoothly (for exploring such questions, researches can build on established literature strands, e.g. on policy instrument choice or on the conditions of successful collaborative governance).

Taking everything into account, it follows from this study that a crucial general guiding question that scholars in the field of sustainability governance should increasingly explore is: *which combination of governance modes functions best in different situations to bring about sustainable results - and what does an appropriate meta-governing of this mixture look like*? A shift in the mainstream research perspective in this direction would be constructive not only for the scientific debate, but as a consequence also for sustainability governance in practice.

References

Note: Reviewed documentation of the case studies is given separately below.

Adelt, F., Weyer, J. & Fink, R.D. (2014). Governance of complex systems: results of a sociological simulation experiment. *Ergonomics, 57*(3), 434-448. doi:10.1080/00140139.2013.877598.

Adger, W.N., Brown, K., Fairbrass, J., Jordan, A., Paavola, J., Rosendo, S., & Seyfang, G. (2003). Governance for sustainability: Towards a "thick" analysis of environmental decision-making. *Environment and Planning A, 35*(2003), 1095-110. doi:10.1068/a35289.

Adger, W.N., & Jordan, A. (2009). Sustainability: exploring the processes and outcomes of governance. In W.N. Adger & A. Jordan (Eds.), *Governing sustainability* (pp. 3-31). Cambridge: Cambridge University Press.

Afgan, N.H., Carvalho, M., & Hovanov, N.V. (2000). Energy system assessment with sustainability indicators. *Energy Policy, 28*(9), 603-612. doi:10.1007/978-1-4615-4479-1.

Andrews, R., & Entwistle, T. (2010). Does cross-sectoral partnership deliver? An empirical exploration of public service effectiveness, efficiency and equity. *Journal of Public Administration Research & Theory, 20*(3), 679-701.

Anheier, H., & List, R. (2013). Governance: issues and frameworks. In H. Anheier (Ed.), *Governance: challenges and innovations* (pp. 3-21). Oxford: Oxford University Press.

Ansell, C., & Gash, A. (2008). Collaborative governance in theory and practice. *Journal of Public Administration Research and Theory, 18*(4), 543-571. doi:10.1093/jopart/mum032.

Arnouts, R. (2010). *Regional nature governance in the Netherlands: four decades of governance modes and shifts in the Utrechtse Heuvelrug and Midden-Brabant.* Wageningen: Wageningen University.

Arnouts, R., & Arts, B. (2009). Environmental governance failure: the 'dark side'of an essentially optimistic concept. In B. Arts, A. Lagendijk & H. van Houtum (Eds.), *The disoriented state: shifts in governmentality, territoriality and governance* (pp. 201-228). Heidelberg: Springer.

Arnouts, R., Van der Zouwen, M., & Arts, B. (2011). Analysing governance modes and shifts - Governance arrangements in Dutch nature policy. *Forest Policy and Economics, 16*(2012), 43-50. doi:10.1016/j.forpol.2011.04.001.

Armitage, D.R., Plummer, R., Berkes, F., Arthur, R.I., Charles, A.T., Davidson-Hunt, I.J., ... & McConney, P. (2009). Adaptive co-management for social-ecological complexity. *Frontiers in Ecology and the Environment*, *7*(2), 95-102.

Arthur, S., & Nazroo, J. (2006). Designing fieldwork strategies and materials. In J. Ritchie & J. Lewis (Eds.), *Qualitative research practice. A guide for social science students and researchers* (pp. 109-137). London: Sage.

Arts, B. (2014). Assessing forest governance from a 'Triple G' perspective: Government, governance, governmentality. *Forest Policy and Economics*, *49*(2014), 17-22. doi:10.1016/j.forpol.2014.05.008.

Arts, B., Leroy, P., & van Tatenhove, J. (2006). Political modernisation and policy arrangements: a framework for understanding environmental policy change. *Public Organization Review*, *6*(2), 93-106.

Arts, B., & van Tatenhove, J. (2005). Policy and power: A conceptual framework between the "old" and "new" policy idioms. *Policy Sciences*, *37*(3-4), 339–356. doi:10.1007/s11077-005-0156-9.

Arts, B., van Tatenhove, J., & Leroy, P. (2000). Policy arrangements. In J. Van Tatenhove, B. Arts & P. Leroy (Eds.), *Political modernization and the environment. The renewal of environmental policy arrangements* (pp. 53-69). Dordrecht: Kluwer.

Arts, K., Fischer, A., & Van der Wal, R. (2014). Political decision making, governance shifts and Scottish animal reintroductions: are democratic principles at stake?. *Journal of Environmental Planning and Management*, *57*(4), 612-628. doi:10.1080/09640568.2012.758627.

Ayre, G., & Callway, R. (Eds.). (2005). *Governance for sustainable development.* London: Earthscan.

Bache, I., & Flinders, M. (Eds.). (2004). *Multi-level governanace*. Oxford: Oxford University Press.

Bäckstrand, K. (2004). Civic Science for sustainability: Reframing the role of experts, policy-makers and citizens in environmental governance. *Global Environmental Politics*, *3*(4), 24-41.

Bäckstrand, K., Khan, J., Kronsell, A., & Lövbrand, E. (2010). The promise of new modes of environmental governance. In K. Bäckstrand, J. Khan, A. Kronsell & E. Lövbrand (Eds.), *Environmental politics and deliberative democracy: examining the promise of new modes of governance* (pp. 3-27). Cheltenham: Edward Elgar.

Baker, S. (2009). In pursuit of sustainable development: A governance perspective. *Ljubljana: 8th International Conference of the European Society for Ecological Economics.* Conference Proceedings.

Baker, S., & Eckerberg, K. (Eds.) (2008). *In pursuit of sustainable development: New governance practices at the sub-national level in europe.* London: Routledge.

Barnes, P.M., & Hoerber, T.C. (2013). Linking the discourse on sustainability and governance. In P.M. Barnes & T.C. Hoerber (Eds.), *Sustainable development and governance in Europe: The evolution of the discourse on sustainability* (pp. 19–33). New York: Routledge.

Bartolini, S. (2011). New modes of European governance: An introduction. In A. Héritier & M. Rhodes (Eds.), *New modes of governance in Europe: Governing in the shadow of hierarchy* (pp. 1-18). Palgrave: Houndmills.

Bell, S., & Hindmoor, A. (2009). *Rethinking governance: the centrality of the state in modern society*. Cambridge: Cambridge University Press.

Bell, S., & Hindmoor, A. (2012). Governance without government? The case of the Forest Stewardship Council. *Public Administration*, *90*(1), 144-159. doi: 10.1111/j.1467-9299.2011.01954.x.

Bell, J., & Morrison, T. (2015). A comparative analysis of the transformation of governance systems: land-use planning for flood risk. *Journal of Environmental Policy & Planning*, 17(4), 516-534. doi: 10.1080/1523908X.2014.986567.

Bell, S., & Park, A. (2006). The problematic metagovernance of networks: water reform in New South Wales, *International Public Policy 26*(1), pp.63–83.

Bellamy, R. (2011). Symposium on democracy and new modes of governance: Introduction. *Government and opposition*, *46*(1), 56–57. doi:10.1111/j.1477-7053.2010.01329.x.

Benz, A. & Dose, N. (Eds.). (2010). *Governance – Regieren in komplexen Regelsystemen. Eine Einführung.* 2nd edition. Wiesbaden: VS Verlag für Sozialwissenschaften.

Bevir, M. (Ed.). (2011). *The sage handbook of governance*. Thousand Oaks: Sage Publishing.

Bevir, M., & Rhodes, R.A.W. (2016). The ′3Rs′ in rethinking governance: ruling, rationalities and resistance. In M. Bevir & R.A.W. Rhodes (Eds.), *Rethinking governance: Ruling, rationalities and resistance* (pp. 1-22). New York: Routledge.

Biddle, J.C., & Koontz, T.M. (2014). Goal specificity: A proxy measure for improvements in environmental outcomes in collaborative governance. *Journal of environmental management*, *145* (2014), 268-276. doi: 10.1016/j.jenvman.2014.06.029.

Biermann, F. (2007). "Earth system governance" as a crosscutting theme of global change research. *Global Environmental Change*, *17*(3), 326–337. doi:10.1016/j.gloenvcha.2006.11.010.

Biermann, F., Betsill, M.M., Gupta, J., Kanie, N., Lebel, L., Liverman, D., Schroeder, H., Siebenhüner, B., & Zondervan, R. (2010). Earth system governance: a research framework. *International Environmental Agreements, 10*(4), 277-298.

Blatter, J. (2007). *Governance - theoretische Formen und historische Transformationen. Politische Steuerung und Integration in Metropolregionen der USA (1850-2000).* Baden-Baden: Nomos.

Blum, S., & Schubert, K. (2011). *Politikfeldanalyse. Eine Einführung.* (2nd ed.). Wiesbaden: VS Verlag für Sozialwissenschaften.

Böcher, M. (2012). A theoretical framework for explaining the choice of instruments in environmental policy. *Forest Policy and Economics, 16,* 14–22. doi:10.1016/j.forpol.2011.03.012.

Bogner, A., Littig, B., & Menz, W. (2014). *Interviews mit Experten. Eine praxisorientierte Einführung.* Wiesbaden: VS Verlag für Sozialwissenschaften.

Bogner, A., Littig, B., & Menz, W. (2009). *Interviewing experts. Methodology and practice.* Basingstoke: Palgrave Macmillan.

Böhling, K., & Arzberger, M.B. (2014). New modes of governance in Bavaria's alpine forests: The 'Mountain Forest Initiative' at work. *Forest Policy and Economics, 49*(2014), 43-50. doi: 10.1016/j.forpol.2014.01.004.

Bolis, I., Morioka, S.N., & Sznelwar, L.I. (2014). When sustainable development risks losing its meaning. Delimiting the concept with a comprehensive literature review and a conceptual model. *Journal of Cleaner Production, 83*(2014), 7-20. doi:10.1016/j.jclepro.2014.06.041.

Bond, A., Morrison-Saunders, A., & Pope, J. (2012). Sustainability assessment: the state of the art. *Impact Assessment and Project Appraisal, 30*(1), 53-62. doi: 10.1080/14615517.2012.661974.

Booher, D.E., & Innes, J.E. (2010). Governance for resilience: CALFED as a complex adaptive network for resource management. *Ecology and Society 15*(3): 35-51.

Bornemann, B. (2013). *Policy-Integration und Nachhaltigkeit. Integrative Politik in der Nachhaltigkeitsstrategie der deutschen Bundesregierung.* Wiesbaden: VS Verlag für Sozialwissenschaften.

Bornemann, B., Lange, P., & Burger, P. (*forthcoming*). Towards systematic understandings of sustainability governance - a conceptual meta-framework. Submitted to *Environmental Politics.*

Borras, S., & Edler, J. (2015). *The governance of socio-technical systems: Explaining change.* Cheltenham: Edward Elgar Publishing.

Börzel, T.A. (2006). New modes of governance and enlargement. When theory meets reality. *Interim Report, NEWGOV, New Modes of Governance:* Free University of Berlin.

Börzel, T.A., & Panke, D. (2007). Network governance: effective and legitimate?. In E. Sørensen & J. Torfing (Eds.), *Theories of democratic network governance* (pp. 153-166). Houndsmills: Palgrave Macmillan.

Börzel, T.A., & Risse, T. (2010). Governance without a state: Can it work? *Regulation & Governance, 4*(2), 113–134. doi:10.1111/j.1748-5991.2010.01076.x.

Bourdieu, P. (1977). *Outline of a theory of practice.* Cambridge: Cambridge University Press.

Bourdieu, P. & Eagleton, T. (1992). Doxa and common life. *New Left Review,* 111-121.

Brand, K.-W. (Ed.) (2002). Politik der Nachhaltigkeit. Voraussetzungen, Probleme, Chancen - eine kritische Diskussion. Berlin: Edition sigma.

Bressers, H.T.A. (2004). Implementing sustainable development: how to know what works, where, when and how. In W.M. Lafferty (Ed.), *Governance for Sustainable Development. The Challenge of Adapting Form to Function* (pp. 284–318). Cheltenham, Northampton: Edward Elgar.

Bressers, H.T.A., & Kuks, S.M.M. (2003). What does governance mean? From conception to elaboration. In H.T.A. Bressers & W.A Rosenbaum (Eds.), *Achieving Sustainable Development. The Challenge of Governance Across Social Scales* (pp. 65-88). Praeger: London.

Bressers, H.T.A., & Rosenbaum, W.A. (Eds.). (2003). *Achieving sustainable development: the challenge of governance across social scales.* Westport: Praeger Publishers.

Brinkmann, S. (2013). Qualitative interviewing. Understanding qualitative research. Oxford: Oxford University Press.

Brodmann, U., Gubler, F., & Walter, F. (2001). *Nachhaltigkeit: Kriterien und Indikatoren für den Energiebereich - Schlussbericht.* Bern: Bundesamt für Energie.

Brousseau, E., Dedeurwaerdere, T., & Siebenhuner, B. (2012). *Reflexive governance for global public goods*. Cambridge: MIT Press.

Brownill, S. (2009). The dynamics of participation: modes of governance and increasing participation in planning. *Urban Policy and Research*, *27*(4), 357-375. doi:10.1080/08111140903308842.

Buizer, M. (2008). *Worlds apart: Interactions between local initiatives and established policy*. Wageningen: Wageningen University.

Buizer, M., Arts, B. & Kok, K. (2011). Governance, scale, and the environment: the importance of recognizing knowledge claims intransdisciplinary arenas. *Ecology and Society 16*(1), 1-18.

Bulkeley, H., Watson, M. & Hudson, R. (2007). Modes of governing municipal waste. *Environment and Planning A, 39*(11), 2733–2753. doi:10.1068/a38269.

Burger, P., & Christen, M. (2011). Towards a capability approach of sustainability. *Journal of Cleaner Production*, *19*(8), 787–795. doi:10.1016/j.jclepro.2010.06.019.

Bussmann, W., Klöti, U., & Knoepfel, P. (1997). *Einführung in die Politikevaluation*. Basel: Helbing & Lichtenhahn.

Buzogány, A. (2015). Building governance on fragile grounds: lessons from Romania. *Environment and Planning C: Government and Policy*, *47*(2015), 1-18. doi: 10.1177/0263774X15605897.

Capano, G., Howlett, M., & Ramesh, M. (Eds.). (2015a). *Varieties of governance: Dynamics, strategies, capacities*. Houndsmills: Palgrave Macmillan.

Capano, G., Howlett, M., & Ramesh, M. (2015b). Bringing governments back in: Governance and governing in comparative policy analysis. *Journal of Comparative Policy Analysis: Research and Practice,* *17*(4), 311-321. doi: 10.1080/13876988.2015.1031977.

Capano, G., Rayner, J., & Zito, A.R. (2012). Governance from the bottom up: Complexity and divergence in comparative perspective. *Public Administration, 90*(1), 56–73. doi:10.1111/j.1467-9299.2011.02001.x.

Carrozza, C. (2015). Democratizing expertise and environmental governance: Different approaches to the politics of science and their relevance for policy analysis. *Journal of Environmental Policy & Planning, 17*(1), 108-126. doi: 10.1080/1523908X.2014.914894.

Chhotray, V., & Stoker, G. (2009). *Governance theory and practice. A cross-disciplinary approach.* Houndsmills: Palgrave Macmillan.

Christen, M., & Schmidt, S. (2012). A formal framework for conceptions of sustainability - a theoretical contribution to the discourse in sustainable development. *Sustainable Development, 20*(6), 400–410. doi:10.1002/sd.518.

Christopoulos, S., Horvath, B., & Kull, M. (2012). Advancing the governance of cross-sectoral policies for sustainable development: A metagovernance perspective. *Public Administration and Development, 32*(3), 305-323. doi: 10.1002/pad.1629.

Christou, G., & Simpson, S. (2009). New governance, the internet, and country code top-level domains in Europe. *Governance, 22*(4), 599–624. doi:10.1111/j.1468-0491.2009.01455.x.

Colebatch, H.K. (2014). Making sense of governance. *Policy and Society, 33*(4), 307-316. doi: 10.1016/j.polsoc.2014.10.001.

Coleman, J.S. (1990). *Foundations of social theory*. Cambridge: The Belknap Press.

Commission on Global Governance (1995). Our Global Neighbourhood. Oxford: Oxford University Press.

Cowell, R., Ellis, G., Sherry-Brennan, F., Strachan, P.A., & Toke, D. (2015). Rescaling the governance of renewable energy: Lessons from the UK devolution experience. *Journal of Environmental Policy & Planning*, 1-23. Advance online publication. doi: 10.1080/1523908X.2015.1008437.

Craik, N., Doelle, M., & Gale, F. (2012). Governing information: A three dimensional analysis of environmental assessment. *Public Administration, 90*(1), 19-36. doi: 10.1111/j.1467-9299.2011.02002.x.

Dai, L. (2015). China's water resources law in transition. Utrecht: Utrecht University.

Dang, T.K.P., Visseren-Hamakers, I.J., & Arts, B. (2015). A framework for assessing governance capacity: An illustration from Vietnam's forestry reforms. *Environment and Planning C: Government and Policy*, 1-12. Advance online publication. doi: 10.1177/0263774X15598325.

De Búrca, G., & Scott, J. (2006). Introduction: new governance, law and constitutionalism. In G. de Búrca & J. Scott (Eds.), *Law and New Governance in the EU and the US* (pp. 1–12). Oxford: Hart.

Dedeurwaerdere, T. (2005). The contribution of network governance to sustainable development. *Les Se´minaires de l'IDDRI, No. 13.*

Dellas, E., Pattberg, P., & Betsill, M. (2011). Agency in earth system governance: refining a research agenda. *International Environmental Agreements: Politics, Law and Economics*, *11*(1), 85-98. doi: 10.1007/s10784-011-9147-9.

Delli Carpini, M.X., Cook, F.L., & Jacobs, L.R. (2004). Public deliberation, discursive participation, and citizen engagement: A review of the empirical literature. *Annu. Rev. Polit. Sci.*, *7*(2014), 315-344. doi: 10.1146/annurev.polisci.7.121003.091630.

Den Uyl, R.M. (2014). *Navigating toward sustainable development: Conceptual maps of modes of governance vs. practical experiences in the Dutch fen landscape.* Utrecht: Utrecht University.

Den Uyl, R.M., & Driessen, P.P.J. (2015). Evaluating governance for sustainable development - Insights from experiences in the Dutch fen landscape. *Journal of Environmental Management*, *163*(1), 186-203. doi: 10.1016/ j.jenvman.2015.08.022.

Dente, B. (Ed.) (1995). *Environmental policy in search of new instruments.* Dordrecht: Kluwer Academic Publishers.

De Ona, C.R. & Morales, F. (2013). New Modes of Environmental Governance in Central America: Constructing a Biological Corridor Policy in Honduras. *The International Journal of Interdisciplinary Environmental Studies* *7*, 15-32.

Diedrichs, U., Reiners, W., & Wessels, W. (2011). The dynamics of change in EU governance. In U. Diedrichs, W. Reiners & W. Wessels (Eds.), *The Dynamics of Change in EU Governance* (pp. 1–21). Cheltenham: Edward Elgar Publishing.

Dijk, M. (2015). From government to multi-stakeholder governance for sustainable mobility. In F. Mancebo, & I. Sachs (Eds.), *Transitions to sustainability* (pp. 131-140). Dordrecht: Springer.

Dobson, A. (1996). Environment sustainabilities: An analysis and a typology. *Environmental Politics*, *5*(3), 401–428. doi:10.1080/09644019608414280.

Doelle, M., Henschel, C., Smith, J., Tollefson, C., & Wellststead, A. (2012). New governance arrangements at the intersection of climate change and forest policy: institutional, political and regulatory dimensions. *Public Administration*, *90*(1), 37-55. doi: 10.1111/j.1467-9299.2011.02006.x.

Driessen, P.P.J., Behagel, J.H., Hegger, D.L.T., Mees, H.L.P., Almesjo, L., Andresen, S., ... & Verbruggen, A. (2013). *Societal transformations in the face of climate change; research priorities for the next decade.* Brussels: JPI Climate.

Driessen, P.P.J., Dieperink, C., Laerhoven, F., Runhaar, H.A.C., & Vermeulen, W.J.V. (2012). Towards a conceptual framework for the study of shifts in modes of environmental governance - Experiences from the Netherlands. *Environmental Policy and Governance*, *22*(3), 143–160. doi:10.1002/eet.1580.

Driessen, P.P.J., Glasbergen, P., & Verdaas, C. (2001). Interactive policy-making – a model of management for public works. *European Journal of Operational Research*, *128*(2), 322–337.

Duit, A., Galaz, V., Eckerberg, K., & Ebbesson, J. (2010). Governance, complexity, and resilience. *Global environmental change, 20*(3), 363-368.

Dupuis, J., & Knoepfel, P. (2015). *The Politics of Contaminated Sites Management*. Heidelberg: Springer.

Easton, D. (1965). *A Framework for Political Analysis*. Englewood Cliffs: Prentice-Hall, Inc.

Emerson, K., & Nabatchi, T. (2015). Evaluating the productivity of collaborative governance regimes: A performance matrix. *Public Performance & Management Review, 38*(4), 717-747. doi: 10.1080/15309576.2015.1031016.

Emerson, K., Nabatchi, T., & Balogh, S. (2012). An integrative framework for collaborative governance. *Journal of Public Administration Research and Theory, 22*(1), 1–29. doi:10.1093/jopart/mur011.

Engberg, L., & Larsen, J. (2010). Context-oriented meta-governance in danish urban regeneration. *Planning Theory & Practice 11*(4), 549–571. doi: 10.1080/14649357.2010.525379.

Evans, B., Joas, M., Sundback, S., & Theobald, K. (2006). Governing local sustainability. *Journal of Environmental Planning and Management, 49*(6), 849-867.

Evans, J.P. (2012). *Environmental governance*. New York: Routledge.

Falkner, G., & Leiber, S. (2004). Europeanization of social partnership in smaller European democracies? *European Journal of Industrial Relations, 10*(3), 239–260. doi:10.1177/0959680104047020.

Farrell, K.N., Kemp, R., Hinterberger, F., Rammel, C., & Ziegler, R. (2005). From *for* to governance for sustainable development in Europe: what is at stake for further research? *International Journal of Sustainable Development, 8*(1-2), 127–150.

Fawcett, P., & Daugbjerg, C. (2012). Explaining governance outcomes: Epistemology, network governance and policy network analysis. *Political Studies Review, 10*(2), 195-207. doi: 10.1111/j.1478-9302.2012.00257.x.

Fenger, M., & Bekkers, V. (2007). The governance concept in public administration. In V. Bekkers, G Dijkstra, A. Edwards & M. Fenger (Eds.), *Governance and the democtratic deficit: Assessing the democratic legitimacy of governance practices* (pp. 13-43). Aldershot: Ashgate.

Ferlie, E., Fitzgerald, L., McGivern, G., Dopson, S., & Bennett, C. (2013). *Making wicked problems governable: The case of managed networks in health care*. Oxford: Oxford University Press.

Filho, W. L., Platje, J., Gerstlberger, W., Ciegis, R., Kääriä, J., Klavins, M., & Kliucininkas, L. (2016). The role of governance in realising the transition towards sustainable societies. *Journal of Cleaner Production, 113*(1), 755-766. doi: 10.1016/j.jclepro.2015.11.060.

Fischer, F., Miller G. J., & Sidney, M. S. (Eds.). (2007). *Handbook of public policy analysis. Theory, politics, and methods*. London & New York: CRC Press.

Flick, U. (2009). *An introduction to qualitative research* (4th ed.). Thousand Oaks: SAGE Publications Ltd.

Flyvbjerg, B. (2006). Five misunderstandings about case-study research. *Qualitative Inquiry*, *12*(2), 219–245. doi:10.1177/1077800405284363.

Folke, C., Hahn, T., Olsson, P., & Norberg, J. (2005). Adaptive governnace of social-ecological systems. *Annual Review of Environment and Resources*, *30*(1), 441–473. doi:10.1146/annurev.energy.30.050504.144511.

Fotel, T. (2013). Perceptions of effectiveness in governance networks - a comparative analysis. In J. Torfing & P. Triantafillou (Eds.), *Interactive policy making, metagovernance and democracy* (pp. 51–73). Colchester: ECPR Press.

Foxon, T.J., Reed, M.S., & Stringer, L.C. (2009). Governing long-term social–ecological change: what can the adaptive management and transition management approaches learn from each other? *Environmental Policy and Governance*, *19*(1), 3-20. doi:10.1002/eet.496.

Franklin, A., & Blyton, P. (2011). *Researching sustainability: a guide to social science methods, practice and engagement*. Abingdon, Oxon: Earthscan.

Frödin, O. (2015). Researching governance for sustainable development: some conceptual clarifications. *Journal of Developing Societies*, *31*(4), 447-466. doi: 10.1177/0169796X15603236.

Funtowicz, S.O., & Ravetz, J.R. (1993). Science for the post-normal age. *Futures*, *25*(7), 735-755.

Gailing, L., & Röhring, A. (2016). Is it all about collaborative governance? Alternative ways of understanding the success of energy regions. *Utilities Policy*, 1-9. Advance online publication. doi: 10.1016/j.jup.2016.02.009.

Gale, F. (2009). *An ecology of governance: Politics, institutions and regulations*. Launceston, Tasmania: School of Government, University of Tasmania. Eprint. Unpublished manuscript, cited with permission from the author.

George, A.L., & Bennett, A. (2005). *Case studies and theory development in the social sciences*. Cambridge: The MIT Press.

George, C., & Kirkpatrick, C. (2007). *Impact assessment and sustainable development: European practice and experience*. Cheltenham & Northampton: Edward Elgar Pub.

Gerlak, A.K., Lubell, M., & Heikkila, T. (2013). The promise and performance of collaborative governance. In S. Kamieniecki & M. Kraft (Eds.), *The oxford handbook of US environmental policy* (pp. 413-434). New York: Oxford University Press.

Gerring, J. (2007). *Case study research: Principles and practices*. Cambridge: Cambridge University Press.

Gibbons, M., Limoges, C., Nowotny, H., Schwartzman, S., Scott, P., & Trow, M. (1994). *The new production of knowledge: The dynamics of science and research in contemporary societies.* London: Sage.

Gibson, R.B. (2006). Sustainability assessment: basic components of a practical approach. *Impact Assessment and Project Appraisal*, *24*(3), 170–182. doi:10.3152/147154606781765147.

Givoni, M., Macmillen, J., Banister, D., & Feitelson, E. (2013). From policy measures to policy packages. *Transport Reviews*, *33*(1), 1-20. doi: 10.1080/01441647.2012.744779.

Glasbergen, P. (2011). Mechanisms of private meta-governance: an analysis of global private governance for sustainable development. *International Journal of Strategic Business Alliances*, *2*(3), 189-206.

Glasbergen, P. (1992). Seven steps towards an instrumentation theory for environmental policy. *Policy & Politics*, *20*(3), 191–200. doi:10.1332/030557392782718698.

Glasbergen, P., & Driessen, P.P.J. (2002). The paradigm shift in environmental politics. In P.P.J. Driessen & P. Glasbergen (Eds.), *Greening Society: The Paradigm Shift in Dutch Environmental Policies* (pp. 3–26). Dordrecht: Kluwer Academic Publishers

Gläser, J., & Laudel, G. (2010). *Experteninterviews und qualitative Inhaltsanalyse: als Instrumente rekonstruierender Untersuchungen* (4th ed.). Wiesbaden: VS Verlag für Sozialwissenschaften.

Goetz, K.H. (2008). Governance as a path to government. *West European Politics*, *31*(1-2), 258-279. doi: 10.1080/01402380701835066.

Gollagher, M., & Hartz-Karp, J. (2013). The role of deliberative collaborative governance in achieving sustainable cities. *Sustainability*, *5*(6), 2343-2366. doi:10.3390/su5062343.

Grande, E. (2012). Governance-Forschung in der Governance-Falle? - Eine kritische Bestandsaufnahme. *Politische Vierteljahresschrift, 53*(4), 565-592.

Green, J., Willis, K., Hughes, E., Small, R., Welch, N., Gibbs, L., & Daly, J. (2007). Generating best evidence from qualitative research: the role of data analysis. *Australian and New Zealand journal of public health*, *31*(6), 545-550. doi:10.1111/j.1753-6405.2007.00141.x.

Griffin, L. (2010). Governance innovation for sustainability: exploring the tensions and dilemmas. *Environmental Policy and Governance*, *20*(6), 365–369. doi:10.1002/eet.555.

Griffin, L. (2008). Good governance and sustainability. *Geography Compass*, *2*(2), 452-475.

Grin, J., Rotmans, J. & Schot, J. (2010). *Transitions to sustainable development.* New York: Routledge.

Gritsenko, D. (2014). *On governance of quality shipping in the Baltic Sea: Exploring collective action in polycentric contexts*. Helsinki: University of Helsinki.

Grunwald, A., & Rösch, C. (2011). Sustainability assessment of energy technologies: towards an integrative framework. *Energy, Sustainability and Society*, *1*(3), 1–10. doi:10.1186/2192-0567-1-3.

Gubrium, J. F., & Holstein, J. A. (Eds.). (2001). *Handbook of interview research. Context and method*. London: Sage.

Gunningham, N. (2009). The new collaborative environmental governance: The localization of regulation. *Journal of Law and Society, 36*(1), 145-166. doi: 10.1111/j.1467-6478.2009.00461.x.

Gunningham, N., & Grabosky (1998). *Smart regulation: Designing environmental policy*. Oxford: Oxford University Press.

Guston, D.H. (2001). Boundary organizations in environmental policy and science. An introduction. *Science, Technology and Human Values*, *26*(4), 399–408.

Gysen, J., Bruyninckx, H. & Bachus, K. (2006). The modus narrandi: A methodology for evaluating effects of environmental policy. *Evaluation, 12*(1), 95–118. doi: 10.1177/1356389006064176.

Hackett, R. (2013). From government to governance? Forest certification and crisis displacement in Ontario, Canada. *Journal of Rural Studies*, *30*(2013), 120-129. doi:10.1016/j.jrurstud.2013.01.003.

Hajer, M. (2006). The living institutions of the EU: Analysing governance as performance. *Perspectives on European Politics and Society*, 7(1), 41-55. doi: 10.1080/15705850600839546.

Hajer, M., & Wagenaar, H. (Eds.). (2003). *Deliberative policy analysis: Understanding governance in the network society*. Cambridge: Cambridge University Press.

Hanf, K., & Scharpf, F. (1978). *Interorganizational policy making: Limits to coordination and central control*. London: Sage.

Hardiman, N., & Scott, C. (2009). Governance as polity: an institutional approach to the evolution of state functions in Ireland. *Public Administration, 88*(1), 170–189. doi: 10.1111/j.1467-9299.2009.01794.x.

Hardy, C., & Maguire, S. (2008). Institutional entrepreneurship. In R. Greenwood, C. Oliver, R. Suddaby & K. Sahlin (Eds.), *The Sage handbook of organizational institutionalism* (pp. 198-217). Los Angeles: Sage.

Hartley, J. (2004). Case study research. In C. Cassell & G. Symon (Eds.), *Essential guide to qualitative methods in organizational research* (pp. 323–333). London: Sage.

Hatry, H. P. (2006). *Performance measurement: Getting results* (2nd ed.). Washington DC: Urban Institute Press.

Haughton, G., Counsella., D., & Vigarb, G. (2008). Sustainable development in post-devolution UK and Ireland. *Regional studies special issue: sustainable regions 42*(9), 1223–1236.

Head, B.W. (2008). Wicked problems in public policy. *Public Policy, 3*(2), 101-118.

Heidbreder, E.G. (2009). *The heart of political steering: The EU`s arenas of power as template for a governance typology.* Paper presented at the Eleventh Biennial International Conference European Union Studies Association, Los Angeles, California April 23-25, 2009.

Heinelt, H. (2010). *Governing modern societies: towards participatory governance.* London: Routledge.

Heinelt, H. (2007). Do policies determine politics? In F. Fischer, G.J. Miller & M.S. Sidney (Eds.), *Handbook of Public Policy Analysis. Theory, Politics, and Methods* (pp. 109–119). London & New York: CRC Press.

Heinelt, H. (2002). Achieving sustainable and innovate policies through participatory governance in a multi-level context. In H. Heinelt, P. Getimis, G. Kafkalas, R. Smith & E. Swyngedouw (Eds.), *Participatory governance in multi-level context: Concepts and experience* (pp. 17–21). Opladen: Leske and Budrich.

Helfferich, C. (2011). *Die Qualität qualitativer Daten. Manual für die Durchführung qualitativer Interviews* (4th ed.). Wiesbaden: VS Verlag für Sozialwissenschaften.

Helmke, G., & Levitsky, S. (2004). Informal institutions and comparative politics. *Perspectives on Politics, 2*(2014), 725–740.

Héritier, A. (2002). New modes of governance in Europe: Policy-making without legislating. In A. Héritier (Ed.), *Common Goods: Reinventing European and International Governance* (pp. 185–206). Lanham: Rowman & Littlefield.

Héritier, A., & Lehmkuhl, D. (2008). The Shadow of hierarchy and new modes of governance. *Journal of Public Policy, 28*(1), 1–17. doi:10.1017/S0143814X08000755.

Héritier, A., & Rhodes, M. (Eds). (2011). *New modes of governance in Europe: Governing in the shadow of hierarchy*. Palgrave: Houndmills.

Hermans, L.M., & Cunningham, S.W. (2013). Actor models for policy analysis. In W.A.H. Thissen & W. E. Walker (Ed.), *Public Policy Analysis* (pp. 185-213). New York: Springer.

Hey, C., Jacob, K., & Volkery, A. (2007). Better regulation by new governance hybrids? Governance models and the reform of European chemicals policy. *Journal of Cleaner production, 15*(18), 1859-1874. doi:10.1016/j.jclepro.2006.11.001.

Hill, M., & Hupe, P.L. (2014). *Implementing public policy: Governance in theory and practice* (3rd ed.). London: Sage.

Hill, C. & Lynn, L. (2005). Is hierarchical governance in decline? Evidence from empirical research. *Journal of Public Administration Research and Theory, 15*(2), 173-195. doi: 10.1093/jopart/mui011.

Hillman, K., Nilsson, M., Rickne, A., & Magnusson, T. (2011). Fostering sustainable technologies: a framework for analysing the governance of innovation systems. *Science and Public Policy*, *38*(5), 403–415. doi:10.3152/030234211X12960315267499.

Hogl, K., Kvarda, E., Nordbeck, R., & Pregernig, M. (2012). Legitimacy and effectiveness of environmental governance - concepts and perspectives. In K. Hogl, E. Kvarda, R. Nordbeck & M. Pregernig (Eds.), *Environmental governance: The challenge of legitimacy and effectiveness* (pp. 1-28). Cheltenham: Edward Elgar.

Holley, C., Gunningham, N., & Shearing, C. (2012). *The new environmental governance*. London: Routledge.

Homeyer, I. (2006). *EPIGOV Common Framework. EPIGOV Paper No.1*. Berlin: Ecologic - Institute for International and European Environmental Policy.

Hooghe, L., & Marks, G. (2001). *Multi-level governance and european integration*. Maryland: Rowman & Littlefield.

Hoppe, R. (2010). *The governance of problems: Puzzling, powering and participation*. Bristol: The Policy Press.

Howlett, M., & Rayner, J. (2007). Design principles for policy mixes: cohesion and coherence in 'new governance arrangements'. *Policy and Society*, *26*(4), 1-18. doi:10.1016/S1449-4035(07)70118-2.

Howlett, M., Rayner, J., & Tollefson, C. (2009). From government to governance in forest planning? Lessons from the case of the British Columbia Great Bear Rainforest initiative. *Forest Policy and Economics*, *11*(5-6), 383–391.

Howlett, M., & Ramesh, M. (2015). Achilles' heels of governance: Critical capacity deficits and their role in governance failures. *Regulation & Governance*. Advance online publication doi:10.1111/rego.12091.

Howlett, M., & Ramesh, M. (2014). The two orders of governance failure: Design mismatches and policy capacity issues in modern governance. *Policy and Society*, *33*(4), 317-327. doi: 10.1016/j.polsoc.2014.10.002.

Hsieh, H.-F., & Shannon, S. E. (2005). Three approaches to qualitative content analysis. *Qualitative Health Research*, *15*(9), 1277–1288. doi:10.1177/1049732305276687.

Hufty, M. (2011). Investigating policy processes: The governance analytical framework (GAF). In H. Hurni & U. Wiesmann (Eds.), N*CCR North-South Synthesis* (pp. 403–424). Bern: Geographica Bernensia.

Huh, T.W. (2011). Exploring the principles and criteria for governance for sustainable development. *International Review of Public Administration*, *15*(3), 67–78.

Hyden, G. (2001). Operationalizing governance for sustainable development. *Journal of Development Studies, 17*(2), 13-31.

Hysing, E. (2015). Lost in transition? The green state in governance for sustainable development. In K. Bäckstrand & A. Kronsell (Eds.), *Rethinking the Green State:*

Environmental Governance Towards Climate and Sustainability Transitions (pp. 27-42). London: Routledge.

Hysing, E. (2010). *Governing towards Sustainability - Environmental Governance and Policy Change in Swedish Forestry and Transport*. Örebro: Örebro University.

Hysing, E. (2009). From government to governance? A comparison of environmental governing in Swedish forestry and transport. *Governance, 22*(4), 647–672. doi:10.1111/j.1468-0491.2009.01457.x.

IAEA (2005). *Energy indicators for sustainable development: Methodologies and guidelines*. Vienna: IAEA (International Atomic Energy Agency), United Nations Department of Economic and Social Affairs, International Energy Agency, Eurostat, European Environment Agency.

IEA (2012). *Energy policies of IEA countries. Switzerland 2012 Review*. Paris: IEA (International Energy Agency).

In't Veld, R.J. (2013). Transgovernance: the quest for governance of sustainable development. In L. Meuleman (Ed.), *Transgovernance - Advancing Sustainability Governance* (pp. 275-310). Heidelberg: Springer.

Iribarnegaray, M., & Seghezzo, L. (2012). Governance, sustainability and decision making in water and sanitation management systems. *Sustainability, 4*(12), 2922–2945. doi:10.3390/su4112922.

Jacobs, M. (1999). Sustainable development as a contested concept. In A. Dobson (Ed.), *Fairness and futurity. Essays on environmental sustainability and social justice* (pp. 21-45). Oxford: Oxford University Press.

Jänicke, M. (2006). *The "Rio Model" of environmental governance . A general evaluation.* Berlin: FFU-report 2006.

Jordan, A. (2008). The governance of sustainable development: taking stock and looking forwards. *Environment and Planning C: Government and Policy, 26*(1), 17–33.

Jordan, A., & Lenschow, A. (2010). Environmental policy integration: a state of the art review. *Environmental Policy and Governance, 20*(3), 147–158. doi:10.1002/eet.539.

Jordan, A., Wurzel, R.K.W., & Zito, A. (2005). The rise of "new" policy instruments in comparative perspective: Has governance eclipsed government? *Political Studies, 53*(3), 477–496. doi:10.1111/j.1467-9248.2005.00540.x.

Jessop, B. (2011). Metagovernance. In M. Bevir (Ed.), *Handbook of governance* (pp. 106–123). London: Sage.

Jessop, B. (2009). From governance to governance failure and from multi-level governance to multi-scalar meta-governance. In B. Arts, A. Lagendijk & H. van Houtum (Eds.), *The Disoriented State: Shifts in Governmentality, Territoriality and Governance* (pp. 79-98). Heidelberg: Springer.

Jessop, B. (2002). Governance and meta-governance in the face of complexity: On the roles of requistite variety, reflexive observation, and romantic irony in participatory governance. In H. Heinelt, P. Getimis, G. Kafkalas, R. Smith & E. Swyngedouw (Eds.), *Participatory governance in multi-level context. Concepts and experience* (pp. 33-58). Opladen: Leske & Budrich.

Jessop, B. (1998). The rise of governance and the risks of failure: the case of economic development. *International social science journal*, *50*(155), 29-45.

Kajikawa, Y., Tacoa, F., & Yamaguchi, K. (2014). Sustainability science: the changing landscape of sustainability research. *Sustainability science*, *9*(4), 431-438. doi:10.1007/s11625-014-0244-x.

Kardos, M. (2012). The reflection of good governance in sustainable development strategies. *Procedia-Social and Behavioral Sciences*, *58*(2012), 1166-1173. doi: 10.1016/j.sbspro.2012.09.1098.

Kates, R., Parris, T.M., & Leiserowitz, A.A. (2005). What is sustainable development? Goals, indicators, values, and practice. *Environment: Science and Policy for Sustainable Development*, *47*(3), 8–21.

Kelly, J. (2006). Central regulation of English local authorities: an example of metagovernance? *Public Administration, 84*(3), 603–621.

Kemp, R., Parto, S., & Gibson, R. B. (2005). Governance for sustainable development: moving from theory to practice. *International Journal of Sustainable Development*, *8*(1-2), 12–30.

Kenis, P., & Provan, K. G. (2009). Towards an exogenous theory of public network performance. *Public Administration*, *87*(3), 440-456.

Kenis, P., & Schneider, V. (1991). Policy networks in policy analysis: Scrutinizing a new analytical toolbox. In B. Marin & R. Mayntz (Eds.), *Policy networks: Empirical evidence and theoretical considerations* (pp. 25-59). Frankfurt/M.: Campus.

Kickert, W., Klijn, E.-H., & Koppenjan, J. (Eds.). (1997). *Managing complex networks: Strategies for the public sector*. London: sage.

Kingdon, J. (1995). *Agendas, alternatives and public policies*. New York: Harper Collins College Publishers.

Kjær, A.M. (2004). *Governance*. Cambridge: Polity Press.

Klijn, E. H., van Buuren, A., Edelenbos, J. (2012). The impact of governance: a normative and empirical discussion. In D. Levi-Faur (Ed.), *The Oxford Handbook of Governance* (pp. 294-308). Oxford: Oxford University Press.

Knight, J. (1992). *Institutions and social conflict.* New York: Cambridge University Press.

Knill, C. (2004). Modes of governance and their evaluation. *Trames*, *8(4)*, 352–371.

Knoepfel, P., Larrue, C., Varone, F., & Hill, M. (2011). *Public policy analysis*. Bristol: Policy Press.

Koch, P. (2013). Overestimating the shift from government to governance: Evidence from Swiss metropolitan areas. *Governance, 26*(3), 397–423. doi: 10.1111/j.1468-0491.2012.01600.x.

Koehler, D.A. (2007). The effectiveness of voluntary environmental programs - A policy at a crossroads? *Policy Studies Journal, 35*(4), 689-722.

Kohler-Koch, B. (1999). The evolution and transformation of European Governance. In B. Kohler-Koch & R. Eising (Eds.), *The transformation of governance in the European Union* (pp. 14–35). London: Routledge.

Kooiman, J. (2003). *Governing as governance*. London: Sage.

Kooiman, J. (Ed.). (1993). *Modern governance: New government-society interactions*. London: Sage.

Kooiman, J., & Jentoft, S. (2009). Meta-governance: values, norms and principles, and the making of hard choices. *Public administration, 87*(4), 818-836. doi: 10.1111/j.1467-9299.2009.01780.x.

Koontz, T.M., & Thomas, C.W. (2012). Measuring the performance of public-private partnerships: A systematic method for distinguishing outputs from outcomes. *Public Performance and Management Review, 35(*4), 769–786.

Koontz, T.M., & Thomas, C.W. (2006). What do we know and need to know about the environmental outcomes of collaborative management? *Public Administration Review, 66*(s1), 111–121. doi:10.1111/j.1540-6210.2006.00671.x.

Kopfmüller, J. (Ed.). (2006). *Ein Konzept auf dem Prüfstand: das integrative Nachhaltigkeitskonzept in der Forschungspraxis*. Berlin: Edition sigma.

Kopfmüller, J., Brandl, V., Jörissen, J., Paetau, M., Banse, G., Coenen, R., & Grunwald, A. (2001). *Nachhaltige Entwicklung integrativ betrachtet: Konstitutive Elemente, Regeln, Indikatoren*. Berlin: Edition Sigma.

Kopfmüller, J., Coenen, R., & Jörissen, J. (2000). *Konkretisierung und Operationalisierung des Leitbilds einer nachhaltigen Entwicklung für den Energiebereich. Wissenschaftlicher Bericht FZKA 6578*. Karlsruhe: Forschungszentrum Karlsruhe GmbH.

Koppenjan, J., Kars, M., & Van der Voort, H. (2013). Politicians as metagovernors – can metagovernance reconcile representative democracy and network reality?. In J. Torfing & P. Triantafillou (Eds.), *Interactive Policy Making, Metagovernance, and Democracy* (pp. 95-110). Colchester: ECPR.

Krippendorff, K. (2004). *Content analysis. An introduction to its methodology* (2nd ed.). Thousand Oaks: Sage.

Kritzinger, S., & Pülzl, H. (2008). Governance modes and interests: Higher education and innovation policy in Austria. *Journal of Public Policy, 28*(03), 289–307. doi:10.1017/S0143814X08000913.

Kronsell, A., & Bäckstrand, K. (2010). Rationalities and forms of governance: a framework for analysing the legitamcy of new modes of governance. In K. Bäckstrand, J. Khan, A. Kronsell & E. Lövbrand (Eds.), *Environmental politics and deliberative democracy: Examining the promise of new modes of governance* (pp. 28-45). Cheltenham, UK: Edward Elgar.

Kuckartz, U. (2007). *Einführung in die computergestützte Analyse qualitativer Daten* (2nd ed.). Wiesbaden: VS Verlag für Sozialwissenschaften.

Kuhlmann, S., Bogumil, J., & Wollmann, H. (Eds.). (2004). *Leistungsmessung und-vergleich in Politik und Verwaltung: Konzepte und Praxis*. Wiesbaden: VS Verlag für Sozialwissenschaften.

Kvartiuk, V. (2016). Participation and local governance uutcomes: Evidence from Ukraine. *Voluntas: International Journal of Voluntary and Nonprofit Organizations*, 1-29. Advance Online Publication. doi: 10.1007/s11266-016-9687-2.

Lafferty, W. (2004). Introduction: form and function in governance for sustainable development. In W. Lafferty (Ed.), *Governance for Sustainable Development: The Challenge of Adapting Form to Function* (pp. 1–31). Cheltenham & Northampton: Edward Elgar.

Lafferty, W., & Hovden, E. (2003). Environmental policy integration: towards an analytical framework. *Environmental Politics*, *12*(3), 1–22. doi:10.1080/09644010412331308254.

Lange, P., Driessen, P.P.J., Sauer, A., Bornemann, B., & Burger, P. (2013). Governing Towards Sustainability - Conceptualizing Modes of Governance. *Journal of Environmental Policy & Planning*, *15*(3), 403–425. doi:10.1080/1523908X.2013.769414.

Larsson, O. (2015). The Governmentality of meta-governance: Identifying theoretical and empirical challenges of network governance in the political field of security and beyond. Uppsala: Uppsala University.

Lauth, H. J., & Wagner, C. (2010). Gegenstand, grundlegende Kategorien und Forschungsfragen der vergleichenden Regierungslehre. In H.J. Lauth (Ed.), *Vergleichende Regierungslehre* (3rd ed.). Wiesbaden: VS Verlag für Sozialwissenschaften.

Lejano, R., Ingram, H., Whiteley, J., Torres, D., & Agduma, S. (2007). The importance of context: integrating resource conservation with local institutions. *Society and Natural Resources, 20*(2), 177–85.

Levi-Faur, D. (Ed.). (2012). *The oxford handbook of governance*. Oxford: Oxford University Press.

Liefferink, D. (2006). The dynamics of policy arrangements: turning round the tetrahedron. In B. Arts, & P. Leroy (Eds.), *Institutional Dynamics in Environmental Governance* (pp. 45–68). Dordrecht: Springer.

Lin, Y., Hao, P., & Geertman, S. (2014). A conceptual framework on modes of governance for the regeneration of Chinese 'villages in the city'. *Urban Studies*. Advance online publication. doi: 10.1177/0042098014540345.

Lockwood, M. (2010). Good governance for terrestrial protected areas: A framework, principles and performance outcomes. *Journal of Environmental Management*, *91*(3), 754–766.

Lockwood, M., Davidson, J., Curtis, A., Stratford, E., & Griffith, R. (2010). Governance principles for natural resource management. *Society & Natural Resources*, *23*(10), 986–1001. doi:10.1080/08941920802178214.

Loorbach, D. (2010). Transition management for sustainable development: A Prescriptive, Complexity-Based Governance Framework. *Governance*, *23*(1), 161–183. doi:10.1111/j.1468-0491.2009.01471.x.

Lowi, T.J. (1972). Four systems of policy, politics, and choice. *Public Administration Review,* 33(4), 298-310. doi: 10.2307/974990.

Lowndes, V., & Skelcher, C. (1998). The dynamics of multi-organizational partnerships: an analysis of changing modes of governance. *Public Administration*, *76*(2), 313–333. doi:10.1111/1467-9299.00103.

Lund, D.H., Sehested, K., Hellesen, T., & Nellemann, V. (2012). Climate change adaptation in Denmark: enhancement through collaboration and meta-governance?. *Local Environment*, *17*(6-7), 613-628.

Lynn, L.E. (2011). The persistence of hierarchy. In M. Bevir (Ed.), *The SAGE handbook of governance* (pp. 218-236). Thousand Oaks: SAGE.

Mahanti, A., & Manuel-Navarrete, D. (2015). From sustainable development to governance for sustainability. In M. Redclift & D. Springett (Eds.), *Routledge International Handbook of Sustainable Development* (pp. 416-428). New York: Routledge.

March, J.G., & Olsen, J.P. (1989). *Rediscovering institutions: the organizational basis of politics*. New York.: Free Press.

Marsh, D., & Smith, M. (2000). Understanding policy networks: towards a dialectical approach. *Political Studies*, *48*(1), 4–21. doi:10.1111/1467-9248.00247.

Martin, P., & Gunningham, N. (2014). Improving governance arrangements for sustainable agriculture: Groundwater as an illustration. *Australian Journal of Environmental Law*, *1*(1), 5-23.

Mauerhofer, V. (2013). The "Governance-Check": Assessing the sustainability of public spatial decision-making structures. *Land Use Policy*, *30*(1), 328–336.

Mayntz, R. (2003). New challenges to governance theory. In H.B. Bang (Ed.), *Governance as Social and Political Communication* (pp. 27–40). Manchester: Manchester University Press.

Mayring, P. (2015). Qualitative content analysis: Theoretical background and procedures. In A. Bikner-Ahsbahs, C. Knipping & N. Presmeg (Eds.), *Approaches to qualitative research in mathematics education* (pp. 365-380). Dordrecht: Springer.

Mayring, P. (2010). *Qualitative Inhaltsanalyse: Grundlagen und Techniken* (11th ed.). Basel: Beltz.

Mayring, P. (2000). Qualitative content analysis. *Forum: Qualitative Social Research*, *1*(2).

McNeill, D., Bursztyn, M., Novira, N., Purushothaman, S., Verburg, R., & Rodrigues-Filho, S. (2014). Taking account of governance: The challenge for land-use planning models. *Land Use Policy*, *37*(2014), 6-13.

McNutt, K. & Rayner, J. (2014): Is learning without teaching possible? The productive tension between network governance and reflexivity. *Journal of Environmental Policy & Planning*. Advance online publication. doi: 10.1080/1523908X.2014.986568.

Meadowcroft, J. (2011). Sustainable development. In M. Bevir (Ed.), *The SAGE handbook of governance* (pp. 535–551). Thousand Oaks: SAGE.

Meadowcroft, J. (2007). Who is in charge here? Governance for sustainable development in a complex world. *Journal of Environmental Policy & Planning*, *9*(3-4), 299–314. doi:10.1080/15239080701631544.

Meadowcroft, J., Farrell, N., & Spangenberg, J. (2005). Developing a framework for sustainability governance in the European Union. *International Journal of Sustainable Development, 8*(1-2), 3-11.

Meadowcroft, J., Langhelle, O., & Ruud, A. (2012). *Governance, democracy and sustainable development: moving beyond the impasse*. Cheltenham: Edward Elgar Pub.

Mees, H.L.P., Driessen, P.P.J., Runhaar, H.A.C. & Stamatelos, J. (2013). Who governs climate adaptation; getting green roofs for storm-water retention off the ground. *Journal of Environmental Planning & Management, 56*(6), 802–825. doi:10.1080/09640568.2012.706600.

Meuleman, L. (2014). Governance frameworks. In B. Freedman (Ed.), *Global Environmental Change* (pp. 885-901). Dordrecht: Springer.

Meuleman, L. (2008). *Public management and the metagovernance of hierarchies, networks and markets: The feasibility of designing and managing governance style combinations*. Heidelberg: Springer.

Meuleman, L., & In 't Veld, R. (2010). Sustainable development and the governance of long-term decisions. In R. In 't Veld (Ed.), *Knowledge democracy: consequences for science, politics, and media* (pp. 255–283). Heidelberg: Springer.

Meuleman, L., & Niestroy, I. (2015). Common but differentiated governance: A metagovernance approach to make the SDGs work. *Sustainability, 7*(9), 12295-12321. doi:10.3390/su70912295.

Michelsen, G., Adomßent, M., Martens, P., & von Hauff, M. (2016). Sustainable development -background and context. In H. Heinrichs, P. Martens, G. Michelsen & A. Wiek (Eds.), *Sustainability Science* (pp. 5-29). Dordrecht: Springer.

Miles, M. B., & Huberman, A. M. (1994). *Qualitative data analysis: A methods sourcebook*. Beverly Hills: Sage.

Milgrom, P.R., & Roberts, J. (1990). The economics of modern manufacturing: Technology, strategy and organization. *American Economic Review 80*(3), 511–528.

Miller, C.A., & Edwards, P.N. (2001). *Changing the atmosphere. Expert knowledge and environmental governance*. Cambridge: MIT Press.

Miller, T.R. (2013). Constructing sustainability science: emerging perspectives and research trajectories. *Sustainability Science* 8(2), 279–293. doi:10.1007/s11625-012-0180-6.

Mol, A.P. (2016). The environmental nation state in decline. *Environmental Politics*, *25*(1), 48-68. doi: 10.1080/09644016.2015.1074385.

Monkelbaan, J. (2015). Experimentalist sustainability governance: Jazzing up environmental blues?. *Public Participation and Climate Governance Working Paper Series.* Centre for International Sustainable Development Law.

Morse, J.M. (1995). The significance of saturation. *Qualitative health research*, *5*(2), 147-149.

Nelissen, N. (2002). The administrative capacity of new types of governance. *Public organization review: a global journal, 2(*1), 5–22. doi: 10.1023/A:1016019302732.

Newell, P., Jenner, N., & Baker, L. (2009). Governing clean development: A framework for analysis. *Development Policy Review*, *27*(6), 717–739.

Newig, J. (2012). More effective natural resource management through participatory governance? Taking stock of the conceptual and empirical literature–and moving forward. In K. Hogl, E. Kvarda, R. Nordbeck & M. Pregernig (Eds.), *Environmental Governance: The Challenge of Legitimacy and Effectiveness* (pp. 46-68). Cheltenham: Edward Elgar.

Newig, J., & Fritsch, O. (2009). Environmental governance: participatory, multi-level - and effective? *Environmental Policy and Governance*, *19*(3), 197–214. doi:10.1002/eet.509.

Newig, J. & Kvarda, E. (2012). Participation in environmental governance: legitimate and effective?. In K. Hogl, E. Kvarda, R. Nordbeck & M. Pregernig (Eds.), *Environmental Governance: The Challenge of Legitimacy and Effectiveness* (pp. 29-45). Cheltenham: Edward Elgar.

Newig, J., Voss, J.P., & Monstadt, J. (Eds.). (2008). *Governance for sustainable development: Coping with ambivalence, uncertainty and distributed power*. London: Routledge.

North, D. C. (1990). *Institutions, institutional change and economic performance*. Cambridge: Cambridge University Press.

OECD (2002). *Improving policy coherence and integration for sustainable sevelopment: A checklist.* Paris: OECD (Organisation for Economic Co-operation and Development).

OECD (2007). *Institutionalising sustainable development*. Paris: OECD (Organisation for Economic Co-operation and Development).

Ostrom, E. (2010). Beyond markets and states: polycentric governance of complex economic systems. *Transnational Corporations Review*, *2*(2), 1-12.

Ostrom, E. (1998). The institutional analysis and development approach. In E.T. Loehman & D.M. Kilgour (Eds.), *Designing Institutions for Environmental and Resource Management* (pp. 68-90). Cheltenham: Edward Elgar.

Ostrom, E. & Crawford, S. (2005). Classifying rules. In E. Ostrom (Ed.), *Understanding institutional diversity* (pp. 186-215). Princeton: Princeton University Press.

Ostrom, E., Gardner, R., & Walker, J. (1994). *Rules, games, and common-pool resources.* Ann Arbor: University of Michigan Press.

Padt, F., Opdam, P., Polman, N., & Termeer, C. (Eds.). (2014). *Scale-sensitive governance of the environment*. Chichester: John Wiley & Sons.

Pahl-Wostl, C. (2015). Governance modes. In C. Pahl-Wostl (Ed.), *Water governance in the face of global change* (pp. 85-98). Heidelberg: Springer.

Pahl-Wostl, C. (2009). A conceptual framework for analysing adaptive capacity and multi-level learning processes in resource governance regimes. *Global Environmental Change*, *19*(3), 354–365. doi:10.1016/j.gloenvcha.2009.06.001.

Paleo, U.F. (2014). Principles for the evaluation of risk governance and the measurement of performance. In M.B. Dan, I. Armas & A. Goretti (Eds.), *Earthquake hazard impact and urban planning* (pp. 171-193). Dordrecht: Springer.

Parkins, J.R. (2008). The metagovernance of climate change: institutional adaptation of the mountain pine beetle epidemic in British Columbia. *Journal of Rural and Community Development 3*(2): 7–26.

Parsons, D.W. (1995). *Public policy: An introduction to the theory and practice of policy analysis*. Cheltemham: Edward Elgar.

Patlitzianas, K.D., Doukas, H., Kagiannas, A.G., & Psarras, J. (2008). Sustainable energy policy indicators: Review and recommendations. *Renewable Energy*, *33*(5), 966–973.

Pattberg, P.H. (2007). *Private institutions and global governance. The new politics of environmental sustainability*. Cheltenham & Northampton: Edward Elgar.

Payne, G., & Williams, M. (2005). Generalization in qualitative research. *Sociology, 39*(2), 295-314.

Pennings, P., Keman, H., & Kleinnijenhuis, J. (2006). *Doing research in political science. An introduction to comparative methods and statistics* (2nd ed.). London: Sage.

Petschow, U., Rosenau, J., & von Weizsacker, E. (2005). *Governance and sustainability: New challenges for states, companies and civil society.* Greenleaf Publishing.

Pierre, J. (Ed.). (2000). *Debating governance: Authority, steering, and democracy*. Oxford: Oxford University Press.

Pierre, J., & Peters, B.G. (2005). *Governing complex societies.* Basingstoke: Palgrave.

Pierre, J., & Peters, B.G. (2000). *Governance, politics and the state*. London: Macmillan.

Pisano, U., Lepuschitz, K., & Berger, G. (2014). Transformative environmental and sustainability policy: new thematic issues, actor constellations and governance modes. *11th European Sustainable Development Network Workshop - Background and Discussion Paper*.

Pollitt, C., & Hupe, P. (2011). Talking about government: The role of magic concepts. *Public Management Review, 13*(5), 641–658.

Potter, W.J., & Levine-Donnerstein, D. (1999). Rethinking validity and reliability in content analysis. *Journal of Applied Communication Research*, *27*(3), 258–284. doi:10.1080/00909889909365539.

Ramesh, M., Wu, X., & Howlett, M. (2015). Second best governance? Governments and governance in the imperfect world of health care delivery in China, India and Thailand in comparative perspective. *Journal of Comparative Policy Analysis: Research and Practice*, *17*(4), 342-358. doi: 10.1080/13876988.2014.889903.

Raschke, J., & Tils, R. (2007). *Politische Strategie: Eine Grundlegung*. Wiesbaden: VS Verlag für Sozialwissenschaften.

Rauschmayer, F., Berghöfer, A., Omann, I., & Zikos, D. (2009). Examining processes or/and outcomes? Evaluation concepts in European governance of natural resources. *Environmental Policy and Governance, 19*(2009), 159-173. doi: 10.1002/eet.506.

Rayner, J. (2015). The past and future of governance studies: From governance to meta-governance?. In G. Capano, M. Howlett & M. Ramesh (Eds.), *Varieties of governance* (pp. 235-254). Houndsmills: Palgrave Macmillan.

Redclift, M. (2005): *Sustainability: Critical Concepts in the Social Sciences*. London: Routledge.

Reed, M.S., Evely, A.C., Cundill, G., Fazey, I., Glass, J., Laing, A., & Stringer, L.C. (2010). What is social learning? *Ecology and Society*, *15*(4).

Rhodes, R.A.W. (1997). *Understanding governance: Policy networks, governance, reflexivity and accountability*. Buckingham: Open University Press.

Rhodes, R.A.W., & Marsh, D. (1992). New directions in the study of policy networks. *European Journal of Political Research, 21*(1-2), 181–205. doi:10.1111/j.1475-6765.1992.tb00294.x.

Rhodes, M.L., & Murray, J. (2007). Collaborative decision making in urban regeneration: A complex adaptive systems perspective. *International Public Management Journal*, *10*(1), 79-101. doi: 10.1080/10967490601185740.

Rich, R.F. (1997). Measuring knowledge utilization, processes and outcomes. *Knowledge Policy*, *10*(3), 11–23. doi:10.1007/BF02912504.

Rist, S., Chidambaranathan, M., Escobar, C., Wiesmann, U., & Zimmermann, A. (2007). Moving from sustainable management to sustainable governance of natural resources: The role of social learning processes in rural India, Bolivia and Mali. *Journal of Rural Studies*, *23*(1), 23–37.

Ritchie, J., & Lewis, J. (2003). *Qualitative research practice: A guide for social science students and researchers.* London: Sage.

Rittel, H.W.J., & Webber, M.M. (1973). Dilemmas in a general theory of planning. *Policy Sciences 4*(2), 155–169.

Robertson, M. (2014). *Sustainability: Principles and practice*. London: Routledge.

Robichau, R.W. (2011). The mosaic of governance: Creating a picture with definitions, theories, and debates. *Policy Studies Journal*, *39*(2011), 113–131. doi:10.1111/j.1541-0072.2010.00389_8.x.

Rosenau, J.N. (1992). Governance, order, and change in world politics. In E. Czempiel (Ed.), *Governance without Government: Order and Change in World Politics* (pp. 1–29). Cambridge: Cambridge University Press.

Rossi, P.H., Lipsey, M.W., & Freeman, H.E. (2003). *Evaluation: A systematic approach* (7th edition). Thousand Oaks: Sage.

Ruhanen, L., Scott, N., Ritchie, B., & Tkaczynski, A. (2010). Governance: A review and synthesis of the literature. *Tourism Review*, *65*(4), 4–16. doi: 10.1108/16605371011093836.

Runhaar, H.A.C., Driessen, P.P.J., & Uittenbroek, C. (2014). Towards a systematic framework for the analysis of environmental policy integration. *Environmental Policy and Governance*, *24*(4), 233-246. doi: 10.1002/eet.1647.

Sabatier, P.A. (Ed.). (2007). *Theories of the policy process* (2nd ed.). Boulder: Westview Press.

Sabatier, P.A. (1998). The advocacy coalition framework: revisions and relevance for Europe. *Journal of European Public Policy*, *5*(1), 98–130. doi:10.1080/13501768880000051.

Sabatier, P.A. (1986). Top-down and bottom-up approaches to implementation research: A critical analysis and suggested synthesis. *Journal of Public Policy*, *6*(1), 21–48.

Sajeva, M., Sahota, P. S., & Lemon, M. (2015). Giving sustainability a chance: a participatory framework for choosing between alternative futures. *Journal of Organisational Transformation & Social Change*, *12*(1), 57-89. doi: 10.1179/1477963314Z.00000000035.

Sanders, J.R. (2002). Presidential address: On mainstreaming evaluation. *American Journal of Evaluation*, *23*(3), 253-259.

Sauer, A. (2006). European nature conservation policy: Challenges for local implementation in Germany. In: S. Stoll-Kleemann & M. Welp (Eds.), *Stakeholder Dialogues in Natural Resources Management: Theory and Practice* (pp. 173–189). Heidelberg: Springer

Scharpf, F.W. (1997). *Games real actors play: Actor-centered institutionalism in policy research*. Boulder: Westview Press.

Schmidt, B. (2005). Competing realist conceptions of power. *Millenium – Journal of International Studies*, *33*(3), 523–549.

Schmitter, P.C. (1981). Interest intermediation and regime governability in contemporary western Europe and North America. In S. Berger (Ed.), *Organising interests in western Europe: Pluralism, corporatism, and the transformation of politics* (pp. 287-327). Cambridge: Cambridge University Press.

Schneider, F., Bonriposi, M., Graefe, O., Herweg, K., Homewood, C., Huss, M., Kauzlaric, M., Liniger, H., Rey, E., Reynard, E., Rist, S., Schädler, B., & Weingartner, R. (2014): Assessing the sustainability of water governance systems: the sustainability wheel. *Journal of Environmental Planning and Management, 58*(9), 1577-1600. doi: 10.1080/09640568.2014.938804.

Schneider, V., Janning, F. (2006). Politikfeldanalyse. Akteure, Diskurse und Netzwerke in der öffentlichen Politik. Wiesbaden: VS Verlag für Sozialwissenschaften.

Schultz, J., Brand, F., Kopfmüller, J., & Ott, K. (2008). Building a 'theory of sustainable development': two salient conceptions within the German discourse'. *Int. J. Environment and Sustainable Development, 7*(4), 465-482. doi: 10.1504/IJESD.2008.02239.

Schultz, E., Christen, M., Voget-Kleschin, L., & Burger, P. (2013). A sustainability-fitting interpretation of the capability approach: integrating the natural dimension by employing feedback loops. *Journal of Human Development and Capabilities 14*(1):115-133. doi: 10.1080/19452829.2012.747489.

Scott, T. (2015). Does collaboration make any difference? Linking collaborative governance to environmental outcomes. *Journal of Policy Analysis and Management, 34*(3), 537-566. doi:10.1002/pam.21836.

Scott, W.R. (2001). *Institutions and organizations* (2nd ed.). Thousand Oaks: Sage.

Seawright, J., & Gerring, J. (2008). Case selection techniques in case study research: A menu of qualitative and quantitative options. *Political Research Quarterly, 61*(2), 294–308. doi:10.1177/1065912907313077.

Segerson, K., & Miceli, T.J. (1999). Voluntary approaches to environmental protection: the role of legislative threats. In C. Carraro & F. Leveque (Eds.), *Voluntary Approaches in Environmental Policy* (pp. 105-120). Dordrecht: Springer.

Seidman, I. (2006). *Interviewing as qualitative research: A guide for researchers in education and the social sciences.* New York: Teachers College Press.

SFOE (2011). *Schlussevaluation EnergieSchweiz 2001-2010.* Bern: SFOE (Swiss Federal Office of Energy).

Shiroyama, H., Yarime, M., Matsuo, M., Schroeder, H., Scholz, R., & Ulrich, A. E. (2012). Governance for sustainability: knowledge integration and multi-actor dimensions in risk management. *Sustainability Science, 7*(S1), 45–55. doi:10.1007/s11625-011-0155-z.

Shove, E., & Walker, G. (2007). Caution! Transitions ahead: politics, practice, and sustainable transition management. *Environment and Planning A, 39*(4), 763-770.

Sinha, A. (2012). Sustainable development and governance: Complex processes and unpredictable outcomes. *IIM Kozhikode Society & Management Review*, *1*(1), 11–20. doi:10.1177/2277975212001000103.

Smismans, S. (2008). New modes of governance and the participatory myth. *West European Politics*, *31*(5), 874–895. doi:10.1080/01402380802234540.

Sohre, A. (2014). *Strategien in der Energie-und Klimapolitik. Bedingungen strategischer Steuerung der Energiewende in Deutschland und Großbritannien.* Wiesbaden: VS Verlag für Sozialwissenschaften.

Sørensen, E. (2006). Metagovernance the changing role of politicians in processes of democratic governance. *The American review of public administration*, *36*(1), 98-114.

Sørensen, E., & Torfing, J. (2009). Making governance networks effective and democratic through metagovernance. *Public Administration*, *87*(2), 234–258. doi:10.1111/j.1467-9299.2009.01753.x.

Sørensen, E., & Triantafillou, P. (Eds.). (2013). *The politics of self-governance.* Farnham: Ashgate Publishing.

Speer, J. (2012). Participatory governance reform: a good strategy for increasing government responsiveness and improving public services?. *World Development*, *40*(12), 2379-2398.

Stake, R. (2000). Case studies. In N. Denzing, & Y. Lincoln (Eds.), *Handbook of qualitative research* (pp. 435–453). Thousand Oaks: Sage.

Steinke, I. (2004). Quality criteria in qualitative research. In U. Flick, E. Kardoff von & I. Steinke (Eds.), *A Companion to Qualitative Research* (pp. 184–190). London: Sage.

Steurer, R. (2013). Disentangling governance: a synoptic view of regulation by government, business and civil society. *Policy Sciences*, *46*(4), 387–410. doi:10.1007/s11077-013-9177-y.

Steurer, R. (2010). Sustainable development as a governance reform agenda: Principles and challenges. In R. Steurer, & R. Trattnigg (Eds.), *Nachhaltigkeit regieren: Eine Bilanz zu Governance-Prinzipien und -Praktiken* (pp. 33–54). München: Oekom.

Stoker, G. (2006). *Why politics matters: Making democracy work.* Basingstoke: Palgrave Macmillan.

Stoker, G. (2000). Urban political science and the challenge of urban governance. In J. Pierre (Ed.), *Debating Governance* (pp. 91–109). Oxford: Oxford University Press.

Stoker, G. (1998). Governance as theory: five propositions. *International Social Science Journal*, *50*(155), 17–28. doi:10.1111/1468-2451.00106.

Streimikiene, D., & Šivickas, G. (2008). The EU sustainable energy policy indicators framework. *Environment International*, *34*(8), 1227–1240.

Swiss Academies of Arts and Sciences. (2012). *Zukunft Stromversorgung Schweiz - Kurzfassung*. Bern: Swiss Academies of Arts and Sciences.

Taylor, C., Pollard, S., Rocks, S., & Angus, A. (2012). Selecting policy instruments for better environmental regulation: a critique and future research agenda. *Environmental Policy and Governance, 22*(4), 268-292. doi: 10.1002/eet.1584.

Thalmann, P. (2013). Klimapolitik der Schweiz: Musterschülerin mit Fragezeichen. *Die Volkswirtschaft Das Magazin für Wirtschaftspolitik, 11-2013, 35-38.*

Thompson, G., Frances, J., Levacic, R., & Mitchell, J. (Eds.). (1991). *Markets, hierarchies and networks: The co-ordination of social Life*. London: Sage.

Tils, R. (2005). *Politische Strategieanalyse: Konzeptionelle Grundlagen und Anwendung in der Umwelt- und Nachhaltigkeitspolitik*. Wiesbaden: VS Verlag für Sozialwissenschaften.

Timmermans, A. (2001). Arenas as institutional sites for policymaking: Patterns and effects in comparative perpective. *Journal of Comparative Policy Analysis: Research and Practice, 3*(3), 311-337. doi:10.1023/A:1012357518537.

Timmermans, J., Van der Heiden, S., & Born, M.P. (2014). Policy entrepreneurs in sustainability transitions: Their personality and leadership profiles assessed. *Environmental Innovation and Societal Transitions, 13*(2014), 96-108. doi: 10.1016/j.eist.2014.06.002.

Tollefson, C., Gale, F., & Haley, D. (2008). *Setting the standard: Certification, governance, and the forest stewardship council*. Vancouver: UBC Press.

Tollefson, C., Zito, A. R., & Gale, F. (2012). Symposium overview: Conceptualizing new governance arrangements. *Public Administration, 90*(1), 3–18. doi:10.1111/j.1467-9299.2011.02003.x.

Tömmel, I. (2009). Modes of governance and the institutional structure of the European Union. In I. Tömmel & A. Verdun (Eds.), *Innovative governance in the European Union: The politics of multilevel policymaking* (pp. 9–26). Boulder: Lynne Rienner.

Torfing, J., Peters, B., Pierre, J., & Sørensen, E. (2012). *Interactive governance: advancing the paradigm*. Oxford: Oxford University Press.

Torfing, J., & Triantafillou, P. (Eds.). (2013). *Interactive policy making, metagovernance and democracy*. Colchester: ECPR.

Tracy, S.J. (2013). *Qualitative research methods: Collecting evidence, crafting analysis, communicating impact*. Malden: Wiley-Blackwell.

Treib, O., Bähr, H., & Falkner, G. (2011). Social policy and environmental policy: Comparing modes of governance. In U. Diedrichs & W. Wessels (Eds.), *The dynamics of change in EU governance: Policy-making and system evolution* (pp. 103–131). Cheltenham: Edward Elgar.

Treib, O., Bähr, H., & Falkner, G. (2007). Modes of governance: towards a conceptual clarification. *Journal of European Public Policy, 14*(1), 1–20. doi:10.1080/13501760601071406.

Turnhout, E., Hisschemöller, M., & Eijsackers, H. (2007). Ecological indicators: Between the two fires of science and policy. *Ecological Indicators*, *7*(2), 215–228. doi:10.1016/j.ecolind.2005.12.003.

UNCED (1992). Agenda 21. United Nations Conference on Environment and Development. New York: United Nations General Assembly.

UNDP (1997). *Governance for sustainable human development. A UNDP policy document.* New York: United Nations Development Programme.

Van Assche, K., Beunen R., & Duineveld, M. (2014a). *Evolutionary governance theory: An introduction*. Heidelberg: Springer.

Van Assche, K., Van Biesebroeck, J., & Holm, J. (2014b). Governing the ice. Ice fishing villages on Lake Mille Lacs and the creation of environmental governance institutions. *Journal of Environmental Planning and Management,* 57(8), 1122-1144. doi: 10.1080/09640568.2013.787054.

Van Bommel, S. (2008). *Understanding experts and expertise in different governance contexts: The case of nature conservation in the Drentsche Area in the Netherlands*. Wageningen: Wageningen University.

Van Buuren, A., & Klijn, E. (2006). Trajectories of institutional design in policy networks: European interventions in the Dutch fishery network as an example. *International Review of Administrative Sciences,* *72*(3), 395-415. doi:10.1177/002085230606802.

Van de Meene, S.J., Brown, R.R., & Farrelly, M. (2011). Towards understanding governance for sustainable urban water management. *Global Environmental Change*, *21*(3), 1117–1127. doi:10.1016/j.gloenvcha.2011.04.003.

Van der Heijden, J. (2015). Regulatory failures, split-incentives, conflicting interests and a vicious circle of blame: the New Environmental Governance to the rescue?. *Journal of Environmental Planning and Management, 58*(6), 1034-1057. doi: 10.1080/09640568.2014.907135.

Van der Heijden, J. (2013). Is new governance the silver bullet? Insights from the Australian buildings sector. *Urban Policy and Research*, *31*(4), 453–471. doi:10.1080/08111146.2013.769156.

Van der Heijden, J. (2012). Voluntary environmental governance arrangements. *Environmental Politics*, *21*(3), 486-509. doi: 10.1080/09644016.2012.671576.

Van der Wal, M., De Kraker, J., Offermans, A., Kroeze, C., Kirschner, P. a., & van Ittersum, M. (2014). Measuring social learning in participatory approaches to natural resource management. *Environmental Policy and Governance*, *24*(1), 1–15. doi:10.1002/eet.1627.

Van der Windt, H. (2008). Nature conservation in Poland and the Netherland. Bottom–up or bottom line? In J. Keulartz & G. Leistra (Eds.), *Legitimacy in European nature conservation policy: Case studies in multilevel governance* (pp. 149–157). Heidelberg: Springer.

Van Kersbergen, K., & van Waarden, F. (2004). "Governance" as a bridge between disciplines: Cross-disciplinary inspiration regarding shifts in governance and problems of governability, accountability and legitimacy. *European Journal of Political Research*, *43*(2), 143–171. doi:10.1111/j.1475-6765.2004.00149.x.

Van Leeuwen, J., & van Tatenhove, J. (2010). The triangle of marine governance in the environmental governance of Dutch offshore platforms. *Marine Policy*, *34*(3), 590–597.

Van Trung Ho, T., Woodley, S., Cottrell, A., Valentine, P. (2014). A multilevel analytical framework for more-effective governance in human-natural systems: a case study of marine protected areas in Vietnam. *Ocean & Coastal Management*, 90(2014), 11-19. doi:10.1016/j.ocecoaman.2013.12.015.

Van Zeijl-Rozema, A., Cörvers, R., Kemp, R., & Martens, P. (2008). Governance for sustainable development: a framework. *Sustainable Development*, *16*(6), 410–421.

Vera, I., & Langlois, L. (2007). Energy indicators for sustainable development. *Energy*, *32*(6), 875–882. doi:10.1016/j.energy.2006.08.006.

Vermeulen, W.J.V. (2002). Greening production as co-responsibility. In P.P.J. Driessen & P. Glasbergen (Eds.), *Greening Society. The Paradigm Shift in Dutch Environmental Politics* (pp. 67–90). Dordrecht: Kluwer.

Vermeulen, W.J.V., & Kok, M.T.J. (2012). Government interventions in sustainable supply chain governance: Experience in Dutch front-running cases. *Ecological Economics*, *83*(2012), 183-196. doi:10.1016/j.ecolecon.2012.04.006.

Verschuren, P.J. (2003). Case study as a research strategy: Some ambiguities and opportunities. *International Journal of Social Science Research Methodology*, *6*(2), 121−139.

Verschuren, P.J., Doorewaard, H., & Mellion, M. (2010). *Designing a research project.* The Hague: Eleven International Publishing House.

Vodden, K. (2015). Governing sustainable coastal development: The promise and challenge of collaborative governance in Canadian coastal watersheds. *The Canadian Geographer*, *59*(2), 167-180. doi: 10.1111/cag.12135.

Von Blumenthal, J. (2014). Governance im und durch den Staat. In K. Maag Merki, R. Langer & H. Altrichter (Eds.), *Educational Governance als Forschungsperspektive* (pp. 85-107). Wiesbaden: VS Verlag für Sozialwissenschaften.

Von Prittwitz, V. (1994). *Politikanalyse.* Opladen: Leske & Budrich.

Voss, J.-P., Bauknecht, D., & Kemp, R. (Eds.). (2006). *Reflexive governance for sustainable development.* Cheltenham: Edward Elgar Publishing.

Voss, J.-P., & Bornemann, B. (2011). The politics of reflexive governance: challenges for designing adaptive management and transition management. *Ecology and Society* 16(2). Online publication.

Voss, J.-P., Newig, J., Kastens, B., Monstadt, J., & Nölting, B. (2007). Steering for sustainable development: a typology of problems and strategies with respect to ambivalence, uncertainty and distributed power. *Journal of Environmental Policy & Planning*, *9*(3-4), 193–212. doi:10.1080/15239080701622881.

Walter, F., Gubler, F., Brodman, U., & Heer, L. (2001). Nachhaltigkeit: Kriterien und Indikatoren für den Energiebereich. Bern: Bundesamt für Energie.

Wan, Y.K.P., & Bramwell, B. (2015). Political economy and the emergence of a hybrid mode of governance of tourism planning. *Tourism Management*, *50*(2015), 316-327. doi:10.1016/j.tourman.2015.03.010.

WCED (World Commission on Environment and Development) (1987). *Our common future*. Oxford: Oxford University Press.

Webb, K. (2005). Sustainable governance in the twenty-first century: Moving beyond instrument choice. In P. Eliadis, M. Hill & M. Howlett (Eds.), *Designing government: From instruments to governance*. Montreal: McGill-Queen's University Press.

Weber, M., Driessen, P.P.J., & Runhaar, H.A.C. (2014). Evaluating environmental policy instruments mixes: a methodology illustrated by noise policy in the Netherlands. *Journal of Environmental Planning and Management*, *57*(9), 1381-1397. doi: 10.1080/09640568.2013.808609.

Weber, M., Driessen, P.P.J., & Runhaar, H.A.C. (2011). Drivers of and Barriers to Shifts in Governance: Analysing Noise Policy in the Netherlands. *Journal of Environmental Policy & Planning*, *13*(2), 119–137. doi:10.1080/1523908X.2011.572657.

Whitehead, M. (2003). 'In the shadow of hierarchy': meta-governance, policy reform and urban regeneration in the West Midlands. *Area 35*(1): 6–14.

Whittemore, R., Chase, S.K., & Mandle, C.L. (2001). Validity in qualitative research. *Qualitative health research*, *11*(4), 522-537.

Wiek, A., & Larson, K. (2012). Water, people, and sustainability—A systems framework for analyzing and assessing water governance regimes. *Water Resources Management*, *26*(11), 3153-3171. doi:10.10076 s11269-012-0065-6.

Wiek, A., Ness, B., Schweizer-Ries, P., Brand, F.S., & Farioli, F. (2012). From complex systems analysis to transformational change: a comparative appraisal of sustainability science projects. *Sustainability Science*, *7*(s1), 5–24. doi:10.1007/s11625-011-0148-y.

Willer, D., Lovaglia, M., & Markovsky, B. (1997). Power and influence: A theoretical bridge. *Social Forces*, *76*(2), 571–603.

Wolff, F., & Schönherr, N. (2011). The impact evaluation of sustainable consumption policy instruments. *Journal of Consumer Policy*, *34*(1), 43-66. doi: 10.1007/s10603-010-9152-3.

Wurster, S. (2013). Staatstätigkeit II: neue Formen politischer Steuerung. In M.G. Schmidt, F. Wolf & S. Wurster (Eds.). *Studienbuch Politikwissenschaft* (pp. 351-377). Wiesbaden: VS Verlag für Sozialwissenschaften.

Wydra, D., & Pülzl, H. (2013). Sustainability governance in democracies. *International Journal of Social Ecology and Sustainable Development*, *4*(1), 86–107. doi:10.4018/jsesd.2013010105.

Yin, R. (2009). *Case study research: Design and methods* (4th ed.). Thousand Oaks: Sage Publishing.

Young, O.R. (2009). Governance for sustainable development in a world of rising interdependencies. In O.R. Young & M.A. Delmas (Eds.), *Governance for the Environment. New perspectives* (pp. 12-408). Cambridge: Cambridge University Press.

Young, J.C., Jordan, A., Searle, K.R., Butler, A., Chapman, D.S., Simmons, P., & Watt, A.D. (2013). Does stakeholder involvement really benefit biodiversity conservation?. *Biological Conservation*, *158*(2015), 359-370.

Young, O.R., & Zürn, M. (2006). The international regimes database: Designing and using a sophisticated tool for institutional analysis. *Global Environmental Politics*, *6*(3), 121-143. doi: 10.1162/glep.2006.6.3.121.

Zhang, Q. F. (2015). State political identity and meta-governance: Comparative analysis of governance modes in vegetable retail in urban China. *Journal of Comparative Policy Analysis: Research and Practice*, *17*(4), 378-392. doi: 10.1080/13876988.2015.1020630.

Zürn, M. (2008). Governance in einer sich wandelnden Welt – eine Zwischenbilanz. In G.F. Schuppert & M. Zürn (Eds.), *Governance in einer sich wandelnden Welt* (pp. 553-580). Wiesbaden: VS Verlag für Sozialwissenschaften.

Bibliography of case studies

THE CASE STUDIES IN THE CONTEXT OF SWISS ENERGY POLICY

Beyeler, P.C., & Kaiser, T. (2012). *Trialog Neue Energiepolitik - Zusammenfassung Konzept.* Zürich: Energie Trialog Schweiz.

DETEC (2013). *Bericht über die Ergebnisse der Vernehmlassung zum ersten Massnahmenpaket der Energiestrategie 2050 (Energiestrategie 2050).* Bern: DETEC (Department of the Environment, Transport, Energy and Communications).

EnDK (2015). *Mustervorschriften der Kantone im Energiebereich (MuKEn). Ausgabe 2014.* Bern: EnDK (Konferenz Kanonaler Energiedirektoren).

IEA (2012). *Energy Policies of IEA Countries. Switzerland 2012 Review.* Paris: IEA (International Energy Agency).

SFOE (2011). *Schlussevaluation EnergieSchweiz 2001-2010.* Bern: SFOE (Swiss Federal Office of Energy).

Swiss Confederation (2005). *Bundesgesetz über das Vernehmlassungsverfahren (Vernehmlassungsgesetz, VlG) vom 18. März 2005. 172.061.* Bern: Swiss Confederation.

Swiss Confederation (1999a). *Bundesverfassung der Schweizerischen Eidgenossenschaft vom 18. April 1999.* Bern: Swiss Confederation.

Swiss Confederation (1999b). *Bundesgesetz über die Reduktion der CO_2-Emissionen (CO_2-Gesetz) vom 8. Oktober 1999. 641.71.* Bern: Swiss Confederation.

Swiss Confederation (1998). *Energiegestz (EnG) vom 26. Juni 1998. 730.0.* Bern: Swiss Confederation.

Vatter, A. (2014). *Das politische System der Schweiz.* Baden-Baden: Nomos.

CASE 1: THE SWISS CO_2 LEVY

Baranzini, A., Thalmann, P., & Gonseth, C. (2004). Swiss climate policy: Combining VAs with other instruments under the menace of a CO_2 tax. In: A. Baranzini & P. Thalmann (Eds.), *Voluntary approaches in climate policy* (pp. 249–276). Cheltenham: Edward Elgar.

Betz, R., Leu, T., & Schleiniger, R. (2015). Disentangling the Effects of Swiss Energy and Climate Policies. *SML Working Paper No. 5. ZHAW School of Management and Law.*

Brönnimann, S., Appenzeller, C., Croci-Maspoli, M., Fuhrer, J., Grosjean, M., Hohmann, R., Ingold, K., Knutti, R., Liniger, M. A., Raible, C. C., Röthlisberger, R., Schär, C., Scherrer, S. C., Strassmann, K., & Thalmann, P. (2014). Climate change in Switzerland: a review of physical, institutional, and political aspects. *Wiley Interdisciplinary Reviews: Climate Change, 5*(4), 461-481. doi: 10.1002/wcc.280.

Climate Cent Foundation (2014). *Abschlussbericht 2005-2013.* Zurich: Climate Cent Foundation.

DETEC (2005). *Auswertung der Vernehmlassung zu den Massnahmen zur Einhaltung der Reduktionsziele nach dem CO_2-Gesetz.* Bern: Federal Department of the Environment, Transport, Energy and Communications (DETEC).

DETEC (2004). *Massnahmen zur Einhaltung der Reduktionsziele nach dem CO_2-Gesetz. Vernehmlassung zu vier Varianten.* Bern: Federal Department of the Environment, Transport, Energy and Communications (DETEC).

Ecoplan (*forthcoming*). *Wirkungsabschätzung CO_2-Abgabe Modul A: Entwicklung eines Zeitreihenanalysemodells zur Abschätzung der bisherigen Reduktionswirkung der CO_2-Abgabe. Schlussbericht Modul A. Zuhanden des Bundesamts für Umwelt.* Bern: Ecoplan.

Ecoplan (2008). *Volkswirtschaftliche Auswirkungen von CO_2-Abgaben und Emissionshandel für das Jahr 2020. Analyse der volkswirtschaftlichen Auswirkungen mit Hilfe eines allgemeinen Mehrländer-Gleichgewichtsmodell.* Bern: Ecoplan.

Ecoplan, EPFL and FHNW (*forthcoming*). *Wirkungsabschätzung CO_2-Abgabe. Synthese. Schlussbericht. Im Auftrag des Bundesamts für Umwelt.* Bern: Ecoplan.

Elbeze, J., & de Perthuis, C. (2011). *Twenty years of carbon taxing in Europe: some lessons learned.* Les Cahiers de la Chaire Economie du Climat, Information and debates Series, no 9.

EnAW (2014). *Tätigkeitsbericht. Der Partner für Klimaschutz und Energieeffizienz.* Zurich: Energieagentur der Wirtschaft.

EnAW (2013). *Erfolgfreicher Abschluss der Kyoto-Periode. EnAW Teilnehmer reduzieren CO_2 Ausstoss um 25 Prozent.* Zurich: Energieagentur der Wirtschaft.

EPFL (*forthcoming*). *An ex-post evaluation of the effectiveness of the Swiss CO_2 levy.* Lausanne: Ecole polytechnique fédérale de Lausanne (EPFL).

FOEN (2015). Emissionen von Treibhausgasen nach revidiertem CO_2-*Gesetz und Kyoto-Protokoll, 2. Verpflichtungsperiode (2013–2020).* Bern: FOEN (Federal Office for the Enviroment).

FOEN (2014a). *Faktenblatt 1. Schweizer Kyoto Bilanz 2008 bis 2012.* Bern: FOEN (Federal Office for the Enviroment).

FOEN (2014b). *CO_2-Abgabebefreiung für Unternehmen: Bilanz der 1. Verpflichtungsperiode.* Bern: FOEN (Federal Office for the Enviroment).

FOEN (2013). *CO_2-Abgabebefreiung ohne Emissionshandel. Ein Modul der Mitteilung des BAFU als Vollzugsbehörde zur CO_2-Verordnung.* Bern: FOEN (Federal Office for the Enviroment).

FOEN (2012). *Verordnung über die Reduktion der CO_2-Emissionen (CO_2-Verordnung). Erläuternder Bericht.* Bern: FOEN (Federal Office for the Enviroment).

FOEN (2010). *Synthesebericht zur Volkswirtschaftlichen Beurteilung der Schweizer Klimapolitik nach 2012 (VOBU).* Bern: FOEN (Federal Office for the Enviroment).

IEA (2012). *Energy Policies of IEA Countries. Switzerland 2012 Review.* Paris: IEA (International Energy Agency).

IEA (2007). *Energy Policies of IEA Countries. Switzerland 2007 Review.* Paris: IEA (International Energy Agency).

Ingold, K. (2011). Network structures within policy processes: Coalitions, power, and brokerage in Swiss climate policy. *Policy Studies Journal, 39*(3), 435-459. doi: 10.1111/j.1541-0072.2011.00416.x.

Ingold, K., & Varone, F. (2012). Treating policy brokers seriously: evidence from the climate policy. *Journal of Public Administration Research and Theory, 22*(2), 319–346. doi:10.1093/jopart/mur035.

Jochem, E., & Ott, V. (2005). *Verteilungseffekte einer CO_2-Abgabe auf Brennstoffe für die Schweizer Wirtschaft. Eine Kurzstudie. Endbericht. An das Bundesamt für Umwelt, Wald und Landschaft (BUWAL) sowie das Bundesamt für Energie (BFE).* Zurich: Swiss Federal Institute of Technology.

Krysiak, F. C., & Oberauner, I. M. (2010). Environmental policy à la carte: Letting firms choose their regulation. *Journal of Environmental Economics and Management, 60*(3), 221-232. doi:10.1016/j.jeem.2010.07.001.

Meng, S., Siriwardana, M., & McNeill, J. (2013). The environmental and economic impact of the carbon tax in Australia. *Environmental and Resource Economics, 54*(3), 313-332. doi: 10.1007/s10640-012-9600-4.

Niederberger, A. A. (2005). The Swiss Climate Penny: An innovative approach to transport sector emissions. *Transport Policy, 12*(2005), 303-313. doi:10.1016/j.tranpol.2005.05.003.

OcCC (2005). Gute Gründe für die CO_2-Lenkungsabgabe. Bern: Organe consultatif sur les changements climatiques (OcCC).

Prognos (2004). *Aufdatierung der Standortbestimmung CO_2-Gesetz. CO_2-Perspektiven und Sensitivitäten Stand: März 2004*. Basel: Prognos.

Sager, F., Bürki, M., & Luginbühl, J. (2014). Can a policy program influence policy change? The case of the Swiss EnergieSchweiz program. *Energy Policy*. Advance online publication. doi: 10.1016/j.enpol.2014.07.005.

Schwegler, R., Spescha, G., Schäppi, B., Iten, R. (2015): *Klimaschutz und Grüne Wirtschaft – was meint die Bevölkerung? Ergebnisse einer repräsentativen Bevölkerungsbefragung. Schlussbericht.* Zurich: INFRAS.

SFOE (2009). *Evaluation der Zielvereinbarungen der Wirtschaft zur Reduktion des Energieverbrauchs und zur Begrenzung der CO_2-Emissionen*. Bern: Swiss Federal Office of Energy (SFOE).

Sumner, J., Bird, L., & Dobos, H. (2011). Carbon taxes: a review of experience and policy design considerations. *Climate Policy, 11*(2), 922-943. doi: 10.3763/cpol.2010.0093.

Swiss Climate Foundation (2014*). Klima schützen. KMU stärken*. Zürich: Swiss Climate Foundation.

Swiss Confederation (2011). *Bundesgesetz über die Reduktion der CO_2-Emissionen (CO_2-Gesetz) vom 23. Dezember 2011. 641.71.* Bern: Swiss Confederation.

Swiss Confederation (2005). *Verordnung über die CO_2-Abgabe (CO_2-Verordnung). SR 641.712.* Bern: Swiss Confederation.

Swiss Confederation (1999). *Bundesgesetz über die Reduktion der CO_2-Emissionen (CO_2-Gesetz) vom 8. Oktober 1999. 641.71.* Bern: Swiss Confederation.

Swiss Federal Council (2015). *Umwelt Schweiz 2015. Bericht des Bundesrates.* Bern: Swiss Federal Council.

Thalmann, P. (2013). Klimapolitik der Schweiz: Musterschülerin mit Fragezeichen. *Die Volkswirtschaft Das Magazin für Wirtschaftspolitik, 11-2013, 35-38.*

Case 2: The electricity saving fund in the canton Basel

AUE (2015). *Haushaltsflyer Stromsparfonds 2015*. Basel: AUE (Amt für Umwelt und Energie).

AUE (2007). *Umweltbericht beider Basel 2007*. Basel: AUE (Amt für Umwelt und Energie).

AUE (2002a). *Der Stromspar-Fonds Basel Ein Kurzüberblick über die Lenkungsabgabe auf Strom und den Bonus für Haushalte und Betriebe*. Basel: AUE (Amt für Umwelt und Energie).

AUE (2002b). *Erläuterungen zum Stromspar-Fonds Basel*. Basel: AUE (Amt für Umwelt und Energie).

AUE (2000). *Stromspar-Fonds Basel. Rechenschaftsbericht 1999. Kurzform mit Erfolgen, Problemen und Lösungsansätzen*. Basel: AUE (Amt für Umwelt und Energie).

Boogen, N. (2010). *Analyse der Effektivität von Stromeffizienz- Massnahmen in der Schweiz*. Zurich: Swiss Federal Institute of Technology.

Brutschin, C (2012). *Lenkungsabgabe - kein Schreckgespenst. Gastkommentar. 15.10.2012*. Zurich: NZZ.

Governing Council of the Canton of Basel-City (1999). *Verordnung zur Lenkungsabgabe und zum Strompreis-Bonus. Vom 11. Mai 1999. 772.140*. Basel: Governing Council of the Canton of Basel-City.

Great Council of the Canton Basel-City (2015). *Bericht der Umwelt-, Verkehrs- und Energiekommission zum Leistungsauftrag und den Gesamtinvestitionen der IWB Industrielle Werke Basel für die Periode 2015-2018*. Basel: Great Council of the Canton of Basel-City.

Great Council of the Canton of Basel-City (1998). *Energiegesetz (EnG). Vom 9. September 1998. 772.100*. Basel: Great Council of the Canton of Basel-City.

Häne, S. (2015). *Wirkungslose Stromabgabe. 10.03.2015*. Zurich: Tagesanzeiger.

IWB (2015). *Stromtarife 2015 für Haushalte und Gewerbe mit Doppeltarif*. Basel: IWB (Industrial Works Basel).

IWB (2004). *Was sind Lenkungs- und Förderabgaben?*. Basel: IWB (Industrial Works Basel).

Leimbacher, J. (2008). *Rechtliche Überlegungen: Elektrizitätsabgabe im Kanton Bern. Schlussbericht zuhanden des Amtes für Umweltkoordination und Energie der Bau-, Verkehrs- und Energiedirektion des Kantons Bern*. Bern: Amt für Umweltkoordination und Energie.

Rechsteiner R. (2008). *Schweiz erneuerbar. Unterwegs zur Vollversorgung mit erneuerbaren Energien*. Basel.

Rechsteiner, R. (2002). *Basler Lenkungsabgabe senkt Umweltbelastung. 04.11.2002*. Basel: Basler Zeitung.

SFOE (2009). *Effizienzmassnahmen im Elektrizitätsbereich Grundlagen für Wettbewerbliche Ausschreibungen.* Bern: SFOE (Swiss Federal Office of Energy).

SFOE (2007). *Instrumente für Energieeffizienz im Elektrizitätsbereich Ausländische Erfahrungen und Instrumenten- Mix für die Schweiz.* Bern: SFOE (Swiss Federal Office of Energy).

SFOE (2004). *Stromspar-Fonds Basel ist ein Erfolg.* Bern: SFOE (Swiss Federal Office of Energy).

SFOE (2003). *Evaluation des Stromsparfonds Basel.* Bern: SFOE (Swiss Federal Office of Energy).

Statistical office of the canton Basel-City (2015). Energiestatistik Kanton Basel-Stadt. Basel: Statistisches Amt des Kantons Basel-City.

Suna, D., Loew T., & Zeschmar-Lahl, B. (2013). *Förderung von Energieeffizienz und erneuerbaren Energien bei Endverbrauchern.* Technische Universität Wien: Wien.

CASE 3: THE FUEL CONSUMPTION COVENANT IN SWITZERLAND

Alberini, A., Bareit, M., & Filippini, M. (2014). *Does the Swiss car market reward ruel efficient cars? Evidence from hedonic pricing regressions, matching and a regression discontinuity design.* Economics Working Paper Series. Zurich: Swiss Federal Institute of Technology.

ASIA (2002-2012). 6-*17. Berichterstattung im Rahmen der Energieverordnung über die Absenkung des spezifischen Treibstoff-Normverbrauchs von Personenwagen.* Bern: Association of Swiss car importers (ASIA).

Börner, A. (2010). *Voluntary agreement of Swiss car importers.* Zurich: Swiss Federal Institute of Technology.

De Haan, P. (2007). *Erforschung des Autokaufverhaltens hinsichtlich Treibstoffeinsparung und Technologieakzeptantz. Berichte zum Schweizer Autokaufverhalten.* Zurich: Swiss Federal Institute of Technology.

DETEC (2013). *Strategie Nachhaltige Entwicklung 2012-2015.* Bern: DETEC (Federal Department of the Environment, Transport, Energy and Communications).

DETEC (2003). *Gut unterwegs. 2. Jahresbericht EnergieSchweiz 2002/03.* Bern: DETEC (Federal Department of the Environment, Transport, Energy and Communications).

Lienhard, A. (2006). Public private partnerships (PPPs) in Switzerland: Experiences – risks - potentials. *International Review of Administrative Sciences*, *72*(4), 547-563. doi: 10.1177/0020852306070083.

Quandt, A. (2010). *Voluntary approaches in climate policy: comparing European and Swiss transport legislation.* Bern: Swiss National Competence Centre for Climate Research.

SFOE (2015). *Energieverbrauch und Energieeffizienz der neuen Personenwagen 2014. 19. Berichterstattung im Rahmen der Energieverordnung.* Bern: SFOE (Swiss Federal Office of Energy).

SFOE (2011a). *Schlussevaluation EnergieSchweiz 2001-2010.* Bern: SFOE (Swiss Federal Office of Energy).

SFOE (2011b). *Wirkungsanalyse EnergieSchweiz 2010. Wirkungen der freiwilligen Massnahmen und der Förderaktivitäten von EnergieSchweiz auf Energie, Emissionen und Beschäftigung.* Bern: SFOE (Swiss Federal Office of Energy).

SFOE (2009). *Schweizer Autos sind immer noch zu durstig.* Bern: SFOE (Swiss Federal Office of Energy).

SFOE (2007). *Lenkungsabgaben zur Senkung des CO_2-Ausstosses beim Neuwagenkauf. Hintergrund, Mechanismen, Prognosen.* Bern: SFOE (Swiss Federal Office of Energy).

SFOE (2005). *Massnahmen zur Absenkung des Flottenverbrauchs Abschätzung der Wirkung.* Bern: SFOE (Swiss Federal Office of Energy).

SFOE (2003): *EnergieSchweiz, Quantitative Befragung, Segment „Mobilität".* Bern: SFOE (Swiss Federal Office of Energy).

Spielmann, M., & Althaus, H.-J. (2007). Can a prolonged use of a passenger car reduce environmental burdens? Life Cycle analysis of Swiss passenger cars. *Journal of Cleaner Production, 15*(11-12), 1122–1134. doi:10.1016/j.jclepro.2006.07.022.

Swiss Confederation (1999). *Bundesgesetz über die Reduktion der CO_2-Emissionen (CO_2-Gesetz) vom 8. Oktober 1999. 641.71.* Bern: Swiss Confederation.

Swiss Confederation (1998a). *Energiegestz (EnG) vom 26. Juni 1998. 730.0.* Bern: Swiss Confederation.

Swiss Confederation (1998b). *Energieverordnung (EnV) vom 7. Dezember 1998. 730.1.* Bern: Swiss Confederation.

Touring Club Switzerland (2008). Controlling energieEtikette (gemäss Anhang 3.6 EnV). Schlussbericht 5. Kontrolljahr 1.7.2007 bis 30.6.2008. Emmen: Touring Club Switzerland.

Volken, T. (2010). *Energiepolitische Landschaft: Massnahmen für mehr Energieeffizienz von Neuwagen. Präsentation Forschungsresultate im Verkehr.* Bern: SFOE (Swiss Federal Office of Energy).

Case 4: The energy trialogue Switzerland

AUE (2012). *Energiestrategie 2012. Strategie des Regierungsrates für die Energiepolitik des Kantons Basel-Landschaft.* Basel: AUE (Amt für Umwelt und Energie).

Beyeler, P. C., & Kaiser, T. (2012). *Trialog Neue Energiepolitik – Zusammenfassung Konzept.* Zurich: Energie Trialog Schweiz.

Büsser, M. (2010). *Der Prozess Energie Trialog Schweiz für eine Energie-Strategie 2050.* Bern: Proceedings of the Wassertag 2010, Bern.

DETEC (2013). *Bericht über die Ergebnisse der Vernehmlassung zum ersten Massnahmenpaket der Energiestrategie 2050 (Energiestrategie 2050).* Bern: Federal Department of the Environment, Transport, Energy and Communications (DETEC).

Energieforum Schweiz (2009). *Energie Trialog Schweiz präsentiert Energie-Strategie 2050.* Argus Medienbeobachtung: Bern.

Energie Trialog Schweiz (2013). *Trialog Neue Energiepolitik. Energiestrategie 2050 aus Sicht des Energie Trialogs. Schlussbericht der Lenkungsgruppe.* Zurich: Energie Trialog Schweiz.

Energie Trialog Schweiz (2009). *Energie-Strategie 2050 – Impulse für die schweizerische Energiepolitik, Grundlagenbericht.* Zurich: Energie Trialog Schweiz.

Energie Trialog Schweiz (2007). *Energie Trialog Schweiz: SEPImpulse für eine nachhaltige und wettbewerbsfähige Energiepolitik der Schweiz. Grundlagenpapier.* Zurich: Energie Trialog Schweiz.

Kaiser, T. (2012). *Was heisst "Führen eines partizipativen Prozesses"? Erfahrungen in der Energiepolitik - Energie Trialog Schweiz. AoeL -Tagung 202.* Zurich: Energie Trialog Schweiz.

Kaiser, T., & Schips, B. (2013). *Trialog Neue Energiepolitik. Persönliche Eindrücke zum Schlussbericht „Energiestrategie 2050 aus Sicht des Energie Trialogs".* Zurich: Energie Trialog Schweiz.

Meier, J. (2010). Streit um neue Energiestudie. *Handelszeitung (10)*2010. Zurich: Handelszeitung.

Metrobasel (2010). *Standortbestimmung und Grundlagen für eine Energie-Strategie der Metropolitanregion Basel. Erste Ansätze zur Umsetzung der Energie-Strategie Schweiz 2050 des Energie Trialog Schweiz in der Metropoitanregion Basel.* Basel: Metrobasel.

PSI (2008). *PSI Scientific Report 2008.* Villigen: PSI (Paul Scherrer Institute).

Schips (2013). Die Energiestrategie 2050 aus volkswirtschaftlicher Sicht. *Die Volkswirtschaft. Das Magazin für Wirtschaftspolitik, 10*(2013), 60-62.

Sharma, A., & Kearins, K. (2011). Interorganizational collaboration for regional sustainability. What happens when organizational representatives come together?. *The journal of applied behavioral science*, *47*(2), 168-203.

Studerus, K. (2011). *Die Defizite des Energie Trialog Schweiz (ETS).* Bern: Aktion für vernünftige Energiepolitik Schweiz.

Swiss Federal Council (2013). *Botschaft zum ersten Massnahmenpaket der Energiestrategie 2050 und zur Atomausstiegsinitiative*. Bern: Swiss Federal Council.

Turcotte, M.F., & Pasquero, J. (2001). The paradox of multistakeholder collaborative roundtables. *The journal of applied behavioral science*, *37*(4), 447-464.

Weidmann, N. O. (2013). *Transforamtion strategies towards a sustaianble swiss energy system: an energy-economic scenario analysis*. Zurich: Swiss Federal Institute of Technology.

CASE 5: THE SWISS BUILDING LABEL MINERGIE

Beyeler, F., Beglinger, N., & Roder, R. (2009). Minergie: The swiss sustainable building standard. *Innovations*, *4*(4), 241–244.

Bharathi, K., & Nicol, L. A. (2013). Between research and practice: Experts on implementing sustainable construction. *Buildings*, *3*(4), 739-765. doi:10.3390/buildings3040739.

Carassus, J. (2007). Innovation in buildings: a socio-eco-technical approach. *Proceedings of the CIB World Building Congress" Construction for Development*, 2331-2343.

EnDK (2015). *Mustervorschriften der Kantone im Energiebereich (MuKEn). Ausgabe 2014*. Bern: EnDK (Konferenz Kanonaler Energiedirektoren).

EnDK (2014). *Energieverbrauch von Gebäuden. Fact Sheet.* Bern: EnDK (Konferenz Kanonaler Energiedirektoren).

EnDK (2004). *Praxistest Minergie. Erfahrungen aus Planung, Realisierung und Nutzung von Minergie-Bauten. Zusammenfassung Schlussbericht.* Bern: EnDK (Konferenz Kanonaler Energiedirektoren).

Feige, A., Wallbaum, H., & Krank, S. (2011). Harnessing stakeholder motivation: towards a Swiss sustainable building sector. *Building Research & Information*, *39*(5), 504–517. doi:10.1080/09613218.2011.589788.

Hässig, W., Lalive, A., Fotsch, P., Steinle, P. (2003). Gesundheitliche Aspekte der Komfortlüftungen im Wohnbereich. Zurich: Basler & Hofmann.

IEA (2007). *Energy Policies of IEA Countries. Switzerland 2007 Review*. Paris: IEA (International Energy Agency).

Kriesi, R. (2009). *Minergie – Fortschritt am Bau nach Schweizer Art*. Bern: Minergie Association.

Kriesi, R. (1995): Erfahrungen aus dem Pilotprojekt Wädenswili: Null Energie zum Wohnen? *Umweltpraxis 6(1995), 25-26.*

Minergie (2015). *Geschäftsbericht 2014*. Bern: Minergie Association.

Minergie (2011). *Minergie - auf dem Weg zum nachhaltigen Bauen*. Bern: Minergie Association.

Minergie (2008). *10 Jahre Minergie – Eine Erfolgsgeschichte.* Bern: Minergie Association.

Sager, F., Bürki, M., & Luginbühl, J. (2014). Can a policy program influence policy change? The case of the Swiss EnergieSchweiz program. *Energy Policy,* 74(2), 352-365. doi:10.1016/j.enpol.2014.07.005.

Salvi, M., Horehájova, A., & Neeser, J. (2010). *Der Minergie-Boom unter der Lupe.* Zurich: Center for Corporate Responsibility and Sustainability, University of Zurich.

Salvi, M., Horehájova, A., & Neeser, J. (2008). *Der Nachhaltigkeit von Immobilien einen finanziellen Wert geben – Minergie macht sich bezahlt.* Zurich: Center for Corporate Responsibility and Sustainability, University of Zurich.

Salvi, M., & Syz, J. (2011). What drives "green housing" construction? Evidence from Switzerland. *Journal of Financial Economic Policy, 3*(1), 86–102. doi:10.1108/17576381111116777.

SFOE (2015). *EnergieSchweiz. Das Programm des Bundesrats zur Förderung von Energieeffizienz und erneuerbaren Energien.* Bern: SFOE (Swiss Federal Office of Energy).

SFOE (2014a). *Evaluation Art. 9 EnG (Gebäudebereich) und der kantonalen Mustervorschriften im Energiebereich (MuKEn 2008).* Bern: SFOE (Swiss Federal Office of Energy).

SFOE (2014b). *Standard nachhaltiges Bauen Schweiz – Hochbau.* Bern: SFOE (Swiss Federal Office of Energy).

SFOE (2013). *Wirkung kantonaler Energiegesetze. Analyse der Auswirkungen gemäss Art. 20 EnG, Aktualisierung für das Jahr 2012.* Bern: Swiss Federal Office of Energy (SFOE).

SFOE (2011a). *Schlussevaluation EnergieSchweiz 2001-2010.* Bern: SFOE (Swiss Federal Office of Energy).

SFOE (2011b). *Wirkungsanalyse EnergieSchweiz 2010. Wirkungen der freiwilligen Massnahmen und der Förderaktivitäten von EnergieSchweiz auf Energie, Emissionen und Beschäftigung.* Bern: SFOE (Swiss Federal Office of Energy).

SFOE (2005). *Internationaler Vergleich von Energiestandards im Baubereich.* Bern: SFOE (Swiss Federal Office of Energy).

Wallbaum, H. (2010). Stärkung des Netzwerkes nachhaltiges Bauen Schweiz. Zurich: Swiss Federal Institute of Technology.

Appendix

List of conducted interviews

Interview 01-01: September 24, 2015; face-to-face interview, Bern
Interview 01-02: October 05, 2015; face-to-face interview, Zurich
Interview 01-03: September 29, 2015; face-to-face interview, Zurich
Interview 01-04: October 10, 2015; face-to-face interview, Zurich
Interview 01-05: September 24, 2015; face-to-face interview, Bern

Interview 02-01: April 15, 2015; face-to-face interview, Basel
Interview 02-02: December 08, 2014; face-to-face interview, Basel
Interview 02-03: May 11, 2015; face-to-face interview, Basel
Interview 02-04: December 08, 2014; face-to-face interview, Basel
Interview 02-05: April 15, 2015; face-to-face interview, Basel

Interview 03-01: November 06, 2015; face-to-face interview, Bern
Interview 03-02: November 09, 2015; face-to-face interview, Bern
Interview 03-03: November 10, 2015; face-to-face interview, Bern
Interview 03-04: November 04, 2015; face-to-face interview, Bern
Interview 03-05: November 09, 2015; face-to-face interview, Bern

Interview 04-01: August 26, 2015; face-to-face interview, Aarau
Interview 04-02: September 01, 2015; face-to-face interview, Aarau
Interview 04-03: September 01, 2015; face-to-face interview, Aarau
Interview 04-04: August 19, 2015; face-to-face interview, Aarau
(Written Statement 04-01)
(Written Statement 04-02)

Interview 05-01: July 22, 2015; face-to-face interview, Bern
Interview 05-02: August 06, 2015; face-to-face interview, Zurich
Interview 05-03: July 20, 2015; face-to-face interview, Zurich
Interview 05-04: August 06, 2015; face-to-face interview, Zurich
Interview 05-05: July 22, 2015; face-to-face interview, Bern

Example of an interview guide (translated)

Note that this is only for illustration purposes, since each specific interview guide was different. I used two overall guides (with regard to governance and impacts) that gave each individual one the same basic structure. However, the specific questions varied in view of the expert (e.g. in terms of whether the actor was directly affected or a general expert with regard to results) and the knowledge base on the case study at the specific time of the interview - and thus the focus of interests. Each interview guide was composed of platform questions to generate impulses for narrating, supplemented by specific inquiries.

<table>
<tr><th colspan="2">Impacts</th></tr>
<tr><td colspan="2">
• 1.) So, basically - I would like to explore, which changes have been induced - directly and indirectly. Simply put, what things became different through the levy and all the developments that were connected to it? So, when you look back, which things were triggered, which effects resulted? (...) What was the reason for this?
• 2.) Thank you! When we now look concretely at the affected groups of actors. Who was influenced in which way by the levy?
• 3.) Now I would like to look in more detail at the influences on political and socio-economic structures. First of all, what would you say, in how far was there an influence on the general political agenda? (...) How would you estimate the influence on socio-economic environments?
</td></tr>
<tr><td>
• 1.) Realized actions and institutionalization processes / side effects

• 2.) Affected actors
- Influence on goals
- Influence on means

• 3.) Strategy environment
- Politics
- Society
- Economy
</td><td>
• In view of energetic effects and emissions... In 2014, the SFOE has announced that the goals of the Kyoto protocol have been reached (for the period of 2008-2012)? The target for the fossil combustible fuels was slightly missed? (...) Which role did the levy play in this regard?
• Other developments, which were triggered or influenced and are now established...? Perhaps not only direct influences of the levy but also of the development around it? (...) for instance, in view of the consultation phase?
• Did you notice indirect effects, maybe also unintended side effects?

• How did the public receive the levy, in terms of praise or resistance? (...) How was the reaction of the economy? (...) In which way did societal groups react?
• In view of the refunding mechanism - what would you say when looking at the effects on households, e.g. in terms of income and so on? (...) What were the effects of the refunding when we look at companies?
• Do you think, the perspective on questions of energy have changed, respectively the attitude of the affected actors?
• Would you say that the interests of the specific actor groups we talked about have changed?
• In view of the capacities of actors to accomplish their interests - can you think of certain changes? Did some actor groups gain or lose influence in the field?
• Were there changes in the mutual influence of actors - for instance in view of supporters and opponents, the evolvement of new groups etc.?

• In how far have other energy-political measures been influenced in their evolvement or effect (...) The climate cent - would this measure been realized without the levy? In how far was it influenced by the levy? (...) What about the reduction commitments of companies - or the emission trading scheme? (...) When we look at the building refurbishment program - or the technology fund?
• For instance, in terms of growth effects? (...) effects on employment? (...) Distributional effects among the branches of firms? (...) Supply security and energy dependence on foreign countries? (...) In terms of stimulating innovation? (...) What about health effects?
• Are there evaluations of the levy? (...) ex-ante impact assessments - ex post? (...) I have read about one project conducted by the Rütter Soceco AG?
</td></tr>
<tr><th colspan="2">Relationship to the mode</th></tr>
<tr><td colspan="2">
• Very well. Thank you very much! Now I would like to have a closer look at the way of steering, that is, the manner in which societal changes are triggered. When we look at the arrangement around the levy - a top-down way of steering, based on a legal basis and a coercive measure – here, public authorities were responsible for implementation. Which role did these aspects play in terms of triggering changes in society? (...) Today, there are also other ways to induce changes in society. For instance, there are partnerships among different groups from state and society that strive for collaboration, such as the Energietrialog (...) There are also bottom-up movements, for instance when you look at the evolvement of the voluntary building standard Minergie (...) When you see these different forms of steering in comparison, where do you see advantages and drawbacks?
</td></tr>
<tr><td>
. Triggers within the dimensions of governance /

key characteristics of the mode of governance
</td><td>
• The ways of steering in comparison - what would you think, how can one best reach at changes in society?
• So in view of the different steering forms you were talking about - what are in your opinion important factors to induce changes in society?

• Having a look at the way of proceeding and mechanisms of the levy... Do you think it was an advantage that the competences were in the hand of a small group of political-administrative authorities? (...) How would you estimate the importance of the consultation phase? (...) Advantages and drawbacks...?
• Would you say, it was an advantage that formal ways of institutional structures, like laws, were used?
• In how far was it relevant that the levy was a coercive instrument?
• Do you see some potentials of improvement in terms of the proceeding of the levy, that is, the way of steering?
</td></tr>
</table>